THE MISSING COURSE

THE MISSING COURSE

Everything They Never Taught You
about College Teaching

David Gooblar

Harvard University Press

Cambridge, Massachusetts, and London, England   2019

Copyright © 2019 by the President and Fellows of Harvard College
All rights reserved
Printed in the United States of America

First printing

CIP data for this book is available from the Library of Congress

ISBN 978-0-674-98441-7

This book is dedicated to Katarina

Contents

THE MISSING COURSE

Introduction
The Students Are the Material

TEACHING IS DIFFICULT because success and failure depend on the extent to which you help other people learn. The most knowledgeable and prepared teacher in the world is a failure if her students don't learn. It took me many years, and two continents, to learn this.

When I was a graduate student, teaching was not a priority. I did my PhD in England, at University College London, writing my dissertation on the work of Philip Roth. While most graduate students in the United States receive little to no instruction on pedagogy, in Britain the attention given to teaching is almost nonexistent. The entirety of the teaching instruction I received during my graduate studies was a single sentence uttered by a big-shot professor as he was leaving the classroom I was entering. "No matter how little you know," he said, "they know less."

Although I taught throughout my degree, teaching was not required, and any supervision I had was cursory. The message was clear: the important part of an academic's life, the aspect that separates those who succeed from those who don't, was research. Teaching was marginal—something academics had to do to satisfy the terms of their employment, but mostly separate from the real work.

When I did teach, first in one-on-one tutorials, then in seminars, and then in larger classes, my approach was unimaginative. Like many literature students who find themselves in the front of a classroom, I did what most of my own teachers had done over the years: expound at length my brilliant interpretations of novels and stories and poems. The preparatory work of teaching, I assumed, was in reading texts over and over again, pencil in hand, looking for new and interesting meanings to sniff out. I could present those meanings to presumably grateful students who would then have a new appreciation for these classic works of literature. What the students brought to the class, or even what they would be doing while I was doing all this expounding, never crossed my mind. My job was to show them the value of litera-ture, and, if I'm being honest, to show them how smart I was.[1]

I don't think my experience is at all uncommon. With few excep-tions, graduate programs still focus overwhelmingly on training stu-dents to become researchers and writers, and expect the teaching to take care of itself. But the career path for most academics is not one in which research plays a dominant role. Those academics lucky enough to secure a full-time job at an American college or university generally spend around three times as many hours on teaching as they do on research, according to the most recent numbers from the Na-tional Center for Education Statistics.[2] And that's just full-timers. American postsecondary institutions now employ nearly as many part-time faculty as they do full-time. Part-time faculty spend 88 percent of their time on teaching, compared with just under 4 percent on scholarship (the remaining 8 percent seems to be spent in meetings).[3] The job of the American academic, clearly, is teaching. Why don't we train academics for that job?

I finished my PhD in early 2008, right when the academic job market was gearing up for a historic crash. According to the Modern Language Association (MLA), there were 2,700 fewer jobs posted on its *Job Information List* in the six-year period after my graduation than in the six years that preceded it.[4] It was not at all uncommon to apply for jobs with 1,000 other applicants. It was, and remains to a great extent, a terrible time to be on the job market, particularly in the humanities.

My wife and daughter and I moved to Iowa at the end of 2010, after my wife accepted a tenure-track position teaching philosophy at the University of Iowa. The following August, I got a last-minute opportunity to teach as an adjunct at Augustana College in Illinois. I was to teach two sections of a first-year writing course called Rhetoric and the Liberal Arts.

From the beginning, this was a different sort of teaching experience. There were some required texts (some short readings on the liberal arts and Gerald Graff and Cathy Birkenstein's *They Say / I Say*, a terrific book on academic writing that I still use), but for the most part I was left on my own to create the syllabus.

My previous experience, in which I'd spend a certain amount of time on one novel or on one era of literary history, didn't help me here. Rather, my task was to help students develop certain crucial *skills*: academic writing, critical reading, critical thinking. Although I was excited for the opportunity, a low-level panic set in. What were the students supposed to be studying, exactly? Oh sure, I found some readings to assign and came up with assignments for essays. But once classes began, I often felt rudderless, unsure what my focus should be. If the point of the class wasn't to gain a better understanding of the material (and what was the material, anyway?), then what *was* it?

About halfway through the semester, it dawned on me: *the students are the material.* My task wasn't to master the essence of some text and then convey it to the students' hungry and waiting brains. The students themselves were what I had to study, assess, and work with to achieve something together. They were the subject of action, consideration, discussion, and feeling; their learning was the point of the whole enterprise. If I was going to be a good teacher, I was going to need to master the mysterious art of helping people change.

That shift—from a content-coverage model to one that centered on students—was a sea change for me. Putting students and their skill development at the heart of teaching, no matter how obvious a move it seems in retrospect, made me see teaching as a much more complex and interesting discipline than I had before. It was a challenge every bit as intellectual as those I faced in doing my research. My task was to help my students become better writers, become better students, become better citizens. How was I supposed to do that?

I wasn't sure how to proceed, but I certainly threw myself into the job, drawn in by the challenge. I set to work selling students on the utility of academic skills and thinking about how best to help them develop and practice those skills. It was like a whole new career.

In January 2013, I went to the MLA conference in Boston. On the first day of the conference, I attended the session "New Approaches to Teaching the Literature Surveys," chaired by James Lang. I was going to be teaching an American literature survey that spring at Mount

Mercy College in Cedar Rapids, Iowa, and hoped to get a few good ideas. Did I ever.

I can legitimately say that attending that session changed my life. There were five or six speakers sitting at the front of the room, and each one had prepared a short paper detailing an innovation he or she had developed in teaching a literature survey course.[5] In the question-and-answer period afterward, members of the audience chimed in with their own innovations. I scribbled in my notebook as fast as I could—I couldn't believe how many great ideas were being thrown out.

What struck me was the community that revealed itself during that question-and-answer period. When you put a bunch of teachers together in a room, it turns out, they pool their wisdom and share the strategies that have worked for them. What's more, many of these teachers actually pursued scholarship in pedagogy. Teaching wasn't just an annoying requirement of their university positions; it was a calling they devoted themselves to.

All of this was eye-opening for me. Up to that point the entirety of my teaching experience had taken place (a) within a graduate program that completely ignored teaching as something to be learned, and then (b) as an adjunct with little to no institutional support and few colleagues to talk to. The idea, so vividly illustrated by this MLA session, that teaching was a discipline with innumerable possibilities for creativity, and that collegial collaboration might be a huge help, was a world changer.

An idea came into my head almost immediately: Why not try to replicate such a collaborative community on the web? Wouldn't a web-based resource where teachers could share the sort of concrete teaching strategies I heard at the MLA session be useful? I knew I could benefit from it; I imagined others could too.

In my excitement, I fired off an overly enthusiastic email to Lang, heaping praise on the session he organized and asking if he knew if any such resource already existed. He didn't, and he encouraged me to pursue the idea.

It took me eight months of brainstorming and procrastination and false starts, but in August 2013, I launched Pedagogy Unbound, with the tagline "A place for college teachers to share practical strategies for today's classrooms." College instructors from any discipline could submit teaching tips up to 500 words in length. I would decide whether they were acceptable, lightly edit them, and publish them with full credit for the author. I seeded the site with tips from the pedagogy books that were quickly becoming my scholarly obsession: Lang's *On Course*, Peter Filene's *The Joy of Teaching*, Ken Bain's *What the Best College Teachers Do*, and Robert Magnan's *147 Practical Tips for Teaching Professors*.

With a little bit of promotion and a big stroke of luck—James Lang, quickly becoming the fairy godmother of this story, wrote a column about me and the site in the *Chronicle of Higher Education*—Pedagogy Unbound began to attract some attention. Instructors were sending in tips, and I posted them and sorted them into categories. People were visiting the site and reading the tips.

That September, I got an email from Gabriela Montell, an assistant editor at the *Chronicle of Higher Education*. She was part of a team setting up a new site—to be called Vitae—focused on higher education as a career, and wrote to ask if I wanted to contribute. I eagerly accepted, proposing a fortnightly column highlighting the most interesting submissions to Pedagogy Unbound. I would write about teaching tips, adding context and suggesting practical applications for readers.

For a few months, that was the column: each of my first pieces was inspired by a submission to Pedagogy Unbound. But then a strange thing happened: the submissions started to dry up. Certainly part of this was due to my lax promotion of the site. But I also think it had something to do with a truth that made the site's concept an uphill battle. Academics are busy people and are much more likely to be looking for teaching tips than looking to contribute their own.[6]

In retrospect, this was another stroke of luck. Because I so quickly ran out of tips to write about, and because I had a deadline every two weeks, I started to do some research. I began reading journals in the flourishing field of the scholarship of teaching and learning. I read anything I could find about teaching, whether it was K–12 or college or corporate training. I became conversant with the rudiments of cognitive science and theories of learning. Suddenly finding myself with a pedagogical advice column, I worked hard to make myself someone worthy of it.

It turns out that the bulk of the scholarship I was reading confirmed the lessons I intuited during that first semester teaching at Augustana. My shift—from content-focused to student-centered—echoed a larger shift sketched by many pedagogy scholars. A great body of literature had developed, advocating for active learning strategies, for pedagogical approaches that focused on skill development, for a move away from the "sage on the stage" model of college teaching. Much of this scholarship was based on actual evidence, too, on peer-reviewed studies instead of institutional lore.

But I was aware of this body of literature only because I was writing a teaching column. Nothing in my experience as a student, either as

an undergraduate watching my professors or as a graduate student os-
tensibly training for the profession, prepared me to teach in a way
backed up by evidence. This is the case for most academics: as graduate
students they are trained almost exclusively to be researchers and
writers and are expected to pick up whatever pedagogical training
along the way, perhaps by osmosis. When they get in front of a class,
most fall back on what their own professors did (which probably
doesn't stray all too far from what *their* professors once did).[7]

Once in a full-time job, an academic has even less time to work on
her teaching. The job of an academic in America, for the majority of
us, now falls into one of two camps: the tenure-track position that in-
centivizes research above all else, and the instructional faculty or
adjunct position with a teaching load so large that there's little time
for the kind of preparation and reflection that best prepares instructors to teach well. Teaching—the practice of helping others learn—is
a discipline every bit as challenging and intellectual as anything we
tackle in our research. But as long as the industry doesn't value the
pursuit of that discipline, too many will remain mostly unfamiliar
with its lessons. This book is for those people.

In the fall of 2015, after years in the adjunct wilderness, I was hired
as a lecturer in the University of Iowa's Rhetoric Department. My position is not on the tenure track and the pay's not great, but I have
pretty good job security and, as importantly, I can pursue what I now
know to be my calling with almost complete freedom. I teach University of Iowa students how to write, speak, read critically, and discover what they believe about the world. Students are my discipline,
and every semester they change and I have to try to become proficient
in that discipline all over again. I've learned so much about teaching

(and about myself) as I've taken advantage of the stability of a full-time position. Teaching for a living is a wonderfully challenging and fulfilling pursuit.

But it's also, of course, a difficult one. To return to where I started, what makes teaching so difficult is that you're working to help other people learn. There's no guarantee that if you do everything the right way, your students will succeed. In fact, thinking that there's one "right way" that guarantees success may be what dooms you to failure. If there's a unifying principle to what I've learned over the past seven years in the classroom, it's that we must grant attention and thought to every aspect of the instructor's task; let nothing go unquestioned except the requirement to help students help themselves. It's the unifying principle of this book, as well.

There's a sense in which my current position, in a department of rhetoric, is the perfect one for understanding such a principle. As a rhetoric instructor, I am heavily focused on students and what they can do. Most of the content I teach is in the service of teaching students transferable skills and knowledge. So if I assign readings on feminism and related issues, as I often do, I'm more concerned with teaching students how to recognize, understand, and respond to the arguments in the readings than I am with them "learning the material." I don't give a test that asks students to remember three out of four of Rebecca Solnit's mansplainers. But I will assign an exercise that asks students to write a personal narrative like Solnit's that embeds an argument in its story. I'll ask them to study Solnit's writing for "moves" that they can appropriate into their own writing. We'll chart out Solnit's argument to see if the logic holds up. The content serves the skills.

I've written more about balancing skills and content in Chapter 1, but my point is this: teaching courses with skills at their core has allowed me to see more clearly that students, not course content, need to be at the center of our conception of our jobs. This is true even if you want students to learn a lot of content; we must begin with students, in every course. As someone who began his career holding the unexamined belief that teaching was the brilliant presentation of course material, I've come a long way. Insofar as I obsess over course content now, it's because I want to ensure it engages students. If they're not interested in it, they won't care enough to learn the skills I'm laboring to teach them. But even if course content is more important to you than it is to me, I think you'll still find a lot of useful advice in these pages.

My particular path has made me into the teacher I am today, one who sees students as the material, who goes to work every day eager to see what the students are ready to do. Teaching is human work— we work with people and try to help them develop. That doesn't require the teacher to be the smartest person in the room, but it does require the right mind-set and a set of strategies to help that development happen.

It's taken me a long time to become a better teacher; I only hope I can keep improving as I continue to teach. I'd like this book to kickstart your own improvement as a teacher. I'm sure it'll take you a lot less time than it took me.

In writing this book, I asked myself, What would have best prepared me for my career? What would a thorough and inspiring pedagogy course look like? If I had fifteen weeks to teach other scholars the lessons of evidence-based pedagogical research, how would I do it?

Many of the ideas in this book began life in the form of short columns written for Vitae and the *Chronicle of Higher Education*. So while I've worked to present a coherent and thorough approach to college teaching in these pages, many of the tips here can be taken and applied without remaking your whole course. My hope is that the book is valuable to both readers and browsers.

I begin with a call to use active learning strategies. The concept of active learning is so important to my way of thinking about pedagogy that I don't think it can be overemphasized. To many of us who, for the most part, were taught by professors content to talk at us for hours on end, it is all too easy to fall back on the simplest mode of content delivery. We have to always remind ourselves that students learn through active engagement and that our task is to entice them into that engagement.

Following that sentiment, that task is a lot easier if students take our courses to be their own. Chapter 2 offers strategies to encourage student ownership. Forcing students to learn, or even coercing them through the threat of negative consequences, is at best an inefficient way to teach; at worst it's a recipe for failure for both teacher and student. Much better, of course, is that the students' goals line up with our own. This chapter outlines some ways to make that happen.

Chapter 3 examines some common aspects of the college course—tests, readings, assignments, and others—and asks how we can improve them to better encourage student learning. With diverse classrooms full of students with varying backgrounds, capabilities, and goals, it's impossible to expect the same level of improvement in each of them. But with some conscious attention to our course design, we can set up the elements of our courses to create the conditions that will help us obtain the outcomes we're after.

With that diversity in mind, Chapter 4 looks at ways to tailor our teaching to the students in front of us. No teaching strategy works all the time, with every group of students. This chapter offers ways to learn about your students so that you can help them help themselves.

Next up is a look at assessment, both summative (aimed at measuring past behavior) and formative (aimed at influencing future behavior). Giving students feedback is an important part of the instructor's job. Whether they come in the form of tests, quizzes, returned essays, or more informal feedback, assessment opportunities offer us the chance to speak with students when we know they'll be listening.

Chapter 6 offers ways for instructors from any discipline to model process in their classrooms. One of the strengths of my department is the way the faculty teaches rhetoric—on the whole, our focus is on the replicable processes of writing and speaking rather than on just the finished essays and speeches of one particular semester. It's a great way to ensure that the lessons students learn are ones they can take with them when the course is over. This chapter offers strategies that can help us not lose sight of process, even as we hold our students' products to high standards.

Chapter 7 offers some advice for teaching within our particular era, one of political upheaval, "fake news," and increasing diversity. When the world outside the classroom undergoes radical change, we cannot keep teaching in the way we always have. How do we educate a new generation of citizens when so many forces seem arrayed against that project?

Finally, Chapter 8 offers ways to improve as a teacher, even within the frenetic and overburdened life of the twenty-first-century professor. As with any practice, teaching well involves a near-constant series of adjustments to improve. This chapter provides some advice on how to build on successes and learn from mistakes as you go.

What follows is my attempt to synthesize all I've learned as I've gone from a teaching-indifferent graduate student to a struggling adjunct to a pedagogy writer to a rhetoric lecturer. Each of those identities has helped me understand the challenge of teaching, but then again, all aspects of life can shed light on the challenge of teaching. Once you realize that the core of teaching is the attempt to help other people change, you start to see object lessons everywhere.

It's my belief that all academics should be excellent teachers; teaching should be at the center of our profession. If it is true, as Derek Bok has written, that "a fundamental aim of college is to help students grow to fulfill their potential," then surely it is a problem of existential import that we generally ignore the training and development of effective teachers.[8] We don't emphasize teaching in graduate school, we don't sufficiently reward teaching in our institutions, nor do we take great pains to assess the effectiveness of teaching in our classrooms. All of this must change if universities are to fulfill their missions.

I titled this book *The Missing Course* because I believe that extensive pedagogy training should be a required element of graduate programs across the disciplines. When we treat teaching with the seriousness it deserves, we'll see that it is an essential part of scholarship, not a distraction from it. We'll recommit ourselves to an inspiring model of higher education: as we explore new frontiers of knowledge, we will take our students with us.

It takes continual work to be an excellent teacher, but it's not rocket science. Anyone can be a great teacher as long as she has the requisite commitment to properly understand and help her students. Let's make that drive—how do I help these students transform themselves?—underlie everything we do in the classroom.

1

Helping Students Revise Themselves
Active Learning Strategies

ANYONE WHO TEACHES will come up against a difficult truth: you can't make someone learn. It sounds obvious, but it's actually a crucial insight, one that more professors need to take to heart if our universities are going to more effectively teach their students. Long-term, significant learning gains are produced neither by merely telling students information nor by giving them the right books to read. Helping students learn requires us to create the conditions in which students can revise their previous understandings of the concepts and skills we're trying to help them acquire. Such revision is necessarily an active process; when all we ask of students in class is to sit and listen to us lecture, we make this revision far less likely to occur. It's far better to fill our class periods with "active learning strategies": activities designed to get students to engage with the material, confront the limits of their understanding, see how their thinking must change, and practice the skills we hope they will develop.

In 2013, a group of researchers, led by the University of Washington's Scott Freeman, set out to thoroughly examine the relevant research on active learning as an alternative to lecturing. They eventually produced a meta-analysis of 225 studies that compared student performance in science, technology, engineering, and mathematics (STEM) courses taught by traditional lectures versus those that used active learning strategies. Using a cautious methodology to avoid conscious or unconscious biases, the study found a marked difference between the two categories. Average grades in those courses that used active learning were a half grade higher (that is, a B rather than a B–) than those taught by lecture. Moreover, students in lecture courses were one and a half times more likely to fail than their counterparts who engaged in active learning. It was pretty clear cut.

How clear cut? So much so that the authors mused that if this had been medical research instead of an educational study, the project might have been "stopped for benefit"—that is, discontinued out of an ethical responsibility to those enrolled. In the not-too-distant future, it is now imaginable that researchers will refuse to study lectures as a mode of teaching because to do so would be an unethical imposition on the poor students who have to suffer through them. Consequently, the authors suggested that future studies move on from the active learning versus lecturing question and focus instead on determining what *kinds* of active learning work best.[1] As Carl Wieman, who authored a comment on the study, added, "If a new antibiotic is being tested for effectiveness, its effectiveness at curing patients is compared with the best current antibiotics and not with treatment by bloodletting."[2]

It's not as if these results were unexpected. The Freeman et al. meta-analysis dramatically underlined what most educational researchers have been saying for years: students learn best not from passive listening to an expert but from actively taking part in their own education, utilizing higher-order thinking, and collaborating with each other.[3] The demonstrated advantages aren't restricted to the straightforward ones revealed in the meta-analysis, either. A number of studies have shown that active learning strategies can have a disproportionately positive impact on traditionally underprivileged groups of students, lowering so-called performance gaps between male and female students and between white students and students of color.[4] Other studies suggested that active learning increases student enthusiasm for learning.[5] Another found that students who engaged in active learning in their courses were significantly more likely to have developed those higher-order skills we expect higher education to provide—critical thinking, creative thinking, problem-solving skills—than students who had mainly taken lectures.[6] The evidence for active learning has been so convincing that some educational researchers simply refer to it as "research-based instructional strategies."

Active learning rests on a constructivist view of human learning—meaning we *construct* new knowledge by building on our previous knowledge. Although this will not be an in-depth look at the science behind our current understanding of how we learn, it's important to understand this model.[7]

We used to think learning was like filling up a jar. If you wanted to teach students something, you gave them the relevant information. Once they understood that information, it stayed in their brain to be used as needed. Students who didn't yet fully understand the information needed to study harder—usually this meant reading and rereading the information until it was memorized.[8] This was certainly how I went about learning through much of my undergraduate career.

Now we understand that learning is much more like an act of revision. All of our students bring to our classes certain ideas about the world, and about our subjects, and these preconceptions are a crucial part of the process of learning new ideas. For a student to be taught, she must revise her current understanding to become a new understanding—it doesn't just happen automatically. "A critical feature of effective teaching," according to the National Research Council's landmark report *How People Learn*, "is that it elicits from students their pre-existing understanding of the subject matter to be taught and provides opportunities to build on—or challenge—the initial understanding."[9] That word, *elicits*, is a crucial one for successful pedagogy: the teacher's task is to draw out students' preconceptions and entice them to engage in the work of revision.

This is a highly simplified version of constructivism, and yet it gets across, I think, the central differences between our old and new ways of conceiving of learning. Rather than seeing students as a passive jar that waits to be filled up, we now believe that students must actively participate in the learning process if real learning is to occur. You cannot make someone learn something without their willingness and without their work. It is in this sense that lecturing is severely restricted in its effectiveness. It is very difficult to get someone to change his mind or alter his beliefs just by telling him that he's wrong. Even when people are provided with proof that their beliefs are mistaken, they tend to cling to those beliefs rather than revise them.[10] The kind of revision needed for lasting learning is difficult and sometimes painful, and it doesn't happen because someone external forces it to happen. The student has to take an active role.

In this sense, "active learning" has come to encompass a huge body of teaching practices in the literature; it's essentially "anything but lecturing." Anything that asks students to actively take part in their own learning—frequent testing with immediate feedback, group work, discussion, role-playing games—seems to be better than students passively sitting and listening to a lecture. But, as a curious study led by Tessa Andrews suggests, this definitional looseness might mean that we need to add a caveat or two to the unanimity of the research so far.

I say "curious" because Andrews et al.'s study is more or less on its own in the literature in suggesting that there may be limits to the effectiveness of active learning. The study, "Active Learning *Not* Associated with Student Learning in a Random Sample of College Biology Courses," indeed found that active learning offered no apparent advantages over lecturing. The details of the study are fascinating and, I think, offer up a few important questions that need to be answered.[11]

In many studies of teaching methods, the authors noted, the instructors of the courses being studied are educational researchers—the ones who designed the studies. Shouldn't we expect these educational researchers, who have devoted their professional lives to the study of education, to be unusually informed and committed teachers? What would happen if we designed a study that compared active learning with lecture in courses taught by "ordinary" instructors? That's just what this study sought to answer.

The researchers took a random sampling of introductory biology courses taught at major colleges and universities in the United States; they ended up with twenty-nine courses taught at twenty-eight institutions by thirty-three instructors. They gathered data on both the teaching methods used (in particular, the frequency of active learning strategies) and the student learning (measured through pre- and posttests) in the courses. I already mentioned the article's title, so you know the results, but it's worth repeating: the study found *no* significant relationship between the amount of active learning a class engaged in and how much students learned in the course. If students learned more in one class than in another, it wasn't because their teacher gave them more opportunities for active learning.

So what does this mean?

To the authors of the study, the findings confirmed the concerns that prompted the study in the first place: "Most of the faculty using active learning in previous studies had backgrounds in science education research. The expertise gained during research likely prepares these instructors to use active learning more effectively."[12] In one sense, this is obvious; expert teachers produce better results than novices. But it also underlines an important point: active learning strategies in and of themselves are not a magic bullet. You can't just use the strategies; you have to know how to use them well.

What kind of expertise do educational researchers have that "ordinary" instructors lack? The study's authors suggested that perhaps the instructors in the study didn't fully understand the constructivist model of learning. "Without this expertise," the authors suggest, "the active-learning exercises an instructor uses may have superficial similarities to exercises described in the literature, but may lack constructivist elements necessary for improving learning." Fully understanding constructivism may be necessary to properly put active learning strategies into practice. This idea is supported by the fact that the frequency with which instructors addressed student misconceptions—that is, the degree to which instructors worked to help students revise their prior knowledge—*was* positively associated with student learning.[13] Maybe you have to know why active learning works to be able to know how it works best.[14]

Active learning as a subject of scientific inquiry is still a relatively young phenomenon. Despite the fact that its overall advantages over traditional lecturing seem pretty well settled at this point, there is still

So What Do I Need to Know about Constructivism?

- Constructivism understands truth not as something to be discovered or revealed but as something contestable, contingent, and created by humans engaged in social communities of discourse. This means that we can't just tell students what they need to know and be done with teaching; students need to create their own understanding of the world through active engagement. Our task is to create the conditions for such engagement.

- Constructivism understands learning as a process that begins with confronting the differences between preexisting models of the world and new insights that diverge from those models. Contradictions and disequilibrium are the precursors to learning. This means that good teaching begins with the drawing out of students' preconceptions. If someone calls you up and asks for directions to your house, the first thing you ask is "Where are you now?" Once you—and students—know where students are, you can help them get where they need to go. This begins with designing activities that reveal to students where their current understanding falls short.

- Learning involves constructing new models of reality to reconcile prior models with new information. This often requires reflection in order to generalize and draw conclusions from new experiences. The activities we design for our students should allow them to raise questions, come up with hypotheses, and try out possible solutions. We should be giving our students plenty of opportunities to reflect on the activities they do for our courses, giving time and space for students to cement their learning, abstracting from the particular to the general.

- Constructivism also understands humans as social beings who continually negotiate their understanding of the world through social activities and debate within communities. This means we should take advantage of the classroom environment as much as possible, creating conditions in which the students can form authentic communities to test out ideas, debate conclusions, and understand other perspectives.

much we don't know. As more research is done, we'll learn more and more about the mechanisms behind active learning, what kinds of strategies work better than others, and how best to put these strategies into practice.

In the meantime, one of the goals of this book is to help instructors put active learning strategies to use with a specific and nuanced understanding of their purpose. I don't think you need to be a career education researcher to be able to give your students the benefits of active learning. But I do think that mind-set matters: knowing what you want to achieve in the classroom and having a plan for how your teaching methods will help you reach those goals is just about the best way to ensure you are giving yourself, and your students, the best shot at success.

The first order of business, once you've adopted a constructivist view of the learning process, is to change your approach to your teaching. If we accept that students learn best when they take part in the kinds of activities in which they hold their preconceptions up to the light and revise them, then we must adjust our focus. What this requires is a shift from *What am I going to cover today?* to *What are the students going to do today?* and *How am I going to entice them to do it successfully?*

Introducing Active Learning and Combating Resistance

The work of enticement begins, for me at least, on the first day of class. Many of our students may be used to doing schoolwork at home and using class time to sit and listen and absorb whatever the professor wants to communicate. Active learning requires students to break from the passive role of merely listening to a lecture and taking notes. They must become protagonists in the class's activities. At least some resistance to your methods is normal and to be expected. Part of your job, particularly at the beginning of the semester, is to be a salesperson for the active learning practices you want to introduce.

I think it's important to be explicit up front. As I've noted, a course in which students are expected to be active participants can be a bit of a shock for some. So make the case for your pedagogical choices. I tell my students that we're going to be using active learning methods, and I make clear what's expected of them. Read up on the benefits of active learning and, particularly at the beginning of the semester, let your students know that there are well-researched reasons behind the way you've designed the course. Treat students like colleagues whose cooperation you need, and they will be much more likely to buy into new approaches.

I ask my students about their other courses, particularly their big lectures. I try to get them to both think about and talk about their experiences as learners: Do they think they learn a lot from lectures? What were their best teachers like? What have been their favorite courses? I explain some of the science behind active learning methods, give them a brief summary of constructivism, and ask if that conception of learning jibes with their own experiences. Sometimes I will ask them to recount their most memorable learning experiences, to get them to see that the most significant learning occurs when the learner is actively engaged in the process.

Because active learning methods require full student participation for their success, you can't take that participation for granted. Throughout the semester, get into the habit of explaining the justification behind each activity as you introduce it. Let your students know why a particular exercise or topic will be useful to them, either for their final grade or (better yet) in their lives outside the classroom walls. Use rubrics or annotated examples of past student work to show them how you'll be assessing their work. Give updates on their course performance early and often. Students are less likely to resist your pedagogy if you cultivate a relationship of openness throughout.[15]

Some students may resist your attempts to integrate active learning strategies simply because you rely too heavily on one kind of activity. If your way of keeping students active is always to break students into small groups to discuss the reading, you may run into some problems. You want your teaching to benefit both the extrovert who loves collaborative exercises and the bookworm who excels at in-class writing assignments. Mix it up on a regular basis and keep everyone on their toes.

Creating a High-Participation Classroom

One of the main things that changes when you make your classroom an active learning classroom is that student participation becomes nonnegotiable. Active learning strategies require that students take the lead, so if you are going to start to introduce more of these strategies into your classroom, you need to work to ensure that students participate. How can we create conditions in which participation is the norm, not the exception?

Among the drafts and notebooks and juvenilia found in the late David Foster Wallace's archives, housed at the University of Texas's Ransom Center, are some of his teaching materials. I'm particularly fond of this passage in one of his syllabi (I include something similar in my own):

You are <u>forbidden</u> to keep yourself from asking a question or making a comment because you fear it will sound obvious or unsophisticated or lame or stupid. Because critical reading and prose fiction are such hard, weird things to try to study, a stupid-seeming comment or question can end up being valuable or even profound. I am deadly-serious about creating a classroom environment where everyone feels free to ask or speak about anything she wishes. So any student who groans, smirks, mimes machine-gunning or onanism, chortles, eye-rolls, or in any way ridicules some other student's in-class question/comment will be warned once in private and on the second offense will be kicked out of class and flunked, no matter what week it is. If the offender is male, I am also apt to find him off-campus and beat him up.[16]

This may be a little too forward for your own style of teaching, but Wallace's emphasis on creating a safe and supportive community points to an essential ingredient in the active learning classroom. Research suggests that, even more than any particular characteristics or behavior of the instructor, it's the students themselves, their personal characteristics and the overall character of the group, that most influence whether students participate. But there's plenty that instructors can do to help shape this classroom community.

In the 1990s, Polly Fassinger, then a professor of sociology at Concordia College in Minnesota, was curious about the research she'd read about why students participate—or don't—in college classrooms. Most of the studies she'd seen focused on the instructor's actions, on how some instructors seemed to create a classroom environment that made it less likely for students to speak up or take part. But her training as a sociologist led her to wonder whether this approach was missing something crucial: students in classrooms are groups. There is a long tradition within sociology of studying groups, of paying attention to the ways that group characteristics can have strong effects on individual behavior. Fassinger set out to survey students, in the middle of a semester, not just on how often they participate but also on their individual traits, the characteristics of the group, and their perceptions of the instructor.

In a series of articles, Fassinger detailed her results, some of which were surprising. She found that "professors' interpersonal styles"— whether professors promote discussion, or give students adequate time to respond, or interrupt students—"do not have a direct effect on whether students talk in class."[17] Instead, she found that the biggest contributors to student participation are student confidence and students' perception of the classroom climate. The more confident students feel in class, the more likely they are to speak up and to participate fully. What's more, Fassinger found that the biggest factor associated with students' confidence in class was their sense of the class as inclusive, encouraging, and attentive.[18] It seems that students' perceptions of their peers, and of the extent to which the group of students is a friendly one, are even more important, when it comes to participation, than students' perceptions of the instructor.[19]

But that doesn't mean that the instructor is irrelevant. Fassinger, along with many of the researchers who have confirmed her results over the years, has been quick to point out that just because students don't attribute their participation to instructor behavior doesn't mean it's not significant. Students may not always know exactly why they feel comfortable speaking in one class rather than another. And teachers have a big role to play in shaping the environment of the classroom so that an inclusive student group can take shape. Even if no single action on behalf of the professor leads students to participate more, we can try to create the conditions in which more participation occurs.

Particularly at the beginning of the semester, we should be focused on creating a classroom environment in which students feel respected, listened to, and encouraged to be themselves. But we can't forget that, whether we like it or not, students have a significant part to play in shaping that environment. Chapter 2 is devoted to strategies to encourage student ownership of our courses, but it's worth underlining this social aspect here: students will have a better chance of succeeding in your course if the classroom environment is supportive and encouraging.

In the early days of the course, give students plenty of opportunities to talk to each other informally, to get to know each other as people beyond what they bring to the topic up for discussion in any given class period. If your class isn't massive, insist that students learn each other's names. Many instructors have students make name cards at the beginning of the semester: three-by-five cards with their names, and sometimes relevant information as well. You can use these cards to help students quickly get to know each other—give the cards to a different student at the beginning of each class period to hand out. Or keep them yourself and shuffle them to randomly determine who gets called on. When students are able to know and trust each other, they are more likely to open up in class and to take full part in the class's activities. And that's our goal, remember. Full participation—in which each student is fully present in the day's activities—is a prerequisite for active learning strategies to succeed. So laying the groundwork by encouraging your students to connect as human beings is a good idea.

Jay Howard, whose excellent book *Discussion in the College Classroom* surveys a wide variety of research on the subject, suggests looking for ways, early in the semester, for students to collaborate on coursework. Have their participation be mostly with each other, in pairs or small groups, before you ask them to participate with you, in front of the whole class.[20] I put students in small groups all semester long, but leaning on groups in a course's opening weeks allows students who are just getting to know each other the opportunity to communicate in a format that doesn't feel quite so public. Having students work together to define certain course policies (as I suggest you do in Chapter 2) is another good way to encourage students to start building a cohesive classroom community.

Getting Students to Talk

The kind of student participation you'll probably be most concerned with from day to day is whether students talk in class. As anyone who has taught for more than a week will tell you, the most clever and carefully planned classroom strategy can fall flat in the face of the wall of student silence. We've all had classes in which, for whatever reason, students just don't want to talk. What do we do then?

The first step, I think, is to prioritize discussion. It's important that you let students know that discussion is integral to the course, to their learning, and to their grades. Early in the term, be explicit about why you want everyone to take part in discussions. Devote a section of your syllabus to laying out that reasoning as well. Make participation at least 10 percent of students' final grades (I do 20 percent), and hand out interim participation grades regularly to remind students of their responsibility. Although overly emphasizing participation points can backfire,[21] the simple fact that participation counts as much as a major assignment sends a signal to students about your priorities.

You can also enshrine discussion in the regular rhythm of a class period. Begin each class with a discussion question. Do that every time—perhaps allowing a few minutes for students to write down their thoughts first—and they will get in the habit of coming to class ready to talk. Or if you'd rather start class with a short lecture or

My Syllabus's Participation Policy (Feel free to steal this; I've stolen parts of it from other teachers.)

The importance of actively taking part in class activities is difficult to overstate. Research has consistently shown that students who participate in the learning process learn more, and retain their learning for longer, than students who do not. You won't learn very well by passively listening to someone lecture at you. Therefore, this class will ask a lot of you. You are expected to come to class ready to engage with me and your fellow students on the topics of the day. You will practice the skills we are learning through in-class exercises, in groups and otherwise. What's more, you will play a vital role in your peers' education—you'll help them learn more, and they will, in turn, help you.

Your participation mark will be based on your demonstrated ability to contribute to class activities and discussions in ways that *raise the level of discourse*. Talking all the time is not necessarily the same thing as great participation; indeed, talking too frequently can even lead to imbalance and discomfort for others. Actively listening to classmates, responding with relevance to others' comments, and reflecting and building on your classmates' ideas lead to a strong participation grade.

I am very serious about helping to create a classroom environment in which anyone feels free to ask questions, raise concerns, make brilliant points, and so on. This classroom is your classroom. Please don't keep yourself from asking a question because you fear it will sound stupid or unsophisticated or obvious. Sometimes, clichés are true: in here at least, there are no stupid questions.

Although I am committed to a democratic classroom in which students exert a great measure of control, I recognize that I have institutional authority as the instructor. I choose to use that authority to forbid any behavior that would make anyone else in the class feel uncomfortable or the subject of ridicule. You are expected to behave courteously and respectfully to your classmates and to me. All students need to feel that this is their classroom; I am committed to protecting those conditions.

presentation, try writing an open-ended discussion question on the board first so that students can start thinking about the discussion that your lecture will lead up to.

Even if you have to lecture for most of the class period (I hope I've convinced you otherwise), break it up with frequent opportunities for discussion. You need to convey that participation is nonnegotiable. Opening up the floor to discussion early and often works a lot better than talking at them for an hour and then asking, "Any questions?"

You can model the curiosity you'd like students to exhibit in class by asking rhetorical questions, admitting when you're unsure about something, and thinking out loud. Let students know, through your actions, that it's OK to fumble for an answer—in fact, it's encouraged. In that vein, thank students for their contributions even when they are wrong. You don't need to lie to them or be insincere, just honestly grateful that they are participating.

And don't be afraid of silence. After asking a question of the class, be prepared to wait a full ten or even fifteen seconds without a response. If, when no one immediately responds, you rush to answer your own question, students will get the message that they don't really need to speak up. Instead, let your question hang in the air. If need be, rephrase it. But don't give up on the discussion just because nobody answers right away.

What about cold calling?

Calling on students is hard for many teachers, myself included. It just doesn't fit with the kind of teacher I want to be. I don't want to be the authority figure in front of whom students cower. I get no pleasure from putting students on the spot, from scaring them into knowing the material. I don't teach law, and I have no need to grill students to see how they hold up under pressure. My feeling is that if

I have to force my students to participate in discussions, I must be doing something wrong.

As well, doesn't calling on students, demanding they give us an answer, seem to undermine the positive classroom climate I was just suggesting we strive to create?

Well, some intriguing research on the subject indicates that we shouldn't shy away from cold calling; we just need to change how we think of it. In a 2013 study that included sixteen sections of an undergraduate accounting course, Elise Dallimore and her colleagues at Northeastern University found that as the frequency of cold calling increased, so, too, did the frequency of students' voluntary contributions to discussions. What's more, in those classrooms in which instructors regularly called on students, voluntary participation increased as the semester went on.[22]

The study's results suggest that participating in a class discussion in college is a skill—and like all skills, it requires practice. Calling on students gets them to talk and gives them practice at speaking up. That practice then leads to further, voluntary participation, without the need to be called on. In the words of the study's authors: "Cold-calling encourages students to prepare more and to participate more frequently; the more they prepare, and the more frequently they participate, the more comfortable they become when participating."[23] I think the emphasis on student comfort in that explanation can help us shift our model of what cold calling is, and can be. We don't want a classroom in which students aren't comfortable participating; we're trying to achieve the opposite. So instead of seeing cold calling as an antagonistic demand for students to prove they are up to snuff, let's think of it as a warm invitation to contribute to a discussion.

Try to remember: the thing that often keeps us from calling on students—the concern that they might be uncomfortable speaking up in class—is actually a good reason to call on them. If we don't encourage students to come out of their shells for fear of putting them on the spot, we may be doing them a disservice. As well, being able to speak in front of other people, being able to keep your cool when asked questions, is something students will need to do throughout their lives. Just as we ask students to write essays or take tests, we should be asking them to respond to course material in class.

So call on students in class discussions—but with the right attitude. You're not trying to put them on the spot. You're curious about their views and their understanding of the issues being discussed. What they think is important—both to their own learning and to that of their peers. An earlier study (also led by Dallimore) suggests that one student's participation has a positive effect on another's learning—student participation is a tide that lifts all boats.[24] So there's little point in frightening students into taking part in class discussions. We need to invite them in.

Can I Still Lecture Sometimes?

For reasons of class size, course content, or departmental policy, you might not have the option of abandoning a lecture-dominated course. Not to worry. Many of us were educated by professors who mainly lectured; we still learned plenty (right?). I still have fond memories of a lecture Michael Bristol gave, at McGill University twenty years ago, in which he riffed for ten minutes or so on the "funeral baked meats" in *Hamlet*. It is important to remember, even as the field moves away from lectures toward active learning strategies, that lecturing per se is not the problem. It's lecturing *only*, what the pedagogy scholar Derek Bruff has called "continuous exposition by the teacher," that we need to avoid.[25]

To figure out when, and how, to lecture, we need to understand what *telling* is good for and what it is not.

If you know something important that you think your students should know, there is nothing wrong, of course, with just telling them. If a friend calls you up and asks you how to make that risotto you're famous for, you wouldn't start in on the Socratic method and make her work to discover the recipe by herself. You'd just tell her. Telling is an excellent method for communicating specific information. And there are plenty of occasions when our students need specific information. To communicate important facts, to illustrate a concept with a concrete story of its application, to explain the historical origins of a conflict, you can take the easiest route from A to B and just tell your students.

What telling is not good for is teaching students complex ideas, conceptual knowledge, or difficult skills. In his 2000 book *Teaching with Your Mouth Shut*, Donald Finkel uses the example of giving directions: "When I tell my friend how to get to my house, I allow him to solve a specific problem (how to get to my house), but I do not enrich his understanding of geography, transportation, navigation, or anything else. He doesn't have to think differently after he has digested my instructions; he has neither deepened nor broadened his understanding of the world. He simply has gained some facts he needs for a specific purpose."[26] For our students to gain more than specific information—to gain understanding rather than just knowledge of a set of facts—we need to design learning experiences in which they gain that understanding for themselves, that is to say, *actively*. If you're just lecturing without giving your students a chance to take part—to try to solve problems on their own, to work together on answering a question, to predict the consequences of a complex phenomenon—you might as well be showing them a video.

The goal is to engage, and it's self-defeating to attempt to elicit that engagement solely through the force of your skillful way with words. Many, if not all, of the strategies described in this book can be used to break up a lecture, although some you will have to modify for your purposes. Even just pausing your lecture now and again and asking students about their prior knowledge about the topic under consideration can help get them in the revising state of mind (and make sure they're staying awake to boot). Here are a few other ideas, some possibilities to ensure your students remain active and engaged, even when you can't leave the lectern.

Mick Charney, an associate professor of architecture at Kansas State University, has written about using quizzes to maintain students' attention during lectures. At the beginning of class, he hands out a ten-question, multiple-choice quiz and tells students that the answers can be found in that day's lecture. Students need to pay attention to get the answers right, but if they do, it's a gimme of a quiz: you're telling them the answers. You collect the quizzes at the end of class and grade them for a small portion of the final grade. The marking shouldn't take too much time—it's multiple-choice and, again, most students should get all the answers right.[27]

It's a simple, relatively low-effort way to keep students engaged during a lecture. Even better, I think, would be to have students quickly attempt to answer the quiz questions before you start lecturing, and then correct their own answers as the lecture sets them straight. That approach can help demonstrate to students what they don't yet understand, and get them thinking about their thinking—a key behavior of successful learners (I discuss the value of metacognition—thinking about thinking—in more detail in Chapter 2).

That move—giving students a quiz before you deliver the lecture that provides them with the answers—is what a number of scholars at the University at Albany have called a "naive task." In a naive task, the instructor asks students to complete a challenge for which they don't yet have the necessary knowledge or skill to complete. Often the challenge requires students to make predictions. A physics professor might give students a puzzle: "A canary is inside a sealed bottle on top of a scale. What will happen to the reading on the scale if the canary takes flight inside the bottle?"[28] Students work together to try to predict what will happen, but they won't be able to explain it properly without the relevant knowledge of mass and force. According to Bill Roberson and Billie Franchini, both of the University at Albany, "making and defending a decision before having access to key information promotes the perception that the information, when it is eventually provided, will be a valuable tool or resource."[29] When, after students attempt to complete a naive task, you deliver a short lecture that provides them with the information they have been missing, they will be primed to learn it. Naive tasks work well because they reveal to students the gaps in their knowledge—gaps that your lecture can fill. Having been primed by attempting to complete a task armed only with their own preconceptions, they will be more likely to connect the information you give them to larger concepts.

But I Teach Science—How Can I Abandon the Lecture?

Many instructors in the sciences may read this section with skepticism—the lecture is so embedded in college science instruction that moving away from it may seem impossible. But much excellent work has been done to discover more effective ways to teach science[30]—particularly since the 1990s, when a great number of calls went out to remake science education in the wake of studies showing a marked decline in enrollment in science majors. Here are a few specific suggestions to help you move away from only telling.

Shift your approach from deductive to inductive

Angela Bauer-Dantoin has written about one way that professors, particularly in the biological sciences, have moved away from dependence on the lecture: by moving from a deductive mode of teaching to an inductive mode. "Rather than teaching theories or general principles and then progressing to applications of those theories or principles (the deductive method of teaching typically employed in biology lectures), instructors who teach inductively facilitate learning by presenting students with problems or case studies to solve (typically in small groups), and relevant principles or theories are explored or discussed once students have established the need to know them."[31] By having students engage in problem-solving or predictive activities before introducing general theories, you encourage students to construct conceptual knowledge for themselves—they'll see why the theory or principle exists, and understand its utility.

Have students teach each other

Harvard's Eric Mazur has gotten plenty of well-deserved attention over the years for his "peer instruction" method that he evolved in his physics classes.[32] Prompted by the discovery that even students who did well on his course's exams weren't learning much more than how to "plug and chug," Mazur developed a system in which students engage deeply in thinking about and explaining concepts to each other, and the instructor is able to respond to their needs.

Peer instruction typically proceeds like this:

- A brief lecture (typically five to seven minutes) introducing a concept or problem.

- Students take a quiz on the lecture, with questions based on past student difficulties. They enter their answers on clickers or phones, and the class's collective response is displayed on screen at the front of the room.

- Students then turn to a partner and try to prove that their answers are right.

- After discussion, students again answer the questions through the clicker system.

- Finally, the instructor delivers another short lecture, explaining why the common errors are wrong and why the correct answers are right.

Mazur has reported that even two minutes of student discussion leads to significantly more correct answers on the second quiz. The approach is a great way to use technology to make sure that when you do lecture, you are responding to the students in the room.

Teach in cycles

Many science professors have found that the 5E instructional model is a helpful alternative to the lecture.[33] This is a cyclical approach to the class period that originated in the K–12 world. By cycling through a number of student activities, you can avoid monotony while making sure students are actively engaging with the material in a constructive way. In each class period, follow this cycle:

- Engagement: introduce a short activity or reading or video clip that gets students interested in the topic and primes them to want to learn more. This is also an opportunity to find out about students' prior knowledge and possible misconceptions.

- Exploration: engage students in an activity that gives them hands-on experience of the concept and how it works.

- Explanation: ask students to try to analyze and explain the phenomenon; can they put it into words? Entice students to describe their understanding and highlight what they don't yet know.

- Elaboration: deepen student understanding by offering new applications and contexts for the central concept. Students put their assumptions to the test by applying them in new circumstances.

- Evaluation: work to assess how much students have learned, either through a test or through more informal means, like having students test each other.

Another idea comes from Tamara Rosier, a former academic who now leads the consultancy Acorn Leadership. Called "knowledge ratings," this approach asks students to pay attention to how much or how little they know about a particular topic during class.[34] Begin by asking students to rate their knowledge of the topic on a scale from 0 to 3, where 0 means no knowledge of the subject and 3 means very knowledgeable. Tell them that the goal is to get everyone up to a 3 before the end of that class period.

Halfway through the class period, take a timeout and ask students to reassess their knowledge ratings. Have they improved? Then ask students to write down the questions they still have about the topic. What gaps in their knowledge are keeping them from getting to a 3? If you have the time, it's a good practice to ask students to voice these questions aloud so that you can focus your teaching in the second half of the class period on what students still don't understand. Repeat the exercise at the end of class, explaining that they should aim to get themselves to a 3 before beginning that evening's homework or reading.

Group work is a commonly used component of active learning pedagogies, and dividing students into small groups is a good way to get them involved in the day's topic during a lecture. Especially in large classes, breaking students into groups can help counteract the students' sense of sitting in a theater, watching a performance.[35] I often think the best kind of groups are groups of two.

Pairing students up rather than getting them into larger groups has the advantage of being a lot quicker: there's no time spent deciding who is in which group (just turn to the person next to you), and far less time actually getting into the groups. It also has the benefit of leaving students with nowhere to hide. Each person is accountable to a partner in a way that isn't always the case with larger groups.

What do you do with them once they're paired up? The "classroom assessment technique" of think-pair-share is a classic for a reason.[36] You interrupt your lecture to ask an important and open-ended question. Have the students take a minute or two to write down a response and then share their answers with their partners. You can then call on students to share their responses aloud with the whole class.

Another useful strategy: pair students up and, at various points throughout the lecture, pause and ask the pairs to share and compare notes for the previous section of the lecture. This is a good way for students to discover if they've missed anything important, and for misconceptions to reveal themselves quickly.

Another classic technique is known as the "muddiest point" exercise. You ask students, either midway through or at the end of your lecture, to take a couple of minutes and write down the muddiest point from the day's class. What don't they understand? What isn't quite clear yet? Whether or not you collect their answers (collecting them is particularly useful if you do the exercise at the end of class), I think it's important that you immediately follow this exercise by calling on students to read their responses aloud. Put aside any reluctance you might have to put students on the spot; you've given them the opportunity to write down an answer first.

That exercise, in addition to asking students to think critically about the lecture and providing you with valuable feedback about their understanding, also lets students know that others might share their confusion. Whenever I've done this activity, I always notice heads nodding when students read their muddiest point to the class.

Building this into your lecture routine—a formalized ritual that acknowledges that the lecturer does not always make things crystal clear—is a great way to break students out of the role of passive listeners, unable to question the wisdom of the great sage in the front of the classroom. If you introduce this exercise early in the semester, and use it often, your students might even ask a question of their own accord sometimes.

Lecturing is a time-tested and efficient way to communicate information. But the most effective teaching involves looking to communicate information in *inefficient* ways—that is, in ways that make students work to understand the information and not just listen passively.[37] So if we lecture, we need to supplement periods of telling with activities in which students can then put to use the information we tell them. We need to design activities that allow students to integrate the new information into their prior knowledge and construct new concepts. And we'd be wise to think about how to prime students to receive a lecture, by creating activities that reveal to them the gaps in their own knowledge. A big benefit of engaging students in active learning is that it can reveal—to us and to them—what they don't yet understand. If we only lecture, we can tell them all we want, but whether they're listening is anyone's guess.

Skills *and* Content (but Skills First)

One of the oldest—and most tired—debates in the education world is about skills versus content. For years, especially in K–12 circles, teachers, administrators, and education researchers have debated whether skills or content is more important for students to learn.

The apparent dichotomy has proved surprisingly sturdy. In an April 2016 *Chronicle of Higher Education* report on skills as "the new canon," Dan Berrett detailed an effort at Emory University to shift faculty focus toward teaching the skill of using and evaluating evidence. The story quoted the Emory lecturer Robert Goddard, who worried that the move to skills-focused courses was "doing a disservice to the students by not having a more coherent, uniform body of content to deliver."[38] Such a conception suggests a zero-sum game: more time spent on skills necessarily means less time spent on content.

But if a consensus has emerged in this long-standing debate, it's one that pushes against an either-or approach.

I would argue that skills versus content is a false choice; our students need both. As John Schlueter, an instructor of English at St. Paul College, wrote in a 2016 essay for *Inside Higher Ed*, "Classrooms must move beyond being places where content is delivered and become places where students learn how to process that content."[39] Content is present in both cases. What matters is whether we merely "deliver" it or teach students the skills that allow them to put that content to use.

Much research has suggested that skills by themselves—isolated from any knowledge of disciplinary content—are very difficult, if not impossible, to teach.[40] We learn important skills through practice in specific domains, and transferring those skills to other domains is not straightforward. Similarly, content without the skills to apply it is merely trivia. What good is it to know a lot about a subject if you don't know what to do with that knowledge?

So we need both skills and content. But for instructors who want to integrate active learning into their classrooms, I think it still matters which one has a priority in our thinking. The way we conceptualize our tasks as teachers can have a great impact on how we teach. While rejecting the skills-content dichotomy, I think it's important that we focus on skills first and let content follow.

When we define our courses by their content, we almost necessarily force ourselves into a "coverage" mind-set. Many of us still show up to class with a plan that lists the topics we'll go over. By focusing on what material we need to cover, or even on what content students need to learn, the danger is that we just tell students the material, which seems like the most efficient way to get it to them. But we know pretty confidently that just telling students information is not a very good way to help them retain it.

By contrast, when we focus on skills first, when we define our courses by the skills they impart, we are much more likely to use the sort of classroom activities that researchers have found to be most effective for long-term learning. By conceptualizing the class period as a time when students will practice a certain skill, we almost automatically ensure that they will be active learners. When we prioritize skills, we ask, *What will students do today?* instead of *What will I cover today?* The former question builds active learning into your approach, no matter what content you have to cover.

If you take this approach, you're not choosing skills at the expense of content; it isn't one or the other. Luckily, when you lead with skills, it's easy for content to follow. Begin your course planning by thinking about what skills you want students to practice. Design class activities that help students learn how to execute those skills on their own. Then make the "what" of your activities the content that you want your students to learn. It's not difficult to integrate content into the skills you ask your students to practice. In fact, it's much easier to start with skills and then add content than it is to do the reverse.

If you want students to practice the skill of revision, for example, have them revise one of the course readings according to a set of specifications ("What if the author wanted to use the same evidence to argue the opposite point?"). If you want students to practice making a computational engineering model, have them try to project what happens to a bridge when an earthquake of a certain magnitude hits. If you want students to work on their research skills, have them find, compare, and evaluate two sources with opposing views on that week's topic. By using skills to engage with course content, students will learn that content more easily and will be more likely to retain it as well.[41]

As I mentioned in the introduction, I feel blessed to teach in a department that places such a big emphasis on skills. In my rhetoric classes, I feel very little pressure to lecture, because I feel very little pressure to communicate to my students a large body of material. But a focus on skills can be a part of even the most content-heavy courses. Take a look at how the University of Iowa's Ned Bowden and Rebecca Laird introduce their Organic Chemistry class in their syllabus:

> In this class you are going to learn how to think *critically*. Organic chemistry is more than the memorization of a bunch of facts and it is certainly more than applying a few simple rules to get the right answer. . . . You will have a bunch of facts and you must learn how to think critically to solve problems. Therefore, you must learn to think like a detective and piece answers together with everything that you know. We will help you as much as we can to learn these skills.[42]

Right from the start, students in this course are informed that above all they will be learning how to solve problems. They get a sense that they will have plenty of opportunities to practice such problem solving and that the professors can certainly help. But any preconceived notion that memorizing the periodic table will earn them an A is thrown out the window.

When defining your course, both to your students and to yourself, emphasize the skills students will learn, in particular the skills they will be able to carry forward to future applications. It will help students stay motivated as you engage them in activities that let them practice those skills. And it will help you on those days when you feel like you have run out of material to cover.

What I'm suggesting is more about your mind-set as a teacher than anything else, but then again, so is much of our task as educators. We may not want to always be the center of attention in our classroom, but how we approach our task still has the power to shape our students' learning environment. When you commit to active learning as a pedagogical principle, you start to see the classroom as a different place. I like to think of the process as analogous to photography. Many photographers will tell you that they don't photograph subjects— people or landscapes or objects; they photograph *light*. What light is to the photographer, students are to the teacher. No matter what subject we're teaching, our students are always our real subjects, the human beings we are tasked with helping.

When we keep our focus on our students and their development, we give ourselves the best chance of success, no matter which particular strategies we use.

2

Let Students Own the Course

SOMEONE MUCH SMARTER than me once called active learning a "staged collaboration."[1] I love this phrase. As teachers, all we can do ahead of time is the staging: we can come up with activities, determine elements of the environment, set the rules, and generally have an idea about how things will go. But all that staging is for naught unless the students buy in. There is no such thing as a one-sided collaboration; instructors cannot implement active learning strategies on their own. If we are committed to using active learning strategies in our classrooms, we need to be committed to enticing our students to join us as partners.

In the hopes of making teaching tips seem easily implementable, too much writing on pedagogy treats the classroom as a static environment where instructors can put into place whatever methods they wish and get the desired result every time. But at the heart of the idea of active learning is the students themselves—the students *must* collaborate in their own learning. So any coherent approach to active learning must make it a priority to bring students on board.

All the knowledge, preparation, and pedagogical techniques in the world won't help you in the classroom if you can't motivate students to come along with you.

Most of the time, our main weapons in the fight to motivate students are the grades we give out. To be sure, grades also exist to give an accurate picture of student performance. But grades typically exist as both rewards and punishments to nudge students into approaching the course the way we think they should. When we construct our syllabi, we devote a higher percentage of the final grade to assignments we think are more important or difficult. We assign regular quizzes when we want to make sure students come to class prepared. To encourage punctuality, we threaten to dock grades if students turn lab reports in late. This is the unspoken agreement in higher education: students understand the rules of the game, and if they fail to follow them, their grades (and presumably their prospects) will suffer.

The tricky thing is that, while it's easy to come up with any number of carrots and sticks to prompt students to do better, decades of research have shown that such so-called extrinsic rewards and deterrents are not particularly effective tools. In fact, in many studies, subjects who were offered extrinsic rewards to complete a complex task actually performed worse than when they weren't given rewards.[2]

When grades are the main driving force behind our students' motivation, instead of trying to master the material for their own benefit and assimilate it into their prior knowledge, students figure out what's expected of them to attain a good grade and act accordingly. Extrinsic motivators are additionally problematic if we want students to develop a lifelong interest in our subjects; after graduation, when the rewards for learning are gone, the interest disappears.

Ken Bain, whose book *What the Best College Teachers Do* provides a useful overview of the research into extrinsic and intrinsic motivation, puts it succinctly: "If students study only because they want to get a good grade or be the best in the class, they do not achieve as much as they do when they learn because they are interested."[3]

So how do we keep students interested? How do we teach so that they are motivated to learn because they want to learn, not just because they have to jump through the hoops we've set up? This chapter features strategies that you can use—from the initial process of course design through the last day of the semester—to encourage student ownership of your courses. Without their investment, you may be teaching, but they very well might not be learning.

Salesmanship and Something Bigger

Why should students take your course?

It's a question not enough instructors ask and answer seriously. If you suspect that the answer is "to get three credits toward my major," don't be surprised if you have a problem motivating students.

Many professors no longer have to write the little blurbs that advertise their classes in course catalogs, but the exercise is a valuable one. My colleague Megan Knight and I teach a graduate writing course at the University of Iowa. Because it's a relatively new course, and because it's cross-disciplinary, not originating in any of the students' home departments, we have to do a little marketing to get students to enroll. In the past few summers we've worked together to come up with an email that pitches the course to directors of graduate studies across our university. We figure if we can sell the utility of the course to a director, she might well turn around and recommend it to students in her department. The email blitz is usually successful in filling our class, but just as important is that composing the email, writing the paragraph or two that make clear what our course can do for students, helps Megan and me get clear on the course's raison d'etre, its essential features and its potential benefits. It's an invaluable planning exercise that gets us thinking, well before the semester starts, about how to entice our students to invest themselves in the course.

Ask yourself: Why should students take this class? What do you want students to know and be able to do when they complete your course? Why will it be valuable to them? What's your pitch?

This salesmanship should be an integral part of making your syllabus. The syllabus is a lot of things—contract, calendar, instruction manual—but we shouldn't forget that it's also something like a promotional brochure for your class. Among other reasons, students read syllabi to get an idea of what the course will be about, what will be asked of them, and what they might get for their efforts. You should see it as an opportunity to sell your course to the students.

When drafting your syllabus, focus on big, fundamental questions and fascinating problems. You want to present students with issues that, in their difficulty and intrigue, seem to invite further inquiry. Think through which aspects of your subject might be engaging to nineteen- and twenty-year-olds. Remember, although it can be useful to think about what draws you to your discipline, your students—who lack your experience with the history and minutiae of your field—may need a different angle to spark their interest. The burden is to demonstrate the significance of your subject, to answer the question lingering in the head of every student in your class: So what?

Rice University history professor Caleb McDaniel takes this mission to heart, structuring the syllabus for his American history survey course through a series of questions he imagines students will have: What is different about this course? What should I be able to do by semester's end? What are we going to be doing, and when? How will my learning be assessed and graded? By asking and answering these questions, McDaniel places the students and their experience of the course, rather than the course's content, front and center.[4]

This salesmanship can continue in the classroom throughout the semester. You can't assume that students will understand the purpose of your teaching methods, assignments, or readings if you don't tell them. Don't rely on grades alone to push students into taking an active part in the course. Explain to them what they will gain if they understand the readings or dive deep into their research projects. Emphasize what skills they might attain through mastery of a subject and how those skills might be of help in the future. Strive to tie your subject matter to your students' lives, looking for ways to make it relevant to them.[5]

Of course, there are limits to trying to sell your subject to your students. Different students are going to find different tasks more or less interesting depending on, well, their interests. Even more importantly, the learning process is not uniform. Mastering a subject requires students to engage in a variety of learning tasks, and it's natural that some of those tasks will be more interesting than others. Some may be—in fact, almost certainly will be—boring, repetitive, or without any obvious payoff. What then? How do we entice our students to keep at it even when the going gets dull? Are there conditions that make it more likely that students will persist through those necessary but tedious tasks? What separates the students who stick with something even when it's less than interesting from those who quickly lose motivation?

Those were exactly the questions asked by a group of scholars, led by David S. Yeager of the University of Texas at Austin, who published the results of their research in 2014 in the *Journal of Personality and Social Psychology*. Their paper, "Boring but Important: A Self-Transcendent Purpose for Learning Fosters Academic Self-Regulation," details the four studies they designed, involving nearly 2,000 high school and college students, which attempted to zero in on the causes of student persistence at uninteresting skill-building tasks.

Their conclusions were surprising, at least to me. They found that giving students a "self-transcendent purpose for learning" made it much more likely that they would persist through tasks. By "self-transcendent" they mean a purpose not motivated strictly by self-interest. Students who saw their learning as ultimately beneficial to others, to an important cause, or to the world at large stayed with uninteresting schoolwork much longer than those students who saw their learning as beneficial only to themselves.[6]

I found the results surprising because, as I wrote above, I often think that part of our task as teachers is to make our subjects relevant to students' lives. We're told—particularly those of us who teach in the humanities—that we need to show them how the learning in our courses will benefit them down the road, how it will help them have a more successful career or land a high-paying job.

But no subject is always interesting. Mastering it may be easier if you fall in love with the topic or see it as integral to your future success. But such motivations tend to vanish when students are faced with the sort of skill-building tasks that are necessary for mastery but difficult to find enjoyable or relevant. Think about how much practice is necessary to become proficient in advanced calculus, say, or to master a foreign language. No matter how much your students love German, that love tends to fade when practicing declensions for hours at a time. Interestingly, the research team led by Yeager did not find that the students who persisted in learning those boring tasks enjoyed doing them more; rather, the connection between "enjoying a task" and "completing a task" weakened. Students were more likely to follow through on a tedious task—regardless of how much they enjoyed it—if they saw learning as driven by a goal bigger than themselves.

The findings suggest that one of our goals should be to dislodge the idea that learning is only a means of self-improvement. I don't think this means we should abandon our attempts to make our courses interesting for our students. But we should be looking for ways to tie their learning to bigger things, to causes outside of themselves and their future lives.

How might mastering this subject help students to help others? Can you sell your course as part of a more significant education—one that enables students to be a part of something bigger than themselves?

Ways to Use Your Authority to Cede Control

My ten-year-old daughter takes piano lessons. One of the biggest challenges my wife and I have faced has been getting her to play for herself, not for her parents. Often I'll ask her how she thought she played a song and I'll get a shrug in return. She plays, but she doesn't listen to herself play. That lack of listening, I fear, is a sign that she's playing just because we're making her.

She takes lessons from a very good teacher, but my wife and I oversee her practices six nights a week. We don't choose which songs she works on or decide on the pace of progress, but we do actively monitor her playing at home. If she makes a mistake, we let her know. If her left hand is louder than her right hand, we let her know. If she forgets to repeat at the end of a song, we let her know.

Given all that, is it any surprise that she doesn't know how well she plays? Why would she need to pay attention when we do it for her?

For active learning strategies to really work, we need students to want to learn for themselves, not to satisfy our requirements or to get a certain grade. I often think about this when I'm handing out essay prompts. I've learned, through painful experience, that when giving students these prompts, it's best to lay out in fine detail the manner in which they are to complete an assignment. I don't want there to be any confusion as to the font size, line spacing, word count, paragraph format, and subject matter required. I nip potential misconceptions in the bud with mini-lessons on argument, thesis statements, evidence marshaling, and other elements of a good essay. All of those elements are important. And of course I've found that when I don't make those details explicit, I receive papers that veer off course in maddening ways.

But doesn't that litany of regulations send the message to students that I am in charge, that satisfying my stipulations is their ultimate goal? Should we be surprised that they aren't invested in their work when we tell them, by our actions, that their role is to fill in the few blanks that we've left them?

I don't think the answer is to throw up our hands and just let students do whatever they want in the name of student ownership. But my experience with my daughter suggests there's more we can do.

In the college classroom, there is much that reinforces faculty ownership of the course. In the eyes of the university, we are responsible for the courses we teach. And students have been trained over many years to be obedient and subservient in class. Those traditions and habits, among others, serve to reinforce faculty domination of the classroom space and encourage students to remain passive, deferential, and apathetic. And that limits how much students will care about a course. I'm more and more convinced that it's not enough to allow students some control over aspects of the course; we have to actively work to hand over some of our own control. If we're serious about our students taking ownership of our courses, we need to divest some of our ownership first.

Here are some small things you can do to use your authority to give students more power.

In a 2015 essay called "The Silent Professor," Joseph Finckel wrote about losing his voice in the middle of a semester and being forced to teach without speaking. He found that his silence provoked students to speak up more and take a more active role in class. He still came up with classroom activities—prompted by instructions and questions projected on the board—but found that students, not able to rely on the teacher to tell them the answers, worked to find those answers on their own. Finckel now "loses his voice" every semester and offers tips to those who want to follow his example (even including silent office hours).[7]

You don't have to pretend you have laryngitis to make a conscious effort to speak less in your classroom. My colleague Megan Knight keeps her eyes down on her notebook and takes notes during some class discussions. She tells students she's going to do this in advance (so as not to seem rude) and then she spends the discussion looking down at her desk. I've been a witness to this (in the class we co-teach), and the effect is remarkable. In the absence of an instructor to make eye contact with, students inevitably cast about for someone to direct their comments to. They start slowly, unused to the situation, but are soon doing the only thing they can: talking to each other. It's amazing to watch happen.[8]

I've tried to become more aware of how much I talk, how much I fill in the silences during class. Try to let those silences linger. Every time we tell our students an answer we deprive them of an opportunity to figure it out themselves.[9]

When you do talk, let yourself be human. We can make space for students to own the classroom by chipping away at the traditional teacher persona. If we hold ourselves at a remove or pretend we have all the answers, we do our students a disservice. Better to admit our uncertainties, express what we're excited about, and show ourselves to be flawed and strange sometimes.

In her 1994 book, *Teaching to Transgress*, bell hooks wrote about the benefits that come from a truly engaged instructor, one who opens up to students: "When professors bring narratives of their experiences into classroom discussions it eliminates the possibility that we can function as all-knowing, silent interrogators."[10] Share yourself with your students, let them see that you're risking something by being there, and they'll take risks as well.

And when students do talk, really listen. Managing a class discussion is one of the hardest skills teachers have to learn. Too often, because of the difficulty, we set up discussions with leading questions and shut off debate once we get the answer we're looking for.

If we're always trying to steer students to our point, or if we cut off discussion after a certain amount of time because we've got something else planned, students will understand that the game is rigged—it doesn't really matter what they say. But if we truly listen to students, and let what they say change the trajectory of the class period, we can open up the classroom for students to take the lead.

That isn't easy, of course. We've all got a lot on our minds when we teach, and it's not always possible to distinguish between a pointless tangent and an intriguing change of topic. But try to remember that the answers students arrive at on their own—right or wrong—are almost always more valuable than the ones you tell them. Yes, we need to balance our desire for students to drive the discussion with our own goals for what students will learn (for instance, we may want students to surface and revise a common misconception). But the side effect of taking a step back—students feel that there are real benefits to participating in a discussion—will pay off again and again.

With my daughter, I've been trying to keep my mouth shut. Now I tell her: I'm not allowed to make any comments when you play—not even to tell you when you've played a bum note. You're in charge, I tell her. If she thinks she needs to play a song again, she does; if she's satisfied, then she moves on to the next one. It's really hard for me to keep quiet. But she does seem to be listening to herself more when she plays now.

The Blank Syllabus and Other Ways to Give Students Options

The blank syllabus is an idea that originates from Chris Walsh, the director of the Arts and Sciences Writing Program at Boston University.[11] When I heard him discuss it at that panel on pedagogy at the 2013 MLA conference I was instantly sold. It's a great way to build student ownership into your syllabus, though it does require a bit of trust on the instructor's part.

The syllabus isn't really blank, of course. What's left blank are some of the course readings, which students themselves choose.

Here's how it worked when I did it, in a survey of American literature I taught in the semester immediately after that conference. The textbook we used was a big anthology of readings (the *Norton Anthology of American Literature*), and I decided that, for each class period, the students would read both prose (either a short story or a portion of a longer narrative) and poetry. I picked the prose readings and listed them on the syllabus, but I left blank spaces next to each class period for a poem or poems to be determined by the students. The class was small—only seventeen students—so I was able to ask each of them to choose a reading for one day of class. Those instructors with larger classes can have students select and then vote on the readings that will be included on the syllabus.

On the first day of class, after distributing the syllabus and introducing the students to the course, I explained the concept of the blank syllabus. The first assignment, due three weeks later, was an essay in which each student, having picked a poem from the anthology to include on the syllabus, would make a case for why students should study this poem. On the day a student's poetry selection was slated for class discussion, that student would lead things off by recounting her argument.

The strategy had a number of benefits. First, it got my students to actually look at the anthology. Instead of reading only the pieces that I assigned, they spent the first few weeks of the term browsing through the book, reading unfamiliar poems, looking for one that appealed to them. Any course that uses a textbook is a prime candidate for a blank syllabus assignment—in addition to whatever you know you have to cover, let students choose other sections of the text to study, and ask them to come up with discussion questions for their classmates.

Second, it got them thinking about the value of the texts we were studying. Why read one poem instead of another? Why read poetry at all? Instead of a reading list dictated from on high (these are the most important texts), it became a reading list produced by everyone in the class (Which are the most important texts? What does "important" mean when it comes to our subject?).

This brings us to the third benefit: the blank syllabus showed students that they were crucial players in the class's dynamic and outcomes. It signaled to them, right from the start, that I saw them as partners in their education. It was their course as much as mine, and we would study the texts they wanted to study. It helped instill in them an increased sense of responsibility toward the coursework, the instructor, and not least of all, their classmates.

Mine is hardly a scientific study, but I had a lot of success with this approach. I can't say whether having a hand in choosing the course readings made the students feel more empowered. But there's no question that the blank syllabus led them to engage better with those readings and each other than my previous classes. The students were much more enthusiastic about reading poetry—always a challenge, I find—and the open-mindedness and curiosity with which they approached their peers' choices was great to witness.

One of the reasons the blank syllabus is such a successful idea, I think, is that it extends the domain of student ownership to the first assignment. Assignments are often stubbornly owned by instructors—we set the terms and *assign* students tasks to complete. But assignments are actually great opportunities to give students control. The key is to think clearly about your goals for your assignments.

For example, in the first-year rhetoric course I teach, I have a number of goals for my students' final writing assignment: I want

---

Can I Use the Blank Syllabus in a Science Course?

Caroline Wilson, a clinical associate professor of health sciences at Chapman University, has had success using the blank syllabus in a neurophysiology course.[12] In a team-based learning course, Wilson split her class into three teams for the whole semester.[13] The blank syllabus came into play in the course's final four weeks. For that period, each team selected a topic in the textbook that hadn't been covered yet. They were then responsible for that topic in class—they came up with quiz questions, wrote a study guide, and when it was their turn, led the other teams in an application activity. Wilson, of course, supervised all this, checking and approving what the students did. Wilson reported that the approach led her students to be more self-directed and more enthusiastic about class activities.

them to understand and gain experience with the research process, I want them to learn how to navigate multiple sources and their own views on a subject, I want them to practice writing a longer essay, and so forth. I don't have any explicit goals about content—I'm much more concerned with the skills they'll master than any particular body of knowledge they'll learn.

With those goals in mind, I am free to leave a lot of the decisions about the subjects of their essays up to the students. As long as the subject each student chooses lends itself to a serious research project, with multiple sources to engage with, and enough substance to justify a 2,000-word essay, I'm fine with it. I use a modified version of Ken Macrorie's "I-Search" paper, which requires that students come up with their own research questions that they find interesting or thought-provoking or fun.[14] I can assure you that essays on subjects that the students actually care about are *far* easier to read and grade than essays on subjects dictated by me.

The process is similar even if you can't be as flexible with content as I am. Come up with your goals for the assignment, and look for areas that you don't need to dictate. Be as transparent as possible with your students about those goals, and give them the freedom to be creative in how they attempt to reach them. The more you can leave for the students to decide, the better the chances they'll take the assignment seriously.

Another way to promote student ownership is to allow students to have a say in some of the course policies. In this, I'm inspired by Cathy Davidson, a professor and scholar of technology and pedagogy at the Graduate Center at the City University of New York, who has been working for years on the nuts and bolts of creating a more democratic and student-centered classroom. She argues that the classroom is "one of the least egalitarian spaces on the planet" but that there are changes we can make—on our own, right now—that can help our institutions become more just for students and instructors alike.[15]

Broadly, Davidson asks us to think about the elements of our courses that we absolutely have to control: Does your department require you to assign a certain textbook? Will the course be a failure if it doesn't cover certain topics? Is the course a prerequisite for other classes and thus needs to leave students with particular skills? Work hard to come up with the bare minimum of what you need to dictate to the students.

On everything else, she writes, let the students decide. The more control you relinquish—in creating policies, organizing the calendar, designing assignments—the more the students will see the course as theirs and will commit in a way that makes deep learning much more likely.

But Students Don't Know Enough to Write the Syllabus, Do They?

It may feel unwise to leave parts of your syllabus to the students to create—how can they write the syllabus for a course they haven't taken yet? But thinking about ceding some control over your syllabus does not mean undermining your expertise or your ideas for how the course should go. In particular, your sense of what students will need to learn to gain mastery of the course's subjects is essential. Your knowledge of the subject and the discipline's necessary skills is needed for a successful course. But there's plenty on your syllabus that doesn't have to do with that expertise; this is the stuff that governs how the class is run, what exactly students do during class, how students are assessed, and other issues. For anything that falls into that category, it's worth thinking about giving students control. If nothing else, such a move sends a powerful signal to students about ownership of the course, helping to communicate to them that their full engagement is essential for success.

Perhaps none of a college course's policies are as controversial as the one that governs the use of technology in the classroom. Many instructors have strong views on the subject (I was strictly anti-device for many years), and what seems like thousands of pages has been written on the pros and cons. I'd like to suggest that a technology policy is a perfect opportunity to give students choices, and ownership.

Simon Bates and Alison Lister, both of whom teach in the physics and astronomy department at the University of British Columbia, have done precisely this: they allow their students to collaborate on an acceptable-use policy for technology in the classroom. Bates and Lister introduce the concept on the first day of class. They direct students to a collaborative online space, where they have posted a basic document with a number of guidelines for the students to consider. The students are given a set amount of time (say, a week) to contribute to the document and to edit the rules as they see fit. A vote is then held in class to decide the fate of any rules that the students are divided on. In this way the class works as a unit to devise its own guidelines for what is (and isn't) appropriate.

This strategy is an ingenious way to navigate the tricky terrain of technology in the classroom. And discussing what is acceptable and unacceptable in class may also get students thinking about what you're trying to accomplish as an instructor. Mostly, the hope is that it will prompt them to consider valuable questions that are connected to the course's overall goals: How do we think our class time should be spent? How does learning best occur? How do we create an environment that accommodates everyone's needs?

Recent research suggests that ceding control on this particular topic may pay bigger dividends than most. A 2018 study found that restrictive technology policies negatively influence student perceptions of their rapport with instructors.[16] Leaving these decisions to students, it seems, is a great way to establish early on that you trust students.

Davidson goes even further, having students collectively write a class constitution, in which "all the terms of our engagement for the semester becomes subject to review, discussion, and examination."[17] You may not want to go this far. But inviting students to collaborate on other policies, from plagiarism to late work to the weight given to various assignments in final grades, can have hugely positive effects on your class dynamic. Once you begin to trust that students are invested in these decisions, you may find that they take them as seriously as you do.

Encouraging Student Ownership within the Semester

The First Day of Class: A Gimmick

In my experience, the best way to encourage the sort of student ownership I've been writing about is to emphasize *why* a class does what it does rather than *how*. If we can foreground our course goals, going out of our way to meticulously explain what we're hoping students will learn, we can feel more comfortable allowing students much more leeway in figuring out how to reach those goals in their own way.[18] In a sense, this is another permutation of Cathy Davidson's directive to control what we absolutely have to control and leave the rest to the students.

An emphasis on course goals can, and should, begin on the very first day of class.

If you search the web for "first day of class activities," what you'll find are a lot of gimmicks: long lists of icebreakers and all manner of unusual and goofy ways to get students to read the syllabus. Most of the suggestions take for granted that teachers need to try to "hook" students on the first day.

There are good reasons why teachers may want to begin with activities that differ widely from the tone of the rest of the semester. For one, students have a lot on their plates in the first week, with up to five new courses to attend, so diving right into the material may feel like giving them more than they can handle. Something fun that gets them comfortable with their classmates and the teacher is a gentler beginning.

Second, instructors want to get students interested in and excited for the course, and convince the uncertain ones not to drop it. Just as you might begin a conference paper with a humorous anecdote or quotation to spark your listeners' interest, a gimmicky activity in the first class starts things off on a memorable note, priming students for the more serious and rigorous class periods to follow.

My first-day gimmick satisfies those requirements while foregrounding course goals in a way that I think really encourages students to begin investing in the class.

On the first day of class, teach the last day of class.

When your students file in to class for the first time, act as if you've seen them all before, every week, for the previous fifteen weeks. Turn around and write the date of your last class session on the board, along with the main concepts that your exam will cover. And then launch into it: start summing up the course, exactly as you would on the last day of the term. Review the important ideas that the course will have covered. Refer frequently to exciting details that the students would surely remember. Let them know what they should study if they want to do well on the exam. Make a point of reminding them that this is stuff they should know, that you've gone over it before (you want them to get the joke).

How long you can keep up this charade will vary according to your temperament and how game your students are. But try to do it for at least five minutes before breaking character. The idea is certainly a gimmick, designed to be a memorable and disarming start to the course, drawing students in with an initial mystery: what's going on here? But it's more than just silliness. It starts off class exactly how you should be starting off class—by thinking about, and encouraging students to think about, the desired outcomes of the course.

Before the first class, spend some time thinking about how you'd like the last class to go. Ideally, what will your students have learned by the end of the semester? What will they be able to do? If everything goes as planned, how will you conclude the course? By beginning at the end, even as a joke, you remind students that they're not in class just to get course credit. There are clear course objectives, a destination you're all traveling toward. Use this approach and you'll start planting answers in your students' heads to the most important question they'll have on the first day: What's the point?

After you end the playacting, use the rest of the class period (or most of it; you'll probably have to go over the syllabus at some point) to build on the exercise and start a class discussion about the course, its objectives, and what students are expecting from it. This last item is not unimportant.

Understanding what students hope to get from the course can help you tailor it further (or help you nip any wild misconceptions in the bud). You can explain that you have very specific things in mind that you'd like the students to be able to do at the end of the term, and that you've constructed the course in a way to help them get there. But it's important that you ask students what they hope to get from the class and that you listen carefully to their answers. This discussion can lead naturally into a goals-oriented first assignment.

A Student Goals Assignment

In a study published in 2015, a group of researchers based in the Netherlands and Canada looked at the effects of a writing assignment in which students had to articulate their goals—both academic and otherwise—to see whether an intervention would lead to better academic performance.[19] The results of the study, which was conducted at a business school in the Netherlands, indeed demonstrated that students who completed the assignment performed significantly better than a control group of students who hadn't. What's more, the assignment seemed particularly helpful for the kinds of students who typically struggled academically: it significantly narrowed the gender and ethnicity gap among students.

Why would the writing assignment have that effect? And how might we apply the lessons of these findings in our own classrooms?

The Dutch business students were asked to write about goals both small and large, short-term and long-term. They wrote briefly and informally about things they would like to do better, subjects they would like to learn more about, and habits they would like to improve. They wrote about their ideal future, and the future they would like to avoid. The assignment prompted them to be specific in articulating and prioritizing their goals, anticipating potential setbacks, and strategizing how exactly they would reach their objectives. Students were also required to make a public commitment to what they considered to be their most important goal.

The Netherlands study built on decades of research about "goal-setting theory," a conception of motivation developed by the psychologist Edwin Locke beginning in the 1960s. His theory—much loved in corporate circles—claims that setting specific and challenging goals improves performance, even in the face of obstacles. The act of putting your goals into words and then breaking those goals down into specific, challenging, but attainable subgoals significantly improves your chances of success.[20]

Why might the same approach help students do better academically? Remember, goal setting has been shown to increase self-regulation, particularly if the student's goal is "self-transcendent," that is, not motivated strictly by self-interest. Breaking big goals into smaller, more easily attainable targets can help foster students' confidence, allowing them to feel a sense of accomplishment each step of the way. And setting goals also seems to help students avoid uncertainty and apathy, reducing anxiety and avoidance behaviors that can interfere with performance.[21] All of this suggests that we should be looking to bring goal setting into our classrooms.

Take a look at the Dutch study if you'd like to try out the researchers' assignment. But even if you don't want to spend so much time having your students write about their ideal future, a more focused assignment might have similarly positive effects.

In the opening days of the semester, have your students write about their goals. But ask them to specifically reflect on their goals for the course. Why are they taking it? What do they hope to learn by the end of the semester? What skills do they want to develop? What concept do they hope to understand better? Have them brainstorm some broad, big-picture goals and then write out a plan to achieve those goals through smaller, more easily attainable steps.

By encouraging students to set such goals, you make it more likely that they will buy into your course objectives. The assignment signals to students that their goals are important, at least as important as the instructor's. You are essentially asking students to write the story of their progress through the course, from their present state to a revised—and hopefully improved—version.

With the goals down on paper, you can revisit them throughout the term, monitoring student progress and adjusting your approach as needed. Perhaps more importantly, with the goals of the course— both yours and theirs—cemented so early, you give yourself the freedom to let students take the lead as the class progresses, secure in the knowledge that the important stuff, the stuff you have to control, has already been established.

Metacognition I: Maintaining Student Ownership

Once the term gets going in earnest, you can shift your focus from establishing goals to encouraging and maintaining student ownership. The challenge here is to encourage students to take responsibility for their learning. We want to give them the tools to monitor their learning so they will be able to make adjustments along the way. The way to do that is through metacognition.

Metacognition is essentially "thinking about thinking." It's the processes through which we analyze, monitor, and regulate our thinking and learning practices, with an eye to bettering those practices. There's now more than thirty years of research into the value of metacognition in the classroom, and that research has led to a whole host of conclusions.[22] But it's fair to say that, broadly speaking, better metacognition equals better learning.

Without training, many students don't think about the best way to study for an exam, write an essay, or take notes in class. Students who do poorly on a test will, more often than not, prepare for the next test in exactly the same way as before. Too often, we assume that students know enough about themselves that our comments and suggestions will be enough to provoke positive change. But self-awareness and self-reflection (not to mention good study habits) are not skills all students possess. Promoting those skills in class can make our lives as teachers a lot easier. If we can encourage metacognitive thinking in our students, the burden of keeping them on target throughout the semester doesn't need to fall solely on us.

Here are some relatively easy ways to spark metacognition in your students.

One good strategy, generally attributed to Marsha Lovett, a teaching professor of psychology at Carnegie Mellon University, is called "exam wrappers."[23] It begins when students get back their first graded test of the semester, although this tactic could easily be adapted to any assignment, including an essay. Along with their graded exam, the students receive an exam wrapper—a brief questionnaire designed to get students to review their performance. They go over their exams and then answer the questions on the exam wrapper. The questions are all metacognitive in nature: How did you prepare for this exam? Where did you make errors on the test? What could you do differently next time?

Students fill out the questionnaire and then return it to you. That way, you can go over their answers and assess how they're doing (and how you're doing). You might find information that helps you adjust your teaching going forward. You can then return the exam wrappers to the students as they begin to prepare for the next test or assignment. The idea is that students can then think about their comments and alter their approach, if necessary, for the next exam. Exam wrappers help tests become formative teaching tools that pay off as the semester goes on.

Metacognition can be similarly cultivated through a questionnaire about study and learning habits. Ask students how they usually study for exams, whether they take notes by hand or on a laptop, and how much (or how little) they know about the course's subject matter. Many of my students are in their first year at university, so this questionnaire often leads to a lively discussion of the differences between high school and college, and their expectations for the latter. At various points in the semester you can revisit the questionnaires with the class, both to review the students' previous answers and to see how those answers have changed as the course has progressed. By encouraging students to reflect on their progress, you'll be reminding them that they are both responsible for that progress and able to alter their trajectory.

Tamara Rosier's "knowledge ratings," which I discussed in Chapter 1, are another way to get students to think about their own learning practices. The goal here is to make students' behavior visible

But I Don't Have Time for All These Metacognitive Activities

I sympathize with those instructors who feel they have too much material to cover to make time for activities such as the ones I'm highlighting here. I get it: I often feel as if there's never enough time in a semester to get to everything. But that's the thing—there *is* never enough time, so it's even more important to be thoughtful about how we spend our time to reach our course objectives. Improving student metacognition is a proven way to improve student learning. Don't think of these activities as taking time away from other elements of the course; think of them as helping your students make the most out of those other elements.

to themselves, with an eye toward gaining better control over that behavior.

Metacognition II: Midterm Evaluations

You can also encourage the class as a whole to engage in some metacognition. Every class has its own character, its own dynamic, and it's worth taking the class's temperature midway through the semester.

Peter Filene, in his book *The Joy of Teaching*, has a tip for times when a course seems to be headed off the tracks, when the dynamic just isn't working for everybody. The idea works well in courses of all kinds, even those without obvious problems. He suggests a sort of midterm full-class evaluation, a diagnostic session that the students undertake, with your guidance, to prompt an open discussion of the course's progress.[24]

You begin by handing out blank index cards and then ask the students to answer, anonymously, a few general questions about the class. I often ask students to note, on one side of the card, something that has really helped them, and on the other side, something that hasn't worked. Stress that you want students to be completely honest (the anonymity helps with this), that they should not hold back if they have criticisms to make.

After collecting the cards, you can take them home, ponder the answers, and think about how to switch gears for the rest of the semester. But I think an even better idea is to shuffle the cards and redistribute them to the students (make sure students don't get their own cards back). Have the students read the cards out loud, and allow the answers to prompt an open discussion about the way the course is going. Try not to be defensive, listen to everyone's suggestions, and work with the students to come up with a plan to fix what can be fixed.

Some Possible Questions for a Midterm Evaluation

What has worked well? What aspects of the course have helped you learn? Of the topics we have covered and the activities we have done, which have been the most helpful to you?

What needs to be improved or changed? What aspects of the course have worked against your learning? Of the topics we have covered and the activities we have done, which could we have done without?

What should we be doing more of? What should we be doing less of? What should we keep the same?

What is one aspect of our subject that you want to be sure we address before the end of the semester?

Has the course been moving too quickly or too slowly? Are the readings (or assignments or tests) too difficult?

Even if the conclusions are modest—more time for discussion, say, or a bit more guidance on the readings—I've found that the exercise itself helps clear the air and leads to a better class dynamic. At the very least, it signals to the students that you value their input and encourages them to take ownership of the course and the way it's going.

Metacognition III: Self-Assessments

Metacognition is also a valuable tool at the end of a course, when there are so many opportunities for self-reflection. At that point, students have been working on the same subject for more than three months; before they move on to other courses and other professors, give them time and space to reflect on what they've done and how they've done it.

A self-evaluation is a great way to get students to assess how they approached the course with an eye to improving their learning strategies in the future. It can also help cement the particular skills they learned in your course—in effect, they remind themselves of the skills they've acquired and may be more likely to be able to put them to use in the future.[25]

Additionally, asking students to reflect on their own practices during your course may make them better equipped to evaluate your teaching in a way that accurately reflects how much they've learned.

A self-evaluation can take many forms. One approach is to first explicitly talk to students about the value of metacognitive thinking. Ask them to reflect on the learning strategies they used in the course and think deeply about their own habits of thinking. Explain that the act of reflection is itself a valuable learning strategy. With that introduction, you pave the way to ask students general questions: What strategies did they use for the course? What worked? What didn't? The nature of the questions you ask will probably vary with your course (I've included some sample questions below). The value of this kind of exercise is that it asks students to consider that which usually remains unnoticed and unquestioned. Even if their answers tend to be vague, engaging in this kind of self-evaluation can go a long way toward helping students develop valuable metacognitive practices that can help their learning going forward.[26]

Along those same lines is what Kimberly D. Tanner, a professor of biology at San Francisco State University, has called "retrospective postassessments."[27] Essentially, she asks students to compare where they are at the end of the course with where they were at the beginning. You can give students explicit statements to finish: "Before this course, I thought Marxism was _____. Now, I think Marxism is _____." Alternatively, you can ask students to write about the specific ways they have changed their thinking about the topics you

A Sample Self-Assessment Prompt

Looking back on the semester, how do you think you did? This self-assessment is designed to help you think about your experience in the course and draw lessons for the future—both in future courses and beyond.

1. Thinking back to the beginning of the semester, what were your goals for this course? To what extent did you meet them? Did they change as the semester went on? Which goals did you not meet, and why do you think you fell short?

2. What are the three most important things you learned in this class? Can you describe *how* you learned them?

3. What strategies did you use to help yourself learn in this class? How did you approach the assignments? How did you prepare for the tests? Which strategies worked well? Which ones didn't work so well?

4. If you had to do the course all over again, what are three things you would change in your approach? What do you think those changes would accomplish?

covered. Either way, you bring students face to face with their own learning, asking them to reflect on the distance they've traveled.

Tanner's approach is particularly effective if you ask students for their preconceptions about the course topics at the beginning of the semester, as many instructors already do (this can be a part of your beginning-of-term goals assignment). Then, as part of their self-evaluations, students can compare their current thinking with explicit evidence of their past thinking.

Perhaps you didn't ask students to do such a "pre-assessment" at the beginning of the semester? You can still have them reckon with their past selves at the end of the course. One approach I particularly like is to ask students to revisit their first assignment, using it as the basis for self-reflection. What would they have done differently? What did they succeed at, by chance? What did they learn from the assignment that they put into practice later in the semester?

Even better, ask students to assemble a portfolio of all the work they've done over the semester, read it over, and write an analysis of how they've progressed. Some instructors may prefer this approach to a more general one because it keeps students focused squarely on the black and white of their demonstrable contributions to the course.

A Gimmick for the Last Day of Class

I like to end the semester with one final metacognitive gimmick, a parting shot that gets my students to think about what we did, and what it meant, in a way that's creative and maybe even fun. One of your objectives as the semester winds down should be to get students to synthesize the myriad course topics, and student metacognition should help toward that goal.

I ask my students to write letters to future students of the course. It's a relatively straightforward assignment. I explain that they've now been through almost the entirety of the course and are well placed to render judgment on it. They can reflect on its high points and low points and offer advice to those who will sit in their places next fall. What do they wish they had known going in to the class? What do they wish they would have done differently? What should future students know about the course and—gulp—about the professor?

Like the beginning-of-term charade I proposed earlier, this exercise has value that makes it more than just a gimmick. If you can convince your students to take the assignment seriously, I see a number of benefits.

First of all, by writing the letter, students are pushed into actually thinking about the course as a whole and their role in it. In this sense, the exercise is sneakily metacognitive. By asking students to advise other students on how to approach the class, they are forced to reflect on their own approach and to think about what they would have done differently. Try including specific questions in your prompt. The idea is to turn the letter-writing exercise into a kind of course review that could be useful in helping students prepare for the final exam. Ask the following: What are the most important aspects of the course subject? What were the most insightful readings, and why? What remains unclear at the end of the semester? Having students answer such questions is a great way to get them to review the material. Writing the letter naturally encourages students to think back to where they were at the beginning of the semester. It puts into their heads the distance they've traveled between then and now, asking them to take stock of what they've learned.

Second, the students' letters offer benefits to you as the instructor. Think of these letters as an additional, more casual, set of student evaluations. Don't pitch the assignment so that it's focused on your teaching. However, letters about students' experiences in a course will inevitably take the professor into account. Either way, the letters can provide you with insights into how successful your teaching was this semester. You'll get a better idea of what worked and what didn't, of whether what you thought was important is what students actually thought was important. You'll be left with some solid recommendations, both implicit and explicit. It's notoriously difficult to take much practical guidance from student evaluations, with their numbered rankings of generic aspects of a course. The letters should be helpfully specific, and the letter format should encourage students to be a bit more informal and, you'd hope, honest.

The third main benefit is to your future students. Beginning your fall class with letters from the previous spring's students is yet another way to give new students a snapshot of the course's end. Of course, you're under no obligation to share all the letters; any that you judge to be counterproductive or nonsensical, or that reflect poorly on you, can be conveniently held back.

But I'd encourage distributing a wide variety of letters. Ideally, reading them will get new students thinking about the course, what they should expect, and how they should approach it. But also, the exercise should plant in their heads the idea that different students can have vastly different experiences in the same course. It should underline the fact that their own experience will be mostly shaped by their own approach, what they put into the course. It will also spark some of the metacognitive thinking that you'll be looking to encourage all semester long.

3

Building a Better Course

EVERY MORNING, BEFORE the coffee kicks in, I unload the dishwasher. This is more or less mindless work, but there often comes a moment when I'm forced to pause. I take out the silverware basket, put it on the counter, and look at the disorganized jumble: forks and spoons and knives sticking out every which way. For a split second, I am overwhelmed with a kind of paralysis—I don't know where to begin. Of course, I soon snap out of it and start putting everything away; luckily it doesn't much matter how I put away the forks and spoons.

At the beginning of a new semester, instructors—particularly novice ones—often confront a similar experience. It can be overwhelming to think of all the choices you have to make to put a college course together, especially because these choices *do* matter to most instructors. What are your objectives for the students? How will you assess whether they meet those objectives? How will you spend time in class so that they will succeed on those assessments? And where will you start?

This chapter focuses on many of those choices and looks to guide you in creating course elements that will lead to better outcomes for your students. If we're committed to improving our teaching, we need to give attention to all of these elements: how we organize our syllabus, how we encourage our students to approach the material, how we tackle readings and assignments, study sessions and exams. By putting the students' experience first, and by building on insights from research in the learning sciences, we can improve these elements and create the conditions in which our students are more likely to learn.

Create Desirable Difficulties

A few years ago, the psychology researchers Pam Mueller and Daniel Oppenheimer set out to study the effectiveness of student laptop use in the classroom.[1] They weren't interested in examining whether students were distracted by the internet. Rather, they wanted to look at how effective laptops were at their ostensible academic function: note taking. They had a group of college students watch a series of TED Talks. Half of the students were given laptops (disconnected from the internet) and told to take notes on the video lectures as they normally would in class. The other half were given the same task, only with pens and paper. When the students were tested on the material, the results were clear: students who took notes by hand did substantially better on conceptual questions than those who used laptops. What accounts for this?

When a student takes notes on a laptop, the authors concluded, the ease of data entry makes her more likely to transcribe everything the professor is saying. A student who takes notes in longhand, by contrast, cannot write fast enough to get everything down and so must be selective. It is everything that goes into that selectivity—

summarizing, thinking about what's most important, predicting what might be useful down the road—that helps those who take notes on paper. Students who use laptops end up with neater, more easily searchable notes, but they may be denying themselves the opportunity to do the upfront processing that is a crucial factor, it seems, in long-term retention of class material.

There's a sense in which, as teachers, we should be trying to make things easier for our students. As designers of learning environments, we want to remove any barriers between our students and their learning. But there's another sense in which ease is not at all what we want. The easiest thing in the world for a student to do is sit back and listen (or not listen) to a lecture. As I discussed in Chapter 1, there's now plenty of research that indicates that this is not a good way to learn. Students learn best when their brains are working, when they are actively processing new information and new skills. This simple concept—an active brain learns better—also underpins what the UCLA cognitive psychologist Robert Bjork has termed "desirable difficulties."[2] Simply put, we should be looking for ways to design learning tasks that make students' brains work a little bit harder.

Mueller and Oppenheimer's note-taking study should remind us again that our brains don't work like empty vessels, just waiting to be filled up. Our memories are cemented through frequent neural activity, through repeated encoding and retrieval processes. So although it's easier for laptop note takers to record material for future study, that ease is doing our students no favors. The human brain may not be a muscle, but the analogy isn't completely without merit; the more our brains work while acquiring knowledge, the better they are at retaining it.

We could ban laptops from our classrooms to encourage longhand note taking, but there are good reasons why such a policy is unwise.

Most pressingly, banning laptop use creates a needlessly more difficult learning environment for those students who need laptops because of a disability.[3] So how else can we introduce desirable difficulties into our classrooms?

One way is to vary learning conditions. When students get used to always learning, or practicing, under the same conditions, it can be difficult to then transfer that learning to other situations. It seems that variation itself is a desirable difficulty, training the brain to become more flexible. In a 1978 study conducted by Robert Kerr and Bernard Booth, children practiced throwing beanbags at a target. One group of kids practiced throwing at a target three feet away, while another group varied their practice, throwing at targets two and four feet away. After a delay, all the children were tested on their ability to throw a beanbag at a target three feet away. The second group—the one that practiced throwing at targets at varying distances—outperformed the group that practiced throwing at the distance being tested.[4] Such results have been echoed in more recent studies that show the benefits of varied practice in learning not just motor skills but also cognitive skills.[5]

Keep this in mind when teaching in your classroom. Try to come at your material in a variety of ways so that your students learn within a variety of contexts. The same material can be learned through listening to a lecture, reading at home, problem solving in small groups, doing class presentations, engaging in research, and on and on. When teaching a skill, try to give students the opportunity to apply that skill in a variety of domains. Even varying the environmental setting helps: a 1978 study that Bjork helped lead found that people who studied the same material in two different rooms performed better on tests than those who studied twice in the same room.[6] Try to remember that the next time your students ask you to have class outside in the sun.

A similar principle suggests we should be mixing up the different topics we teach in our classrooms. The practice, usually called "interleaving," forces students to change gears often, encouraging them to "reload" their memories of a subject each time you return to it. That extra mental work is the kind of difficulty we're looking for here. Instead of spending a whole class period on one subject and then another class period on another subject, try shuffling shorter periods of focus. Twenty-minute sessions on individual topics, with frequent switching between topics, can help promote long-term retention. What you are looking for, according to Elizabeth Bjork and Robert Bjork, is for students to start forgetting material before you return to it: "Forgetting (losing retrieval strength) creates the opportunity for increasing the storage strength of to-be-learned information or skills."[7]

The benefits of forgetting (the Bjorks' lab at UCLA is called the Bjork Learning and Forgetting Lab) can inform students' study practices outside of class as well. When students cram at the last minute for an exam, squeezing all of their exam preparation into one coffee-fueled session, they may perform well on the test, but they usually forget most of the information soon afterward. This accounts for my current ignorance of the finer points of psychological statistics, a course I aced back in college. One reason such cramming is ineffective for long-term learning is that students think they're learning more than they are. The familiarity that comes from reviewing a chapter in a textbook repeatedly during one long session fools students into thinking they've mastered the material. The most durable learning, much research has confirmed, comes when students have to relearn material a number of times, forcing their brain to do the difficult work of encoding and reencoding information.

Our students are better off studying throughout the term, returning frequently to material they've already studied, than they are putting off their studying until exam week. As instructors, we can encourage such spaced study. We should also move away from having a single exam-prep session at the end of the term in favor of repeated, and shorter, review sessions spread throughout the semester.

Give More Tests: Understanding the Testing Effect and Taking Advantage of It

Perhaps the most effective desirable difficulty we can introduce into our classes is the test. Now, I write this as someone who by instinct and training generally avoids tests, who many times has included exams only because of departmental requirements. When I teach literature or writing, I generally think that a package of essays, assignments, presentations, and a participation grade is a more appropriate means of assessment than an exam, which can seem unimaginative, a blunt instrument. But, as I explain more fully in Chapter 5, assessment is not just a tool to measure how well students are learning; it can also be a *formative* device, something that promotes learning itself. It turns out that being tested on something, being asked to retrieve and present something previously learned, is a *very* good way to learn that something better.

Henry L. Roediger III, a professor of psychology at Washington University, in St. Louis, has spent years looking into the so-called testing effect—the strange fact that the act of taking a test seems to help students retain class material. In 2006, working with his then graduate student Jeffrey D. Karpicke, Roediger conducted experiments with college students, asking them to read texts that covered general scientific topics.[8] After all of the students read their passages, half of the students were told to restudy the passage, while the other half were given a test on it. The results showed that studying the material provided a modest short-term benefit—the students who studied knew the passage better in the minutes after studying. But those who were tested without studying remembered significantly more about the passage both two days and one week later. Repeated variations of this experiment provided consistent results: taking a test was a better means to long-term retention than studying.

In another paper, also published in 2006, Roediger and Karpicke reviewed nearly a century's worth of studies on the testing effect and concluded that it was a durable and scientifically uncontroversial phenomenon.[9] They surveyed scores of laboratory and classroom studies (the paper has more than 150 references) and found, over and over again, that groups of students who were tested on material retained that material better than groups of students who only studied the material. This effect held up even when students performed poorly on the initial tests and when students received no feedback on their tests.[10]

Knowing what we know about desirable difficulties, about the importance of making our brains process and relearn information, this phenomenon should not be so surprising. What is a test but a circumstance in which we must *rack our brains* trying to remember the right answers. Tests force us to try to recall what we've learned, and it is this trying that helps us learn something better.

Those who want to learn more about the ins and outs of the testing effect should read *Make It Stick*, the book Roediger wrote with Peter Brown and Mark McDaniel. It offers a more detailed picture of the research into the testing effect and other desirable difficulties. Here, I'd like to propose a few ways we might make use of the testing effect in college classrooms.

One is to simply give more tests. I know that a lot of students dread taking exams: they think that tests don't accurately measure what we do in a college classroom. They have probably had more than a few run-ins with poorly designed standardized tests in high school. Some may bring to high-stakes exams a nearly crippling anxiety. But there's nothing forcing us to use the same tactics as standardized tests, nor do we have to make the results of our tests determine our students' final grades. If we're giving tests not primarily to evaluate how much students have learned but rather to promote further learning, it makes far more sense to give frequent, low-stakes tests throughout the semester.

There are a couple of immediately appealing features of such a scheme. For one, regular tests ensure that students are studying regularly throughout the term, not waiting until just before the big exam to relearn everything at once. We know that such spaced study is more effective for long-term learning. Second, frequency breeds comfort: if tests are a regular, perhaps weekly, part of your class's schedule, students' performance anxiety should lessen considerably. They'll get used to taking tests in your class. No longer will there be a sense that everything (or a significant portion of everything) is riding on how they do on one or two tests. Making the tests count for a relatively small portion of students' final grades will help with this as well.

Near the end of their survey of testing effect studies, Roediger and Karpicke mention their colleague Kathleen McDermott, also a psychology professor at Washington University, who gives her students a test in every class period. She devotes the last ten minutes of every class to a test on the assigned readings and the lecture material. The students know they must come to class prepared, and the quizzes help students retain important information from each class.[11]

You can also encourage your students to test themselves. The educational studies that showed that being tested was a more effective way to learn material than studying should tell us something about traditional study techniques. Reviewing material—rereading the textbook, going over notes, and so on—is not a very effective way to learn. It's too easy. Students who read and reread their notes get a false sense of mastery; each time they go over a page it becomes more familiar, and their brains do less work in processing it. Better to test themselves on the material. Flash cards, in which students have to frequently recall definitions of concepts or explanations of phenomena, are a great way to make the brain retrieve information that's not so close at hand. Tell students about the testing effect, and suggest that they put it to use for themselves.

Getting Your Students to Read

No matter your discipline, no matter your pedagogical approach, you will no doubt expect your students to do some reading for your course. You will assign readings on your syllabus, and you will plan out your teaching each day with the expectation that students will have read those pages. In many courses, mine included, the readings, and what the students make of them, are integral to the learning process. And yet a number of studies have consistently demonstrated that the majority of college students—perhaps as many as 80 percent—regularly come to class not having done the reading.[12]

This is a problem. If you have any experience in front of a classroom, you know how frustrating it is to try to lead a discussion or engage students in an activity when they're not prepared. I'm of the opinion that if you have done the hard work of getting your students invested in your course, if they genuinely care about learning what you hope they will learn, they will *want* to do the reading. But there are things we can implement to specifically encourage our students to do the reading ahead of class.

Perhaps the most obvious tactic is to give reading quizzes. If you're looking to introduce regular, low-stakes testing into your classroom as a way to make use of the testing effect, reading quizzes start to look very attractive. Quizzing students on concepts found in the reading can help students better learn those concepts. And, of course, if students know that they will be tested on material found in the reading, and if those tests have some bearing on their final grade, more students will do the reading.

I've found as well that even one or two surprise reading quizzes, deployed whenever you feel students have started to slack off, can be very effective in reminding them of their responsibilities for class.

If you're wary of the punitive flavor of reading quizzes, reading response questions can be a gentler method. Accompany each reading with a brief list of questions for students to answer, asking them for feedback as to how the reading should be handled in class. Ask students which parts of the reading they grasped easily and thus don't need explained further. Ask them to tell you the parts that aren't clear to them. Ask them which points are most helpful to understanding the topic. By asking questions that point to the use you'll make of the reading, you'll underline the fact that the reading is indeed integral to the course. You'll also provide yourself with useful information to guide your lecture or class discussion (particularly if you have students submit their answers before class).

Such questionnaires can still be used to monitor your students' reading: when you collect them it will be pretty clear who has done the reading and who has not. But this approach has the added benefit of treating students like the mature intellectuals you hope they'll become, whose reactions to the reading will shape the class's discussion of it, instead of like disobedient pupils who need to be watched over by a surrogate parent.

We also need to make sure that our required reading is actually required. I'm the first to complain when my students don't prepare for class; but if I don't regularly make use of the stuff I'm asking them to read, I can't really blame them for not wasting their time. Many of our students have an enormous number of responsibilities—multiple courses, a part-time or even full-time job, family duties, a demanding social life—that force them to be pragmatic prioritizers. If they figure out that it's not really necessary to read everything you assign, they won't read everything you assign. Most students will do the reading only if *not* doing it will lead to a poor result. Otherwise, they've got better things to do.

So go through your syllabus and make sure that all of your reading assignments are there for a reason and that it's actually necessary to complete the readings to meet the course objectives. Be ruthless and honest with yourself about what students need to read, whether they can get it all done in a reasonable amount of time, and whether *you* have enough time in class to cover it all. When you have assigned readings, actually discuss them in class.

It's also helpful to discuss your rationale behind the readings you assign. You don't have to bend over backward to sell each reading, or make unrealistic promises about what they'll get if they read. But remember that you are asking students to do something; the least you can do is tell them why. In the last five minutes of class, for example, remind students what they have to read for next time, and also tell them what they can expect. Why is this reading on the schedule? How does it add to what you've been doing so far? How will the next class build on the knowledge they get through their reading? What will they need to understand from the texts to take full part in the discussion? What questions should they be looking to answer through their reading? Peter Filene suggests giving students a handout for each reading that includes an "invitation" (which lays out the reasoning behind assigning the reading), "reading questions" (which help guide students through their reading), and "discussion questions" (which students can ponder before coming to class).[13]

Finally, make use of reading material in class without rehashing it. Many teachers, particularly those who suspect that students haven't done the reading, spend a large amount of class time summarizing the most important parts of the reading assignment for students. While many disciplines require readings to be the main subject of a class discussion, it's important to make sure you're not doing all the work for your students. If you're just going to tell them what they need to know, why should students spend all that extra time reading? So aim to have in-class activities build on the readings rather than recap them.

Make Your Assignments Better

An important part of designing your courses will be designing your assignments. What should guide you in creating your assignments, and how can you ensure they are successful?

Your assignments need to reflect your goals for the course, what you want students to be able to do or be able to demonstrate that they know. Assignments are a way for students to show you how well they can perform the requisite skills or apply the requisite knowledge you are teaching them. But they can't do that if you're not clear on what you're looking for.

Research done by the Transparency in Learning and Teaching Project has shown that offering students a clearer and more transparent picture of their assignments before they start can lead to better results, particularly among student populations that typically perform poorly.[14] That means explaining the overall goals you have for the assignment (what knowledge you want students to gain, what skills you want them to practice), the particular steps you expect them to follow in completing the work, and the specific criteria you will use to evaluate them. Putting in extra work at the outset to make sure that students fully understand what's being asked of them can save you work when it comes time to grade.

What about rubrics? It seems like there are a lot of good reasons to use rubrics in your classroom. As a document that explains the criteria you'll be using to assess students, a rubric is essentially a tool for just the sort of openness that I often lobby for. A good rubric will make clear to students what you expect of them. Students come from various backgrounds—as do faculty—and yet many instructors still make students guess exactly what "A work" consists of in each particular classroom. A rubric aims to cut through that confusion. It has the added benefit of preempting student complaints about grading. When a student stays after class to beg for an extra couple of points to be lifted out of C range, you can just point to the rubric ("See? This is where you fell short").

Another benefit of using a rubric is that creating one can improve your teaching by forcing you to clarify your pedagogical goals. Having to actually think about what you're hoping students do on assignments and exams can make your objectives that much clearer to you. Rubrics can help give you a structure to provide more effective feedback to students, zeroing in on the skills they're still lacking. In that sense a rubric can also provide you with valuable information about which aspects of your course are working well and which are not.

In my experience, though, rubrics often fail in practice because they're not good rhetorical tools. Most rubrics do not speak a language that students understand. Too often, in trying to isolate the skills we want students to master, we fall back on vague and abstract language that means little to them. I don't know about your students, but telling mine that they should "employ language to better control their ideas" or "reflect the generativity of the topic" doesn't really help them understand why they can't seem to do better than a C+. Yes, you can work to use more effective language on your rubric, but the problem remains that, because they deal in abstractions, rubrics often fail to show students what is expected of them in real terms.

Although the goal of clearly communicating expectations to students is a good one, rubrics are ill suited to the task because they are abstracted from the work that students actually do. Better to spend the time you would have used making a rubric to give better and more detailed feedback to your students on their work. If you are going to use a rubric, try to make it—or revise one you already have—with real student work in front of you. The perfect time to make next semester's rubric is right after you've graded this semester's papers.

In that sense, I think that giving your students examples of how other students have completed the assignment can be an effective supplement or replacement for a rubric. Begin by finding examples of completed assignments from past years at various levels of achievement. If you're doing a brand new assignment, try to find examples that typify the kind of work students will be doing. You can have them read the examples as homework or, better yet, break them into groups and have them read them in class. Give out those sample assignments without the grades attached, and have each group discuss the strengths and weaknesses of each sample assignment and give it a grade. Then take the discussion to the whole class and go over each sample, having the groups explain what grade they think each anonymous student should have gotten. Finally, reveal the grade each sample assignment actually got, and explain why in detail.

At this point, your students will be pretty familiar with the examples at hand and will be able to properly understand your reasoning for the grades. They will hear your expectations spelled out, not in the abstract but in relation to the actual work they'll be doing. You can point out what the "A" example did that the "B" example didn't do, and students will see what it actually looks like to "use evidence to support your argument," or whatever it is you're hoping they demonstrate in their work. You'll communicate your expectations to your students without having to hand out a jargon-loaded document that they would probably ignore anyway. It's a good idea to keep such samples online so that students can refer to them as they work on their own assignments.

The University of Victoria's Allyson Hadwin has suggested making "task analysis" a graded part of assignments.[15] That is, ask students to answer, in writing, questions about the goals of the assignment, the tasks necessary for completion, the teacher's expectations, and so on. Remember that being able to complete a college-level assignment is itself a skill, and some students—particularly first-years—may need help in understanding all that they have to do. Hadwin suggests such questions as "Why are you being assigned this task?" and "How does this task fit in with other course readings, lectures, and activities?" I think it's also a good idea to ask students what steps they need to take to successfully complete the assignment, and ask them to think through how exactly they'll accomplish those steps. In any case, check in frequently with students to make sure they're not straying too far off course as they do their work. Taking a few minutes in class to remind students what they should be doing for their assignments can pay dividends down the line.

Finally, you can do your assignments yourself. It's one of those ideas that sound both radical and obvious. Jennifer Gonzalez, who writes about teaching on her Cult of Pedagogy website, wrote in 2015 about "dogfooding"—the tech-world practice of trying out a product like a consumer before bringing it to the market.[16] Completing your

> ## Sample Task Analysis / Task Planning Handout
>
> The following is something you might give your students as they start work on a big assignment.
>
> 1. Reread the assignment prompt.
> 2. What are the goals of this assignment? What will you achieve or understand if you complete this assignment successfully? What will you need to demonstrate to satisfy the assignment requirements?
> 3. Write down all the steps you'll need to take to successfully complete the assignment.
> 4. Go through the list of steps, and note next to each one how much time you think you'll need to complete the step.
> 5. Given the assignment due date, make yourself a plan: a schedule for completing each step along the way in this assignment. Try to be realistic, given your other commitments, academic and otherwise.

own assignments before giving them to students, Gonzalez argues, has many clear benefits. You'll be able to notice, in advance, potential problems. You'll be able to write clearer instructions. And you may very well discover that the assignment doesn't match up with your course goals and that you need to redesign it.

Improve Peer Review

For every essay I assign in my classroom, students have to take part in a peer review session; students read each other's rough drafts and offer critiques and suggestions for revision. Before embarking on this process, I always make sure to ask my class about their previous experiences with peer review. "With a show of hands," I'll ask, "who here has been a part of a useless peer review session?" Nearly everyone puts their hands up. "Now raise your hand if peer review has helped improve your writing in the past." Many fewer hands go up this time.

When I press students about it, most report to me that peer review is often a waste of time: their classmates are too nice, or don't care enough, or don't know how to be constructive, and so it's rare that anyone receives much helpful advice. Research seems to echo my experience; a 2014 study of student perceptions of peer review found "a modest overall downward shift in positive perceptions" of peer review after students engaged in it in four different subjects.[17]

How can we remedy this? Peer review is an activity that courses in almost any discipline can benefit from—from the sciences to the humanities to engineering, any course that requires student work can have students read and respond to each other's work along the way.[18] Students receive feedback from people besides the instructor, they get to see how others have tackled the same project, and the instructor doesn't have to do all the heavy lifting for once. What's more, a number of studies have suggested that the process of reviewing other people's work helps the reviewer herself become a better writer.[19] But we can't assume that students know how to give helpful feedback—as my students' past experiences attest, just having students trade papers and tell each other what they think is not the answer.

I've evolved an approach that I think addresses some of the main weaknesses of most poor peer review sessions. It's a process that can be applied to any discipline, even those that don't traditionally put a lot of emphasis on writing.

I have students pair up with two different partners during the session, one after another, so that they get more than one perspective. During the class before the workshop, I tell them they'll need to bring two hard copies of their drafts, each one with a memo page stapled to the front. The memo page—an idea I got from Oakland University's Christina Moore—has two parts: a context paragraph and a series of questions.[20] In the context paragraph, writers give a brief report about where they are with their draft—what they've done so far, what they haven't done yet, what they're unhappy with, and so on. The questions are requests for specific kinds of feedback: Are my paragraphs too long? Do you think the third example is strong enough? Do I need to write a conclusion?

Both parts of the memo page provide guidance to readers, helping ensure that the feedback students get is the kind they actually need.

On the day of the workshop, after pairing students up, I give them at least five minutes to talk before reading. I ask them to discuss their drafts and the prospect of revising those drafts. That amplifies the positive effects of the memo page and underlines an important aspect of the peer-review workshop: the whole point here is to help each other. I try to do everything I can to encourage students to see the process as allowing them to do something for each other—instead of for themselves or for me.

Next, I hand out feedback forms. The best way to make sure students don't just praise each other's work generically is to structure their feedback for them. So I provide a two-sided sheet with a series of questions they have to answer about the draft. Linda B. Nilson, in a 2003 essay in *College Teaching*, points out that the kinds of questions we ask peer reviewers to answer may impede their ability to offer constructive feedback.[21] Questions that ask students to judge whether the work is well written or whether the research is adequate may lead right into the too-nice problem: ask students a yes-or-no question about the quality of their peers' work and most will default to a yes. In addition, your students are probably not expert readers. You can't expect them to be able to evaluate their peers' work consistently or helpfully. Better instead to ask them to read carefully and describe what they find. Ask them to think about the important elements you want to see in their assignments—a complex thesis, responsible use of sources, support for their claims, perhaps—and look out for those components. For example, I ask students to find the author's thesis and restate it in their own words. Any lack of clarity in the original thesis is usually reflected in this "translation." Descriptive questions allow students to help their peers rather than judge their peers.[22]

Likewise, the final questions on my feedback form encourage constructive criticism and a focus on influencing the revision work to come, instead of appraising the work that's already been done. So the form asks things like, What is the biggest unresolved question in the draft? What do you want to read more about in this essay? What are the draft's biggest strengths? And, crucially, what are the most important things the author should do to improve the draft?

Here, again, the goal is for students to give each other helpful advice, instead of being forced into an evaluative role they're not equipped for. It also has the benefit of emphasizing the importance of revision.

Finally, this workshop shouldn't be the only time undergrads talk with each other about their papers. A successful peer-review process requires students to develop a scholarly camaraderie—they need to see themselves as members of the same team rather than competitors for a limited number of good grades. One way to encourage camaraderie is to give students opportunities to talk about their projects as they're working on them. If you have time in class, you can set up mini-workshops on such aspects as topic choice, thesis development, research, and revision. Even giving students five minutes here and

---

Some Sample Prompts and Questions
for a Peer Review Worksheet

Read through the draft twice. As you read, place a question mark next to any part of the paper that is unclear to you, that you don't understand, or that you want to ask the author about.

Underline the thesis of the paper as you see it. *In your words*, what is the paper's main argument?

Find and underline the main point or topic sentence of each paragraph. Is each paragraph organized around one main idea? If not, are there paragraphs that could be reorganized? Which ones? How?

Has the writer used sufficient evidence to support her argument? Would any of the author's points benefit from more evidence, different evidence, or more effective explanation of the evidence used? Please explain.

Are there aspects of the assignment that this draft failed to address?

What questions, if any, does this paper leave unresolved? Does the paper seem to be missing anything? As a reader, what do you want to know more about?

What is the biggest strength of this draft?

What are the most important things the writer should do to improve this paper?

---

there to pair up and discuss their progress on their assignments can be helpful. All of this lays the groundwork for your workshop, for peer review to work, and for students to actually see themselves as peers.

Peer review, of course, is an important part of the professional life of scientists. It is impossible to think about the creation of scientific knowledge in the absence of peer review, either formal, as in the review of journal articles or grant proposals, or informal, as in the scientific debates that determine whether a given insight or discovery is accepted. Science, like every academic discipline, is a social practice in which collaboration, controversy, uncertainty, and socially determined norms reign.

But as Christine Cunningham and Jenifer Helms pointed out in an excellent 1998 piece in the *Journal of Research in Science Teaching*, many high school and college science classes still portray science as an individual pursuit, in which the lone scientist performs experiments and verifies results completely apart from any broader community. "Contrary to popular depictions and belief," they write, "research science is neither practiced nor governed by a rigid scientific method that produces incontestable facts. Instead, controversies rage, personal and societal values play important roles, and accepted methodologies and knowledge change, as in any other discipline."[23]

Cunningham and Helms suggest that one goal of a university-level science course should be to disrupt students' assumptions about scientific knowledge as straightforwardly discovered and verified. Writing in 2009, Nancy Trautmann offered a similar point, arguing that "students are unlikely to learn about the nature of science simply by conducting their own experiments. Instead, explicit attention needs to be devoted to the role of research and communication in the construction of scientific knowledge."[24] One way to introduce students to the difficult questions and judgments that scientists confront in almost every aspect of their work is to incorporate peer review into the classroom.

Jianguo Liu, a professor of fisheries and wildlife at Michigan State University, integrated a peer review process into his Systems Modeling and Simulation course. Liu calls attention to the two stages at which peer review regularly appears in scientific work: at the proposal stage and at the publication stage. Grant proposals, a hugely important part of a working scientist's professional life, are peer reviewed to determine whether they will be successful. Similarly, academic journals rely on peer review to determine whether to publish a given piece.

Students in Liu's course complete a computer simulation model as a term-long project; Liu has them review each other's work at both proposal and "publication" stages. Students have to write a research proposal before getting to work in earnest on the development of their model. This proposal is reviewed by three classmates as well as the instructor (who also reviews the reviewers' remarks). Those reviewers look for weak points and suggest how the proposal's author can improve the proposed project. Students then revise their proposals on the basis of the reviewers' comments. A similar process occurs when students complete their models and write up draft project reports. The same three classmates who reviewed a student's proposal review that student's report, and the instructor looks over and supplements the reviewers' reports. At both proposal and report stages, reviewers are given detailed instruction on how to give helpful and constructive feedback, and the instructor has a chance to emphasize which aspects of the reviewers' reports are most pertinent and which can be safely ignored.[25]

Such a process almost inevitably improves student coursework. It builds revision into the students' approaches and encourages them to think metacognitively about their own process. By making students review their peers' work, the process teaches students valuable lessons about scientific work more generally, and about the variety of approaches that can lead to good and bad outcomes. And the process introduces students to a significant part of the professional life of the scientist, letting them experience what it's like to belong to a community of scholars and to have to stand behind one's work within that community. "Perhaps the most important variable affecting learning gains through peer review," Nancy Trautmann suggests, "is the extent to which students apply time, effort, and critical thinking in all steps of the process."[26] Rather than conducting experiments or constructing a model, writing it up in isolation, and turning the project in for a grade, students get a vivid illustration of the social nature of science, of the way that scientific knowledge is produced through complicated interactions between real human beings. Look for ways to introduce such interactions to your classes.

Why Students Cheat, and How to Make It Less Likely That They Will

Cheating, or, as my institution calls it, "academic dishonesty," isn't usually thought of as a factor of course design. Rather, it's framed as a disciplinary issue, an unfortunate infraction that must be dealt with (increasingly, by administrators) as it pops up. But nothing happens in a vacuum, and it's worth thinking about *why* students cheat and how we might design our courses to make such incidents few and far between.

James Lang, whose book *Cheating Lessons* investigated this very question, writes that cheating is "an inappropriate response to a learning environment that [isn't] working for the student."[27] That is to say, students cheat only when it seems like cheating will help them. In a well-designed learning environment, one in which students are motivated to learn rather than just to achieve a certain grade, students have no need to cheat. While we have to work to curtail such an inappropriate response—with the threat of discipline, for example—we also should look for ways to shape the learning environment within our courses to make cheating less likely.

We're all familiar with direct approaches to combating academic dishonesty. Automatic failures, disciplinary action from on high, honor codes: instructors and institutions are working hard to weed out cheating, and understandably so. But threatening severe punishment or asking students to promise they won't plagiarize certainly doesn't seem to have eliminated the problem. While it's not clear that cheating is on the rise—that's a controversial subject—I don't think anyone would argue that these direct measures have banished cheating from our classrooms.[28] So it's worth thinking about indirect approaches, strategies that look to prevent cheating before it occurs.

Lang found, after reading up on the current scholarship on academic dishonesty, that students are more likely to cheat when they are less invested in the course material. When students are motivated intrinsically (by curiosity or by a genuine desire to master the material) rather than extrinsically (by the desire for a good grade or to avoid a bad one), they are far less inclined toward dishonest behavior. This makes sense: cheating won't help the student who actually wants to learn what you're trying to teach her. If you've read this far in this book, this will come as something of a relief: Chapter 2 outlines a number of ways for you to design your class so that your students are intrinsically motivated to learn. Keep your attention, especially early in the semester, on drawing students into your course, on enticing them to buy into your learning objectives, and you will see incidences of cheating go way down.

Another indirect approach comes from Sandra Jamieson and Rebecca Moore Howard, the English professors who began the Citation Project, an empirical study of the way students use sources in their writing. Their study analyzed 174 student papers from 16 institutions, classifying a total of 1,911 citations. The findings are striking: only 6 percent of the citations came in the form of summary; the remaining 94 percent were either direct quotations (42 percent), passages copied without quotation marks (4 percent), patchwritten[29] (16 percent), or paraphrased (32 percent), all shallow ways of using secondary sources.[30]

The low incidence of summarization suggests that even students who are not plagiarizing are not fully engaging with the ideas within the sources they cite. To write a summary, the student must read the whole text (perhaps multiple times), think deeply about the most important aspects, and synthesize observations into a concise rendering of the text's substance. Instead, far too often it seems, students find a book or an article on their topic, quickly find a quote to copy and paste, and move on. This sense is further cemented by the fact that in Jamieson and Howard's study, 46 percent of the citations came from the source's first page (70 percent came from the first two pages).

For Jamieson and Howard, plagiarism is not the product of unethical student behavior; rather, students plagiarize most often because they have an inadequate understanding of how to use secondary sources in their writing. We can do a better job of teaching students not only how to properly cite others' work in their own writing but also how to distinguish good sources from bad. Even more importantly, we can help students understand the value of proper research, how to read sources critically, and how the best scholarship builds on other people's ideas. In an essay published in the *Chronicle of Education* in 2018, Rebecca Schuman details what she calls "the baby bibliography": a document that notes for each source its thesis, its impact on the field, some representative quotes, and the writer's opinion about the source.[31] Most scholars have their own systems for keeping track of and summarizing secondary sources in their research; even a brief demonstration of how you engage with sources can show your students a way forward. If you give students the tools necessary to legitimately incorporate other sources into their work—let them know that it's OK to get ideas from other people—incidents of plagiarism should become rare. I've written about more ways to teach information literacy in Chapter 7.

If your assignments require students to do research and to integrate that research into their finished product, think about ways you can teach responsible scholarship in your class. In my rhetoric classroom, I spend a substantial amount of time discussing and having students practice the skills of quotation, summarization, and citation. But even courses that do not have as much time to spend on the nuts and bolts of writing can address some of these issues. Try an ungraded homework assignment in which students have to summarize a secondary source, perhaps one they are using for their paper, followed by a brief in-class discussion of what makes for a good summary. Or take a few minutes in class to discuss your own research process with students. Tell them how you find information, take notes on sources, and make sure to give proper credit for others' original ideas. Give them some sense of how academic discourse functions and you'll encourage them to want to join in. Whatever your discipline, I'm sure it's important to know how to engage with the work of other people; we can't assume our students already know how to do that well.

Connect One Class with the Next

Much of the time, when we think about course design, we envision a semester-long course as one long interval. We try to map things out so that there's a logical progression to the skills students learn and the knowledge they acquire. We envision the term as a sort of unified narrative, with a beginning, middle, and end, and we hope that our students get to the end having discovered the moral of the story. But of course the forty or fifty hours we spend with students over the course of a semester do not happen continuously; the term is broken up into parts. How we connect these parts—how we make individual class periods not feel like discrete entities—is an important part of getting the most out of our courses.

There's so much happening in our students' lives that we're not privy to. Other courses, jobs, families, friends: it's easy to forget that our courses are not the only thing our students have to worry about. And while we should respect the fact that our students have busy lives, there are some steps we can take to ensure that they don't completely forget about our courses when they're away from the classroom. Here are some ways to connect our class periods.

One of the easiest ways to ensure continuity is to bring some regularity to the way you teach. If you have a similar progression in every class period, your students will gain a familiarity with the class that allows them to more easily get back into it after time away. In my rhetoric courses, I start every class period with a five- to ten-minute writing exercise. I'll write a prompt on the board and students respond to it in writing. After a few classes, students get used to the habit and already have their notebooks out at the beginning of class.

Some teachers repeat a more comprehensive structure every class. The British teacher and writer David Didau has written about a sequence in which the teacher explains a concept and lays out its context, models and deconstructs how the concept can be applied, and then provides a "scaffold" with which the students can practice application with the teacher's help, before giving students the opportunity to apply the concept themselves, on their own.[32] Without wanting to be too formulaic or too beholden to the length of a single class period, I like the idea of each class period following a similar pattern. Students will know what to expect and can therefore focus on what we want them to be learning. And the fact that each period shares the same structure lends continuity to the course.

Another idea comes from Robert Hampel, a professor of education at the University of Delaware.[33] Hampel suggests a commonly cited teaching tip: end each class by asking students to respond, in writing, to a couple of pointed questions about the day's lecture and / or discussion. These can be retrospective in nature ("What is the most important aspect of British modernism?") or forward-looking ("Given what you now know about the origin of cancer cells, how do you think early treatments approached them?"). But Hampel goes further. He asks students a couple of questions, collects the responses, and reads them after class. Then he begins the next class period by summarizing the responses, exploring their implications, and using them to provoke a discussion that leads into the next topic. The process constructs a natural bridge between class periods, tying up the loose ends of one class while laying the foundation for the next. And it encourages further participation by demonstrating that students' views are taken seriously. It also gives instructors opportunities to see whether students understand the material and to quickly correct any misperceptions they hold. It's a great idea.

A further way to make connections between class periods is to introduce some online elements of your course. Discussion boards, course blogs, wikis, and other resources accessible to everyone can encourage the conversations you have in class to continue outside of class. For my graduate writing course, we use a course blog for all of the students' writing. Every week, a number of students respond to a prompt by writing a short blog post; the other students read and comment on the blog posts on their own time. There's an ongoing conversation between classes and an easy beginning to discussions in class ("Let's take a look at what you all have written on the blog this week").

Most colleges and universities now use course management software that offers options such as discussion boards and wikis. It's worth exploring these, even if you are usually technology averse, for the benefits they offer in creating continuity. If you want your students to be thinking about your course all week long, not just when they are physically present, giving them more opportunities to interact can help.

Finally, not enough instructors (and not enough students) take advantage of the pedagogical benefits of office hours, another opportunity to keep classroom conversations going between class periods.

In a 2015 issue of *College Teaching*, Lydia Eckstein Jackson and Aimee Knupsky wrote about research that suggested many benefits accrue to students who take advantage of office hours.[34] The advantages include better relationships with professors, with the latter more likely to take on active mentoring roles for students who attend office hours; a higher likelihood of completing a degree, especially for students from underrepresented groups; and the development of important skills for college and the workplace, such as planning, long-term thinking, and self-efficacy.

What's more, in a 2013 study published in the *Journal of Political Science Education*, Mario Guerrero and Alisa Beth Rod found that the number of office-hour visits a student makes during a semester is positively correlated to his or her academic performance in the course.[35] Even when controlling for such variables as GPA, family income, and gender, Guerrero and Rod still found that each office-hour visit increases the probability that a student will get a higher grade. In the study, which tracked 406 undergraduates over a four-year period, students who never made use of office hours could expect to finish with a final grade of 82 percent, a low B. By contrast, students who made more than five office-hour visits during the term finished, on average, with an A.

Maybe attending office hours made a difference, or maybe students who tend to get good grades are more conscientious than others (it's also possible that instructors unknowingly give conscientious students more generous grades). For me, the distinction is not really important. What is important is that meeting with students one-on-one allows me to be a better teacher—to reach students more effectively, regardless of whether the meetings lead to higher grades. In private meetings, students may feel more comfortable asking questions they cannot ask in class. You can take time to explain a concept to a confused student or to encourage a slacker to be more responsible about coursework. Most importantly, I think, students can feel that there's someone in a position of authority who actually cares about their academic progress.

So how do we encourage students to take advantage of our office hours?

One important, and easy, change to make is to arrange your office hours in different blocks of time. Being in your office during the gap between your classes on Tuesdays and Thursdays may be convenient for you, but any student with class during those hours will be out of luck. So try to give your students a few options.

Frequently mention your office hours (and the location) in class, and let students know that you're willing to schedule a meeting outside of office hours if necessary. Many students assume that we are available to meet only during our exact office hours. Make sure they know that isn't the case. You might also tell your students about the research linking office-hour visits and higher grades. Talking about the intangible benefits of stopping by your office might not get through to them; the prospect of an A could work better.

But the best way to get students to come to your office hours, of course, is to require them to visit. I know some teachers who include a minimum number of office-hour visits as a part of the participation mark. As I discuss in Chapter 5, I've had a lot of success requiring students to come in for one-on-one conferences to go over their drafts. Either way, you have to be available during office hours; why not use that time to improve your teaching?

4

Teaching the Students in the Room

IT CAN BE easy to forget—while finding readings, coming up with assignments, planning out lesson sequences, and catching up on the latest research—that we teach students, not just subjects. All the work that goes into preparing to teach can go up in smoke if it's not tailored to the students who have signed up for our courses. If we've committed to judging our teaching by its effect on people—how much we've helped students develop—then a crucial factor is who those students are.

In a 2013 essay in *CBE—Life Sciences Education*, Kimberly Tanner wrote about the need to design college biology courses with the knowledge that "learning is the work of students." She argues that whether students learn in our courses has as much to do with who they are as it does with what we teach or how we teach it. She writes, summarizing a vast amount of research, that

"each student's prior experience and attitude and motivation toward the material being learned, confidence in his or her ability to learn, and relative participation in the learning environment are all thought to be key variables in promoting learning of new ideas, biological or not. Finally, bringing together individual students in classrooms produces group interactions that can either support or impede learning for different individuals."[1] We do not teach generic students. The particularities of the human beings in our classrooms—what they know, what they think of our subjects, what they can and cannot do, how they interact with each other—are not incidental to our task. Knowing that, the traditional approach of a college professor on the first day of class, in which he gives out the syllabus and tells the students what the course will be, suddenly seems callous and potentially absurd. How can we plan out a course before we know who our students are?

Now I don't want to suggest that we disavow all course planning and wait until we meet our students before mapping out the semester. There's much we can do before we get to know our students. The very existence of this book implies that I believe we can do a lot of productive thinking about our teaching even in the absence of our students. But the best teachers are responsive to their students. They adjust on the fly, paying attention to their students' progress throughout. They make sure they are teaching the students in front of them rather than the fantasy students envisioned back in July. Above all, they cultivate *flexibility*, planning for their plans to change as the facts on the ground demand. Your students are the facts on the ground. Your pedagogy must make space for them.

Centering Accessibility

One of the ways that I've come to see flexibility as crucial to the instructor's task has been through engagement with scholars of disability studies. These scholars, in their focus on the educational experience of students for whom our institutions are often not designed, are among some of our keenest thinkers about pedagogy.[2] It is in seriously reckoning with every student's experience, especially those who are often overlooked, that a truly responsive pedagogy can emerge.

For many instructors, accessibility is a topic handled by a brief section toward the end of a syllabus—a paragraph detailing the steps a disabled student can take to receive accommodations. Such policies are very much figured as an exception to the norm, an appendix pinned onto the end of the syllabus, as if to say, "Oh yeah, and if you've got a disability, we can probably work to find some kind of solution."

At my institution, as I imagine it is at most institutions, the burden for receiving such accommodations falls on the student. A student with a disability at the University of Iowa meets with Student Disability Services, which works with the student to figure out what kinds of accommodations might help that student succeed in her courses. For instructors, then, dealing with disabled students is a matter of waiting for them to come forward and adjusting accordingly.

I once briefly worked with a graduate instructor who was worried about one of her students. The student was struggling academically and, halfway through the semester, was on pace to get an F. The instructor suspected that the student was on the autism spectrum, but he had not disclosed a disability to her. The instructor didn't know what to do—it was illegal to help this student without a formal accommodation request, she said, and there couldn't be a formal accommodation request if the student didn't disclose his disability. Because the student hadn't come forward and formally requested special treatment, the instructor felt that her hands were tied.

Now, it should go without saying that it's never *illegal* to help our students. I explained that while there were probably some accommodations she couldn't give without a formal disclosure—she probably couldn't significantly alter the way this student was assessed, for example—that didn't mean she shouldn't try to help a student who was clearly struggling academically. It is not our place as instructors to diagnose students, nor can we make decisions about which accommodations students are legally required to be given. But we have to teach the students we have in the room. We can't assume that our standard practices are ideal for every student who might walk through the classroom door. The work of Anne-Marie Womack, director of writing at Tulane University, has helped me see these issues more clearly.

In a 2017 essay in *College Composition and Communication*, Womack argues that "accommodation is the most basic act and art of teaching. It is not the exception we sometimes make in spite of learning, but rather the adaptations we continually make to promote learning."[3]

Although we must constantly make adjustments to teach the students in our classrooms, seeing accommodations as after-the-fact exceptions obscures the fact that accommodations are central to the very idea of teaching. Think about note taking, Womack writes. We view students taking notes in our classes as a normal part of the learning process, but it's actually an accommodation that allows them to process and retain more information than they could otherwise. Using a PowerPoint presentation during a lecture is an accommodation to help students better remember what we're saying. Conducting an exam-review session near the end of the term is another. Our entire higher education system is designed to make it easier for students to learn complex material. We don't just hand students a big stack of books and tell them to get learning.

So we're wrong to think of accommodations as exceptions that detract from our normal way of doing things. Accommodating students *is* our normal way of doing things. But we don't always accommodate every student.

The line between what we think of as normal practice and special accommodations is a thin one, and it's often based on very little of substance. No matter our students' ability, we need to try—within reason—to eliminate barriers that keep them from fully participating in our courses. We need to work to ensure that students have equal opportunities to succeed. That's true whether our students are disabled or not.

Of course some of our students will be disabled, and we need to consider their needs ahead of time, when we're planning for the semester. Treating accessibility concerns as an afterthought can make disabled students feel unwelcome and, even worse, can erect further barriers to their learning. Better to plan for a diverse student population—making sure that accessibility is threaded throughout your teaching practice—than to assume all of your students will be some shade of "normal" and be surprised later when that's not the case.

Even if your classes have no disabled students, thinking about accessibility in advance can have great benefits for your teaching. The flexibility needed to adjust to students of varying needs requires that we think critically about our teaching priorities. For Womack, her "work with accommodations began when a student requested longer quiz time; [she] questioned whether there was a good rationale for stricter timing in [her] context and removed the requirement for all."[4] Such epiphanies are the kind we should all be chasing. I often ask the graduate instructors I work with to list all of the rules they have for their classroom. I then ask them to think hard about which of those rules are absolutely necessary for students to achieve their learning goals. Keep the ones that are integral to student learning; but if a rule isn't necessary, why have it?

Reading about Universal Design for Learning, the educational application of Universal Design, can help make your classroom a space that works for all of your students. Universal Design seeks to respond to the fact of disability by creating spaces, both physical and otherwise, that suit the needs of the full diversity of humanity. The University of Waterloo professor Jay Dolmage has written a great introduction to Universal Design for Learning in *Disability Studies Quarterly*, in an article that links to a living wiki with a list of places to start if you want to make your classroom a more accommodating place.[5]

You don't need to bend over backward to cater to every possible student or every possible need.[6] But thinking about these possibilities in advance can help you shape a course that's more likely to work for more students. The more you can design your course to respond to a variety of student abilities and needs, the less that students with special needs will have to come forward and ask for accommodations.

We can also help plan for diversity by imagining different kinds of students who may come through our classroom doors. How would your intended approach to teaching your course have to change if one of your students were deaf? Perhaps you would put more of your classroom communications on paper or in PowerPoint presentations. Here's the thing, though—such a change would benefit more students than just the deaf student. A student with high anxiety, or even just someone who's forgetful, would likely benefit from having class announcements typed out on paper or on a learning management system.

What if you have, as my classes often do, students with poor English skills? Or students who are working two jobs and have little time for coursework? Would your assignments need to change if some of your students have very little knowledge of American culture? What will you do if a student can't afford a textbook or a computer? Have you been assuming that all of your students are nineteen years old? What if you have some nontraditional students? Thinking about these hypotheticals can prompt you to make your teaching clearer and more accessible regardless of whether any of your students request official accommodations. Again, I'm not suggesting you plan for every single eventuality, only that thinking through some of these possibilities will help you adjust to a diverse classroom.

As Womack and Louisiana State University's Rick Godden wrote in a 2016 essay, "Seeing a student body as an undifferentiated group leads to strict rules and single solutions."[7] To put it another way, adopting strict rules and single solutions assumes your students are an undifferentiated group. Your students are not an undifferentiated group. Plan for diversity and be less surprised when students turn out to be individuals.

"Where Are You Now?" Finding Out What Your Students Know

In the early 1970s, Rosalind Driver, then a graduate student in education at the University of Illinois, had a peculiar notion. To understand how children learn important scientific concepts, she argued, we first need to grasp how they see the world before they start school. Children do not come into their first science classrooms as blank slates, with no sense whatsoever of the natural world or of the way objects move in space. Talking to children, Driver showed, often revealed that they had quite fully developed (if usually incorrect) ideas about scientific phenomena. By patiently interviewing students about the way they saw the world, Driver provided the first detailed information not just about where students tended to go "wrong" but how.[8] She established a new area of research in science education, laying the groundwork for a great many studies of how students understand important concepts.

Her crucial—and radical—insight was that learning is dependent on our preconceptions. We learn by revising our understanding of things. Reflecting in 1983, Driver wrote that "if a visitor phones you up explaining he has got lost on the way to your home, your first reaction would probably be to ask, 'Where are you now?' You cannot start to give sensible directions without knowing where your visitor is starting from."[9] It follows, Driver suggested, that we cannot begin to teach our students until we understand where they are starting from.

Of course, it's well and good to advocate for teaching that responds to students; but how exactly are we supposed to find out what the students need? How are we supposed to find out what they know—and what they don't know? Finding out what students know and don't know about a topic gets more and more difficult as class sizes go up. In a lecture hall with 200 students, opening class by asking, "Now what do you all know about preindustrial America?" may not be the most effective strategy. Class time, as well, is an issue. Most instructors have a lot of ground to cover over the semester, and not enough time to handle it all. Adding in time for informal chats about students' prior knowledge and current understanding may feel impossible.

So how do we understand our students' preconceptions and still leave room for other pedagogical priorities?

One of the easiest ways to find out what your students know (and think they know) is to administer a survey. Surveys can be short or long, pointedly about subject matter or more generally about the course approach, filled out in class or at home, on paper or online. You'll want to ask students about their prior experience with the topics you'll cover, their self-assessed strengths and weaknesses as students, and their expectations for the course. James Lang suggests a "student information sheet," on which students write a few paragraphs in response to two or three questions about their current understanding of ideas crucial to the course.[10] If you opt for a more complex survey, with many questions, I'd recommend using Google Forms or another online tool to collate and interpret student answers.

Akin to a survey but perhaps better suited to writing-centric courses is a low-stakes assignment that can double as a writing diagnostic. Almost any prompt can be used for such an informal assignment: ask students to write about their personal history with your subject, or about a short and lively reading, or about their thoughts on a hot-button issue in your field. Reading these pieces is my first real introduction to the students as students. It's important to me, as a rhetoric instructor, to quickly understand my students' writing capacity, how well they write, and to what level I should pitch my instruction. But getting a sense of students' level of understanding as they begin your course is valuable no matter your field. The student goals assignment I discussed in Chapter 2 lends itself very well to this sort of thing. The assignment kills at least two birds with one stone: the students begin developing the metacognitive mind-set that will help them learn throughout the semester, and I get an early sense of how well they can write and what they might need to work on.

As the semester goes on, you can continue to solicit feedback from your students without necessarily taking as much time as a full survey requires. Many instructors have had success with the "one-minute paper," one of the more popular "classroom assessment techniques" from the 1993 book of the same name by Thomas A. Angelo and K. Patricia Cross.[11] You simply stop class a few minutes early and ask students two basic, but important, questions: "What is the most important thing you learned during this class?" and "What important questions remain unanswered?" Students write their responses in the minute or two remaining in the class period and hand in their answers on their way out the door. You're left with a stack full of brief responses to help guide your next class period. Students are left with a better understanding of your teaching, the result of having to evaluate the class at its conclusion.

A similar, but more technologically advanced, way to find out what students know is to make use of clickers—classroom response systems. Derek Bruff, who wrote the definitive book on the subject, defines them as "instructional technologies that allow instructors to rapidly collect and analyze student responses to questions posed during class."[12] Whether you distribute physical remote controls (many institutions make these "clickers" available for instructors or students to borrow) or, as is more common these days, use an online service that lets students use their phones, classroom response systems are a surprisingly easy way to poll your students. I'm something of a pedagogical technophobe, but I've found setting up questions on polleverywhere.com to be straightforward and quick. Asking a few multiple-choice questions about important content at the end of each class period, and letting students enter their responses anonymously, can give you an easy-to-understand overview of your class's current understanding of what you're trying to teach.

If the one-minute paper or clicker questions take up more class time than you're comfortable with, why not move outside the confines of the classroom altogether? Try treating homework assignments as formative, rather than strictly summative, assessments. That means constructing your assignments so that students' answers can help you update your teaching approach and help students better understand their own progress. For example, swipe a trick from Just-in-Time Teaching, the pedagogical approach developed by instructors in a number of physics departments in the late 1990s.[13] Instead of collecting student work in class, have them upload their assignments to the course-management system at least a few hours before class. That way, you'll be able to look at their answers and alter your approach in the classroom that day accordingly, offering students an almost immediate pedagogical response to their feedback.

A few years ago, I started doing this with reading-response paragraphs in a literature course. I had students turn in a weekly paragraph in response to their reading. It was due every week, the day before class. Students were able to see their peers' answers after they turned in their own, which allowed them to come to class with an awareness of how others had responded to the material. It allowed me to go into class with a good idea of what students understood and what they didn't, and let me use their answers as examples in class to help illustrate important points. I still do something similar in my rhetoric class, and many a class has been saved by looking at student responses just before class starts—it's sometimes very clear what I need to focus on.

Any of those strategies will help you learn more about what, and how, your students are learning, and make your teaching more effective. They'll also offer students a way to actively evaluate their own learning, understand their progress in the course, and see just how far they have left to go.

Of course, the work that your students do for the course over the semester can be a valuable source of information for your teaching approach. It's baffling to me how few teachers make use of the wealth of material that students provide them with every semester. A 2012 collection of essays, *Teaching with Student Texts: Essays toward an Informed Practice*, edited by Joseph Harris, John Miles, and Charles

Paine, has been helpful in my thinking on this topic. Because most of the contributors teach composition—a subject with a long tradition of using a writers' workshop model—many of the essays discuss ways to make pedagogical use of the papers written by current students. Joseph Harris, for example, creates handouts with multiple excerpts from student essays, demonstrating different ways to solve the same writing problem. "If I've chosen them well," Harris writes, "the excerpts on the handout will show, not a single correct solution to the problem, but a range of responses to it."[14] Such a process turns the traditional writers' workshop on its head: instead of a whole class offering feedback to a writer, a few writers' texts are used to offer lessons to the whole class. I can easily imagine instructors in other disciplines making similar handouts—showing a number of incorrect attempts at solving a physics problem, say, to demonstrate to students the potential wrong turns they should learn to avoid.

By using examples of students' work—especially from that very class—you make sure your teaching responds to their actual needs, instead of whatever ideal version of them you have in your head. Margaret Marshall, in her essay in *Teaching with Student Texts*, writes about using student papers in a graduate pedagogy seminar: "It is the ability to see patterns that lets a teacher treat student writing as primary pedagogical texts rather than inferior products in need of improvement. . . . We teach, we assess what they learned via the writing produced, and we modify our subsequent teaching accordingly."[15] When I grade papers now, I keep a running tally of common problems I come across, whether as small as punctuation issues or as big as misunderstood concepts. On the day I return papers I like to review with the class some of the issues I came across when reading their work. Student writing—or other kinds of student work—can be a source of valuable information that we can use to help students improve. This strategy can be used in almost any discipline, not just in writing-intensive courses.

When I use excerpts from student work, I remove all names from the samples and take out any identifying details, but it's still a good idea to email the students in question and get their permission before using their work in class. Some teachers request permission from students in advance, to potentially use their work with future classes. Do that, and you'll be on your way to creating a library of material full of pedagogical inspiration.

Encouraging Community

Tailoring your teaching to your students is not just about learning about your students and working on their weaknesses; it can also entail stepping back at times to let students form supportive and constructive communities. An important lesson that many beginning instructors need to learn is when to back off, so that students can reveal themselves not just to you but to each other.

One thing I remember vividly from my first semester of teaching was the terrifying sense that I had no safety net. If I ran out of things to say—if I got to the end of my lesson plan—there would just be nothing: total silence. All of the responsibility for keeping the class going fell on me alone. I continually felt like Wile E. Coyote, never sure when I would look down and find I had just run off a cliff. That sensation—that you as the teacher control everything in the classroom and that disaster is just a moment away—is a scary feeling. It's one that we really shouldn't have to feel.

As I've gotten more experienced in the classroom, I've come to realize that the best courses I've taught—when the students seemed to learn the most—were the ones in which they formed a real bond with each other. They came to know and trust each other, and seemed to honestly like spending time together as a group. Those are the classes in which I have to quiet the students down at the beginning of class because they are too busy animatedly talking with each other. The benefits of this kind of community have been well established by research.

In Chapter 1, I discussed Polly Fassinger's research into the sociology of students in classes—remember that she found that student perception of the classroom climate was the biggest factor that contributed to students' likelihood of participating. But it's not just participation that's affected by the nature of the student group. Robert J. Sidelinger and Melanie Booth-Butterfield, in a study of more than 400 students at a mid-Atlantic university, found that when students "feel a sense of connection with their peers," they were more likely to be well prepared for class.[16] In 2009, Ali Sher surveyed thirty sections of an online course at a Washington, DC, private university and found that student-to-student interaction—the degree to which they felt a sense of community with each other—was significantly associated with their learning.[17] Likewise, Gloria J. Galanes and Heather J. Carmack interviewed students at a large midwestern university on their perceptions of classroom climate and found that a positive learning environment—one in which other students modeled positive academic behavior and offered each other support—has "a major impact on student learning."[18]

So what can we do to help our students form supportive, cohesive communities? Here are a few of my strategies.

Begin by encouraging students to share their individual learning goals with each other. This is a good way to respect, and even cultivate, their differences. Emphasize to students that although you have your own goals for their learning, *their* own goals are as important. If you are creating a survey early in the semester to learn about your students' goals and preconceptions, why not let them share their answers with each other as well.

They may not have ready answers. Let them work in pairs to discuss the survey questions and their answers, and then revisit them throughout the term as students develop their goals. You want them to hear each other out, get to know each other as learners with different motivations, and understand the class as a whole as a diverse site of many students chasing different targets together. By asking students to reflect on their own goals, and by having them share those goals, you encourage students to see their involvement in the course as something both personal and shared.

Another way to encourage the formation of a cohesive community is to make time for nonacademic conversations in class. Clearly students have interests beyond those that apply to our course material. Give them a chance to be themselves in class. My colleague Benjamin Hassman starts every class with a "question roll."[19] He asks a question—usually something apparently unrelated to the day's topic—and his students go around the room giving their answer. Questions can range from "What's your favorite word in the English language?" to "What's the closest you've ever come to dying?" I now do a question roll at the beginning of each class period; the one time I forgot to do it (we had a busy day!), the students were up in arms that I would overlook such a crucial ritual.

The point is to get students to feel that your classroom is a space where they are allowed—encouraged, even—to be themselves. You want them to see your course as something they can integrate into their lives, into their sense of themselves. College courses don't need to be isolated from and unrelated to everything else students are doing. Look for ways to show students that "your" course is theirs—a meaningful part of their lives.

You can also look to create conditions in which students depend on each other for success in the course. Steve Fishman and Lucille Mc-Carthy, in a 1995 essay in *College English*, describe a philosophy class in which one student takes notes—a sort of narrative of what happened that day—for each class period.[20] The next day, the note taker reads those notes out loud, reminding everyone of what happened in the previous class, before choosing another student to be the next note taker. Students in that course quickly understood that they were members of a community who would benefit if they could rely on one another.

Group work can be designed to encourage interdependence. For two-stage exams, which I cover in more detail in Chapter 5, students take tests both on their own and in groups, an activity structured so that students need to listen and cooperate in order to get good grades. Jigsaw groups require students to contribute individually and work together to understand a topic fully.[21] Think about how to make your classroom less competitive and more cooperative.

Finally, you can build community through your own actions. Learn about your students, where they're coming from, and what they're good at, and then turn to them when their expertise might help the class as a whole. Let students know that they are a necessary part of the community, that it is important they are there, and that others depend on their knowledge and generosity.

It also makes sense to focus a little more at the beginning of the semester on low-stakes, collaborative activities that enable students to form the kinds of bonds that can help their academic performance. Give your students the time and space to find their footing as a social group, even if it means proceeding a little more slowly than you usually do. Be alive to your students' experience of the class—not just their relationships to you but also their relationships with each other. The group dynamic may be mostly out of your hands, but your approach, and your attitude, can go a long way toward creating the conditions in which good relationships can thrive in your classroom. When students know and are able to trust each other, they are more likely to take full part in the class activities and to be more fully involved in the course overall.

Practice Compassion

If you spend any time listening to other teachers (particularly online, where complaining is almost an art form), you'll soon hear about an epidemic of grandparents dying in the last two months of the semester, when big assignments are due and final exams start to get closer. Students will do anything to take advantage of us, the chorus sings, and the only defense is a strict adherence to the rules: sorry, kid, but the syllabus clearly says "no extensions."

That attitude seems even more desirable when you read some of the criticisms of so-called permissive-indulgent instructors. Such teachers "fear doing anything that might create stress for students, stifle their personal growth, or hurt their self-esteem," writes the psychologist Douglas Bernstein. They coddle students, being careful not to be too harsh for fear of discouraging them. Even worse, those faculty "are eager to help students succeed, even if it means lowering standards for success."[22]

Such criticism takes as its model established research on parenting styles and translates it to the classroom. Those parenting styles—the research builds on work done by Diana Baumrind—typically consider two parameters: how involved the parent is and how demanding the parent is.[23] So there are "authoritarian" parents, who aren't very involved in their kids' lives but nonetheless enforce rules like a drill sergeant, and "permissive-neglectful" parents, who are neither involved nor rule bound. Neither type, it should go without saying, makes for very good parenting. Another model is the "authoritative" parent—the apparent ideal, a parent who is both responsive and demanding. And then there is the "permissive-indulgent" parent, who is responsive to a child's needs but not very strict. The latter is the modern-day stereotype of the coddling parent afraid to let children experience anything that might negatively impact their fragile self-esteem. This parent, according to Baumrind, "presents herself to the child as a resource for him to use as he wishes, not as an active agent responsible for shaping or altering his ongoing or future behavior."[24]

It's the specter of the permissive-indulgent parent that prompts calls for instructors to be strict and unfeeling in their enforcement of classroom policies. Critics fear the alternative, which, as Bernstein writes, is the sort of teacher who sees students "as children who need help and support to come to class, do their reading, and get good grades."[25]

But aside from that obvious straw-man argument—who would disagree that college instructors shouldn't treat their students like young children?—I think it's worth questioning the assumption that strict discipline is the same thing as demanding a lot from our students.

I think it's possible to be a demanding professor without being an officious one. You can care about your students and make allowances for them without fear that they'll walk all over you. It is precisely because our students are not young children that we can be lenient sometimes, allowing extensions and makeups on a case-by-case basis, showing them that we care more about their learning than about whether they checked all the boxes.

There are those who say we as faculty should treat our students like adults, and when they mess up they should face the consequences. I understand that argument. It makes sense, and you are certainly within your rights to state your course policies on your syllabus and then expect students to follow them. But when complicating events inevitably occur—illnesses, crises, those dying grandmothers—you do have a choice.

To me, when we choose to be strict, no exceptions, we signal to students that adherence to the rules is more important than any other learning goal we have for them.

And we encourage "satisficing"—the pursuit of "good enough" at the expense of, well, something better. When our rules and policies appear to be so important, we encourage students to strive only to satisfy our criteria, rather than to pursue their own goals. Edward Deci and Richard Ryan, the pioneers of self-determination theory (thought by many to be the most convincing account of human motivation), distinguish between autonomy-supportive environments and controlling environments. "To the extent that people do feel controlled by extrinsic motivators," they write, "their need for autonomy will be thwarted and some negative motivational, performance, and well-being consequences are likely to follow."[26] If we're led by our predetermined rules rather than our students and their learning goals, we'll undercut our efforts to motivate them. Students who do things just because the teacher made them do it are less likely to learn, and less likely to retain what they learn for the long haul.[27]

There's also a sense in which an emphasis on rules and discipline is itself a form of coddling. By granting so much importance to a set of teacher-imposed policies, you signal to your students that they are children who can't be trusted to figure it out for themselves.

Better, I think, to be flexible with the rules and strive to create a learning community where you don't have to worry about students taking advantage of you. I let my students know at the beginning of the semester that there are penalties for turning in assignments late. But I also tell them that if they have a legitimate reason to need more time, they should ask me for an extension. I tell them that I care most of all that they are able to do good work—it usually doesn't matter to me if it takes them an extra week. I try to signal to my students that their learning is far more important to me than my rules, with the hope that their learning will become important to them as well.

As I wrote in Chapter 2, I now allow my students to come up with a technology policy themselves. I bring up a number of possible concerns, but otherwise let students decide which devices can be used in class, whether phones should be put away or just kept silent, whether students can listen to music when working on class work, and so on.

So far, I've found that students are much more likely to follow a policy they came up with themselves than one that I impose. What's more, the policies they come up with have almost always been more strict than I would have expected. It turns out that most students don't like it when their classmates are texting during class discussion either. I have much less of a problem with texting in class now, and I don't need to police the room either.

Take a moment to ask yourself about the hypothetical student with the fictional dead grandmother: What have you done to make this student think that lying to get an extension is preferable to doing the work on time? What have you done to make this student think that lying is preferable to coming to you with an honest explanation about why they need an extension? Strive to create a classroom environment in which there's no need for students to lie.

Students need to be responsible for their actions, certainly, but instructors need to be responsible for creating an environment that encourages students to learn. We should look to create courses in which students want to do the work on time, because we've successfully made the case that doing the work on time will benefit them. We should also look to make students trust us enough that if tragedy strikes—sometimes family members do die—they feel comfortable coming to us and explaining why they need some extra time. In my classroom at least, there are more important lessons to learn than the value of following the rules.

Justify Your Teaching

To be committed to adapting our teaching to our students means we have a responsibility both to justify our pedagogical decisions to our students and to take student complaints seriously. Even if our instinct when our pedagogical authority is challenged is to get defensive, we have to take students' role as equal partners in the classroom seriously, which means taking their opinions seriously.

The class I teach most often, as I have mentioned, is called Rhetoric. It is focused, as the title suggests, on helping students become college-level writers, readers, speakers, and thinkers. But of course, to practice reading skills you actually need to read something. So I designed a course that focuses, in its assigned readings, on feminism and related issues. About half of our readings have something to do with feminism, gender, and / or sexuality (the other half are mostly readings about the writing process).

About halfway through a semester a few years ago, I sent an email to a student asking him about his poor attendance and participation in the course. In response, after some earnest apologies and promises to do better, the student wrote: "My expectation for this class was to learn how to write and read at a college level. But so often, I feel like I am taking a gender issues class and not a writing and reading course—which frustrates me."

The question of the extent to which we are bound by our students' expectations for our courses is a tricky one. When he signed up for a course called Rhetoric, this student couldn't have known about my emphasis on readings about gender and feminism; it's certainly reasonable that he might have felt a little bit tricked by what the course turned out to focus on. At the same time, I believe strongly that reading about feminism and discussing the issues in class is a great way for students to develop and practice the high-level reading and writing skills my course is charged with teaching. Feminism, itself a practice of critical reading, offers a model of questioning the world that I think benefits students immensely. I stand behind my approach to teaching rhetoric this way. But it's up to me to sell this approach to my students.

I've written before about the benefits of leaving aspects of course design up to students. Yet as the professor, I take for granted that I have a certain amount of freedom to teach my courses in the ways I see fit. My training, expertise, and position of authority all qualify me to set the conditions of a course and to shape the reading list, assignments, and terms of assessment. But we as faculty should admit that this freedom comes at a price.

The authority to unilaterally decide on how we teach our classes, I would argue, comes with a responsibility to explain and justify those methods to our students. I view it as an ethical necessity—I'm going to take up a substantial amount of their time, ask for a substantial amount of their effort, and assess them on my terms. At the very least, I should have good reasons for doing what I'm doing. That's also a pedagogical necessity. Relying on "because I said so" doesn't get you very far when you're trying to persuade students to come on board with you.

In my classes, I spend a lot of time explaining why we do the things we do, and that starts on the first day. In walking students through the syllabus, I am careful to discuss why we will read the particular texts listed, what I hope students will gain from the experience, and how I came to that conclusion. Although we inevitably talk about the content of the readings, I often try to steer the discussion to the aspects of the readings they should pay attention to as writers: the rhetorical moves, the way they are constructed, the ways a reading differs in approach from a previous piece.

All of that said, when I received the email complaining about the focus on feminism, I definitely thought about what might have gone wrong. Did I work hard enough to explain to students the purpose of my approach? Had I let the class veer off course? Was our focus on feminism turning the class into a gender studies course? I recommitted myself to laying out for my students the reasons why we were doing what we were doing.

I once wrote a column in the *Chronicle of Higher Education* arguing that student evaluations are far from worthless. It provoked some predictable responses in the comments section. One poster noted: "The very idea that an 18-year-old knows enough about my subject to evaluate my teaching of that subject is ludicrous." Another claimed that "student comments are largely useless" and "usually never rise above whiny complaining—which is what you would expect from 18-year-olds."

Maybe I should have adopted that same attitude in responding to my student—dismissed his complaint out of hand because he can't possibly understand my methods.

I don't think so. I'm convinced we must listen to our students. If our mission is to help them develop, then the students themselves have to be an important source of feedback. They may not be completely reliable judges of their own learning, but clearly they know better than anyone else how they're experiencing something.

Listening to our students does not mean we have to give equal credence to every comment or gripe from every student. Not only are students sometimes unreliable judges of their own learning, but there are many times when the fault for their lack of learning lies with them, not with us. We have an obligation to keep our ears open to student concerns nonetheless, whether they come to us in person, via email, or anonymously through an evaluation form.

Centering students in our pedagogy is not easy, especially if we ourselves were taught by teachers who didn't always prioritize our learning. But if we are committed to helping each one of our students develop and learn, we have a responsibility to commit ourselves as well to the values of openness and honesty in the classroom. Our students are our material; let's make sure we don't forget that.

5

Assessment Isn't Just Assessment
Giving Students the Right Kind of Feedback

MUCH OF LEARNING IS FAILING. Think about how you learned to ride a bike, or play an instrument, when you were a kid. Every skinned knee or wrong note was a signal that you had more to learn, that you needed to make an adjustment. As Carol Dweck's mind-set research has convincingly demonstrated, being able to see your failures and other setbacks as learning opportunities—and not as indications of lack of talent or intelligence—is crucial to achieving success in almost any pursuit.[1]

Figuring out how to discuss those failures and setbacks with students is an important part of any teacher's job. When I supervise my daughter's piano practices, I can tell her when she's playing too fast or too slow—I've played string instruments all my life—but when it comes to errors of technique, I'm more or less useless. My wife, however, who played piano seriously for many years in her youth, can diagnose such problems and work with her to change her approach going forward. Her expertise is crucial in being able to give our daughter the right kind of feedback to correct her mistakes.

How do we give our students the right kind of feedback? How do we help them see where they've gone wrong in a way that entices them to keep working? How do we give them opportunities to understand their strengths and weaknesses so they can better direct their attention and shape their approach? The right kind of feedback requires that we *see* where students are and that we *tell them* in a way that allows them to improve. It requires a deep knowledge of our subjects, an understanding of the learning process, and real attention to the students in our classrooms.

Perhaps the most important kind of feedback, for a number of reasons, comes in the form of assessment: of assignments, of tests, of any kind of student work.

It's important to distinguish, as educational researchers have, between two types of motivations we have for assessing students. The first (and more typical) way of thinking about why we assess students is referred to as summative assessment. This attempts to measure students' progress to see how well they have learned the material. Summative assessment is a judgment, an indication of how the instructor thinks a student has performed. It's a necessary evil, often required to make students—and instructors—externally accountable.

In contrast to summative assessment is formative assessment, which is aimed not at measuring past performance but at influencing future performance. The idea of formative assessment acknowledges that the feedback we give students has strong effects on how they conduct themselves in our courses. Giving thoughtful feedback on student work helps students develop into independent learners, able to accurately track their own progress (or lack thereof) and adjust their approaches accordingly.

One simple way to think of the learning process is as a feedback loop:

1. The student makes an attempt (to answer a question or complete a task) and fails.
2. The teacher identifies the error or errors and helps the student understand why the failure occurred.
3. The student makes an adjustment and then makes another attempt.

Formative assessment includes all the work that goes into getting step 2 right. What's the best way to communicate to students about their failures so that they can understand them and learn from them? Helping students understand why they made mistakes is just about the core of the teaching process. It is essential, and it is difficult.

In Chapter 4, I wrote about ways to make use of feedback from our students in order to tailor our teaching to them. Here, the subject is the reverse: thinking about how students receive feedback from us, so that they can learn better.

To be sure, the grades we give students count as a kind of feedback. In addition to functioning as an evaluation of how students performed on the test or assignment in question, the grades also communicate to them something about how well they're meeting our expectations and whether their current approach is working. But grades are a pretty blunt instrument.

I think about this when I get a paper so bad I don't know how to grade it. I'm not talking about a late paper, or one that's been plagiarized, or is too short or off topic. Rather, this kind of essay checks all of the superficial boxes but is so poorly written, so shoddily done, that it seems to demand a special response.

I am always unsure about how to handle papers like these—especially because I build in so many checkpoints in my courses, specifically to make sure students don't miss the boat so badly. But one of my colleagues suggested to me that in these cases, a really low grade, particularly on the first major assignment of the semester, can serve as a wake-up call. A properly bad grade might serve a pedagogical purpose in motivating the student to straighten up and fly right.

But research on extrinsic and intrinsic motivation suggests that we shouldn't expect a bad grade in and of itself to be very helpful in motivating students. Extrinsic motivation can actually have a negative effect on intrinsic motivation, so dangling the prospect of a terrible final grade might make a student even less engaged. To the extent that students are motivated to get better grades, they'll do what they think will get them those grades, which won't necessarily align with what you're looking to see (that is, real evidence of learning).[2]

But as most students *do* care about grades, I think there's still room to acknowledge that they can be a tool in producing intrinsic motivation.[3]

In an exhaustive review of the literature on formative assessment, two researchers at King's College London drew on a number of sources that have documented a phenomenon familiar to many faculty—that is, students' "reluctance to be drawn into a more serious engagement with learning work."[4] They quote the Swiss scholar Phillippe Perrenoud, who argues that many students "do not aspire to learn as much as possible, but are content to 'get by,' to get through the period, the day or the year without any major disaster."[5] For these students, a properly bad grade might be just such a disaster. A bad grade might be the jolt that lets those students know their current approach is not working.

But even if a bad grade contributes to an increase in a student's intrinsic motivation, it still doesn't say much at all about what specifically the student needs to change going forward. When I give a D to a terribly written paper, the grade communicates only that I thought the student performed poorly. It doesn't say anything, on its own, about what the student should have done differently—how the paper could have met my criteria. If students' learning process is a three-step feedback loop, our process of giving formative assessment should have three steps as well:

1. We indicate to students that their performance isn't good enough.
2. We show them where they fell short and what they should have done.
3. We help them understand what they need to do to improve in the future.

A bad grade accomplishes only the first step. Is it possible that a bad grade will jolt students out of complacency, make them investigate a better way to approach their studies, and turn their performance around? Yes. But that's unlikely without further feedback. We need to provide context with a bad grade—specific reasons why the student did poorly and specific tasks to improve.

I often decide to give Ds to those terrible papers. But I always make sure to spend extra time giving feedback about such assignments. We need to make sure that struggling students understand what they did wrong, exactly what we were looking to see, and what they missed out on through their initial approach. We should also emphasize concrete ways students can get better results on future assignments, both in terms of process (maybe the student needs to do more re-search before completing the assignment) and in terms of specific subject knowledge (maybe the student needs to brush up on her knowl-edge of polynomial equations). In the end, we need to convince stu-dents that engaging more fully with the course is in their own best interest.

Helping Students Learn from Their Mistakes

When thinking about the importance of formative assessment to stu-dent learning, something always bothers me. To go back to my daughter and the piano, when she makes a mistake playing a song, what happens next is intuitive: we correct the mistake and try to un-derstand why she made it ("you didn't keep your fingers arched"), and then she plays the song again, this time adjusting her approach. This reattempt, the third step in the feedback loop, is necessary to learning. But with students in the college classroom, most of the time we point out their mistakes, *maybe* work with them to understand why they occurred, and then swiftly move on to the next subject. How can this be effective?

Even when our assessment approach leans toward the formative rather than the summative, we rarely spend much time in class re-flecting on students' failed attempts. I think I'm like most instructors in not allowing redos on graded assignments. We want students to carry the lessons of one assignment forward to the next one, but it's easy to see how such lessons get forgotten along the way to the next assignment. Real learning comes from practice and from awareness of past missteps. But if we don't give students space to think about and learn from those missteps, we may be denying them opportuni-ties to learn valuable lessons.

I got to thinking more specifically about these issues after reading a blog post by the high school teacher and education writer Jessica Lahey. In the run-up to the first important tests of the school year, Lahey worried that many of her students would do badly. But, she reasoned, "often a poor result on a test is just what some students need to get serious about figuring out what they were supposed to have learned in class." Her students did indeed fare poorly, but Lahey then used the tests, and their wrong answers, to help her students learn the difficult concepts they were struggling with. She made the students retake the test in class—in pairs, and this time with their books open—and had each pair explain not only why their chosen answer was correct but also why the other answers were wrong.[6]

I know many professors still hand back exams and expect students to go over what they missed on their own. Instead, devote class time to reviewing the results. If the test was worth giving, if it tested important concepts and skills that you want your students to understand, then it's worth taking the time to make sure they got them right. Howard Aldrich, a professor of sociology at the University of North Carolina at Chapel Hill, has written about his practice of breaking students into small groups to review their test results.[7] He asks the groups to go over each question and help each other understand why they made their mistakes. Within the groups, students quickly shift roles between "teacher" and "learner," depending on the question.

Aldrich also notes that he makes sure that his final exam is cumulative—that is, the tests given throughout the semester cover ground that will also make an appearance on the final exam. Aldrich tells his students that up front and allows them to keep their tests. This gives them extra motivation to make sure they understand where they went wrong before moving on to the next subject.

Another idea that Aldrich suggests is to give a follow-up quiz after each test. Give the quiz in class after you review the test results, or make it a take-home quiz. It should be short and focus on the material that gave students the most trouble. The quiz offers students an opportunity—and an incentive—to figure out how to master the most difficult concepts.

Similarly, I like the idea of a wrong-answers test near the end of the semester. This is more easily accomplished with a small class, but it's not impossible with larger classes. Near the end of the term, give each student a personalized test made up of questions the student got wrong (or similar questions) on the earlier tests. Students know the test is coming, and so they can take time to study their previous mistakes to prepare for it. It does require some extra work on the instructor's part, but with a little foresight and preparation, it's easily manageable.

Two-Stage Exams

You can also try changing the nature of the tests you give. Two-stage exams have a simple concept that offers a myriad of benefits: students first take the test individually and then immediately retake it in groups. The group test counts—so students are motivated to work together to figure out the correct answers—but for only 15–20 percent of the whole test grade. Most of the grade (80–85 percent) comes from the results of the individual tests. Because the individual portion of the test is worth so much, students still have to study hard on their own. But they also are rewarded for the work they put into understanding and correcting their mistakes.

With two-stage exams, students receive immediate feedback on their wrong answers while at the same time gaining exposure to alternative approaches to difficult problems. They can see what they did wrong and then almost instantly learn how they might be able to get it right. This works particularly well on tests that require students to show their thinking along with their answers.[8]

A more elaborate version of two-stage exams comes from a systematic pedagogical approach initially developed by Larry Michaelsen, called team-based learning.[9] Here the tests are frequently low stakes.

Every time a new topic is introduced in class, the teacher assigns a modest amount of reading beforehand. In class, the students first take a test on the material, typically consisting of fifteen to twenty multiple-choice questions. After they take their tests, the students move into small groups (in team-based learning, students stay in the same groups throughout the term) and retake the same test as a group. Students are encouraged to discuss each question and work together to determine, as a group, the answers. They're given special scratch-off cards that tell them right away whether each answer is right or wrong. If they're wrong, groups must continue to discuss the question and try again.

Next, the teacher gives each group the opportunity to appeal any question it got wrong but thinks it should have gotten right. The groups do this in writing, pointing out any ambiguity they see in either the question or the readings, and supporting their arguments with evidence. This part of the process, in contrast to the tests, is open-book, allowing students to immediately review those parts of the readings that led to wrong answers. The appeal process invites students to apply their knowledge as part of an argument that can win them further points. The teacher collects these appeals and evaluates them after class.

The process concludes with the teacher giving a short, clarifying lecture informed by the students' test results. (Ideally, while teams are writing their appeals, the teacher can take some time to review these results.) You can ask students which parts of the readings they found difficult or mystifying. Their answers, combined with the test questions that most students got wrong, can help identify which topics need to be further explained in this concluding lecture.

Even if you don't embrace the whole elaborate process in your classroom, it's easy to see the value in such a strategy. In a relatively short period of time, students must review important material four distinct times—during the initial test, the group retest, the appeals process, and the clarifying lecture—and it's not difficult to imagine initiating a class-wide discussion in between two of those segments to add a fifth iteration. The whole process may seem overplanned, but I find it difficult to believe that many students would emerge from a class like this not knowing the most important material well.

Giving Feedback on Assignments

If, like me, you don't give many exams, taking a lesson from the field of rhetoric and composition might help you build this same strategy into your assignments. Many rhet / comp instructors (me included) require students to submit multiple drafts of each assignment. Asking your students to turn in a draft of their assignment, whether it's a writing assignment or something else, offers you the opportunity to give them feedback that they can actually use and that they might actually pay attention to. The biggest reason students don't engage with the feedback we leave on their assignments is that those assignments are now behind them; it's difficult for assessment to be formative if students no longer care about what's being assessed. Once we put a final grade on something, it is effectively dead to most students. It is no longer something they can improve on, and so it is no longer something they will spend much time thinking about. Your students may want to do well in your course, but if your comments only (a) point out mistakes they made on an assignment they've already turned in, or (b) offer lessons to be applied on some far-off-in-the-future assignment, there's not much incentive for them to pay attention now.

One possible remedy to this problem is "minimal marking," an idea developed by Richard Haswell.[10] Knowing that students didn't make much use of his corrections, particularly of surface errors, Haswell simply stopped making those comments. Instead, he'd add a checkmark next to any line of text that contained one of those errors. Lines with two errors would get two checkmarks. Haswell handed back the checkmarked papers without grades. Each student would then have to find, circle, and correct all the errors before receiving her grade. By holding back student grades—and thus delaying the moment at which students stop caring about the paper—minimal marking forces students to actually engage with the instructor's remarks.

But minimal marking really only works with the most basic of mechanical errors. An even better idea is to give feedback earlier in the process, on drafts, rather than on the final product. We need to conserve our time and energy and give students comments when they might actually be useful—while the students are still working on their assignments. In his late-1980s study of what makes the best college courses, the Harvard professor Richard Light found that "an overwhelming majority" of students surveyed "are convinced that their best learning takes place when they have a chance to submit an early version of their work, get detailed feedback and criticism and then hand in a final version for a grade."[11] Of course, such a scheme requires that you build draft deadlines into your course schedule, which I know is not easy for every course. But don't worry that this approach will double your workload. If you explain to students that you want to give feedback when it will most benefit them, you can then hand back their final drafts with just a grade at the bottom. Students who want more of an explanation of their grade can schedule a meeting to talk about their assignment.

Have students turn in a first draft at least a week before the final version is due. If they are late with a draft or fail to turn it in, penalize them just as you would for any other late assignment. Leave yourself enough time so that you can return their marked-up drafts at least three or four days before the final due date. And focus your comments on what students need to do to make their drafts better. You can certainly note surface errors. But spend most of your time on the elements that you find most important in an excellent completed assignment. Teach your students how to revise their work.

I've taken to requiring students to meet with me to discuss paper drafts. I find this saves me time: rather than scrawl comments in the margins (or in addition to my scrawled comments in the margins) I can walk through in person what the student needs to work on in the essay. I make sure to end each conference with a clear takeaway: following the practice of my colleague Naomi Greyser, I write down a brief to-do list for each student to take home from the meeting.

The idea here isn't to give you more work to do, but rather to take time that you have to spend anyway and make it pedagogically useful. Conducting student conferences may seem like a lot of work, but they can replace some of the time you would have spent marking up drafts, and offer the possibility that students might actually understand and make use of your corrections the first time you make them (instead of repeating the same mistakes over and over). I think I'm much better at responding to a student's work in person; there's something about a written comment that just begs to be misinterpreted (or ignored).

Commenting on Student Work So They Listen

In many disciplines, giving feedback on student work is so simple a computer can do it: students lose points for wrong answers and gain points for correct ones. But in any situation where the feedback you give is more complex than that—when you want to tell students *why* their answer is wrong and how they can avoid the mistake in the future—the task becomes much more challenging.

Peter Elbow, a hugely influential scholar of writing studies, has written extensively about responding to student writing; much of his advice can apply to responding to student work of all kinds, in most disciplines. Here are a few of his tips.

Respond as a human being first

Elbow insists that one of the most powerful things we can do as instructors responding to student work is to try to temporarily shed our identities as teachers.[12] Instead of always reading student work as the authority who judges what's right and what's wrong, first read as an interested bystander, and write down your reactions. You don't have to give all of these reactions to the student, but even just shifting your perspective a little ("I found this confusing" rather than "This is confusing") can help.

How does it help? First, students will trust your reaction more if you respond as a human being than if you respond as the voice of God, dictating right and wrong on the basis of your impeccable judgment. Elbow sees this as a problem of epistemology; students "know that the alleged authorities to whom they write often contradict each other."

Second, responding as a human being first treats students as scholars who are doing real work, rather than as supplicants begging for a teacher's approval. Treating students as scholars does not mean you approve everything they do; rather, it means you respond to them with the assumption that they will want to know how their work is seen by other people.

Giving feedback on students' process

As I wrote above, meeting with students or responding to their work earlier in the process is a good idea. But if it's not possible to give feedback on drafts, you can still comment on their process. Most of us do this all the time, guessing as to why students went down the wrong path (I often find myself writing something like, "I think a few more drafts would have improved this paper"). But commenting on process doesn't have to involve guesswork. Elbow recommends having students turn in a cover letter with big assignments, explaining what went into the creation of what they're turning in. What approach did they take? What choices were they faced with and which did they choose? How do they think they did?

With that cover letter in hand, you can better offer advice in your feedback, pointing forward to how the student can build on the experience. ("I noticed that many of your answers suffered from simple arithmetic mistakes. I also noticed that you reported that you didn't start work on the assignment until the night before it was due; maybe getting started earlier next time to leave yourself time to check your work will help with this.") Elbow's cover letter is an example of what's known as "process writing," another example of which is Jody Shipka's "statement of goals and choices," which I discuss in Chapter 6.

Use grids

As a sort of middle ground between just giving a grade and using a more fleshed out (and abstract) rubric, Elbow's grids are an easy way to give more constructive feedback without a lot of extra effort. Come up with a list of basic criteria for the assignment, and grade each aspect on a simple three-point scale: weak, OK, and strong. Without doing much more than assessing whether any element of the student's work was notably good or notably bad, you can give the student a much more detailed picture of how they performed.

Here's an example of a basic grid that Elbow uses for writing assignments:

Weak	OK	Strong	
			Content, insights, thinking
			Organization, structure, guiding the reader
			Language: sentences, wording, voice
			Mechanics: spelling, grammar, punctuation, proofreading
			Overall[13]

In person, I can tell pretty easily when my brilliantly worded constructive criticism goes right over a student's head; I can rephrase it until the student gets it.

Feedback during the Semester

Here's an illustration of feedback making a tangible difference. Mark Salisbury, assistant dean and director of institutional research and assessment at Augustana College in Illinois, noticed that students often complained that they didn't receive enough feedback from instructors until late in the term. So he and his team inserted a question into their freshman surveys: "I had access to my grades and other feedback early enough in the term to adjust my study habits or seek help as necessary." (This is one of those questions that isn't a question; students signal their level of agreement with the statement on a five-point scale.) The wording of that statement gives an indication of what they were looking to show: if assessment helps students monitor their learning, shouldn't more of it, early on, help students perform well?

The responses fell on a fairly typical bell curve, with relatively even distribution of answers among the five choices, ranging from "strongly disagree" to "strongly agree." But here's what was most interesting: the answers to this "early feedback" question correlated with the answers to several other ones.

Those students who felt that they received useful feedback early enough to do something about it were more likely to feel that their interactions with professors in general had a positive effect on their progress. They were also more likely to think that faculty members treated them like individuals. And here's the best part: the more strongly students agreed with the early feedback statement, the more likely they were to say that they worked harder to meet their instructors' expectations, "whether or not the extra effort might improve one's grade." It's a small sample size, but the implication is clear: if students are given a chance to monitor their progress in a class, they may actually put more effort into that class.[14]

This research confirms an intuitive conclusion: we should be aiming to give our students as much constructive and specific feedback as possible, and we should be giving it to them early in the semester. Students want to know how they're doing, what they're doing wrong, and what they should do going forward. We should be telling them these things.

We can make sure we do so, first of all, by not leaving all of the major assignments for the second half of the semester. It can be tempting to delay important graded work, to give students a chance to adjust to the course, to find their feet. But remember that assessment is at least as important in how it guides future learning as in how it measures performance. We do students a disservice when they go months before learning about their progress. Assign graded work early on.

If you give out a participation grade, as many instructors do, interim marks can help as well. The appeal of participation grades is easy to see, and is a good example of the way we already assume that assessment can goad students into learning. Devoting a portion of our students' final grades to their participation signals to them that a significant part of their learning will depend on their contributions in class. For those of us who believe in the value of active learning, including a participation grade is putting our money where our mouths are. It puts in writing—in language students can understand—that we expect them to play an active role in the classroom.

There's also the hope that a participation mark will act as a spur to that participation. We want it to be both carrot and stick: a promised reward for those students who (blessedly) rescue class discussions with insightful comments and a threat of a penalty for those who doze through class after class. But if we give students their participation marks only as part of their final grade, we take away much of the mark's usefulness as formative assessment, as a catalyst for increased student involvement in class. It's as if you gave a number of assignments throughout the term but didn't give students their grades until the end of the semester. Grades can work to motivate students, but the participation grade loses that function when it's held back until after the final class.

A solution is relatively simple: give each student an interim participation grade every two weeks. This may seem like a lot of added work for the teacher, but I think you'll find it actually saves work in the long run. By keeping a running tally of each student's participation progress, you'll never again have to squint at a series of illegible pencil marks on your attendance sheet to work out whether a student spoke five times or six over the course of three months. It's much easier to assess each student's participation over a two-week period than it is over the whole term.

More importantly, students—and your class discussions—will benefit. Just as a bad grade on an essay can spur a student to put in extra work on subsequent assignments, a poor interim participation grade can be just the thing to motivate a quiet student to speak up and contribute to class discussions. Students will no longer be in the dark about how they are doing on this measure.

With more and more classes taking advantage of learning management systems like Canvas and Moodle, it's getting easier and easier to give students interim grades throughout the term. Of course, you don't need to do this as often as every two weeks; every month, or even just once, at the halfway point, would serve a similar function. Any of these options would go some distance to making the participation grade pull more of its weight.

What Happens When Students Fail?

It is a truism that every failure contains a great opportunity to learn. But most of the time, when our students fail our courses, they're left, pedagogically speaking, on their own. When we fail a student, it's usually the final act in the teacher-student relationship: we file the grades; the students deal with them (or don't). Why do we suddenly abandon these students at the moment of their greatest need?

It's pretty hard to fail one of my classes. I'm no pushover, but I do everything in my power throughout the term to reach out to struggling students, give extensions when warranted, and try to understand how to help. When I have to give an F at the end of the semester (or even a D), it is often with deep regret and even antipathy. The student's failure can feel like a personal affront: after all I've done for you, you still couldn't do even the bare minimum?

That emotional reaction feels justified, doesn't it? The failing students have neglected their work, avoided multiple chances to right the ship, and clearly did not satisfy the basic performance requirements. They've broken the implicit contract between teacher and student. Why should we go out of our way to try to reach kids who clearly don't care?

That's a perfectly valid response, and I don't begrudge anyone who wants to file the offending grade and walk away like an action star calmly ignoring an explosion. But something about the scenario of aggrieved teacher and cast-out student bothers me—even though I've done the casting out on a number of occasions. I end up feeling like those students failed me, let me down, when in fact they only failed themselves (or, worse, it's I who has failed them). But hurt feelings are not a good basis for pedagogy, and their failure turns into a missed opportunity.

Faculty and students often have differing explanations as to why students fail. According to a series of studies reported in a 2014 paper, "Why Do Students Fail? Faculty's Perspective," students are most likely to blame their failures on a lack of motivation, whereas instructors most often see a lack of academic preparedness as the main culprit.[15] What that disconnect should tell us is that it's not always obvious why students fail, and what they should learn from that failure.

When we discard these students, filing their grades and closing the book on the semester, we in effect tear up a semester's worth of work. Students may turn to academic advisers or other mentors to reckon with a failed class, but it's the instructors who are best placed to impart whatever lessons can be learned from that experience.

So reach out to those students one more time. Ask them to come for a meeting to discuss the semester. If a face-to-face meeting is impossible, have a conversation over email. Be explicit about your intentions—explain that you want to figure out what happened and what the student can do in the future to prevent it from happening again. Resist the urge to expend a lot of energy justifying the grade, and instead focus on tangible steps the student can take going forward. Just as it's important to give specific feedback when handing out a bad grade during the semester, we need to take student failure as an opportunity to help those students come to grips with what went wrong. It's a simple step to try—one last time—to teach.

Grade Inflation and Blind Grading

Although most of my focus in this chapter is on formative assessment, summative assessment is important too. We should take seriously our responsibility to grade our students' performance fairly and as objectively as possible. And yet that seriousness has caused many well-meaning people to panic about the problem of grade inflation.

Grade inflation is one of those things that sounds much worse than it is. It does certainly sound bad. Did you hear about the high school with 117 valedictorians?[16] Maybe you read the (shocking!) news that the median grade at Harvard is an A–?[17] Or perhaps you've visited gradeinflation.com, with its detailed graphs showing just how pervasive the phenomenon is, and its ominous conclusions about grade inflation's connection to declining literacy rates.

Rebecca Schuman, writing in *Slate* in 2014, confessed that she is a chronic grade inflator. Tough grading, she says, is not worth the barrage of student emails that is a C's inevitable consequence. She convincingly argues that grade inflation is a natural outgrowth of the consumer model of education that seems to be more and more present on American campuses.[18] Considering the outraged and alarmed tone of much of the writing about the subject, one could be forgiven for thinking that grade inflation is the *cause* of the consumer model of education. Either way, the consensus seems to be that grade inflation is a very bad thing indeed.

But the fact of the matter is that grade inflation is probably a victimless crime. There have been no convincing studies that demonstrate that higher grades lead to poorer learning outcomes for students.[19] Some argue that giving better grades to more students does a disservice to those students who are truly exceptional, who deserve to stand head and shoulders above their peers. But a professor's job is to educate all of her students—to help as many of them as possible to thrive in their studies—not to foster competition between them to separate the wheat from the chaff.[20] Let employers and graduate schools come up with their own ways to evaluate students; you've got more important things to do.

Remember, our goal should be to get students to want to excel in our classes because they genuinely want to master the material. As Alfie Kohn pointed out in his 2002 demolition of "The Dangerous Myth of Grade Inflation," "A focus on grades creates, or at least perpetuates, an extrinsic orientation that is likely to undermine the love of learning we are presumably seeking to promote."[21] When we focus heavily on grades, our students will too.

Please don't get me wrong. I am not advocating giving everyone an A and calling it a day. I do not think that grade inflation is something we should be actively pursuing as a goal, only that we should not let fear of grade inflation influence our assessment decisions. We should aim to provide assessment to our students that gives an honest accounting of their work.

But if you put in a good-faith effort to grade your students fairly, do your best to remain objective when evaluating their coursework, and still end up with more As and A minuses than anything else, don't sweat it. Your set of final marks will not be the straw that finally breaks the back of American education, and you are not responsible for the dumbing down of the next generation. Your top-heavy grade book is not the ultimate and damning consequence of a permissive culture of degraded standards and thin-skinned student-customers. I bet your students earned those As.

The "case" against grade inflation assumes that a final grade offers an objective and transparent measurement of a student's performance. For a grade to be seen as "inflated," one has to assume that there's a (lower) grade that the student was supposed to have earned. Again, I think instructors need to take assessment very seriously and should do their absolute best to evaluate students fairly. But we shouldn't kid ourselves and believe that most faculty, especially those of us who cannot rely on multiple-choice exams, are able to exactly quantify a student's performance over a semester. Grades are subjective by nature, influenced by all sorts of circumstances outside the control of both student and instructor, not least the quality of other students' work.

All of that said, insofar as I do inhabit the role of evaluator, I want to make sure that my grading is as fair as possible. Knowing that grades are indeed used to judge, reward, and punish students should make us feel duty bound to grade them evenhandedly. To that end, I've often wondered how much my own unnoticed biases affect my grading. Over the past couple of decades, there has been an increasing amount of research looking into grading bias.

John Malouff, Ashley Emmerton, and Nicola Schutte—all researchers from Australia's University of New England—set out to examine the halo effect: the hypothetical boost given to students who have performed well in the past. The halo effect says that if a student's first essay garners an A, we are more likely to give a higher grade to that student's subsequent work. In their 2013 article in *Teaching of Psychology*, the authors report on a study of 126 instructors who graded both a videotaped oral presentation and a short essay from a psychology student.[22]

Half of the instructors were shown a poor presentation (one in which the student had very little time to prepare); the other half were shown a better presentation (produced after the student was given time and coaching). All of the study participants graded the same written work. The results were significant: those who had seen the better oral presentation before marking the essay gave it a grade that was four points higher, on average, than the grade given by those who saw the poor presentation. We categorize students, unconsciously or not, and generally expect them to perform at an established level.

Another study by Malouff and Einar Thorsteinsson looked at twenty other studies, encompassing a total of 1,935 graders, to see if they could establish how much of a problem bias in grading really is. They determined that grading bias is real, that knowing such details as the students' racial or ethnic identity, gender, or prior educational performance can lead to unintentional bias effects.[23] Other studies have provided conflicting results. A 2016 study by Phil Birch, John Batten, and Jo Batey—lecturers in sport and exercise science at the Universities of Chichester and Winchester—set out to examine the influence of student gender on grading but found no apparent difference between papers apparently written by male students and those written by female students.[24] Likewise, a 2016 study carried out at a Dutch university by the researchers Jan Feld, Nicolás Salamanca, and Daniel S. Hamermesh also found no bias along gender lines and showed that instructors favored students of their own nationality without discriminating against those of other nationalities.[25]

The natural solution to the problem of grading bias, it seems, is to grade blind. That is, if knowing who produced the work we're grading increases the risk that our unconscious biases affect our objectivity, then we shouldn't know who produced the work. Some universities require students to submit work anonymously so that instructors do not know whose work they are grading.

I think it's safe to assume that each of us does have biases that affect how we grade our students. For that reason, there are probably some courses, and some assignments, for which blind grading is a good solution. But I'm not ready to give up the pedagogical benefits of knowing who has completed the assignments I'm grading.

If I were to grade blind, I wouldn't be able to chart a student's progress throughout the term, from one assignment to another, nor would I be able to tailor my grading to the specific skills each student is working on. What's more, I would need to abandon my practice of giving in-class feedback on students' ideas for assignments. For instance, I would spoil students' anonymity the moment I reviewed their thesis statements in advance. And students could no longer come to my office hours to discuss their papers; once they revealed to me the nature of their problem, my attempts to grade blind would be dashed.

What blind grading does is sever the connection between the formal feedback we give on an assignment (written in the margins of an essay, say) and the informal feedback we should be giving all the time. It isolates the feedback we can give students on their graded work from the broader work they do in class, and significantly reduces the opportunities to make our assessment formative. It's not that I don't think grading bias is an issue, but there's simply too much to sacrifice by grading blind.

For me, at least, grading is as much a tool for pedagogy as it is a tool of assessment. Each assignment is an opportunity for student learning, and our personalized feedback is a crucial part of that opportunity. We should strive to grade as fairly and as objectively as possible. But to make sure we do that wisely as well, we need to keep our eyes open. Otherwise, we might lose sight of the fact that we are still teachers when we grade, and the authors of the papers are still our students.

Grades are a necessary evil of our educational system. There are many occasions when inhabiting the role of the assessor (the person

Besides Grading Blind, How Can I Combat My Bias When Grading?

As I discuss in more detail in Chapter 7, every one of us has implicit biases that are, by their very nature, invisible to us. If, like me, you are resistant to making the kinds of pedagogical changes necessitated by blind grading, you can still take steps to minimize your own bias while grading. Here are a few tips:

- Cover up student names when grading. Yes, you've worked with students on their projects and so the work isn't truly anonymous. But even just hiding the name from yourself during the time you're grading can help you keep your focus on the work, instead of the student. Most learning management systems allow students to submit assignments anonymously; take advantage and try to trick yourself out of your knowledge.

- Grade by question or section instead of by student. Daniel Kahneman, in his book *Thinking, Fast and Slow*, notes that when he graded student exams, he would favor those students who performed well on the first essay question. "The mechanism was simple: if I had given a high score to the first essay, I gave the student the benefit of the doubt whenever I encountered a vague or ambiguous statement later on." The halo effect, which explains why we tend to more favorably grade those students who do well early on, also influences us when we're grading individual students. Kahneman's simple solution is easy to follow: grade all students' answers to the first question first, then move on to the second question, and so on.[26]

- Get clear on what you're looking for, ahead of time. Cognitive biases often work to fill in the gaps left by uncertainty—when we're not sure what grade to give a student, we fall back on other cues, like the student's past performance, to help us decide. Thinking about, or even better, writing down, the kinds of things you're looking for in A-quality work can help you stay clearheaded as you grade. Remind yourself of your criteria as much as possible and explain to yourself why you're giving each assignment its particular grade.

who determines students' grades) seems to get in the way of inhabiting the role of the coach (the person who works with students to help them learn and do their best work). By their nature as extrinsic evaluation, grades seem to work against intrinsic motivation: as long as students measure their progress by my standard, it's difficult to get them to develop their own.

But grades are unavoidable for most of us, and so we must find ways to make them work in the student-centered classroom. Think about grades as feedback, just one kind among many, that we can use to help students revise their understanding. It's totally understandable that students think about grades as important indicators of their progress, but we don't have to. Even as students fixate on grades as summative assessment, it's up to us as instructors to take advantage of their formative role, their ability to help shape student behavior and encourage students to learn from their mistakes.

6

What Will We Do Today?
Emphasizing Process

EARLY-CAREER INSTRUCTORS ARE given a host of advice, much of it confusing, about teaching personae. How are you supposed to comport yourself in the classroom? Half of the time the advice is to "just be yourself," as if the self is a stable and known entity, always the same no matter the context. Others advise that new teachers wear the mask of the authoritative professor or else emulate a favorite professor from their own education. But these tactics can often overlook the way that such masks don't fit all faces; not everyone feels comfortable pretending to be someone else.

Both of these kinds of advice suffer from a misplaced focus on identity, I think. It's not easy, nor is it advisable, to try to change who you are. Much better to try to change what you do. It's much more useful to think about your teaching persona as made up of deliberate choices you make about how you will act in the classroom—for specific reasons—than it is to try to *be* a certain kind of teacher. If you are guided by actions, instead of identity, you can choose those actions to further your pedagogical goals. This has little to do with what kind of person you are, and much more to do with what kind of class you want to create.

The same logic applies to our students. If we set ourselves the task of changing who our students *are*, we will almost inevitably fail. Conceived of instead as the challenge of changing some of what our students *do*, teaching becomes much more concrete and achievable. We need to keep our attention—and encourage our students to keep their attention—on the choices and actions our students undertake. This is the way to ensure that whatever it is we want students to learn how to do—whether it is solving complicated equations, designing computer programs, or writing effective essays—they'll be able to do it after they leave our classrooms, when they encounter situations unlike those they've faced before.

This chapter offers some ways to emphasize process, both in how you think about your role as an instructor and in what your students are doing. Like the imperative to start with skills and let content follow, focusing on process ensures that students learn more than how to get a good grade on a single assignment.

Modeling Confidence, and Stupidity

In 1961, a Stanford University psychologist named Albert Bandura conducted a soon-to-be famous experiment. He had young children watch adults interact with an inflatable "Bobo" doll in a toy-strewn room. Half of the children observed an adult acting aggressively toward the doll: pummeling, hitting, and attacking the defenseless toy with mallets. The other half watched an adult playing nicely with Bobo, as the children's parents might want them to play with other kids. All of the children were then left alone in the room with the doll.

The resulting behavior will surprise no one today: children who watched the aggressive adult were themselves much more likely to be aggressive; the other children played nice.[1]

The results were part of a new idea that Bandura helped pioneer called "social learning theory." It revolutionized our way of understanding cognition by showing that learning does not entirely depend on the threat of punishment or the promise of reward. Instead, social learning theory, and its descendant "observational learning," posits that we learn to behave in large part by watching others. That notion is a commonplace now, influencing everything from advertising (ads show celebrities using a product) to psychotherapy (therapists demonstrate how to talk about a problem) to the parenting-advice industry (just try to find a parenting book that doesn't advise modeling appropriate behavior to your children).[2]

Almost everything we do in the classroom—the way we speak, how we make use of technologies, what we demand of our students—provides a model for students in some way. It's worth thinking about the sort of example you want to set for your students. And that begins by thinking about what kinds of things you want students to be doing.

The first thing you want to model in the classroom is confidence in the course itself. Many students are coming to your classroom without much more than a course description to go on. It's important, especially early in the semester, that they trust you, that they believe you've designed a learning experience that will ultimately improve their lives. You're going to ask them to do things—to work hard, to confront their shortcomings, to revise their previous understanding. You need to give them reasons to believe that they won't be doing those things in vain. I've written a lot, in Chapter 2, about ways to get students to buy into our courses. Acting as though you've bought in yourself is a great way to start.

Once you've started modeling confidence (in your course), you can start thinking about modeling uncertainty. So much of learning arises from the gaps in our abilities, those places where we recognize that we don't know enough, or haven't practiced enough, or haven't been doing things the right way. So an instructor who comes across as having never made a mistake in his life is not exactly a good example.

In a 2010 article for Faculty Focus, Matthew Fleenor, an associate professor of math, computer science, and physics at Roanoke College, wrote of his attempts to "model stupidity" in the classroom.[3] His piece built on a 2008 Martin Schwartz essay in the *Journal of Cell Science* titled "The Importance of Stupidity in Scientific Research." Schwartz argues that "the more comfortable we become with being stupid, the deeper we will wade into the unknown and the more likely we are to make big discoveries."[4] Indeed, alighting on a seemingly unanswerable question is often the first step along the way to real scholarship. Fleenor argues that, as instructors, we should be looking for opportunities to display our ignorance in order to help students learn how to respond on occasions in which they don't have the answers.

Fleenor's research area is in galaxy environments and evolution, so when he taught an upper-level astrophysics course, there was plenty in the subject matter that was outside of his wheelhouse. He writes of a class period on the subject of "interacting binary systems with black holes." When students asked questions, he reluctantly admitted that he didn't know all of the answers. That apparent failure became an opportunity: "By voluntarily admitting that I did not know but would like to find the answers, I was able to demonstrate to the students how to search the archives of the *Annual Review in Astronomy and*

Astrophysics, locate and retrieve relevant titles, and scour an article for pertinent graphical and textual information." In addition to the specific pathways that he showed students how to take—what to do when faced with a tough question in astrophysics—Fleenor's improvisation showed his students that ignorance is not something to be hidden or ashamed of. Our ignorance can be an engine for discovery, a signal that we need to learn more.

Many early-career instructors feel insecure in front of a room full of undergraduates and think that any admission of uncertainty will result in the students revolting, no longer thinking that they need to listen to the instructor. But admitting your ignorance is not a sign of weakness—hiding it is. When you admit that you don't know something, *and then do something about it*, you project a confidence in yourself far greater than if you were to pretend that you know everything already. And this is a kind of confidence that can inspire students to want to respond to their ignorance in the same way.

Look for opportunities to display your ignorance in order to help students feel comfortable "being stupid." You can then use those occasions to point forward to how they might remedy that ignorance: through research, reasoning, or experimentation.

Modeling Scholarly Behavior

You can also model other, more specific academic processes when you teach. Julie Glass has written, also in Faculty Focus, about turning her classroom documents into scholarly documents. At the end of her syllabi, Glass writes, she includes a "works cited" page that lists both sources within her discipline that have influenced course content and articles about teaching and learning that have influenced her pedagogical approach.[5] We can make sure to credit other people for their ideas, even informally, when we teach, to encourage our students to adopt academic practices of citation.

But some of the most important aspects of scholarly behavior are more difficult to show to students. As the Loyola Marymount University professor of philosophy Jason Baehr has written, "If we wish to model intellectual virtues for our students, we must find ways of exposing them to how we think." "Intellectual virtues" is Baehr's term for the sorts of character traits he thinks education can instill in students, and exposing students to how we think is one of the most effective ways to accomplish that task.[6]

Noting Aristotle's argument that we acquire virtues by practicing them, Baehr urges college instructors to not just strive to promote intellectual virtues—such as curiosity, open-mindedness, and intellectual courage—but think through what habitual behavior is associated with those virtues. Each virtue, Baehr argues, has a "characteristic activity," a way of acting that is the practical analogue of that virtue. For example, he writes, "curiosity involves asking thoughtful and insightful questions," while "intellectual humility involves being aware of and willing to 'own' one's intellectual limitations or mistakes," and so on.[7] If we think about which traits we want to model in class, and look for ways to make those traits visible through our behavior, we'll show our students that we value, for example, open-mindedness or curiosity or rigor, instead of just telling them.[8] Our actions in front of our students make a sort of implicit argument: this is how a scholar behaves.

For Baehr, most of this modeling is accomplished through thinking aloud. If we accept that part of what we're trying to teach our students is how to think differently about something, then doing that thinking in front of them needs to be a priority. Baehr thinks we should be "explicitly wondering, formulating hypotheses, giving serious consideration to opposing perspectives, admitting when we don't know something, seeking and communicating explanations, and more. In doing so, we provide our students with a window into how our minds work."[9] This is a real shift for a lot of teachers: instead of pretending that you already have everything figured out, show your students that you are thinking as you teach. Show them that you don't always know what to do next, that your interpretation is just a hypothesis, that you have uncertainty just as they do. Let them into your process, so that they might start to see their own.

Modeling Specific Scholarly Work

Take the time, at least once each semester, to assign students a scholarly article from your discipline. As a classroom activity, you can have students analyze the article not just for its content but as an action, as something the author or authors *did*. In the sciences, this can involve zooming in on the methods section, asking students to consider why the authors proceeded as they did, why they made each particular choice. Showing your students what "real" scientists do can offer them a connection between the practice work you're having them do in class and the world of scientific discovery outside the classroom doors. In any field, you can focus on the research the author did, or her writing, or the way the piece builds on previous work. All these lenses offer opportunities to teach your students about how they might carry out these academic practices.

I've had success, in my rhetoric class, showing students drafts of famous writers' pieces. I use the drafts of E.B. White's 1969 *New Yorker* essay on the moon landing to help teach students practices of revision. The drafts, published in an appendix to Scott Elledge's 1984 biography of White, show how carefully the writer worked to discover what he wanted to say.[10] Through careful study in class, my students and I can see, step by step, how White's ideas form and transform on the page. I can show them, visually, just how much even famous published writers have to revise to make their ideas clear and effective.

Anytime you come across someone in your field reflecting on their process, file it away as something you can use in class. Your students need models for how to behave as scholars in training. Of course, you yourself can be a model of scholarly behavior.

Look for opportunities to talk about your own scholarly work in your class—not to show off but to offer your students a further model of academic behavior. I remember the first time I showed the students a rough draft of something I wrote. I was again looking to teach approaches to revision, and I couldn't think of how to communicate how central it is to good writing. Desperate for an idea, I dug up an early draft of one of my old columns for Vitae. I put it on the overhead projector. I won't pretend now that I wasn't embarrassed. But very quickly I saw how valuable such a lesson could be. I admitted my embarrassment to my students, told them I didn't think the writing was very good, and asked them how they would revise it to make it better. As they called out suggestions, I revised the draft in front of them, thinking out loud as I typed, considering various ways to make the writing better. After ten minutes or so of revising in front of them, I brought up the published version of the piece, explained what I was thinking when I revised it initially, and compared that version with the version we came up with in class.

I then asked them: What guided us as we revised? What questions did we ask? What were we trying to achieve? That discussion allowed me to bring their attention back to their own writing. Of course, I wasn't hoping to turn my class into an army of copyeditors, ready to help me improve my writing. Rather, my draft could be an object lesson for them, an opportunity for me to hold their hands and walk them through my revision process before letting them try it for themselves, on their own writing.

Now, it certainly helps that my course was concerned with such foundational academic tasks as writing, reading, and critical thinking. But this lesson can be applied to any discipline, provided you keep the focus on process rather than product. For example, professors in the sciences or social sciences might walk students through a recent study they carried out, highlighting to students the successes and challenges, the ways in which researchers have to make decisions that have real consequences. By showing students how real scholarly work is created and walking them through your idiosyncratic approach to your subject, you offer them a path to solving their own intellectual problems.

You also show them that there's a point to all this stuff that you've been discussing in class. There's a world out there—your world— where the ideas expressed in their essays and exams matter, even if only to their boring professor. This is truer still if your scholarship is in the field in which you are teaching. In that case, you can model not only scholarly practices in general but also the specific practices that apply in your field.

So look for ways to bring to your classroom a recent project you've been working on: a journal article, an experiment, even a grant proposal. You don't have to make your students care about your work. But if you can show them that you care about your work, maybe you can teach them to care about their own.

Encouraging Students to Focus on Process

In addition to paying attention to our own processes, there are benefits to encouraging our students to put their energy into developing the kinds of processes that will be useful even after they leave our classrooms. Students are understandably concerned about the results of the *products* they make for our classes—the artifacts that we will be grading them on. But whenever possible, we should try to steer their attention to their process, to the way they do their work. One way to do that is to highlight, in class, works in progress.

One of the benefits of having taught for more than a semester or two is that you begin to amass a body of student work that can become a secret weapon in your teaching. Student work can teach us much about how students respond to our teaching; it can also offer future students a window into how their peers approach the work you are asking them to do. As I mentioned in my discussion of teaching with student writing in Chapter 4, you should get permission from your students to use anonymized versions of their work with future classes.

One thing I often do is show students portions of a past student's rough draft. I remember the first time I did this. I wanted students to think about essay introductions, so I found a rough draft from a past student and put her opening paragraph up on the projector. I told my students this was a student's first attempt at an opening paragraph, and I wanted them to take a look at it and critique it. What happened next was incredible. What had been a usually quiet group of students suddenly sprang to life. Instead of their usual sleepy-eyed silence, these students were making creative suggestions left and right about how this writer should have written the paragraph. They relished the opportunity to "fix" the work of their unnamed peer.

Since that day in class, I've made frequent use of past student work in my classroom—in part because it allows me to discuss specific examples as opposed to generalities, and also because student writing, to underline the obvious, is the kind of writing my students do. I can directly highlight the particular challenges they are facing in their work. And they can work with material that looks familiar to them. I don't need to make the case for its relevance. Such a strategy can easily be adopted to less writing-intensive courses. Why not show students wrong answers from past years' exams? Break students into groups and have them analyze attempted solutions and find the critical errors. Or talk about common mistakes past students have made in setting up an experiment. Knowing where previous students have gone wrong, and why, can be a learning opportunity for your current students. The more you teach, the more information you pick up about your students' process in doing their work; pass that information on to your current students so they can learn from it.

You can also look for further ways to encourage your students to be metacognitive about their process. Like the tips offered in Chapter 2, these strategies are meant to get students thinking about their thinking—but here, I'm focusing more on getting students to think about what they are *doing*.

Have Students Write in the First Person

There are many ways in which the research paper I assign my rhetoric students is unusual. They get to choose their own topics (the idea is to come up with a question they actually want to know the answer to), research answers to a question through both traditional and untraditional means (including talking to any experts they can find), and then write and turn in a narrative of their search (instead of a traditional argumentative essay). But of all these challenging aspects, the one they struggle with the most is perhaps surprising: they have to write the paper in the first person.[11]

They flood me with questions about it: How can they write in the first person and still be objective? Won't writing the story of how they went about their research come across like a weird kind of diary entry? Many students, particularly the ones who were good students in high school, find the idea deeply uncomfortable. Most of them were not allowed to use the first person in high school writing. To them, it reeks of third-grade "creative writing" assignments: What I Did on My Summer Holiday. They don't understand how writing can be both personal *and* scholarly.

Resistance to first-person writing is not restricted to first-year undergraduates. The reaction is much the same in a graduate course I teach on writing and in tutoring sessions with graduate students at our campus writing center. Many graduate students, especially those in the sciences, are loath to use the first person in their writing, and some have advisers who expressly forbid it.

But writing in the first person carries many benefits for our students and is not as radical a choice in academic writing as it once was.

In her 2012 book *Stylish Academic Writing*, Helen Sword presents research showing that use of the first person is far more widespread—yes, even in the sciences—than you might guess. She found extensive use of personal pronouns in prominent journals from such fields as medicine, evolutionary biology, and computer science but identified only one journal (in history) that forbids the first person altogether. Style guides across the social sciences and sciences, she noted, have long encouraged the use of *I* or *we*.[12]

And yet, in my experience, many graduate students in the sciences are still taught that use of the first person will diminish their apparent objectivity, the hallmark of any scientist's legitimacy. Subjectivity and objectivity, in fact, have nothing to do with which grammatical person you choose to use. It's as easy to come up with examples of subjective writing in the third person ("The results of the experiment suggest a link between vaccines and autism") as it is to conjure objective writing that uses the first person ("We measured the thickness of the diploë using morphometric analyses"). To always insist on the third person is to pretend that there is no researcher and no writer, that the scholarship "just happened." That's not objectivity; that's playacting.

It's in puncturing this illusion that the first person holds value for students in any discipline. When students write in the first person, they have to reckon with the fact that they are involved in their work. They have to admit, even only subtly, that it is *their work*. It encourages students to take responsibility for their work. Writing in the first person teaches students that they need to maintain objectivity precisely because they *are* present. This is particularly important in STEM fields. Students in these disciplines won't produce objective scholarship by pretending they don't exist; rather, they must acknowledge their biases, understand how their presence affects their subject, and indicate to the reader that they are taking every possible step to mitigate such effects.

Most importantly, practicing first-person writing encourages students to begin to see themselves as scholars. If students find using the first person strange and uncomfortable, it suggests that they find the scholarly identity incompatible with their own identity. ("I can't be a serious researcher; I'm just a kid.") That distance impedes their learning. They need to learn that real scholars are real people—people who investigate scholarly problems and write about them. My assignment gives my students the opportunity to practice narrating the story of themselves as scholars. Academic practice is just that—a practice—and the sooner we can get our students to see themselves as practitioners, no matter how modest, the sooner they can leave us behind and start learning for themselves.

Even if you aren't fully comfortable making your students write in the first person in completing their major assignments, you can still

ask them to engage in first-person reflective writing that can serve
some of the same purposes. Jody Shipka, in her excellent book *Toward
a Composition Made Whole*, advocates for what she calls "statements
of goals and choices" (SOGCs).[13] An SOGC is a species of a "process
text," a sort of meta-assignment that students have to complete along-
side their regular assignment. It asks students to reflect on their process in completing the assignment. Shipka's SOGC, as the name suggests, asks students to write about their particular goals in responding
to the assignment (in addition to what the instructor asked them to
do) and the choices they made in trying to achieve those goals.
Building on Donna LeCourt's concept of reflection as something that
can "make the invisible visible so that it can be acted on differently,"
Shipka writes that SOGCs provide her students with "an incentive to
consider how, why, when, and for whom their texts make any kind of
meaning at all."[14] For any kind of assignment that is more complex
than asking students to answer questions on a test, you can ask them
to produce such a document. Have them turn in their SOGC for credit,
either as a portion of that assignment's grade or as a small portion of
a semester-long homework grade.

Again, the goal here is to try to help students be more aware of their
own process. They are doing work in class; part of our job is to help
them become more conscious of that work, pay attention to how they
do it, so that they can continue doing it (and continue to improve)
once they leave our classrooms.

Participation Logs

I discovered this next strategy as I was trying to solve a perennial
problem of the active-learning classroom: How do you keep track of
and assess participation?

If we want our students to learn in our classrooms, they need to participate in class activities. But assessing that participation is actually a really difficult challenge. Although the scholarship on teaching and learning often defines participation strictly in terms of class discussions, in many of our classrooms, there are many other ways that students participate in class: writing, carrying out experiments, researching, and contributing to small group activities are just a few. How do we accurately and objectively measure student participation over the course of a semester? How do we keep track of hundreds, if not thousands, of opportunities for students to engage in class with course activities? And how do we do so without bias?

One answer may be to let students assess their own participation. Tony Docan-Morgan, a professor of communication studies at the University of Wisconsin at La Crosse, wrote in 2015 about the "participation logs" he asks his students to fill out.[15] He distributes a Microsoft Word template with space for students to record their contributions to class discussions, to note how they participated in group work, and to reflect more generally on their activity in class. Students fill out their logs on their own time and submit them to the instructor. Docan-Morgan collects them at midsemester and at the end of the course, but I think asking to see them every two weeks would encourage students to update the logs more frequently.

Even if you don't adopt the template form, giving students an assignment to think and write about what they're doing in your class is a great way to encourage them to focus on their behavior as students. Such assignments can give you a fuller picture of what's happening in your class, helping you assess students' participation, but it's probably more valuable for students than it is for you. It creates a space for students to reflect on why they do what they do during class time. They have to consider what makes a meaningful contribution; what does active participation actually mean? How do they want to spend their time in class?

Docan-Morgan reports that, in his experience, the logs are generally accurate. He attributes that to the fact that he periodically reminds students that he is monitoring their participation. But because students have to stay on top of their own contributions, the instructor doesn't need to play the role of participation policeman nearly as much.

What such an assignment does—like all of these strategies—is elevate the work students do in our class to something worth thinking about and learning from. Class participation isn't ancillary to the real work students do in our classes; in many cases, it *is* the real work. And getting students to think about how they engage in discussion, how they can come up with the next steps in an experiment, or even how to more usefully take notes during a lecture can lead to benefits students will reap for a long time.

Teaching the Rules

I almost always begin my classes with a writing prompt. I give my students a specific question—usually, but not always, related to the day's reading—and ask them to write a response in the first five minutes of class. They don't have to turn in this response; they don't have to do anything but write it. It's a great way to mark the beginning of class and give students space to start thinking.

One day I asked my students to write about a writing rule they were required to follow that they thought was confusing or pointless. After they finished, I asked the class which rules had come to mind. It was remarkable how quickly and productively the discussion sprang to life. Every student, it seemed, had burning questions about writing rules—although some just wanted to know what I would "allow" ("Do you care about formatting and stuff?").

It turns out that talking about the rules of writing is a great way to get into a searching discussion of what it means to write, and to be a writer. Soon we were talking about the best times to write in the first person (see above), the ins and outs of the dreaded five-paragraph essay, and why some teachers require a thesis statement to be one long sentence. Rules—and every discipline has rules—are a surprisingly helpful entry point to discussing students' process. You'd be surprised how much thought students give to following rules, how much these rules have been drilled into their heads throughout their educational careers. We can use that to our advantage.

Most of my students come to my class having been taught that writing is barely more than a series of rules to follow. The problem with such a rules-heavy approach to teaching writing in high school isn't just the rigidity with which students are taught those rules. It's that too often students are taught rules without any context or justi- fication. That's just "the way things are." For example, my students are intimately familiar with the five-paragraph essay form, but none of them know how and why it came to be the standard for high school composition (the explanation has more to do with the ease of grading that form than from any special advantage it offers to a student writer).

Students are left following rules just because a teacher told them to, none the wiser about their function or history. It's a recipe for seeing your subject as foreign or external—something a student is supposed to do but not necessarily understand. Just follow the rules, kid, and there won't be any trouble.

We would do better to treat rules as an opportunity to shift our students' mind-set about the practice the rules are meant to govern. Ask your students: Where do these rules come from? Why are some philosophical arguments considered fallacies? What might French grammar rules tell us about the way the language developed? Why, in music composition, should students avoid parallel fifths? When your students start to pursue answers to these questions, they begin thinking about their practice in a more complex way, and with more agency. Questioning the rules takes away some of the rules' dumb power. Through this questioning, you signal to students that you don't just want them to do what you tell them to do; they are in charge of their own practice, and you want to help them become more independent. They need to decide which rules to follow and which to disregard.

Many of my first-year students are nervous about formatting and citation styles, usually because a teacher in their recent past took off points on papers that were incorrectly formatted. So students are eager to hear my "position" on how to cite correctly for my class. For the first half of the semester I tell them not to worry about such things, that I don't care how they format their papers, and that we'll talk about citation styles when it comes time to write a research paper.

When that day arrives, I lead a class discussion, not about citation styles but about citation itself. Why do we cite? What purpose does it serve? Why should we have conventions for citation? Eventually, of course, we end up talking about style guides, and those students who just want to know whether to put the period before or after the closing parenthesis will get their answer. But they also learn something about why there are so many different style guides. (It has to do with different disciplinary priorities: the exact sentence quoted and its context are important to the humanities; the year the research was published is more important to the sciences.) Students learn about the value of giving credit to people for their ideas, and about the collaborative nature of all scholarly work. What begins as a technicality can end up going pretty deep into the very nature of the writer's task.

Learning the rules is as easy as typing a few words into a search bar. Learning why and how they came about in the first place is a higher-order kind of knowledge. Learning when to follow the rules and when to cast them aside is higher still—the sort of thing we should hope students gain from our courses. Strive to help your students develop flexibility: being able to respond to any situation by making considered choices, not just by blindly following a rule.

Encourage your students, no matter your discipline, to consider the rules they are following, why they are following them, and what they might gain or lose from not following them. Ultimately, all students need to think about their goals and how to best attempt to reach them. When we help students gain a more expansive understanding of the meaning of the rules they've been taught, we help them better understand what those rules are meant to govern.

Teaching Students to Break the Rules

After working to understand the rules, you can work on asking your students to break them, even the ones you think they should be following.

I wrote in Chapter 4 about Rosalind Driver and her work on the prior conceptions that students bring with them to our classrooms. We have to use those conceptions—especially when they are misconceptions—to help us tailor our teaching to what the students think they know about what we're teaching. A similar logic governs the teaching of skills: if we pay attention to where and when students make mistakes, we'll have a better idea of how to teach them to avoid those mistakes. And if we ask students to make those mistakes on purpose, they might start becoming more conscious of where and when they occur by accident.

Gerald Grow, in a 1987 article in the *Journal of Teaching Writing*, argues that "deliberately writing badly can be an effective way to learn to write better, because knowing what is bad is an essential element in knowing what is good."[16] The essay details Grow's overall approach to teaching journalistic writing: at various points in the semester, he asks his students to "do it wrong"—to intentionally break writing rules and make mistakes. One assignment asked students to write a page of prose with as many grammatical errors as possible. He also assigned students a series of article ideas and asked them to write terrible opening paragraphs. At another point, Grow gave his students a list of criteria for good journalistic writing (focus, use of factual detail, paragraph development, and so on) and then asked students to "write a short article that is spectacularly bad in every category."[17]

What's the point of all that deliberate blundering?

Well for one, Grow argues, such exercises are fun for students and help alleviate their fear of failure. The professor is asking them to make mistakes; suddenly it seems OK that they don't always know the right way to do things.

The do-it-wrong strategy seems to work particularly well with students who resist being taught. "This approach," Grow wrote, "seems to activate some capricious side of the self and gives it a job and a voice: producing negative examples for the class to enjoy and learn from."[18] That last bit—that the class shares and learns from each other's deliberate mistakes—is crucial. Each of Grow's assignments has some collaborative element to it: students trade papers, try to fix each other's errors, discuss the rules that were broken, and, ultimately, try to write the correct way in the end.

Teaching students to "do it wrong" could work in almost any college classroom. Mathematics students can construct a solution with an error and then see if their classmates can spot the deliberate mistake. Engineering students can design a bridge that won't hold more than two people at a time. Computer science students can write a simple program that won't run. Each of those exercises could be designed to help students see what the "rules" are and why they are important. The goal is to hold students' mistakes—and in turn their process overall—up to the light. Especially if led by an instructor who has a good handle on common mistakes, these exercises can focus students' attention on how such mistakes happen, why they are a problem, and how to prevent them.

Doing it wrong helps teach skills for the same reason that eliciting misconceptions helps teach content knowledge. By inviting students to write badly, or perform an experiment incorrectly, or botch an equation's solution and then share their mistakes, we can get students to think about their processes of writing or performing experiments or solving equations. Once they start thinking about those processes, we can start helping them do them right.

7

Teaching in Tumultuous Times

THE DAY AFTER Donald Trump's election, I had fourteen student draft conferences scheduled. At twenty minutes each, these conferences are intense exercises in one-on-one teaching. I read through, aloud, each student's draft and then discuss with the student what I think she should do to revise. After twenty minutes, the student leaves, and another student, with another paper, comes in.

That was probably the most difficult day I've faced as a teacher. On very little sleep, in disbelief at the turn my country had taken, immensely fearful about what was coming, I nonetheless had to bring all my mental capacities to bear in responding to my students' work. I also had to be present with those students, who arrived with a varied set of responses to the events of the night before, from tears to anger to apparent ignorance that anything unusual had happened at all.

If teaching has always required a straddling of the worlds inside and outside the classroom, such straddling has only gotten more pressing—and more difficult—in recent years. It no longer seems possible for any teacher to keep the world of politics at bay. We now inhabit a world in which many of the things we took for granted as underpinning our practice cannot be taken for granted anymore. When facts hold little sway in public discourse, when inequality swells to unprecedented levels, when institutions designed for the public good become subsumed by corporate interests, when open bigotry and hatred seem to be on the rise, it is impossible to keep teaching the way we always have.

In times like these, our tasks as instructors are more important than ever. We have the opportunity to foster the values and skills that a fair and representative democracy needs to survive. Critical thinking, reading, research, scientific literacy, tolerance of alternate views, and the ability to respond respectfully and rationally to other people's arguments: the world needs people with those skills if it is to recover. We have the chance to nurture those abilities in the young people in our classrooms.

But such a significant role comes with dangers. How do we approach politics in the classroom? How do we help our students develop into better citizens? How do we grapple with a world in which the very bedrock of academic inquiry seems to be devalued in the public sphere? And as our students' world changes as well, how do we work to ensure the most vulnerable of our students feel safe and able to learn in our classrooms? How do we overcome our own implicit biases? How do we help students navigate an increasingly fraught world?

This chapter takes up these questions and looks to offer advice for teaching in our particular era. With the breakneck speed at which the news seems to happen, it is perhaps folly to write about politics some eighteen months before this book will be published. But no matter what happens between now and then, I write resigned to the fact that these issues—the necessity of inclusive teaching, the difficulty of discussing politics in the classroom, the persistence of falsehoods in our public discourse—will still be relevant for years to come.

The Need for Inclusive Teaching

At a time when many of the values central to the academic mission are under threat, it is more important than ever to think about, and stand up for, those values. The need for a democratic and inclusive university, one that values the pursuit of truth and justice, only grows more pressing when the world outside the university gates grows more antidemocratic, exclusive, and unjust. In an open letter to his students the day after the 2016 election, the Columbia University conservation biology lecturer Joshua Drew wrote that "you are going to be graduating into a challenging time. A time when your science needs to be better, your arguments more convincing, and your commitment to protecting our natural environment fiercer. . . . You are going to have to up your game to operate in a culture that does not value the beliefs you hold dear."[1] In the face of the rapid changes transforming our public life, professors need to up their game as well.

Even if, individually, we cannot change much about the state of the nation's politics, we can use our power as teachers to help make our classrooms more open, more egalitarian, and more focused on helping every student learn. As Cathy Davidson counseled in a 2015 blog post, "Rather than feeling overwhelmed and oppressed by the unfairness of the world, be an activist in the realm where you have control."[2] As the world outside gets less democratic, our charge is to make our classrooms more democratic. As lies proliferate in our public discourse, we must work harder to uphold the values of truth and evidence-based reasoning in our courses. As the powers that be work to enforce and maintain unjust hierarchies, our job must be to structure our classes so that every student has an equal chance at success.

It is this last imperative that I focus on first, not least because so-called inclusive teaching has benefits for learning that you can offer your students regardless of what happens to Trump and his allies. Davidson has argued that the classroom is traditionally "one of the least egalitarian spaces on the planet," in which the conditions of students' learning are, for the most part, outside of their control, and opportunities for inequity are plentiful.[3] Inclusive teaching fights against that, asking us to consciously use our authority as instructors to create a democratic space that is more just for every student. But it also creates a climate that makes it more likely that every student will learn.

What is inclusive teaching? To me, inclusive teaching is an approach to pedagogy that takes seriously the equality of our students and the inequality of the world. It is a series of choices to ensure that the students whom our society and its institutions have marginalized will not be marginalized in our classrooms. According to Grand View University's Kevin Gannon, "It's a realization that traditional pedagogical methods—traditionally applied—have not served all of our students well."[4] It is an imperative: that our classrooms must be spaces of opportunity and learning for all students, not just those who traditionally succeed in higher education.[5]

Just as scholars of disability have argued that a focus on accessibility in the classroom improves conditions for all students, working to ensure that your teaching is inclusive will benefit all of your students, not just marginalized ones. In 2010, Susan Ambrose and her colleagues at Carnegie Mellon's Eberly Center for Teaching Excellence published a highly instructive book called *How Learning Works*. It details seven significant principles for effective learning, taken from research in the learning sciences (studies in psychology, cognitive science, and education) and applied to the context of the contemporary college classroom. The chapter on the sixth principle—"students' current level of development interacts with the social, emotional, and intellectual climate of the course to impact learning"—has much to say about how course climate affects our students' learning and why inclusive teaching is necessary for an increasingly diverse student population.[6]

Defining course climate as "the intellectual, social, emotional, and physical environments in which our students learn," Ambrose et al. follow Christopher DeSurra and Kimberley Church in discussing climate as existing on a continuum between "marginalizing" (in which the student in question feels excluded or discouraged) and "centralizing" (in which individual students feel included and welcomed). It turns out that where students see their courses along this continuum can have significant effects on their learning.[7] A number of studies have shown that a so-called chilly climate can "have a profound negative impact on learning" for those marginalized by their gender, sexual orientation, race, or ethnicity. What's more, "course climate does not have to be blatantly exclusive or hostile in order to have a marginalizing effect on students."[8] Implicit and subtle elements of a course can communicate to some students that they don't really belong. The research presented is clear in its conclusions: the more that students feel marginalized by their courses, the harder it is for them to learn and develop as much as they should. So working to make sure that all your students feel like they belong in your classroom is not just the right thing to do on a human level; it's the right thing to do for their learning.

Not every aspect of course climate is under your control as an instructor, but there's plenty you can do to help ensure every student has a seat at the table.

In your syllabus and on the first day of class, you can set a tone of inclusion and mutual respect. I include in my syllabi a statement that explicitly lays out my expectations for how students will treat each other and me; I let them know how important a welcoming community is to their learning, and that I will not tolerate any behavior that makes anyone feel unsafe, ostracized, or the subject of ridicule. By including such a statement in my syllabus, I am signaling to students at the very beginning of our time together that I take seriously each individual student's experience of being in the course, and that I will work to make the classroom a space where they can feel safe enough to be themselves.

Apart from explicitly addressing issues related to inclusion, how you communicate with your students about anything can also send strong messages about the course climate. I often find myself walking past open classroom doors, astonished to hear professors speaking to college students as if they were third-graders. Condescending to your students, treating them as antagonists or employees or children, does not contribute to a positive environment for learning. It's important to treat your students with respect and to speak to them, from the beginning, as the scholars you hope they will become. You can begin setting this tone in the syllabus as well. In fact, the authors of *How Learning Works* call attention to research that suggests that the tone of your syllabus can have powerful effects on students' perception of the course climate. John T. Ishiyama and Stephen Hartlaub, in their studies of syllabus language, found that "students are less likely to seek help from the instructor who worded those policies in punitive language than from the instructor who worded the same policies in rewarding language."[9] Other studies have extended those conclusions to other aspects of professor communication: how faculty speak to students in the classroom, how they provide feedback to student work, what policies they set for the class.[10] You can influence how comfortable your students feel in your classroom—and how much they will be able to learn—by communicating with them in a way that invites them in. Trust your students, treat them as worthy of that trust, and they'll show themselves that they *are* worthy of that trust.

You can also make the content of your course more inclusive. Decades after the so-called canon wars, battles over who gets covered in college courses still simmer in many disciplines. Put simply, which people and whose work we deem worthy of study sends a message to our students about who belongs—and who doesn't—in our disciplines. We communicate important values to our students by who and what we choose to give our attention to. Can you highlight the work of people from marginalized groups in your field? Do you assign readings by women and people of color? Don't merely repeat the version of your subject that was taught to you; do what you can to model for your students what a more just version of your discipline might look like. Ambrose et al. remind us that course content is more than just course readings and is relevant to more than just humanities and arts courses: content "includes the examples and metaphors instructors use in class and the case studies and project topics we let our students choose." Students are paying attention to what we include in our courses; they pick up signals that tell them whether they are included in our world or are an afterthought. "For students who are developing their sense of identity, purpose, and competence, some of these messages can translate into messages about their own power, identity, and agency and can influence engagement and persistence in the field."[11] Again, we can't control everything. But for those aspects of our courses that we do control, inclusion, the drive to create a course that has room for every one of our students, should help guide our decisions.

Supporting Your Students

Creating a more inclusive classroom requires seeing our students as human beings. As college instructors, we see our students nearly every day and are well placed to tell if they are struggling mentally or emotionally. We're not mental health professionals, but nonetheless we can look out for our students and make sure they get the help they need. Here are three steps to be there for your students.

Notice

Pay attention to your students and look for signs of distress. You're not trained to diagnose mental illness or to know when someone has been the victim of assault, but you can tell when someone is in distress. Maybe you notice a downturn in a student's hygiene, or perhaps a student starts missing a lot of class out of nowhere. If you're looking, you'll notice.

Ask

What do you do if you notice a student in distress? Ask them about it. This can be a brief email or a short conversation after class: "Is everything OK? I've noticed you're not yourself lately." You don't need to cross any boundaries or be an expert. Just ask. Students in distress are often waiting for someone to open up to—someone who shows they care.

Refer

Be ready if a student does open up to you. I keep a sheet in my office with the phone numbers of a number of campus resources that can help students. Do a little research on what services are available to students, so that if students need help, you can point them in the right direction.[12]

Implicit Biases

Among the aspects of teaching that fall outside our control are our own implicit biases—those tendencies and prejudices we hold that we are not aware of. How do we make sure we are not standing in the way of our own efforts to be inclusive?

Most of us now readily accept that behavior is often driven by unconscious attitudes and stereotypes.[13] Even so, if you suggest to people that they themselves may have implicit biases, suddenly the defense mechanisms roar into effect. But we do have implicit biases—every one of us—and as faculty members, it's imperative we take them into account.

In my own classroom, I often ask my students to imagine a world in which 80 percent of the national political leaders are men, 95 percent of the prominent business leaders are men, 70 percent of the established scientists and engineers are men, and 85 percent of the police officers are men. If you grew up in such a world, I ask students, what would your idea of an authority figure be? Wouldn't it be natural, having seen positions of authority held mostly by men your whole life, to associate the masculine with the authoritative? Under those circumstances, wouldn't you, all else being equal, see a man as more qualified than a woman?[14]

Of course, this imagined world is our own. For Patricia G. Devine, a professor of psychology at the University of Wisconsin at Madison, and director of its Prejudice and Intergroup Relations Lab, the repeated exposure to stereotypes is precisely how implicit bias is formed—and may hold the key to how it can be erased.

In work stretching over decades, Devine has put forward a theory that prejudice functions as a kind of habit.[15] We get used to certain associations—say, that students from a marginalized group struggle academically compared with white students—and when we come in contact with a student from that group, our default attitude is to uphold the stereotype. Without conscious work to counteract this automatic "activation," we assume the association is true.

As teachers, we set the tone for the classroom environment, modeling for our students what scholarly behavior should be like. Just as importantly, we function as institutionally backed authority figures. We evaluate students, make judgments, create rules, and often decide who gets to speak and when. If we are serious about our responsibility to create a classroom environment in which every student has an equal opportunity to excel, we need to take a hard look at our own behavior. We have to take whatever steps are necessary to combat anything that might handicap our ability to be fair, including any implicit bias.

The fact that implicit biases are implicit—that is, hidden even from ourselves—means that our perception of what is right may be off. Most employers that favor a white applicant over a black person with the same credentials don't think they are prejudiced and are unaware of their own bias. When such assumptions remain unconscious, they can deform our sense of fairness. As Devine notes in a 2012 article, "Implicit biases persist and are powerful determinants of behavior precisely because people lack personal awareness of them."[16]

That article details an experimental intervention, led by Devine and her colleagues, to help subjects overcome implicit bias. In the years since, she has led many such interventions, both in and out of academe, and has been able to demonstrate remarkable success in reducing prejudicial behavior.[17]

The challenge of confronting our own biases as teachers came to mind as I read news accounts in the fall of 2017 about the controversy

---

Ways to Counter Your Own Implicit Biases

Although not all of us can participate in one of Devine's workshops, we can all make use of her and her colleagues' strategies for countering our own implicit biases. Regularly engaging in these mental exercises can help you neutralize any harmful biases you unwittingly hold.

- "Stereotype replacement" involves recognizing and labeling your own biased behavior or thoughts and replacing them with nonprejudicial responses. For example, if you catch yourself showing surprise when a female student mentions that she's a physics major, you can first recognize that your behavior is likely guided by a stereotype that men are better at science and math. You then reflect on why you had that response, and think about how you will respond in a similar situation next time without relying on stereotypes.

- "Counter-stereotypic imaging" entails thinking of examples of people who defy the stereotypes of their groups. You can do this whenever you find yourself unthinkingly affirming a misleading stereotype.

- "Perspective taking" involves trying to adopt the perspective of someone in a group to which you don't belong. Just imagining what it would be like to walk into class as a Spanish-speaking immigrant, say, can help you better understand the effects of stereotypes about immigrants.[18]

These are mental exercises that anyone can do. Underlying them all is awareness: you have to be conscious of the existence of implicit biases and the probability that you yourself may be influenced by them, before you can do anything about the problem.

---

over "the progressive stack."[19] A graduate student at the University of Pennsylvania reported being pulled from the classroom for using that teaching technique, which aims to offer students whose voices tend to be marginalized in class discussions a greater opportunity to speak.

For all the controversy it has attracted, the progressive stack strikes me as an approach that attempts to respond to the problem of implicit bias in teaching. It developed in the context of Occupy Wall Street meetings, as a way to organize a large number of people trying to speak at the same time. In the college classroom, the progressive stack involves looking for ways to create space for students from marginalized groups. If a number of students raise their hands to talk, the progressive stack means that you call on the marginalized students first, making sure that they get to speak first. Without that conscious intervention, what you think of as a fair distribution of speakers may just be the furtherance of an unhealthy social dynamic: the privileged kids feel free to speak, while the marginalized students stay silent.[20] It's worth thinking, in dealing with the question of who speaks in class, of what it means to take part in class discussion. As I wrote in Chapter 1, it's far more effective to think of calling on students as inviting them to join a conversation than it is to think of it as putting students on the spot, publicly grilling them about their knowledge. In this sense, all the progressive stack suggests is that we make a conscious effort to invite more marginalized students into class discussions; we have a responsibility to show those students, who have been taught by so many institutions that their voices do not matter, that they matter to us and that we want to hear from them.

We may never be completely aware of our own implicit biases. But by assuming that we hold at least some of the pernicious stereotypes that our cultures have handed down to us, we can take steps to counteract them. As faculty members, we have a particular responsibility to work on this. Our role in the college classroom requires us to work toward a perhaps impossible ideal of equity. The first step is to open our eyes and look in the mirror.

How (and Why) to Be Political

What do we mean when we talk about politics in the classroom? It could mean the discussion of politics itself—of elections, campaigns, policy debates, and now, it seems, tweets. Or it could mean the discussion of or inquiry into issues that are considered to be politically sensitive, regardless of whether they are in the news at the moment. Here we might consider questions around race and racism, or abortion, or stem cell research to be political. The first question to ask with either of these kinds of political topics is *why*. *Why* should we include such controversial subjects in our courses? Or perhaps the question is better framed as its inverse: Why shouldn't we keep such subjects out of our courses? Wouldn't it be easier—safer—to put our heads down and stay away from all this stuff?

In a word, no. If our students can learn from them, if they can help our students meet our courses' goals, we shouldn't stop ourselves from including political subjects in our courses. It's not difficult to imagine how such subjects might lend themselves to educational aims. Inquiry into current political events can teach students about issues relevant to the course, the world, and themselves. Investigation of politically sensitive topics can teach students about underlying issues in human behavior, psychology, and interpersonal relationships. How would you teach an environmental science course without referring to the political debate about climate change? Or a course on business without reference to government regulations? Imagine courses in history, gender studies, journalism, or economics without any political content. The borderlessness of politics—what's taken for granted by one person may be controversial to another—means even seemingly apolitical courses like computer science and engineering may take up political subjects as well.

So rather than deny that politics can ever be relevant to your course, it's better to think about, if such topics come up, how you will handle them.

To consider politics in the classroom is inevitably to consider the problem of indoctrination. If we introduce politically sensitive topics in our classrooms, how do we ensure we don't unduly influence students with our views on the issues? What if we're unconsciously pressuring our students to adopt those views themselves? Indoctrination is a serious charge, one frequently leveled at college professors, who are, on the whole, more liberal than the general public.[21] In her 2018 book *The Diversity Delusion: How Race and Gender Pandering Corrupt the University and Undermine Our Culture*, Heather Mac Donald identifies "a growing constellation of gender studies, queer studies, and women's studies departments" as leading to "a pipeline" of graduates who "bring their high-theory indoctrination with them into the federal and state bureaucracies and into newsrooms."[22] The University of Toronto provocateur Jordan Peterson spent much of 2017 talking about creating an online university that would "cut off the supply to the people who are running the indoctrination cults."[23] I quote these critics not because I think they paint an accurate picture of colleges and universities—on the contrary, I think the right wing's critique of higher education is a fanciful caricature—but because the accusation reflects the fact that everyone, of all political persuasions, seems to agree that instructors should seek to avoid indoctrinating their students. But what exactly is indoctrination? And how do we avoid it?

Indoctrination and education used to be synonymous. Webster's 1913 dictionary defines *indoctrination* as "instruction in the rudiments and principles of any science or system of belief."[24] It was well into the twentieth century before the word widely took on the negative connotations it has now. Still, as the philosophers Eamonn Callan and Dylan Arena wrote in 2009, indoctrination "as the name for a species of morally objectionable teaching has no more than rough conceptual boundaries."[25] Luckily, a number of philosophers of education, beginning with Callan and Arena, have since attempted to more clearly define this important concept.

A broad consensus has emerged, highlighting two essential conditions of indoctrination. In the words of Emory University's Rebecca Taylor, these are "the outcome of closed-mindedness and an asymmetry of authority."[26] That is to say, to indoctrinate in the classroom means that we (a) use our authority to (b) promote a closed-minded adoption of a belief by our students. Both aspects are important.

The fact of our asymmetrical authority in the classroom should be plain to see. As professors, we hold what's known as "intellectual authority" (students' perception that we are experts) as well as "practical authority" (the power, by virtue of our position, to influence students' grades, to enforce rules, and so on).[27] There is no question that we have this power, to varying extents. We cannot escape the fact of our authority; we can only choose how to use it. To avoid indoctrination requires that we remain aware of our authority over students, lest we abuse our power and infringe on our students' autonomy. I don't think I need to work too hard to convince you that we must avoid the unethical use of our authority, which derives from our institutionally granted power to evaluate and grade our students. It would be wrong to use that power for anything other than our mission to help our students learn and develop.

It is the unavoidable fact of our authority that makes the promotion of *closed-minded* belief so dangerous, write Callan and Arena: "When someone exploits the asymmetry of power between teacher and learner by instilling close-minded belief, the intellectual self-rule that befits rational beings has been violated." Indoctrination is not just the promotion of certain beliefs in our students; it's when we attempt to change students' beliefs *and* instill in them a fear or reluctance to consider evidence that might conflict with those beliefs. If we do that, we take from students something essential: their ability to think for themselves, to determine their own paths.

Taylor warns that such indoctrination produces students who lack the motivation to pursue knowledge for themselves or to consider available evidence when forming beliefs. They become "closed-minded agents," who are either intellectually arrogant (they downplay the potential that they could ever be wrong) or intellectually servile (they distrust their own intellectual capacities, and therefore defer to and rely on another authority).[28] Clearly, either outcome is a bad one. We're looking to help our students be more confident, competent, and informed. Both arrogance and servility work against those goals.

So how do we guard against such indoctrination? How do we make sure we are not encouraging closed-mindedness? One way is by focusing on its opposite: open-mindedness and intellectual humility.

As I wrote in Chapter 6, a good way to teach intellectual virtues such as open-mindedness is to model it ourselves. If we admit when we're wrong, discuss our failures, and let students know when we're unsure about something, we can guard against closed-mindedness in two ways. First, by modeling the kind of humility that we hope students will adopt, we encourage students to aspire to be something other than intellectually arrogant. We show them that the best way to approach any intellectual activity is to have an open mind. Second, by knocking ourselves down a peg or two, we discourage students from seeing us as an all-knowing authority, someone to defer to at all times. As Jason Baehr writes in his guide to teaching the intellectual virtues, "The 'stronger' we are, the weaker they can feel, and therefore the more reluctant they can be to take the kinds of intellectual risks or to engage in ways that are crucial to their own intellectual development."[29] Instead, by admitting, in front of our students, that we don't have all the answers, we can help students develop the confidence to admit when they are unsure, and the autonomy (and the skills) to do something about that uncertainty.

We can also look to provide opportunities for our students to practice open-mindedness. Wherever possible, try to expose your students to multiple perspectives, even those that you disagree with. In discussing these perspectives, while it's fine to express your own opinions, look for ways to put the emphasis on the students' thinking rather than on whether they've reached the same conclusion as you. I often tell students that I won't express my own view on an issue, because I want them to debate it on their own, without my influence pushing things in one direction or the other. If I do share my opinion, I strive to come across as an equal participant of the discussion rather than as their superior, telling them the correct way of things. I often try to seem less certain than I actually am, in order to leave plenty of space for students to disagree. I want to model a constructive self-doubt and signal that the classroom is a place to work out what we think. And if a student offers an opinion that runs counter to my own views, I go out of my way to give it credence, to be the opposite of dismissive. This sends a message, I hope, that my own views are beside the point—we're trying to understand an issue, or analyze an argument, or find out what we believe, and looking closely at a variety of views can help us achieve those aims.

In that vein, asking students to think through other people's viewpoints can help them resist closed-mindedness. In his philosophy classes, Baehr has his students engage in debates in which they argue in favor of a view they disagree with.[30] They have to defend the view as effectively as possible, giving reasons that support why others should adopt the view. With this kind of role-playing, students are confronted with the fact that their own view is just one of many, and that everyone has their reasons for believing what they do.

But isn't this kind of exposure to multiple perspectives a recipe for *bothsidesism*: the idea that all sides of a debate are equally viable? Doesn't this teach our students that there's no way to sort out the truth—that some people think this way and others think another, and that's as much as we can establish? I don't think it has to. We're not looking to teach our students that every possible perspective on an issue is equally true. Rather, we need to teach students that the consideration of argument and evidence—even if that evidence conflicts with our prior beliefs—should lead us to our conclusions. Teaching inductively, that is, having students engage in problem solving or case studies and asking them to induce general principles from what they learn, can help students practice this crucial skill. If you teach argumentative writing, stress to students that a thesis statement should change as the evidence does. If you teach the history of science, highlight those moments when our understanding of the world shifted because the evidence did. The opposite of closed-mindedness is not a postmodern void in which there's no such thing as truth. The opposite of closed-mindedness is open-mindedness, in which we seek the truth but always keep in mind that we could be wrong.

Emphasizing the practices associated with open-mindedness and intellectual humility can help ensure that even if we handle subjects that we feel strongly about, we won't indoctrinate our students. Of course you have political views, and students will know that you do. You can tell your students, as I do mine, that you will work to ensure that your views do not influence your evaluation of their progress in the course. But it's also important to tell them, and show them, that the content of their beliefs is far less important to you than the process they took to come to those beliefs. I tell my students that most of the time I don't care *what* they think; I just care *how* they think.

Making Citizens

Another way to think about politics in the classroom is as movement in the other direction: not the world of the news coming into our courses, but our students going out into the world. I believe that our mission as faculty members goes beyond helping students learn the knowledge and skills necessary to develop mastery of our disciplines. We should be trying, as well, to help them develop into more capable, ethical, and critical scholars and citizens. I believe that a college education can achieve those aims and that those of us who teach in higher education should devote ourselves to realizing them.

Racism, sexism, injustice, poverty, needless suffering: the problems of the world—whatever you think they are—are mostly made by people. And we teach people.

In her book *Teaching to Transgress*, the writer and scholar bell hooks distinguishes between "ways of knowing" and "habits of being." Most of the time as college instructors, we are concerned with ways of knowing. We want to teach students about our discipline and train them to think like scholars in our field. We are rightly concerned with teaching them how to master the course's subject. But we should not neglect our chance to teach broader skills—ones that transcend the classroom and can be put into practice in the students' lives beyond college. In her book, hooks writes about how her students, returning from Thanksgiving break, described the ways in which the concepts they had learned in class (about race and racism) made them see their parents and relatives in a different light.[31] By trying to help our students develop habits of mind, we are guiding them in the future, whether they continue in our disciplines or not.

Patricia Devine, in her work on implicit biases and stereotypes, also writes about habit. For her, racist and sexist associations are like habits—connections we make so often they become automatic. Breaking such habits is a long process that requires, she writes, "learning about the contexts that activate the bias and how to replace the biased responses with responses that reflect one's nonprejudiced goals."[32] Part of our task as faculty members should be to help students develop new, healthier habits to replace the bad ones we hope they will abandon. If you believe, as I do, that we should help students develop into more capable, ethical, and critical scholars and citizens, then we must take the fifteen weeks we get with our students and look to develop habits of self-scrutiny, metacognition, critical thinking, deliberate decision-making, and open-mindedness, among others. The way you approach your subject in your courses can help students develop those habits.

How, specifically, can you do this in your own teaching? By looking for ways to lessen the distance between your classroom and the world outside, to open doors instead of closing them. Invite students to think about how the events in the newspaper relate to the topics in your course, and vice versa. Encourage them to draw parallels between the kind of thinking you do in your discipline and the thinking they do elsewhere. Look to integrate theory and practice, to demonstrate that chemistry or sociology or engineering doesn't confine itself to the college classroom—that their lives will be enriched by what they are learning. And call attention to the habits of being you are helping them develop, even if those habits are as humble as the quiet discipline of reading carefully before voicing an opinion. We could use more of that in our public life too.

Part of our mission as college educators is to train students to be more critical of themselves and their culture, to be more aware of biases (their own and other people's), and to be more compassionate and diligent in understanding people who are different, and more ethical in acting toward those people. The development of such habits in our classrooms is not just essential to the betterment of our world but essential to our disciplines. Being able to recognize the work of women as equal to that of men, for example, isn't just necessary for good citizenship; it's also integral to being a good scientist or historian or doctor. Being able to recognize and work to correct your own bias doesn't just make you more tolerant of others; it's a crucial skill for getting things right in any discipline. And if students don't learn these habits in our classrooms, they may not learn them at all.

Teaching in an Era of "Fake News"

How do we tell the truth from a lie? How do we know when what we are reading isn't actually true? Such questions are vitally important not only to public life but also to the college classroom. Brendan Nyhan, a professor of public policy at the University of Michigan, and Jason Reifler, a professor of politics at the University of Exeter in Britain, wanted to evaluate the efficacy of factual corrections, such as those found in news reports following a misleading statement made by a public figure, in remedying misperceptions. In 2005 and 2006, they conducted experiments in which subjects read articles that reported politicians making false claims. Some of the articles included an objectively voiced correction. Surprisingly, Nyhan and Reifler found that the corrections often failed to undo belief in the false claims, particularly when the corrections ran counter to the subject's ideological predispositions. In fact, among those subjects most committed to their political positions, such corrections actually strengthened belief in the misperceptions.[33] People resist seeing themselves as wrong.

Similarly, Nyhan and Reifler, writing in 2014 with two other coauthors, reported that public-health communications about vaccines—public-service announcements that refuted claims of a link between vaccines and autism, for example—could actually be backfiring and decreasing the chances that parents will vaccinate their children. Worryingly, "corrective information about controversial issues may fail to change factual beliefs or opinions among respondents who are most likely to be misinformed."[34] Those who need the facts most are too often not swayed by them.

We don't need to look very far these days to see evidence of Nyhan and Reifler's conclusions. The *Washington Post* has been tallying and correcting Donald Trump's many false or misleading claims since he took office. As of January 21, 2019, that tally had passed 8,000.[35] That's more than 8,000 verifiably untrue claims made by the president of the United States over two years. And each of them was reported on and refuted by a national newspaper that reaches millions of readers every day. Although such fact checking has undoubtedly produced some effect (as of this writing, Trump has an approval rating of 41 percent), for the many millions of Americans who still support the president, the corrections do not seem to have changed their view of the man and his trustworthiness.[36]

That the persistence of belief in falsehoods can withstand even direct and authoritative correction is a phenomenon that every teacher should be thinking about. If part of what we hope to do is help our students understand and thrive in the world as it is, don't we need to find some kind of shared understanding of that world, some agreed-upon set of facts? The flourishing of misperceptions, even in the face of corrections, not only makes it harder for us to do our jobs; it presents another challenge in helping our students navigate their academic pursuits. To succeed in our subjects, and beyond them, our students need to be able to tell a truth from a falsehood. And that's not as easy as it seems.

We need to help our students develop strategies for sorting true from false, in tackling both the generalized problem that people resist seeing themselves as wrong and the specific problem of a public discourse increasingly filled with falsehoods. This is an imperative in every subject in the academy, for every student. When students come into our classrooms with misperceptions about the course topics—or about anything, for that matter—we cannot assume that merely correcting them will have the desired effect. Nor can we assume that correcting a student's misperception now will help her avoid making a similar mistake down the road. We need to teach our students the skills to be able to accurately assess the veracity of information, in whatever domain they find it.

What we're looking for are ways to teach *information literacy* within our subjects. Information literacy—the capability to understand, access, evaluate, and apply information to solve problems or answer questions—is a necessary set of skills for any academic discipline. And yet, too much of the time, professors neglect to teach such skills, assuming that students will pick up these abilities on their own. To be fair, many college assignments are designed in part to give students opportunities to practice and develop information literacy; but for the reasons outlined above, it seems to me more important than ever to give explicit attention to this crucial set of skills.

The first step to teaching information literacy in your courses is to visit the library. Many college libraries have staff whose job it is to collaborate with faculty to teach research skills. It's worth developing relationships with these librarians, talking about your goals for your students before the semester starts. It's fairly common at my institution for instructors, particularly when they have a lot of first-year students, to take students to the library for a session on research or else invite a librarian to the classroom for an introduction to the library's resources. But if you meet with a librarian before the term starts, you can work out ways to integrate information literacy instruction at a number of points throughout the semester. You might have a session on finding materials in your library, exercises to help students develop and refine research questions, regular assignments that require various kinds of research, and so on. Collaborating with a librarian can allow you to tailor information literacy instruction to your particular discipline and course subject.[37]

Being able to determine true from false is a particular—and important—aspect of information literacy. Aside from "fake news" and falsehoods uttered by public figures, being able to sniff out and reject shoddy research is a significant part of any scholar's bag of tricks. Which is why the results of a 2017 study by the Stanford History Education Group were so surprising.[38] Sam Wineburg and Sarah McGrew, the study's authors, wanted to compare how well three groups of people could evaluate the credibility of digital information: professional fact-checkers, historians (all with PhDs), and Stanford undergraduates. They set the three groups' tasks, in which they had to read and quickly assess the content from a number of sources. Unsurprisingly, the fact-checkers performed very well, quickly showing that they could spot untrustworthy information. The students, perhaps also unsurprisingly, were quite often fooled by the trappings of pseudo-authority: they trusted material found on websites with professional graphics, .org domain names, and fancy-sounding names. What was most surprising to me is that the historians—academics particularly focused on the nature of sources—fared nearly as badly as the undergraduates. What accounted for the differences? What strategies did the three groups employ to assess information?

One of the tasks the participants had to complete was to read two articles on bullying, one on the website of the American Academy of Pediatrics, the largest professional organization of pediatricians in the world, and one on the website of the American College of Pediatrics, a much smaller splinter group that advocates against LGBT rights. In a timed task, participants had to read the articles and, using whatever online resources they wanted, evaluate their credibility. The fact-checkers, who were much more successful at identifying the latter site's biases, did so for the most part by *leaving* the site in question to search for corroborating information elsewhere. While the historians and college students spent minutes reading a dubious site, trying to detect clues that would let them know whether to trust it, the fact-checkers swiftly googled the site's name, found a host of sources questioning its bias, and were able to read the site's article with immensely helpful context. Wineburg and McGrew call this skill "lateral reading," and they argue that it is a crucial strategy for assessing credibility in the digital age. Instead of just looking for indicators of reliability within a particular site, lateral readers take advantage of prior research and find out what others have said about a source's credibility. According to Washington State University's Michael Caulfield, such strategies are precisely the kind we should be helping our students develop to navigate a world of fake news and sham sources.

Caulfield, who is the director of blended and networked learning at Washington State University Vancouver, argues that too often information literacy is taught to undergraduates by way of checklists: students are trained to ask a series of questions of any source they come across. What is the source? If it's online, does it have a .com, .org, .gov, or .edu domain name? Where on the ideological spectrum does the publication fall? What credentials does the article's author have? To Caulfield, putting so much emphasis on the source (and not on the claims within the source) is an absurd waste of students' time: "To put it in perspective, you got a dubious letter and just spent 20 minutes fact-checking the mailman. And then you actually opened the letter and found it was a signed letter from your Mom. 'Ah,' you say, 'but the mailman is a Republican!'"[39] Credibility checklists are well intentioned but often inefficient; it's more important for students to be able to evaluate *claims* than sources per se.[40] In a thoroughly networked world—and the world of academic scholarship is just as networked, in the era of Google Scholar—our students have access to a wealth of information that can help them assess whether something is true or false.

In addition to lateral reading, Caulfield suggests two other strategies for checking dubious claims: looking for previous fact-checking work and following claims "upstream." The first strategy is pretty self-explanatory; if someone has already disproved a claim, it should be relatively easy to find online. The second strategy involves following the trail of citations. If a source makes a claim, where does the claim come from? If a source is given, you can investigate that source. The idea is to get as close as possible to the original source of information so that you can more clearly assess its plausibility.

Now, Caulfield's work and the Stanford History Education Group's research are specifically targeted at "web literacy" and uncovering false claims in the public sphere. But the skills your students need for information literacy within your academic discipline require very similar thinking. Reading laterally, checking for previous work, and following citations to primary sources are good strategies for research in any domain. What's more, using examples from the world of internet news can be a great way to teach these skills with content your students find familiar and accessible. Our goal should go beyond our students understanding discrete content knowledge; they need to develop the ability to flexibly apply these strategies wherever they are called for. Rather than teach students which journals are reliable, teach them how to verify a claim in any journal.

Politics doesn't disappear when we enter a college classroom. But the classroom offers us a chance to make a space where we can discuss vitally important issues with the civility, selflessness, empathy, and insight so often missing outside the classroom walls. In the classroom we get to imagine and bring into being a parallel world, a world slightly more just than our own, with slightly different realities that we can shape with our students. I can think of no other space that offers this opportunity, and as instructors we are uniquely empowered to help make and maintain this space.

We also have the incredible privilege to be able to work with and influence our students. Our students depend on us to help them, to look out for them, to offer them guidance. They need us now more than ever. We have the chance to be there for our students, to help them adapt to, and struggle with, the uncertainty of the coming years. We have a particular responsibility to help the most vulnerable of our students: people of color, immigrants and children of immigrants, members of the LGBTQ+ community, those with disabilities, the underprivileged, and women. We can show these students that they are valued, work to offer them opportunities denied to them elsewhere, and make clear to them that we are on their side.

If you are worried about the country's political present, remember that you get to spend your days with its future. If your students are going to undo the damage done by their elders, if they are going to make this country and the world a more just place, they're going to need your help. If they're going to save us from the human-made climate disaster on the horizon, they need to understand science well. If they're going to make this country safer for everyone, they need to know how to argue, and they need to develop the empathy that only comes from listening to other people and their ideas. If they're going to make a better democracy, they need to become better citizens. Help them get there.

8

Revise Your Teaching

I REMEMBER VIVIDLY my first day of class as a graduate instructor. I stood at the front of the classroom, swallowing hard, my notes in hand, scarcely much older than the twenty or so undergraduates looking up at me expectantly. What was I supposed to do up there? My own professors had always made it look easy, but this was anything but. I don't remember much more about that first day, but I'm sure I got through the class period mostly by talking continuously at the students.

Today, when I work with graduate instructors before their first semester teaching, I make sure to tell them that they shouldn't lecture. I tell them about the research that has demonstrated how ineffective lecturing is as a mode of teaching, how passive students don't learn very much, usually. Instead, I tell them, you'll want to make your classroom a space in which students *do stuff*. You're going to design activities for students to practice crucial skills, give them feedback on how they do, and allow them to learn from their missteps and mistakes. Practice isn't the only way we learn, but it's one of the best.

It's also an important way we learn as teachers. Teaching college is a vocation and a discipline, but it's also a job. An increasing number of resources are available to help novice instructors become better teachers, but there's no substitute for experience. What you learn in the classroom, through trying things out and understanding why they work—or don't work—creates lessons that stay with you for years. I've come a long way since that first day in the classroom. Every semester I've taught has helped me change my practice and make adjustments that I hope have helped me become a better teacher. That's all we can hope for, really: not to be perfect but to be able to continue to revise our practice as we go, learning from our mistakes and striving to be better.

This chapter offers some advice to help you improve on the job. These are some strategies I've developed over the years to help me do the job of teaching better, to be able to reflect on and analyze my practice, so I can see what I should do differently. Teaching is difficult because success and failure depend on the extent to which you effect change in other people. But that difficulty can be eased if you focus on effecting change in yourself, learning from experience, dedicating yourself to getting better, a little at a time.

Draft Your Teaching

Teaching and writing are the two great common denominators of academic life (the departmental meeting is a third). With few exceptions, no matter your field, you have to teach, and you have to write.

I co-teach a writing course for graduate students, and I'm always surprised at how often discussions of writing drift into discussions of teaching. Both involve thinking about how best to present ideas so they can be understood by other people. In that sense, many strategies that work for planning out a piece of writing can also work for planning out a course.

In the weeks leading up to a new semester, try thinking of your courses like you think about your writing: as the result of a series of drafts. You don't expect to sit down and write a journal article in one go. Why would creating a course be any different? Acknowledge that drafting and revision are essential to any creative project and give yourself plenty of time.

One of my favorite texts to teach in writing courses is a section from Anne Lamott's *Bird by Bird* called "Shitty First Drafts." Reading Lamott, and her advice to write a terrible draft first, completely transformed the way I write. "The first draft," she writes, "is the child's draft, where you let it all pour out and then romp all over the place, knowing that no one is going to see it and that you can shape it later."[1] This last aspect is crucial: once you tell yourself that no one will ever see this draft, you grant yourself the freedom to try out ideas that you would otherwise dismiss. You allow your brain to take risks that ordinarily you would be too cautious to attempt. By separating the composition process from the revision process, you can turn off your inner critic when trying to be creative.

Why not try a similar process for course planning? Give yourself an hour to draft a "shitty" plan for a course you have to teach. Write out the sequence of topics you'll cover. Break up important skills into components and take a swing at a schedule to teach them one by one. Draft a new assignment that takes students out of their comfort zone and pushes them to learn new things. Don't stop yourself from writing something because it's unrealistic or might not work. Put new and risky ideas down on paper. There will be time later to come back and take them out if they are, indeed, untenable. Plan the course the way you'd teach it right this minute, without restrictions, and see what you come up with.

You can also trick yourself into better course planning. When I was a graduate student, I turned a couple of my dissertation chapters into journal articles. I remember the painful process of drastically cutting down one of the chapters to get under a journal's strict word limit. To make myself do it, I told myself that I could always restore the deleted sections to the chapter when it came time to submit my dissertation. That gave me the freedom to "kill my darlings" and make the chapter substantially shorter. I kept the cut sections in a separate file, waiting to be put back in when I needed them.

But when I finished the dissertation and returned to the chapter, I discovered that I liked the chapter much better without the stuff I had cut. I ended up leaving the chapter in its shorter version. It turns out that making those cuts forced me to trim the fat and leave only what was absolutely necessary for the chapter's arguments.

We can try something similar in planning our courses. I like an exercise that the University of Manitoba's William Kops mentions in a 2014 article on teaching summer courses.[2] The idea: how would you teach your course if, instead of fifteen weeks of multiple meetings, you had to teach the whole thing in a single three-hour class period? Sit down and plan out the session. What would you do?

You can't possibly fit everything in, which is exactly the point. The exercise forces you to zero in on your priorities for the semester. What are the most crucial elements of your course? What would you leave out if you had to? What do students absolutely need to know? Later, when you revisit the course plan, you will of course add back in much of what you decided to jettison. But I bet you'll find that some of that material remains on the cutting-room floor.

I've also taken to using Scrivener, the popular writing software, to plan my courses. The features that make the software useful to writers working on long projects—in particular the "corkboard view," which allows writers to organize chapters or subsections as a collection of notecards—also make it a great tool for course planning. Just as Scrivener helps authors organize a great mass of content into a readable whole, it can also help teachers rein in the chaos of a semester's worth of teaching materials into a successful course.[3] But the specifics of the software aren't as important as the approach. Think about the strategies that help you succeed in making a piece of writing; can you apply them to your course planning process?

Adjusting Midsemester

One of the most essential qualities of a good instructor is flexibility: the ability to adapt as situations change, to keep long-term goals in mind as short-term circumstances change, to balance competing priorities amid the cacophony of the semester. If you're serious about creating courses in which students are at the center, then the drafting and revision processes can't stop once the semester starts. Advance preparation and planning can only go so far: what happens if you turn up for class on the first day and discover that your students have very little background knowledge in physics? Or that a significant portion of them struggle with spoken English? Or that they've already taken classes that covered most of what you were planning to cover? What's required is the ability and willingness to change your lesson plans to suit the students you have in the room rather than the students you wish you had.

There's very little benefit to rigidly adhering to your initial conceptions of a course no matter what. Particularly as you get deeper into the semester, beyond the first few weeks, you can start to take stock of your class, paying attention to how your course has diverged from your initial plans. Chapter 4 offers a number of ways to learn about the students in your classroom, to respond to their feedback to better fit your instruction to them. But it's also worth engaging in some self-reflection and reassessment. As you approach a semester's halfway point, look back on what you planned for the semester and decide how faithfully you want to stick to those plans. Take a look at your syllabus, in particular the goals you sketched for the course. How much progress have you made? Are you heading in the right direction? Conducting a midterm evaluation like the one I suggest in Chapter 2 can let you know whether the students see the course in the same way that you see it. Remind yourself of your hoped-for destination and turn the steering wheel accordingly.

Certainly there may be elements of your syllabus that you can't change halfway through the semester, but you don't need to feel completely handcuffed by your initial plans.

In a rhetoric course I taught a couple of years ago, the biggest changes I made had to do with the number of readings on the schedule. Readings take valuable class time to unpack and discuss, and, starting around week six, I started to worry that I wasn't leaving enough time for the practice of skills my students need. Particularly in light of their first papers, which showed that many of the students needed more help with constructing effective sentences and paragraphs, I decided to thin the calendar a bit.

To be flexible is to be able to bend without breaking. To do so in the face of changing circumstances requires both confidence and wisdom: the confidence to remain dedicated to our goals for our students, and the wisdom to know how to adjust our methods to meet those goals when things don't go as planned.

Looking Backward, and Forward, at the End of the Semester

I'm always taken aback by the sudden change that happens at the end of a class period. What just seconds ago was an intense and heady environment is transformed back into an empty room. Something similar happens at the end of a semester. After months of running— of juggling course prep, marking, student conferences, faculty meetings, and any other work you want to get done—suddenly there's stillness and quiet. Suddenly there's time to do all the things on your to-do lists.

I'm usually more than ready for that change. But before I indulge in my well-deserved break from teaching, I find it important to make sure I take advantage of still being completely engrossed in it.

I learn a lot every semester. Getting through a course, trying out new things, learning about and adjusting to my students, I'll inevitably learn about how to teach the course, and how to teach more generally. I always feel better about my pedagogy at the end of the term than I do at the beginning. Curiously, though, these gains don't always carry over from semester to semester. By the time that next semester rolls around, a lot of the lessons we've learned are often forgotten. Did that new approach to a familiar text produce the results you'd hoped for? How did that new topic go over with the students? Was the multipart assignment too much of a headache (for you or them), or was it worth it? A few months later, it can all get kind of hazy.

Part of this can be preempted with good note taking throughout the term. If your course is a living thing, morphing constantly, your pre-semester plans won't be much help as a record of what you actually taught. I cannot count how many times, in the first years of my teaching career, that I cursed myself for my incomplete and unhelpful teaching notes. Even if you don't depend on a written-out plan for each class period, it's important to write down what you did in each class. The best time to do this is immediately after class ends. Sit down for five minutes and type or write out what you did in class, and if you can, make note of what worked well and what didn't. It's worth it, as well, to keep these notes organized in a way that you'll be able to easily find what you're looking for (this becomes all the more important the longer you teach). You'll be grateful for this diligence in the future, when you teach the course again.

At the end of the semester, it's important to do some thinking— both backward- and forward-looking—about your teaching. Although at the end of a course the next semester is just about the farthest thing from your mind, it's best to strike while the iron is hot. Before you close the book on one semester, do yourself a favor that you'll be grateful for down the line. Having just taught them, you will never be better equipped to think through how your courses should change—or not—than right now. A few hours of work now will pay dividends in the future that can't be earned any other way.

Start by getting organized. Go through your notes from the semester and catalog everything you did from the first class meeting to the last. For each class period, I keep a separate document with my notes and title it by the class date. At the end of the semester, I retitle these files to reflect their contents: for example, one document will be titled "Revision skills - Assignment 3 thesis workshop - Steinem essay." That way, I can easily glance at a semester's worth of class sessions and quickly remind myself of what I did. When I want to remember how I taught revision, I can easily find the appropriate notes.

Next, evaluate each class session. Which ones were hits? Which ones flopped? Are the successful classes replicable? Do the failures indicate that you should try something different next time around, or are you not ready to give up on them just yet? That kind of work requires you to be self-critical and clear-eyed—you need an honest assessment of the semester's progress that will be useful to you in the future. You can also do some big-picture thinking at this point: How did your overall approach to the course work? Should you rearrange some of the elements? Should you bring in a fresh set of readings?

Finally, make yourself plan out the next iteration of the course. Write that "shitty first draft" now. If you had to teach the class again, starting next week, how would you teach it? Fill out the calendar with readings, topics, assignments, and in-class activities. Consider the arc of the semester, what you want to achieve, and how you might make the elements of the course best complement each other. Start by figuring out where the best classes from this past semester will go on the fall calendar and then fill in the rest of the course around them. You can certainly change this plan when the time comes. But as with writing, it's easier to revise a course plan than to create one from scratch.

It would be a real shame if you didn't build on the successes you achieved this semester because you forgot how you achieved them. Just as important, drafting a plan now for next time can help ensure that you don't repeat your mistakes.

Make the Most of Student Evaluations

If you've spent any amount of time around other college professors, you've probably encountered more than a few instances of what I call EESS—extreme evaluation skepticism syndrome. That ailment, which seems to infect more and more academics every year, causes ordinarily sensible instructors to utter such statements as "Student evaluations are worthless" or "It's the Yelpification of education." The media are also quick to jump on any study that seems to confirm that students are not qualified to evaluate course effectiveness.

In 2014 and 2015, Betsy Barre, then associate director of Rice University's Center for Teaching Excellence, noticed the rapid spread of EESS and decided to look into the phenomenon. Reading extensively in literature stretching back decades, she tried to sort out the signal from the noise: How good are student evaluations at measuring student learning? In presentations to Rice faculty and in several blog posts, she presented her findings.[4] In short, it's complicated. Because student evaluations are administered with a multitude of instruments, for a multitude of purposes, and at every kind of institution, it's nearly impossible to draw any simple conclusions about their reliability as measures of teaching effectiveness or student learning. But, she concluded, that doesn't mean they are worthless.

On the contrary, Barre found there were many more studies that showed a positive correlation between student evaluations and learning than studies that showed no correlation. She estimated that once you control for known biases like student motivation, class size, and discipline, the correlation between scores and learning was around 0.5. That is a relatively strong but definitely imperfect correlation, meaning there are factors influencing the relationship that we still don't understand. However, she emphasized, while student evaluations are an imperfect tool, "we have not yet been able to find an alternative measure of teaching effectiveness that correlates as strongly with student learning."[5]

That is to say, student evaluations may be flawed, but right now they're the best instrument we've got.

Of course it's those flaws that make the use of evaluation scores in personnel decisions highly controversial. As well, there is ample evidence that student evaluations reflect pernicious biases; many studies have demonstrated that evaluations, unsurprisingly, tend to be more positive if the instructor is white and male.[6] All the more reason for departments and institutions to avoid using evaluations to assess faculty performance for employment decisions. It's clear that taking a handful of numbers from a faculty member's file and expecting them to be a meaningful measure of teaching quality is foolish. Yet Barre's work demonstrates—to me at least—that evaluations probably have some value, particularly for individual teachers. We may have legitimate cause to fear superficial interpretations of evaluation data, but that doesn't mean we should ignore what our students are saying about our courses. As James Lang wrote in his 2010 book *On Course*, "The important thing to remember is that you will get information from students about your teaching, and you should take it seriously."[7] But *how* should we take it seriously? How can we use our student evaluations to revise our teaching going forward? Here's some advice that I hope will help you make something constructive out of your evals.

If you're anything like me, you check your student evaluations as soon as they are available. That makes sense. If your teaching is important to you, you're going to be interested in how students assess your teaching. But the heat of the end-of-semester moment may not be the best time to objectively make sense of your evaluations. It's very easy, and totally natural, to be defensive about low scores and critical comments. You just spent a whole semester working countless hours to teach these students and this is the thanks you get? However understandable, a defensive mind-set is not going to help you learn from your evaluations. Take a week off before coming back and looking at the results again. You'll be better able to see things with a bit more objectivity.

Once you do sit down to properly make sense of your evaluations, don't make the mistake of simplistically interpreting the results, good or bad. Don't be content to just look at the overall average. Pay special attention to the individual questions that target outcomes that mean the most to you. Although it can be tempting to fixate on the questions that straightforwardly evaluate performance ("Was the instructor prepared for each class?"), I focus instead on how my students answered questions about whether their writing and critical reading skills have improved. Our system at the University of Iowa allows me to click on any given comment and see how an individual student (still anonymous, of course) responded to the other questions. I sniff around to see if the negative comments came from a small number of disgruntled students or are more spread out.

Similarly, if you have low average scores overall, or on certain questions, is it because most responses clustered around that low figure, or were your generally high marks brought down by a few low scorers? Two different circumstances might lead you to two very different conclusions. Look for patterns, take notes, and go slowly: it's not easy to draw conclusions from such a small sample, so exercise caution.

Finally, try to see the evaluations in context. Evaluations are anonymous but they're not random numbers reported by unknown students. You already have a lot of information about the courses and the students you just taught. When you look at your evaluations, the challenge is to synthesize this new information with what you already know. Were there students in the class who nursed grudges about their poor grades? Did some students struggle to keep up with the course's level of difficulty? Were there students who routinely came to class unprepared? Keep all of that in mind as you read the comments.

Lang, in *On Course*, also advises early-career instructors to make an appointment with their department chair to discuss their evaluations.[8] Among other things, you might find out that students at your institution always complain about workload, for example, on evaluations. It might not be you.

Above all, look for constructive lessons from your evaluations. Look for patterns—multiple students mentioning the same thing, or a particularly low cluster of scores on a certain question. Look for comments that confirm suspicions you already had about your teaching. And look for common complaints from different classes: if students in two or more different courses make a similar criticism, you may want to look into it. What can you learn that will help you revise?

Revising a Class

Teaching the same class multiple times can be a very good thing. Every time you teach it, your confidence grows, as you build on the successes and failures of past semesters. As well, prepping for class takes less and less time each semester. Having a backlog of assignments and class activities means never having to come up with a class from scratch. But easily filling a class period is not the same as teaching well. Even if your lesson plans are battle-tested and effective, teaching them cold—that is, without spending any time thinking about them before class—is a poor way to operate. It is definitely a good thing to be able to prep for class more efficiently as you gain experience, but that efficiency is counterproductive if it means you are sleepwalking through class.

Here are some ways to combat these dangers and let your prior experience help you, not suffocate you.

First, get down to brass tacks. Before a class, review each class exercise and ask the crucial questions that should apply to everything you do in the classroom:

- What are the goals? What do you want the students to learn?
- How does this activity help them learn?
- Are there ways to more effectively achieve that learning?
- Why is it important that students learn this material or this skill?

Your initial reasoning for designing some particular activity may now be lost to the sands of time, which may be a sign that the original goal was not worth pursuing. Reevaluate the activity to make sure it's doing what you want it to be doing. Remember that your aim should not be to merely cover material, but for students to learn valuable information and skills. This sort of self-interrogation will almost inevitably lead you to revise and improve your teaching.

Even after considering those questions, you may want to teach the unit the same way you always have. That's OK. Just subjecting your approach to scrutiny will improve your teaching. You will operate in the classroom with a refreshed sense of purpose and a clear understanding of both why you're doing what you're doing and why it's important that students go through the experience. And you'll still be spending less time on class prep than you would have starting from scratch.

As well, every group of students is different, and every semester is different. The undergraduates you're teaching now have different strengths, weaknesses, and needs from the students you taught in the past. Maybe you'll notice, as I did a few semesters ago, that your students respond particularly well to questions that steer class discussion to connections between the readings and current events. That may be just the information you need to make an adjustment that helps other class activities succeed. Once you get a few weeks into the semester, you can ask yourself:

- What have you learned about this semester's students so far?
- What do they need extra help with? What do they seem to have mastered already?
- How can you revise your old material so that it fits their needs, not just your own need to have some activity ready to go?

You can also see your familiarity as an opportunity to innovate. The fact that you've taught this course before means you may be comfortable enough to experiment. You have a road map to get to the end of the semester. So why not take a detour? This may be the perfect chance to give students more control over class activities, or try out a new exercise from a colleague, or give students a provocative reading about a topic in the news. The moment you get really comfortable teaching a class may be a signal that it's time to try something new.

Sit In on Someone Else's Class

So much of the work that goes into teaching is necessarily invisible. Nobody sees your best teaching days—when everything clicks, when you get your class to truly see the world differently—except for the students in the room. (Luckily, no one else sees your worst teaching days either.) Most of us don't teach for praise, but it's a shame that our best work in the classroom isn't seen by our peers and superiors. It's also a shame that those instructors who want to improve don't get the benefit of learning directly from the excellent teachers in their midst.

Consider how you learned about your research discipline in graduate school. Sure, you got ideas, advice, and information from your adviser and from other professors, but you also benefited from reading other people's work to see how scholarship in your field was done. You found models. When it comes to developing as teachers, however, most of us haven't been able to learn by watching others. We can hark back to our own teachers, but that's a pretty limited sample.

I remember the first time I co-taught a course, with my colleague Matt Gilchrist. Together we taught a writing course for graduate students, and I learned as much as our students. Being able to see another teacher work, especially one as talented as Matt (he's particularly good at fostering constructive student discussion), was extremely valuable to my teaching practice. When I started co-teaching the course with Megan Knight, I learned a whole new set of strategies.

Of course, not everyone is able to team-teach a course. So how else might you get to see your colleagues in action and learn from their classroom expertise? The answer: ask your colleagues if you can sit in on their classes.

All around you are expert practitioners of your craft, and all that stands between you and their classrooms is a polite request. Most professors, I would bet, would not have a problem with a colleague sitting in on a class. The instructor can explain to students that you aren't there to conduct an evaluation—just to observe for your own benefit. You can be unobtrusive, sit in the back, and take notes.

When you observe someone else's classroom, you notice all the little ways that each instructor differs. What seemed straightforward—the way you begin every class period, perhaps—is now revealed to be a pedagogical choice. The very experience of witnessing a different approach might be the most important benefit from a classroom observation: if someone else can do things differently, so can you. But that won't be the only thing you learn. Think of all your expert strategies, all the wisdom you've developed as you've taught semester after semester. You get the opportunity to take a peek into someone else's bag of tricks to see how their magic is made.

You might want to stick to observing colleagues with a lot of experience; those new to the job may be more self-conscious about being watched. But the request is so low impact—another instructor sitting quietly in the back will not disrupt most classrooms—that there's really no reason not to ask anyone you're curious about learning from.

There's another, more subtle benefit to doing this: you'll get to see the classroom from the students' point of view. Even just the physical difference—sitting in the back of the classroom instead of standing at the front—can be eye-opening. In addition to any strategies you pick up, that change of perspective can be helpful to your teaching. What's your class like for the student at the back of the room?[9]

Ideally, departments should encourage faculty to sit in on each other's classes regularly. It would be pretty easy for most departments to set up a rotation so that every instructor has a chance to sit in on the classes of two or three other teachers each semester. Such a system would encourage the sharing of ideas, lead to better professional relationships (making it easier to find someone to write a teaching-centered letter of reference), and support departmental collegiality and morale.[10]

The ways to approach teaching your subject are more varied than you think. But there's really only one way to get a sense of that variety: see it for yourself. I particularly recommend this practice to graduate students, who should be looking to expose themselves to as wide an array of teaching approaches as possible. But established instructors can benefit, too—sitting in on another teacher's class can provide the push you need to break out of your pedagogical rut. There may be good reasons for doing things the way you've always done them. But watching a colleague teach may give you good reasons to try something new.

Avoiding Burnout

In a 2005 essay in the *Annual Review of Sociology*, the Stanford sociology professor Paula England set out to detail five "theoretical frameworks" that sociologists have used to conceptualize "care work," jobs that require employees to provide care for pay. A number of these frameworks apply to academic work (which is only sometimes considered care work), including what England calls the "prisoner of love" framework: the fact that employees love what they do makes it easier for employers to exploit them. But what I found most striking among England's categories was the "commodification of emotion" framework, which zeroes in on "emotional harm to workers when they have to sell services that use an intimate part of themselves."[11]

Burnout—often defined as a combination of exhaustion, alienation from work, and diminished performance as a consequence—is a concern in many industries, but the nature of the work we do as teachers makes teaching academics particularly susceptible to it.[12] Working closely with students, helping them respond to challenges, and being there for them at a period of their lives often marked by upheaval and stress is emotionally draining work. A British study of workplace stress across twenty-six occupations, conducted in 2005, found university faculty members were among the worst professions in terms of self-reported psychological well-being.[13] A 2011 literature review of studies of faculty burnout found that the phenomenon was comparable to burnout among school teachers and health-care professionals. That study said the problem most likely was related to our role as teachers, finding that "exposure to high numbers of students . . . strongly predicts the experience of burnout."[14]

Of course, if teaching is the main source of faculty burnout, doesn't it follow that our teaching—and our students' learning—will suffer the more stressed and exhausted we become? Good teaching requires reserves of patience and ingenuity that are all too often depleted in overworked faculty members. I haven't seen any research on the relationship between college faculty burnout and student learning, but there have been at least two recent large-scale studies of that relationship in elementary schools. The two studies, both conducted in Germany and published in 2016, found that teachers' emotional exhaustion was directly and negatively related to students' educational outcomes. That is to say, the more teachers reported feeling emotionally exhausted, the worse their students did across the board: on their grades, on standardized tests, on measures of student satisfaction, you name it.[15]

Teaching college is not the same as teaching fourth grade. We don't spend nearly as many hours in the classroom with our students, of course. But faculty burnout is a real phenomenon, and it would be hard to argue that it helps our students.

Caring about students, and sometimes caring for them, is an integral part of most teachers' practice. As much as I want to treat teaching as an intellectual pursuit, the emotional aspects of working closely with students to help them develop cannot be denied. Neither can the emotional costs. We may not always want to admit that we are using "an intimate part" of ourselves when we teach, but there's little doubt that we are. We work with people and try to help them develop; this is a task that requires much more of us than our academic training. If we're not psychologically healthy, it's near impossible to do our jobs well. Here are some suggestions for taking care of yourself while teaching.

First, don't be afraid to ask for help. You've got friends, family, and colleagues who can help you. Your institution likely offers support services; take advantage of them. If you're feeling stressed and emotionally exhausted, it's most likely because you care deeply about your job and believe in the importance of doing it well. But there's no benefit to running yourself into the ground. Let people around you know when you're feeling low, and offer words of understanding and support when you see colleagues struggling to balance it all. It's a hard job.

It's also important to take time off, if only for an evening. From graduate school onward, we're trained to feel like we should always be working. The lack of a nine-to-five workday only contributes to that mentality. If you are able to work at any time of day, any day of the week, shouldn't you be working at all times, every day of the week? But there are significant negative effects of an always-on mind-set.[16] You'll be better able to plan out that class after a good night's sleep. And those emails from students? Rarely is the question so urgent that responding can't wait until morning.

Try to remember that your job is just a job, even if you love it. As academics we are both blessed and cursed with a profession that aligns with our personal intellectual ambitions. Most of us were drawn to our field because we earnestly wanted to find answers to questions that fascinated us, and most of us have probably caught ourselves telling others how lucky we feel to be able to do what we do.

Yet, as many scholars have warned, that devotion to our work makes us prime candidates for exploitation. As Sarah Brouillette has written, "Our faith that our work offers nonmaterial rewards, and is more integral to our identity than a 'regular' job would be, makes us ideal employees when the goal of management is to extract our labor's maximum value at minimum cost."[17] A 2014 study of non-tenure-track faculty members found that the more they identified them-selves with their institutions, the more stressful—and anxiety- and depression-inducing—their jobs were.[18] Do your best to cultivate perspective and outside interests. Just because you love your work doesn't mean that it's the be-all and end-all of your existence. You are more than your job.

That "I do what I love" phenomenon also leads many of us to take on more work than is probably wise. It may be collegial to sit on multiple committees, but there are only so many hours in a week, and you've already got a mountain of papers to grade. Recent research has suggested that this so-called extra-role behavior at work can significantly contribute to workplace stress, and that academic workplaces are particularly prone to that kind of behavior.[19] Take a hard look at your work commitments, both formal and informal, and ask yourself if you absolutely have to do all of them.

What We're Aiming For

One last way to combat burnout also connects with what I see as an ideal to shoot for in our teaching. Sleep is increasingly seen as hugely important to our mental and physical well-being. Most of us, it seems, are not getting enough of it. And sleep deprivation (which kicks in, for most people, when we get fewer than seven hours of sleep a night) can lead to high levels of anxiety, poor decision-making, lack of energy, and lack of concentration.[20] All of your capabilities are needed to be a good teacher, and your fully functioning brain is worth far more than your completely worked-out lesson plans. What is going to be more valuable to your students—that you went over the readings one more time or that you are rested enough to be fully present and responsive in the classroom?

I've been an overplanning kind of teacher for a long time. I once boasted in a job application that, in a single class period, I might make use of a freewriting exercise, a mini-lecture, a discussion of the freewriting exercise, a group activity, a quiz, a role-playing game, and an end-of-class written reflection. Some of that tendency to fill up a class period proceeds from an admirable instinct: there's no one ideal way to teach any class, so it makes sense to use a mix of approaches.

I also think my overstuffed classes were a reaction against the tyranny of the lecture. Instead of a single mode of information delivery, I'd use five. Or ten. But I've begun to see that that manic approach stems more from my own insecurity than from any pedagogical principle. If I had the whole class period planned down to the minute, if I made sure that the students' experience was a whirlwind of activities and exercises, no one could accuse me of being underprepared. No less important, by overscheduling each class period, I could protect myself from the paralyzing prospect of having to think on my feet.

That is the real terror of the novice instructor, isn't it: standing in front of a room full of students and not knowing what to say. A detailed class plan full of bullet points is a security blanket against the fear that the students are about to figure out we don't know what we're talking about. I've started to think that this tendency to overprepare can prevent us from being as effective as we want to be.

I've written, in Chapter 2, about ways to cede control of the classroom, but in that case I was writing specifically about passing the baton to students. It's also important to cede control to the moment—to the time you and your students have together in the classroom. By planning so much, I now realize, I often foreclosed possibility and made sure that almost nothing could happen that I didn't think of in advance. Although I wasn't lecturing, my rigidity and ultimate control over what went on in the classroom remained the same.

I'm working to change that, and I invite you to do the same. I'm not saying you should walk into the classroom with nothing, and just have the students sit around and talk. But as I've gotten more experience as a teacher, I've become more and more convinced that it's important to leave time for my classes to wander off course, for class discussions to function like real discussions and take off on interesting tangents, and for unexpected problems to come up (and be faced).

The ideal is to plan less and think more. Class needs to be more than the place where you execute a previously conceived procedure. If we're serious about all the foundational principles of this book— active learning strategies, student-centered teaching, pedagogy as more than just the poor cousin of academic research—we need to be serious about the classroom as a space where real learning can occur, for both the students and the instructor.

What we need to aim for is the ability to be fully present in the classroom. The best teachers respond to students in the moment, working with them as they figure things out. They don't fear uncertainty but embrace it as a necessary precondition of learning. They see moments of uncomfortable silence not as evidence that the class is a disaster but as valuable opportunities for reflection. They leave open the possibility that they might fail. All of this is frightening. But it's an approach that makes the classroom one of the most exciting and dynamic and fertile spaces we have, a place where anything can happen, where students can walk in curious and walk out transformed.

Notes

Introduction

1. In her essay on the "signature pedagogy" of literary studies, Nancy L. Chick argues that far too often the default mode of the English professor is "professorial packing": rather than unpacking texts, opening them up to reveal multiple possibilities of meaning, professors "pack" texts with their own ideas, foreclosing any opportunities for the students to take an active role in interpreting—and learning how to interpret—literary texts. Chick sensibly deduces that "given [the] context in which most English Ph.D.s are being trained solely in content knowledge and not pedagogy or even pedagogical content knowledge, it's understandable that they rely on their strengths—presenting interpretations—and begin teaching as they were taught." Nancy L. Chick, "Unpacking a Signature Pedagogy in Literary Studies," in *Exploring Signature Pedagogies: Approaches to Teaching Disciplinary Habits of Mind*, ed. Regan A. R. Gurung, Nancy L. Chick, and Aeron Haynie (Sterling, VA: Stylus, 2009), 43.

2. T. D. Snyder, C. de Brey, and S. A. Dillow, "Percentage Distribution of Full-Time Faculty and Instructional Staff in Degree-Granting Postsecondary Institutions, by Level and Control of Institution, Selected Instruction Activities, and Number of Classes Taught for Credit: Fall 2003," Table 315.30, *Digest of Education Statistics 2016*, National Center for Education Statistics, Institute of Education Sciences, U.S. Department of Education, 2018, https://nces.ed.gov/programs/digest/d16/tables/dt16_315.30.asp.

3. T. D. Snyder, C. de Brey, and S. A. Dillow, "Percentage Distribution of Part-Time Faculty and Instructional Staff in Degree-Granting Postsecondary Institutions, by Level and Control of Institution, Selected Instruction Activities, and Number of Classes Taught for Credit: Fall 2003," Table 315.40, *Digest of Education Statistics 2018*, National Center for Education Statistics, Institute of Education Sciences, U.S. Department of Education, 2018, https://nces.ed.gov/programs/digest/d16/tables/dt16_315.40.asp.

4. MLA Office of Research, *Report on the MLA "Job Information List," 2013–14* (New York: Modern Language Association of America, 2014).

5. Among these speakers was Chris Walsh, whose "blank syllabus" I discuss in Chapter 2.

6. This truth seems borne out by the site's numbers to this day. Although I get few submissions, the site attracts a consistent readership.

7. In 2008, Derek Bok pointed out that college faculty—even when they set out to remake their curricula—rarely consider any research on teaching and learning. He argues that such neglect may be rooted in professors' self-interest: They're afraid to find out they have to completely remake their approach in the classroom, and therefore put their heads in the sand. "Shielded in this way, even professors who devote their lives to research continue to ignore empirical work on teaching and learning when they prepare their own courses or meet with colleagues to review their educational programs." Derek Bok, *Our Underachieving Colleges* (Princeton, NJ: Princeton University Press, 2008), 51.

8. Bok, 359.

1. Helping Students Revise Themselves

1. Scott Freeman et al., "Active Learning Increases Student Performance in Science, Engineering, and Mathematics," *Proceedings of the National Academy of Sciences* 111 (2014): 8410–8415.

2. Carl E. Wieman, "Large-Scale Comparison of Science Teaching Methods Sends Clear Message," *Proceedings of the National Academy of Sciences* 111 (2014): 8319–8320.

3. See, for instance, Richard R. Hake, "Interactive-Engagement versus Traditional Methods: A Six-Thousand-Student Survey of Mechanics Test Data for Introductory Physics Courses," *American Journal of Physics* 66, no. 1

(1998): 64–74; Dean Zollman, "Millikan Lecture 1995: Do They Just Sit There? Reflections on Helping Students Learn Physics," *American Journal of Physics* 64, no. 2 (1996): 114–119; and Maria Araceli Ruiz-Primo et al., "Impact of Undergraduate Science Course Innovations on Learning," *Science* 331, no. 6022 (2011): 1269–1270.

4. See Mercedes Lorenzo, Catherine H. Crouch, and Eric Mazur, "Reducing the Gender Gap in the Physics Classroom," *American Journal of Physics* 74, no. 2 (2006): 118–122; and David C. Haak et al., "Increased Structure and Active Learning Reduce the Achievement Gap in Introductory Biology," *Science* 332 (2011): 1213–1216.

5. Richa Thaman et al., "Promoting Active Learning in Respiratory Physiology—Positive Student Perception and Improved Outcomes," *National Journal of Physiology, Pharmacy and Pharmacology* 3, no. 1 (2013): 27–34.

6. David Kember and Doris Y. P. Leung, "The Influence of Active Learning Experiences on the Development of Graduate Capabilities," *Studies in Higher Education* 30, no. 2 (April 2005): 155–170.

7. To read more about constructivism as a theory of learning, see John D. Bransford, Ann L. Brown, and Rodney R. Cocking, *How People Learn* (Washington, DC: National Academy Press, 2000); and Catherine Twomey Fosnot, ed., *Constructivism: Theory, Perspectives, and Practice* (New York: Teachers College Press, 2005).

8. For a compelling explanation of why rereading is an inefficient and often counterproductive way to study, see Peter C. Brown, Henry L. Roediger, and Mark A. McDaniel, *Make It Stick* (Cambridge, MA: Harvard University Press, 2014), 13–17.

9. Bransford, Brown, and Cocking, *How People Learn*, 15.

10. See, for example, Brendan Nyhan and Jason Reifler, "When Corrections Fail: The Persistence of Political Misperceptions," *Political Behavior* 32, no. 2 (2010): 303–330; and Brendan Nyhan et al., "Effective Messages in Vaccine Promotion: A Randomized Trial," *Pediatrics* 133, no. 4 (2014): e835–e842.

11. Tessa M. Andrews et al., "Active Learning *Not* Associated with Student Learning in a Random Sample of College Biology Courses," *CBE-Life Sciences Education* 10 (2011): 394–405.

12. Andrews et al., "Active Learning *Not* Associated with Student Learning," 400.

13. Andrews et al., 400.

14. A 1996 study found that teachers who believed in constructivism were more likely to have "a richer variety of teaching strategies" and were more likely to use "potentially more effective teaching strategies for inducing student conceptual change." Maher Z. Hashweh, "Effects of Science Teachers' Epistemological Beliefs in Teaching," *Journal of Research in Science Teaching* 33, no. 1 (1996): 47.

15. Mary-Ann Winkelmes has done great work in promoting such transparent teaching practices through her Transparency in Learning and Teaching in Higher Education Project. The project's website (http://tilthighered.com) has a wealth of research and practical strategies for using transparency to improve learning outcomes.

16. David Foster Wallace, "Syllabus for David Foster Wallace's class 'English 102-Literary Analysis: Prose Fiction Fall '94,'" David Foster Wallace Papers, Harry Ransom Center, University of Texas at Austin, 3–4.

17. Polly A. Fassinger, "Classes Are Groups: Thinking Sociologically about Teaching," *College Teaching* 45, no. 1 (1997): 23.

18. Fassinger, 23.

19. See also Polly A. Fassinger, "Professors' and Students' Perceptions of Why Students Participate in Class," *Teaching Sociology* 24, no. 1 (1996): 25–33; Polly A. Fassinger, "How Classes Influence Students' Participation in College Classrooms," *Journal of Classroom Interaction* 35, no. 2 (2000): 38–47; Robert J. Sidelinger and Melanie Booth-Butterfield, "Co-constructing Student Involvement: An Examination of Teacher Confirmation and Student-to-Student Connectedness in the College Classroom," *Communication Education* 59, no. 2 (2010): 165–184; Jennifer Moffett et al., "An Investigation into the Factors That Encourage Learner Participation in a Large Group Medical Classroom," *Advances in Medical Education and Practice* 5 (2014): 65–71; and Süleyman Nihat Şad and Niyazi Özer, "Silent Scream: 'I Do Not Want to Participate Professor!,'" *Procedia - Social and Behavioral Sciences* 116 (2014): 2532–2536.

20. Jay R. Howard, *Discussion in the College Classroom: Getting Your Students Engaged and Participating in Person and Online* (San Francisco: John Wiley & Sons, 2015), 38–39.

21. As I explain in more detail in Chapters 2 and 5, too much reliance on extrinsic motivation can actually undercut students' intrinsic motivation.

22. Elise J. Dallimore, Julie H. Hertenstein, and Marjorie B. Platt, "Impact of Cold-Calling on Student Voluntary Participation," *Journal of Management Education* 37 (2013): 305–341.

23. Dallimore, Hertenstein, and Platt, 331.

24. Elise J. Dallimore, Julie H. Hertenstein, and Marjorie B. Platt, "Class Participation in Accounting Courses: Factors That Affect Student Comfort and Learning," *Issues in Accounting Education* 25 (2010): 613–629.

25. Derek Bruff, "In Defense of Continuous Exposition by the Teacher," *Agile Learning* (blog), September 15, 2015, http://derekbruff.org/?p=3126.

26. Donald L. Finkel, *Teaching with Your Mouth Shut* (Portsmouth, NH: Boynton / Cook, 2000), 3.

27. Mick Charney, "Active Processing Using 'Quizzes-on-the-Go,'" *The Scholarly Teacher* (blog), December 1, 2014, https://www.scholarlyteacher.com /blog/using-quizzes-on-the-go.

28. The example is taken from Finkel, *Teaching with Your Mouth Shut*, 16.

29. Bill Roberson and Billie Franchini, "Effective Task Design for the TBL Classroom," *Journal on Excellence in College Teaching* 25 (2014): 281.

30. The work of Deborah Allen and Kimberly Tanner offers an abundance of ideas for the science instructor looking to incorporate more active learning strategies into her classroom. The two biologists collaborated on a series of essays on teaching in the sciences in the journal *CBE—Life Sciences Education*. Those essays were collected in a book that is now very difficult to find; your best bet is to read them on the journal's website, under the collection title "Approaches to Biology Teaching and Learning." See *"CBE—Life Sciences Education,"* The American Society for Cell Biology, accessed January 24, 2019, https://www.lifescied.org; and Deborah Allen and Kimberly D. Tanner, *Transformations: Approaches to College Science Teaching* (New York: WH Freeman, 2009).

31. Angela Bauer-Dantoin, "The Evolution of Scientific Teaching within the Biological Sciences," in *Exploring Signature Pedagogies: Approaches to Teaching Disciplinary Habits of Mind*, ed. Regan A. R. Gurung, Nancy L. Chick, and Aeron Haynie (Sterling, VA: Stylus, 2009), 229.

32. See Eric Mazur, *Peer Instruction: A User's Manual* (Upper Saddle River, NJ: Prentice Hall, 1997); and Mark J. Lattery, "Signature Pedagogies in Introductory Physics," in Gurung, Chick, and Haynie, *Exploring Signature Pedagogies*, 287–288.

33. See Lelia Ballone Duran and Emilio Duran, "The 5E Instructional Model: A Learning Cycle Approach for Inquiry-Based Science Teaching," *Science Education Review* 3, no. 2 (2004): 49–58; and Diane Ebert-May, Carol Brewer, and Sylvester Allred, "Innovation in Large Lectures: Teaching for Active Learning," *Bioscience* 47, no. 9 (1997): 601–607.

34. Tamara Rosier, "Filling in the Gaps: Emphasizing Thinking about One's Own Thinking," *The Scholarly Teacher* (blog), August 1, 2014, https://www .scholarlyteacher.com/blog/filling-in-the-gaps.

35. For more on the benefits of group work in large lecture classes, see James L. Cooper and Pamela Robinson, "The Argument for Making Large Classes Seem Small," *New Directions for Teaching and Learning* 81 (2000): 5–16; Ani Yazedjian and Brittany Boyle Kolkhorst, "Implementing Small-Group Activities in Large Lecture Classes," *College Teaching* 55, no. 4 (2007): 164–169. As well, Eric Mazur's peer instruction method offers a systematic way to keep students engaged and interested during lectures. See Mazur, *Peer Instruction*.

36. The phrase "classroom assessment techniques" originates in the classic book of the same name, by Thomas Angelo and K. Patricia Cross. Although published nearly a quarter century ago, the book remains a useful resource for novice instructors, with a great number of practical strategies for assessing students' progress at any given point within a class period. Thomas A. Angelo and K. Patricia Cross, *Classroom Assessment Techniques: A Handbook for College Teachers* (San Francisco: Jossey-Bass, 1993).

37. For more on what Robert Bjork has called "desirable difficulties," see Chapter 3.

38. Dan Berrett, "If Skills Are the New Canon, Are Colleges Teaching Them?," *Chronicle of Higher Education*, April 3, 2016, http://www.chronicle .com/article/If-Skills-Are-the-New-Canon/235948.

39. John Schlueter, "Higher Ed's Biggest Gamble," *Inside Higher Ed*, June 7, 2016, https://www.insidehighered.com/views/2016/06/07/can-colleges-truly -teach-critical-thinking-skills-essay.

40. See, for instance, Daniel T. Willingham, "Critical Thinking: Why Is It So Hard to Teach?," *Arts Education Policy Review* 109 (2008): 21–29.

41. For example, a 2003 study by Michael J. McInerney and L. Dee Fink centered on a microbial physiology course—a course in which "an enormous amount of information" "is critically needed if the students are to understand how microorganisms function." They replaced lectures with "team-based

learning," an approach that centers on dividing students into persistent teams for the semester and "engag[ing] those teams with challenging, complex learning tasks." McInerney and Fink report that the intervention "improved the students' comprehension and retention of information, critical thinking, and attitudes about the course, and focused student-instructor interactions on learning rather than grades." Michael J. McInerney and L. Dee Fink, "Team-Based Learning Enhances Long-Term Retention and Critical Thinking in an Undergraduate Microbial Physiology Course," *Microbiology Education* 4 (2003): 3–12.

42. Ned B. Bowden and Rebecca Laird, "CHEM:2210 Organic Chemistry I Syllabus" (University of Iowa Chemistry Department, 2016), https://chem.uiowa.edu/sites/chem.uiowa.edu/files/2210_Syllabus_Spring%202017.pdf.

2. Let Students Own the Course

1. That smart person was David Mazella, associate professor of English at the University of Houston, who used the expression on Twitter.

2. See Edward L. Deci, "Effects of Externally Mediated Rewards on Intrinsic Motivation," *Journal of Personality and Social Psychology* 18 (1970): 105–115; and Mark Lepper and David Greene, eds., *The Hidden Costs of Reward* (London: Psychology Press, 2016).

3. Ken Bain, *What the Best College Teachers Do* (Cambridge, MA: Harvard University Press, 2004), 33. For more on the interactions between extrinsic and intrinsic motivation, see the website of the Self-Determination Theory Institute (http://selfdeterminationtheory.org), founded by Richard Ryan and Edward Deci, pioneers in the study of motivation.

4. W. Caleb McDaniel, "The United States, 1848 to the Present" (Rice University History Department, 2015), http://wcm1.web.rice.edu/pdf/hist118sp15.pdf.

5. In their excellent book *How Learning Works*, Susan A. Ambrose and her coauthors sketch a framework for understanding motivation that posits three main variables that influence it: value (how much the student values the goal), expectancies (how likely it is that the student will attain the goal), and environment (how supportive the student's surroundings are). Susan Ambrose et al., *How Learning Works: 7 Research-Based Principles for Smart Teaching* (San Francisco: Jossey-Bass, 2010), 70–82.

6. David S. Yeager et al., "Boring but Important: A Self-Transcendent Purpose for Learning Fosters Academic Self-Regulation," *Journal of Personality and Social Psychology* 107, no. 4 (2014): 559–580.

7. Joseph Finckel, "The Silent Professor," Faculty Focus, November 3, 2015, https://www.facultyfocus.com/articles/teaching-and-learning/the-silent -professor. Amanda Lohiser, in a 2017 *College Teaching* essay, recounts a similarly transformative bout of laryngitis. Unable to speak for a number of weeks, Lohiser prepared PowerPoint presentations of her lectures, and then during the class she passed a microphone around the hall, with each student presenting a slide. Students were encouraged to not just read the slide's text but *present* the material, along with their own interpretations of the significance of the ideas. Amanda Lohiser, "Voiceless in Lecture: A Lesson in Vocal Difficulties and Student-Led Classes," *College Teaching* 65, no. 4 (2017): 204–206.

8. Donald Finkel details a more formalized version of this present-but-silent professor in his book *Teaching with Your Mouth Shut*. In his "open seminar," students arrive to class with questions about a reading, then discuss the text in a circle, led by their own questions, while the teacher sits outside the circle and observes. Donald L. Finkel, *Teaching with Your Mouth Shut* (Portsmouth, NH: Boynton / Cook, 2000), 31–50.

9. A wealth of good ideas for using silence in the classroom can be found in Heather Anne Trahan's 2013 essay "The Silent Teacher: A Performative, Meditative Model of Pedagogy," *Liminalities: A Journal of Performance Studies* 9, no. 3 (2013): n.p.

10. bell hooks, *Teaching to Transgress: Education as the Practice of Freedom* (New York: Routledge, 1994), 21.

11. Walsh published an essay on the blank syllabus: Chris Walsh, "The Blank Survey Syllabus," in *Teaching the Literature Survey Course: New Strategies for College Faculty*, ed. Gwynn Dujardin, James M. Lang, and John A. Staunton (Morgantown: West Virginia University Press, 2018), 102–119.

12. Caroline Wilson, "Integrating a 'Blank Syllabus' with Team-Based Learning (TBL): Student-Designed TBL Modules in a Neurophysiology Course" (presentation, 2018 TBLC Meeting, San Diego, CA, March 2, 2018).

13. For more on team-based learning, see Chapter 5.

14. Ken Macrorie, *The I-Search Paper—Revised Edition of "Searching Writing"* (Portsmouth, NH: Heinemann, 1988).

15. Cathy Davidson, "Why Start with Pedagogy? 4 Good Reasons, 4 Good Solutions," HASTAC, June 18, 2015, https://www.hastac.org/blogs/cathy-davidson/2015/06/18/why-start-pedagogy-4-good-reasons-4-good-solutions.

16. Jeffrey R. Stowell, William E. Addison, and Samuel L. Clay, "Effects of Classroom Technology Policies on Students' Perceptions of Instructors: What Is Your Syllabus Saying about You?," *College Teaching* 66, no. 2 (2018): 98–103.

17. Cathy Davidson, "Getting Started 5: First Class: Collectively Writing a Constitution," HASTAC, August 13, 2015, https://www.hastac.org/blogs/cathy-davidson/2015/08/13/getting-started-5-first-classcollectively-writing-constitution.

18. I finally understood this simple but important point after reading the writing of Chris Friend, who writes about pedagogy often at *Hybrid Pedagogy*, which he directs.

19. Michaéla C. Schippers, Ad WA Scheepers, and Jordan B. Peterson, "A Scalable Goal-Setting Intervention Closes Both the Gender and Ethnic Minority Achievement Gap," *Palgrave Communications* 1 (2015): 1-12.

20. See Edwin A. Locke and Gary P. Latham, "Building a Practically Useful Theory of Goal Setting and Task Motivation: A 35-Year Odyssey," *American Psychologist* 57, no. 9 (2002): 705–717.

21. See Jacob B. Hirsh, Raymond A. Mar, and Jordan B. Peterson, "Psychological Entropy: A Framework for Understanding Uncertainty-Related Anxiety," *Psychological Review* 119, no. 2 (2012): 304–320.

22. To learn more about metacognition, see John D. Bransford, Ann L. Brown, and Rodney R. Cocking, *How People Learn* (Washington, DC: National Academy Press, 2000); and Nancy Chick, "Metacognition," *Center for Teaching* (blog), Vanderbilt University Center for Teaching, accessed March 20, 2019, https://cft.vanderbilt.edu/guides-sub-pages/metacognition.

23. "Exam Wrappers," *Eberly Center* (blog), Carnegie Mellon University Eberly Center for Teaching Excellence and Educational Innovation, accessed March 20, 2019, https://www.cmu.edu/teaching/designteach/teach/examwrappers.

24. Peter Filene, *The Joy of Teaching: A Practical Guide for New College Instructors* (Chapel Hill: University of North Carolina Press, 2005), 71–73.

25. The connection between metacognition and learning transfer is generally well established in the literature, though it is sometimes hard to pin down because of the many different names for metacognitive skills. See Bransford, Brown, and Cocking, *How People Learn*, 12–13, 18–21.

26. For more on the benefits of metacognition to student learning, see Anat Zohar and Sarit Barzilai, "A Review of Research on Metacognition in Science Education: Current and Future Directions," *Studies in Science Education* 49, no. 2 (2013): 121–169; Christine B. McCormick, Carey Dimmitt, and Florence R. Sullivan, "Metacognition, Learning, and Instruction," in *Handbook of Psychology*, 2nd ed. Vol. 7, ed. William M. Reynolds and Gloria E. Miller (Hoboken, NJ: Wiley, 2012), 69–97; and J. Kevin Ford et al., "Relationships of Goal Orientation, Metacognitive Activity, and Practice Strategies with Learning Outcomes and Transfer," *Journal of Applied Psychology* 83, no. 2 (1998): 218–233.

27. Kimberly D. Tanner, "Promoting Student Metacognition," *CBE-Life Sciences Education* 11, no. 2 (2012): 113–120.

3. Building a Better Course

1. Pam A. Mueller and Daniel M. Oppenheimer, "The Pen Is Mightier Than the Keyboard: Advantages of Longhand over Laptop Note Taking," *Psychological Science* 25, no. 6 (2014): 1159–1168.

2. Elizabeth Ligon Bjork and Robert Bjork, "Making Things Hard on Yourself, but in a Good Way: Creating Desirable Difficulties to Enhance Learning," in *Psychology and the Real World*, ed. Morton Ann Gernsbacher and James R. Pomerantz (New York: Worth Publishers, 2011): 59–68.

3. For insight into this issue, see Rick Godden and Anne-Marie Womack, "Making Disability Part of the Conversation: Combatting Inaccessible Spaces and Logics," *Hybrid Pedagogy*, May 12, 2016, http://hybridpedagogy.org/making-disability-part-of-the-conversation.

4. Robert Kerr and Bernard Booth, "Specific and Varied Practice of Motor Skill," *Perceptual and Motor Skills* 46, no. 2 (1978): 395–401.

5. See, for instance, M. K. Goode, L. Geraci, and H. L. Roediger, "Superiority of Variable to Repeated Practice in Transfer on Anagram Solution," *Psychonomic Bulletin & Review* 15 (2008): 662–666.

6. Steven M. Smith, Arthur Glenberg, and Robert A. Bjork, "Environmental Context and Human Memory," *Memory & Cognition* 6, no. 4 (1978): 342–353.

7. Bjork and Bjork, "Making Things Hard," 61.

8. Henry L. Roediger III and Jeffrey D. Karpicke, "Test-Enhanced Learning: Taking Memory Tests Improves Long-Term Retention," *Psychological Science* 17, no. 3 (2006): 249–255.

9. Henry L. Roediger III and Jeffrey D. Karpicke, "The Power of Testing Memory: Basic Research and Implications for Educational Practice," *Perspectives on Psychological Science* 1, no. 3 (2006): 181–210.

10. Although a number of studies have shown that the testing effect persists even when no feedback is given, Brown, Roediger, and McDaniel note in *Make It Stick* that feedback on tests, especially when delayed, can increase the positive effects. "Studies show that giving feedback strengthens retention more than testing alone does, and, interestingly, some evidence shows that delaying the feedback briefly produces better long-term learning than immediate feedback." Peter C. Brown, Henry L. Roediger, and Mark A. McDaniel, *Make It Stick* (Cambridge, MA: Harvard University Press, 2014), 39.

11. Roediger and Karpicke, "Power of Testing Memory," 205–206.

12. See Eric H. Hobson, "Getting Students to Read: Fourteen Tips," *Idea Paper* 40 (2004): 1–10; Michael A. Clump, Heather Bauer, and Catherine Breadley, "The Extent to Which Psychology Students Read Textbooks: A Multiple Class Analysis of Reading across the Psychology Curriculum," *Journal of Instructional Psychology* 31, no. 3 (2004): 227–232; and Colin M. Burchfield and John Sappington, "Compliance with Required Reading Assignments," *Teaching of Psychology* 27, no. 1 (2000): 58–60.

13. Peter Filene, *The Joy of Teaching: A Practical Guide for New College Instructors* (Chapel Hill: University of North Carolina Press, 2005), 65–70.

14. Mary-Ann Winkelmes et al., "A Teaching Intervention That Increases Underserved College Students' Success," *Peer Review* 18, no. 1 / 2 (2016): 31–36.

15. Allyson F. Hadwin, "Do Your Students Really Understand Your Assignment?," *LTC Currents Newsletter* 2, no. 3 (2006): 1–9.

16. Jennifer Gonzalez, "Dogfooding: How Often Do You Do Your Own Assignments?," Cult of Pedagogy, June 10, 2015, https://www.cultofpedagogy.com/dogfooding.

17. Raoul A. Mulder, Jon M. Pearce, and Chi Baik, "Peer Review in Higher Education: Student Perceptions Before and After Participation," *Active Learning in Higher Education* 15, no. 2 (2014): 157–171.

18. For a sampling of the variety of disciplines in which peer review sessions have been studied, see Julie E. Sharp et al., "Four Effective Writing Strategies for Engineering Classes," *Journal of Engineering Education* 88, no. 1 (1999): 53–57; Christine von Renesse and Jennifer DiGrazia, "Mathematics, Writing, and Rhetoric: Deep Thinking in First-Year Learning Communities," *Journal of*

Humanistic Mathematics 8, no. 1 (2018): 24–63; and Sue Odom et al., "Group Peer Review as an Active Learning Strategy in a Research Course," *International Journal of Teaching and Learning in Higher Education* 21, no. 1 (2009): 108–117.

19. See, for instance, Kristi Lundstrom and Wendy Baker, "To Give Is Better Than to Receive: The Benefits of Peer Review to the Reviewer's Own Writing," *Journal of Second Language Writing* 18, no. 1 (2009): 30–43; Young Hoan Cho and Kwangsu Cho, "Peer Reviewers Learn from Giving Comments," *Instructional Science* 39, no. 5 (2011): 629–643; and Kwangsu Cho and Charles MacArthur, "Learning by Reviewing," *Journal of Educational Psychology* 103, no. 1 (2011): 73.

20. Christina Moore, "Frame Your Feedback: Making Peer Review Work in Class," Faculty Focus, June 6, 2016, https://www.facultyfocus.com/articles /teaching-and-learning/frame-feedback-making-peer-review-work-class.

21. Linda B. Nilson, "Improving Student Peer Feedback," *College Teaching* 51, no. 1 (2003), 34–38.

22. John C. Bean, in his book *Engaging Ideas*, has a helpful section on peer review sessions that builds on Nilson's work. John C. Bean, *Engaging Ideas* (San Francisco: Jossey-Bass, 2011), 295–302.

23. Christine M. Cunningham and Jenifer V. Helms, "Sociology of Science as a Means to a More Authentic, Inclusive Science Education," *Journal of Research in Science Teaching* 35, no. 5 (1998): 483–499.

24. Nancy M. Trautmann, "Designing Peer Review for Pedagogical Success," *Journal of College Science Teaching* 38, no. 4 (2009): 16.

25. Jianguo Liu, Dawn Thorndike Pysarchik, and William W. Taylor, "Peer Review in the Classroom," *AIBS Bulletin* 52, no. 9 (2002): 824–829.

26. Trautmann, "Designing Peer Review," 18.

27. James M. Lang, *Cheating Lessons: Learning from Academic Dishonesty* (Cambridge, MA: Harvard University Press, 2013), 2.

28. Here's a thoughtful paper on the complexities of assessing the overall rate of academic cheating: Guy J. Curtis and Lucia Vardanega, "Is Plagiarism Changing over Time? A 10-Year Time-Lag Study with Three Points of Measurement," *Higher Education Research & Development* 35, no. 6 (2016): 1167–1179.

29. Jamieson and Howard define *patchwriting* as "an unsuccessful attempt at paraphrase"—that is, a restatement of ideas from a secondary source that stays close (perhaps too close) to the language of that source. This definition

comes from an excellent interview with Jamieson and Howard in which they expand on their findings and offer suggestions for actions their results point toward. "Unraveling the Citation Trail," *Project Information Literacy Smart Talk*, no. 8, Sandra Jamieson and Rebecca Moore Howard, The Citation Project, August 15, 2011.

30. Sandra Jamieson and Rebecca Moore Howard, "Sentence-Mining: Uncovering the Amount of Reading and Reading Comprehension in College Writers' Researched Writing," in *The New Digital Scholar: Exploring and Enriching the Research and Writing Practices of NextGen Students*, ed. Randall McClure and James P. Purdy (Medford, NJ: American Society for Information Science and Technology, 2013), 111–133.

31. Rebecca Schuman, "Don't Spend Your Holiday Break Writing," *Chronicle of Higher Education*, December 12, 2018, https://www.chronicle.com /article/Don-t-Spend-Your-Holiday/245292.

32. David Didau, "Great Teaching Happens in Cycles—the Teaching Sequence for Developing Independence," *The Learning Spy* (blog), June 24, 2013, http://www.learningspy.co.uk/featured/great-teaching-happens-in-cycles.

33. Robert L. Hampel, "The Final Three Minutes with 100 Undergraduates," *College Teaching* 62, no. 2 (2014), 77–78.

34. Lydia Eckstein Jackson and Aimee Knupsky, "'Weaning off of Email': Encouraging Students to Use Office Hours over Email to Contact Professors," *College Teaching* 63, no. 4 (2015): 183–184.

35. Mario Guerrero and Alisa Beth Rod, "Engaging in Office Hours: A Study of Student-Faculty Interaction and Academic Performance," *Journal of Political Science Education* 9, no. 4 (2013): 403–416.

4. Teaching the Students in the Room

1. Kimberly D. Tanner, "Structure Matters: Twenty-One Teaching Strategies to Promote Student Engagement and Cultivate Classroom Equity," *CBE—Life Sciences Education* 12, no. 3 (2013): 322.

2. In particular, I'm thinking of Jay Dolmage, Anne-Marie Womack, David M. Perry, and Katie Rose Guest Pryal. There are many others, of course.

3. Anne-Marie Womack, "Teaching Is Accommodation: Universally Designing Composition Classrooms and Syllabi," *College Composition and Communication* 68, no. 3 (2017): 494.

4. Womack, 498.

5. Jay Dolmage, "Universal Design: Places to Start," *Disability Studies Quarterly* 35, no. 2 (2015): 4. The wiki can be found at http://universaldesignideas.pbworks.com.

6. I recognize that many of these efforts take time to put into place, time that overworked instructors may feel they don't have. Most of our institutions are still not set up to support instructors who are fully committed to helping every student get the resources they need.

7. Rick Godden and Anne-Marie Womack, "Making Disability Part of the Conversation: Combatting Inaccessible Spaces and Logics," *Hybrid Pedagogy*, May 12, 2016, http://hybridpedagogy.org/making-disability-part-of-the -conversation/.

8. For an introduction to Driver and her work, see Rosalind Driver, "Students' Conceptions and the Learning of Science," *International Journal of Science Education* 11, no. 5 (1989): 481–490; Rosalind Driver, ed., *Children's Ideas in Science* (Milton Keynes, UK: Open University Press, 1985); and Kimberly D. Tanner, "Approaches to Biology Teaching and Learning: Understanding the Wrong Answers—Teaching toward Conceptual Change," *CBE— Life Sciences Education* 4, no. 2 (2005): 112–117.

9. Rosalind Driver, *The Pupil as Scientist?* (Milton Keynes, UK: Open University Press, 1983), 3.

10. James M. Lang, *On Course: A Week-by-Week Guide to Your First Semester of College Teaching* (Cambridge, MA: Harvard University Press, 2008), 31–35.

11. Thomas A. Angelo and K. Patricia Cross, *Classroom Assessment Techniques* (San Francisco: Jossey-Bass, 1993).

12. Derek Bruff, *Teaching with Classroom Response Systems: Creating Active Learning Environments* (San Francisco: Jossey-Bass, 2009), 1.

13. To learn more about this approach, see "Just-in-Time Teaching," Indiana University, accessed June 11, 2018, https://jittdl.physics.iupui.edu/jitt.

14. Joseph Harris, "Workshop and Seminar," in *Teaching with Student Texts: Essays toward an Informed Practice*, ed. Joseph Harris, John D. Miles, and Charles Paine (Logan, UT: Utah State University Press, 2010), 148.

15. Margaret Marshall, "Writing to Learn, Reading to Teach: Student Texts in the Pedagogy Seminar," in Harris, Miles, and Paine, *Teaching with Student Texts*, 176.

16. Robert J. Sidelinger and Melanie Booth-Butterfield, "Co-constructing Student Involvement: An Examination of Teacher Confirmation and Student-to-Student Connectedness in the College Classroom," *Communication Education* 59, no. 2 (2010): 179.

17. Ali Sher, "Assessing the Relationship of Student-Instructor and Student-Student Interaction to Student Learning and Satisfaction in Web-Based Online Learning Environment," *Journal of Interactive Online Learning* 8, no. 2 (2009): 102–120.

18. Gloria J. Galanes and Heather J. Carmack, "'He's Really Setting an Example': Student Contributions to the Learning Environment," *Communication Studies* 64, no. 1 (2013): 61.

19. Benjamin Hassman, "Question Roll 1: Building Community," *Filling the Chalkboard* (blog), June 16, 2014, https://fillingthechalkboard.wordpress.com/2014/06/16/question-roll-1-building-community; and Benjamin Hassman, "Question Roll 2: Integrating Pedagogy," *Filling the Chalkboard* (blog), July 11, 2014, https://fillingthechalkboard.wordpress.com/2014/06/16/question-roll-1-building-community.

20. Stephen M. Fishman and Lucille Parkinson McCarthy, "Community in the Expressivist Classroom: Juggling Liberal and Communitarian Visions," *College English* 57, no. 1 (1995): 62–81.

21. For more on jigsaw groups—in which students in groups are given different tasks to complete and then the groups are mixed up to allow students to learn from each other—see Raymond Benton Jr., "Put Students in Charge: A Variation on the Jigsaw Discussion," *College Teaching* 64, no. 1 (2016): 40–45; and Kimberly Tanner, Liesl S. Chatman, and Deborah Allen, "Approaches to Cell Biology Teaching: Cooperative Learning in the Science Classroom—Beyond Students Working in Groups," *Cell Biology Education* 2, no. 1 (2003): 1–5.

22. Douglas A. Bernstein, "Parenting and Teaching: What's the Connection in Our Classrooms?," *Psychology Teacher Network*, September 2013, http://www.apa.org/ed/precollege/ptn/2013/09/parenting-teaching.aspx.

23. See Diana Baumrind, "The Influence of Parenting Style on Adolescent Competence and Substance Use," *Journal of Early Adolescence* 11, no. 1 (1991): 56–95.

24. Diana Baumrind, "Authoritarian vs. Authoritative Parental Control," *Adolescence* 3, no. 11 (Fall 1968): 256.

25. Bernstein, "Parenting and Teaching."

26. Edward L. Deci and Richard M. Ryan, "Motivation, Personality, and Development within Embedded Social Contexts: An Overview of Self-Determination Theory," in *The Oxford Handbook of Human Motivation*, ed. Richard M. Ryan (New York: Oxford University Press, 2012), 85–107.

27. In a 2008 review of the research on self-determination theory in educational contexts, Frédéric Guay, Catherine Ratelle, and Julien Chanel conclude that "autonomous motivation has been associated with cognitive outcomes such as increased retention and depth of learning." Frédéric Guay, Catherine F. Ratelle, and Julien Chanal, "Optimal Learning in Optimal Contexts: The Role of Self-Determination in Education," *Canadian Psychology / Psychologie canadienne* 49, no. 3 (2008): 235.

5. Assessment Isn't Just Assessment

1. Carol Dweck, *Mindset: The New Psychology of Success* (New York: Random House, 2006).

2. Self-determination theory originators Edward L. Deci and Richard M. Ryan describe the process as follows: when people are driven by the pursuit of rewards or the avoidance of punishments, "their behavior tends to become dependent on the contingencies, so they do not do the behaviors if the contingencies are not operative. To the extent that people do feel controlled by extrinsic motivators, their need for autonomy will be thwarted and some negative motivational, performance, and well-being consequences are likely to follow." Edward L. Deci and Richard M. Ryan, "Motivation, Personality, and Development within Embedded Social Contexts: An Overview of Self-Determination Theory," in *The Oxford Handbook of Human Motivation* (New York: Oxford University Press, 2012), 88.

3. To return to Deci and Ryan, they argue that external motivators such as rewards or punishments can become *internalized* and thus contribute to intrinsic motivation. Part of this is because "people have an inclination, as part of the inherent integrative process, to internalize the regulation of behaviors that are valued by important others in their environments." In that sense, the message that your grading decisions send about what you value may influence your students' intrinsic motivation (Deci and Ryan, 88).

4. Paul Black and Dylan William, "Assessment and Classroom Learning," *Assessment in Education: Principles, Policy & Practice* 5, no. 1 (2006): 22.

5. Phillippe Perrenoud, "Towards a Pragmatic Approach to Formative Evaluation," in *Assessment of Pupils' Achievement: Motivation and School Success*, ed. P. Weston (Amsterdam: Swets and Zeitlinger, 1991), 92.

6. Jessica Lahey, "Things Fall Apart," *Coming of Age in the Middle* (blog), November 6, 2011, http://comingofageinthemiddle.blogspot.com/2011/11/things-fall-apart.html.

7. Howard E. Aldrich, "How to Hand Exams Back to Your Class," *College Teaching* 49, no. 3 (2001): 82.

8. See "Two-Stage Exams," Carl Wieman Science Education Initiative, October 2014, http://www.cwsei.ubc.ca/resources/files/Two-stage_Exams.pdf.

9. See Larry K. Michaelsen and Michael Sweet, "Team-Based Learning," *New Directions for Teaching and Learning* 128 (2011): 41–51.

10. Richard H. Haswell, "Minimal Marking," *College English* 45, no. 6 (October 1983): 600–604.

11. Richard Light, *The Harvard Assessment Seminars* (Cambridge, MA: Harvard University Press, 1990), 24.

12. Peter Elbow, "About Responding to Student Writing," accessed January 30, 2019, http://peterelbow.com/pdfs/Responding_to_Student_Writing.pdf.

13. Peter Elbow, "From Grades to Grids: Responding to Writing with Criteria," accessed January 30, 2019, http://peterelbow.com/pdfs/Grids_for_Grading.pdf.

14. Mark Salisbury, "Revisiting the Value of Early Feedback," *Delicious Ambiguity* (blog), Augustana College, April 30, 2018, http://www.augustana.net/blogs/ir/?p=2415.

15. Abour H. Cherif et al., "Why Do Students Fail? Faculty's Perspective," *2014 Collection of Papers*, Higher Learning Commission Annual Conference, accessed June 13, 2018, https://cop.hlcommission.org/Learning-Environments/cherif.html.

16. Moriah Balingit, "The New Trend in Validating Top Students: Make Them All Valedictorians," *Washington Post*, July 12, 2015.

17. Valerie Strauss, "Harvard College's Median Grade Is an A-, Dean Admits," *Washington Post*, December 4, 2013.

18. Rebecca Schuman, "Confessions of a Grade Inflator," *Slate*, May 14, 2014, http://www.slate.com/articles/life/education/2014/05/why_professors_inflate_grades_because_their_jobs_depend_on_it.html.

19. I did find one study, published in 2010, that found that students at the University of California, San Diego, spent less time studying as their expected final grade increased. Philip Babcock, "Real Costs of Nominal Grade Inflation? New Evidence from Student Course Evaluations," *Economic Inquiry* 48, no. 4 (2010): 983–996.

20. Indeed, fostering competition between students can have unfortunate effects. A 2014 study of an effort at Wellesley College to combat grade inflation concluded that departments that enforced an artificial cap on grades ended up with an expanded racial gap in grades and reduced enrollments and majors. Kristin F. Butcher, Patrick J. McEwan, and Akila Weerapana, "The Effects of an Anti-grade-inflation Policy at Wellesley College," *Journal of Economic Perspectives* 28, no. 3 (2014): 189–204.

21. Alfie Kohn, "The Dangerous Myth of Grade Inflation," *Chronicle of Higher Education*, November 8, 2002, https://www.chronicle.com/article/The -Dangerous-Myth-of-Grade/34252.

22. John M. Malouff, Ashley J. Emmerton, and Nicola S. Schutte, "The Risk of a Halo Bias as a Reason to Keep Students Anonymous during Grading," *Teaching of Psychology* 40, no. 3 (2013): 233–237.

23. John M. Malouff and Einar B. Thorsteinsson, "Bias in Grading: A Meta-analysis of Experimental Research Findings," *Australian Journal of Education* 60, no. 3 (2016): 245–256.

24. Phil Birch, John Batten, and Jo Batey, "The Influence of Student Gender on the Assessment of Undergraduate Student Work," *Assessment & Evaluation in Higher Education* 41, no. 7 (2016): 1065–1080.

25. Jan Feld, Nicolás Salamanca, and Daniel S. Hamermesh, "Endophilia or Exophobia: Beyond Discrimination," *Economic Journal* 126, no. 594 (2016): 1503–1527.

26. Daniel Kahneman, *Thinking, Fast and Slow* (New York: Farrar, Straus and Giroux, 2011), 83.

6. What Will We Do Today?

1. Albert Bandura, Dorothea Ross, and Sheila A. Ross, "Transmission of Aggression through Imitation of Aggressive Models," *Journal of Abnormal and Social Psychology* 63, no. 3 (1961): 575–582.

2. For a history of research into observational learning, see Mitch J. Fryling, Christin Johnston, and Linda J. Hayes, "Understanding Observational Learning: An Interbehavioral Approach," *Analysis of Verbal Behavior* 27, no. 1 (2011): 191–203.

3. Matthew Fleenor, "Responding to Student Questions When You Don't Know the Answer," Faculty Focus, October 1, 2010, https://www.facultyfocus .com/articles/teaching-and-learning/responding-to-student-questions-when -you-dont-know-the-answer.

4. Martin A. Schwartz, "The Importance of Stupidity in Scientific Research," *Journal of Cell Science* 121, no. 11 (2008): 1771.

5. Julie Glass, "Modeling Scholarly Practice Using Your Syllabus," Faculty Focus, December 6, 2013, https://www.facultyfocus.com/articles/faculty -development/modeling-scholarly-practice-using-your-syllabus.

6. Baehr has written much about intellectual virtues, particularly as part of the Educating for Intellectual Virtues project he led at Loyola Marymount. Of particular interest for readers may be his self-published e-book for college instructors: Jason Baehr, *Educating for Intellectual Virtues: An Introductory Guide for College and University Instructors* (self-pub., 2015), https:// jasonbaehr.files.wordpress.com/2013/12/e4iv_baehr.pdf.

7. Baehr, 20.

8. As I discuss in Chapter 7, modeling open-mindedness may be particularly important if we are teaching politically controversial topics.

9. Baehr, *Educating for Intellectual Virtues*, 33.

10. Scott Elledge, *E.B. White: A Biography* (New York: W. W. Norton, 1984): 359–367. I learned of the drafts from a post on the Harvard College Writing Center's website: Laura Saltz, "Revising the Draft," Harvard College Writing Center, accessed March 23, 2019, https://writingcenter.fas.harvard.edu/pages/ revising-draft.

11. My paper is a version of Ken Macrorie's "I-Search" paper, which he detailed in full in *Searching Writing* (Upper Montclair, NJ: Boynton / Cook, 1984).

12. Helen Sword, *Stylish Academic Writing* (Cambridge, MA: Harvard University Press, 2012).

13. Jody Shipka, *Toward a Composition Made Whole* (Pittsburgh: University of Pittsburgh Press, 2011), 113–117.

14. Donna LeCourt, "Critical Pedagogy in the Computer Classroom: Politicizing the Writing Space," *Computers and Composition* 15, no. 3 (1998): 278; and Shipka, *Composition Made Whole*, 116.

15. Tony Docan-Morgan, "The Participation Log: Assessing Students' Classroom Participation," *Assessment Update* 27, no. 2 (2015): 6–7.

16. Gerald Grow, "Teaching Writing through Negative Examples," *Journal of Teaching Writing* 6, no. 2 (1987): 239.

17. Grow, 241.

18. Grow, 240.

7. Teaching in Tumultuous Times

1. Joshua Drew, "An Open Letter to My Class," *The Drew Lab* (blog), November 9, 2016, https://labroides.org/an-open-letter-to-my-class.

2. Cathy Davidson, "Why Start with Pedagogy? 4 Good Reasons, 4 Good Solutions," Hastac, June 18, 2015, https://www.hastac.org/blogs/cathy-davidson/2015/06/18/why-start-pedagogy-4-good-reasons-4-good-solutions.

3. Davidson, "Why Start with Pedagogy?"

4. Kevin Gannon, "The Case for Inclusive Teaching," *Chronicle of Higher Education*, February 27, 2018, https://www.chronicle.com/article/The-Case-for-Inclusive/242636.

5. There is a growing literature on inclusive teaching. Here are a few good places to begin learning more: Christine Hockings, "Inclusive Learning and Teaching in Higher Education: A Synthesis of Research," EvidenceNet, Higher Education Authority, https://www.heacademy.ac.uk/system/files/inclusive _teaching_and_learning_in_he_synthesis_200410_0.pdf; Mathew L. Ouellett, ed., *Teaching Inclusively* (Stillwater, OK: New Forums Press, 2007); and Maurianne Adams and Lee Anne Bell, eds., *Teaching for Diversity and Social Justice*, 3rd ed. (New York: Routledge, 2016).

6. Susan Ambrose et al., *How Learning Works: 7 Research-Based Principles for Smart Teaching* (San Francisco: Jossey-Bass, 2010), 158.

7. Ambrose et al., 171; Christopher J. DeSurra and Kimberley A. Church, "Unlocking the Classroom Closet: Privileging the Marginalized Voices of Gay / Lesbian College Students" (paper presented at the Annual Meeting of the Speech Communication Association, November 19-22, 1994, New Orleans, LA), https://eric.ed.gov/?id=ED379697.

8. Ambrose et al., *How Learning Works*, 173.

9. John T. Ishiyama and Stephen Hartlaub, "Does the Wording of Syllabi Affect Student Course Assessment in Introductory Political Science Classes?," *PS: Political Science & Politics* 35, no. 3 (2002): 567–570.

10. Ambrose et al., *How Learning Works*, 176–177.

11. Ambrose et al., 179.

12. A conversation with Barry Schreier, the director of the University of Iowa's University Counseling Service, helped me formulate this advice. See David Gooblar, "How to Help a Student in a Mental-Health Crisis," *Chronicle of Higher Education*, December 7, 2018, https://www.chronicle.com/article /How-to-Help-a-Student-in-a/245305.

13. See "Understanding Implicit Bias," Kirwan Institute for the Study of Race and Ethnicity, The Ohio State University, accessed February 6, 2019, http://kirwaninstitute.osu.edu/research/understanding-implicit-bias.

14. A 2012 study showed, for example, that science faculty from research-intensive universities consistently rated candidates for a laboratory position as more competent and worthy of a higher starting salary when the application materials were said to be from a male candidate than when the same application materials were said to be from a female candidate. Corinne A. Moss-Racusin et al., "Faculty's Subtle Gender Biases Favor Male Students," *Proceedings of the National Academy of Sciences* 109, no. 41 (2012): 16474–16479.

15. Patricia G. Devine, "Stereotypes and Prejudice: Their Automatic and Controlled Components," *Journal of Personality and Social Psychology* 56, no. 1 (1989): 5–18.

16. Patricia G. Devine et al., "Long-Term Reduction in Implicit Race Bias: A Prejudice Habit-Breaking Intervention," *Journal of Experimental Social Psychology* 48, no. 6 (2012): 1267–1278.

17. See Jessica Nordell, "Is This How Discrimination Ends?" *The Atlantic*, May 7, 2017.

18. Devine et al., "Long-Term Reduction in Implicit Race Bias"; and "Understanding Bias: A Resource Guide," U.S. Department of Justice, accessed February 7, 2019, https://www.justice.gov/crs/file/836431/download.

19. See Chris Quintana and Becky Supiano, "Grad Student Sounds Alarm over Penn's Response to Online Attacks," *The Ticker* (blog), *Chronicle of Higher Education*, October 19, 2017, https://www.chronicle.com/blogs/ticker

/grad-student-sounds-alarms-over-penns-response-to-online-attacks
/120693.

20. For more on this phenomenon, see Sarah L. Eddy, Sara E. Brownell, and
Mary Pat Wenderoth, "Gender Gaps in Achievement and Participation in
Multiple Introductory Biology Classrooms," *CBE—Life Sciences Education* 13,
no. 3 (2017): 478–492.

21. In their 2007 study of the political views of the American professoriate,
the sociologists Neil Gross and Solon Simmons classified 44 percent of faculty as
"liberal," compared with only 9 percent as "conservative." It is perhaps surprising that a plurality of respondents (47 percent) were classified as "moderate."
Neil Gross and Solon Simmons, "The Social and Political Views of American
College and University Professors," in *Professors and Their Politics*, ed. Neil
Gross and Solon Simmons (Baltimore: Johns Hopkins University Press, 2014),
25–26.

22. Heather Mac Donald, *The Diversity Delusion: How Race and Gender
Pandering Corrupt the University and Undermine Our Culture* (New York:
St. Martin's Press, 2018), 166.

23. "U of T Profs Alarmed by Jordan Peterson's Plan to Target Classes He
Calls 'Indoctrination Cults,'" CBC Radio, November 13, 2017, https://www.cbc
.ca/radio/asithappens/as-it-happens-friday-edition-1.4396970/u-of-t-profs
-alarmed-by-jordan-peterson-s-plan-to-target-classes-he-calls-indoctrination
-cults-1.4396974

24. Noah Porter, *Webster's Revised Unabridged Dictionary* (Springfield, MA:
G. and C. Merriam Co., 1913).

25. Eamonn Callan and Dylan Arena, "Indoctrination," in *The Oxford
Handbook of Philosophy of Education*, ed. Harvey Siegel (Oxford: Oxford
University Press, 2009), 105.

26. Rebecca M. Taylor, "Indoctrination and Social Context: A System-Based
Approach to Identifying the Threat of Indoctrination and the Responsibilities
of Educators," *Journal of Philosophy of Education* 51, no. 1 (2017): 40.

27. I take the distinction—apparently a common one in philosophy of
education—from Taylor, "Indoctrination and Social Context."

28. Taylor, 48.

29. Jason Baehr, *Educating for Intellectual Virtues: An Introductory Guide
for College and University Instructors* (self-pub., 2015), https://jasonbaehr.files
.wordpress.com/2013/12/e4iv_baehr.pdf, 31.

30. Baehr, 22.

31. bell hooks, *Teaching to Transgress: Education as the Practice of Freedom* (New York: Routledge, 1994), 43.

32. Devine et al., "Long-Term Reduction," 1268.

33. Brendan Nyhan and Jason Reifler, "When Corrections Fail: The Persistence of Political Misperceptions," *Political Behavior* 32, no. 2 (2010): 303–330.

34. Brendan Nyhan et al., "Effective Messages in Vaccine Promotion: A Randomized Trial," *Pediatrics* 133, no. 4 (2014): e835–e842.

35. Glenn Kessler, Salvador Rizzo, and Meg Kelly, "President Trump Made 8,158 False or Misleading Claims in His First Two Years," *Washington Post*, January 21, 2019.

36. "President Trump Job Approval," Real Clear Politics, last modified February 4, 2019, https://www.realclearpolitics.com/epolls/other/president _trump_job_approval-6179.html.

37. There's a growing literature on the subject of faculty-librarian collaboration. For detailed accounts of collaborations around information literacy, see Ignacio J. Ferrer-Vinent and Christy A. Carello, "The Lasting Value of an Embedded, First-Year, Biology Library Instruction Program," *Science & Technology Libraries* 30, no. 3 (2011): 254–266; K. Kearns and T. T. Hybl, "A Collaboration between Faculty and Librarians to Develop and Assess a Science Literacy Laboratory Module," *Science and Technology Libraries* 25, no. 4 (2005): 39–56; and Marilyn D. Lovett, Selma T. Burrell, and Lawrence O. Flowers, "Fusing Information Literacy Skills in STEM Courses," *Journal of Education and Social Policy* 3, no. 3 (2016): 7–11.

38. Sam Wineburg and Sarah McGrew, "Lateral Reading: Reading Less and Learning More When Evaluating Digital Information" (Stanford History Education Group Working Paper No. 2017-A1, October 6, 2017), http://dx.doi .org/10.2139/ssrn.3048994.

39. Michael Caulfield, "How 'News Literacy' Gets the Web Wrong," *Hapgood* (blog), March 4, 2017, https://hapgood.us/2017/03/04/how-news -literacy-gets-the-web-wrong.

40. In another blog post, Caulfield persuasively argues that the skill of *source* evaluation—how we know which websites are trustworthy, for example—is built much more on knowledge than skills. Michael Caulfield, "Yes, Digital Literacy. But Which One?," *Hapgood* (blog), December 19, 2016, https://hapgood.us/2016/12/19/yes-digital-literacy-but-which-one.

8. Revise Your Teaching

1. Anne Lamott, *Bird by Bird: Some Instructions on Writing and Life* (New York: Doubleday, 1994), 22.

2. William J. Kops, "Teaching Compressed-Format Courses: Teacher-Based Best Practices," *Canadian Journal of University Continuing Education* 40, no. 1 (Spring 2014): 1–18.

3. I got the idea to use Scrivener for course planning from Bryna R. Campbell, "Course Planning with Scrivener," *Smart Women Write* (blog), September 19, 2016, https://smartwomenwrite.com/2016/09/19/course -planning-with-scrivener/.

4. Elizabeth Barre, "Student Ratings of Instruction: A Literature Review," *Reflections on Teaching and Learning* (blog), Rice University Center for Teaching Excellence, February 1, 2015, http://cte.rice.edu/blogar-chive/2015/02/01/studentratings; Elizabeth Barre, "Do Student Evaluations of Teaching Really Get an 'F'?," *Reflections on Teaching and Learning* (blog), Rice University Center for Teaching Excellence, July 9, 2015, http://cte.rice.edu/ blogarchive/2015/07/09/studentevaluations; Elizabeth Barre, "Academic Blogging and Student Evaluation Click Bait: A Follow-Up," *Reflections on Teaching and Learning* (blog), Rice University Center for Teaching Excellence, July 28, 2015, http://cte.rice.edu/blogarchive/2015/07/28/studentevaluationsfollowup; Elizabeth Barre, "Research on Student Ratings Continues to Evolve. We Should, Too," *Reflections on Teaching and Learning* (blog), Rice University Center for Teaching Excellence, February 22, 2018, http://cte.rice.edu/blogarchive/2018/2/20/ studentratingsupdate.

5. Barre, "Academic Blogging and Student Evaluation Click Bait."

6. See Michelle Falkoff, "Why We Must Stop Relying on Student Ratings of Teaching," *Chronicle of Higher Education*, April 25, 2018, https://www .chronicle.com/article/Why-We-Must-Stop-Relying-on/243213 for a good overview of this research.

7. James M. Lang, *On Course: A Week-by-Week Guide to Your First Semester of College Teaching* (Cambridge, MA: Harvard University Press, 2008), 279.

8. Lang, 280–281.

9. For an interesting account of a community college professor who enrolled as an undergraduate at his institution to see what the college

experience was like for his students, see Katherine Mangan, "This Professor Enrolled as an Undercover Student," *Chronicle of Higher Education*, May 30, 2016, https://www.chronicle.com/article/This-Professor-Enrolled-as-an /236649.

10. A number of institutions, including Rice University and Vanderbilt University, hold annual events in which instructors across campus open their doors to faculty visitors. It's a great way to foster collegiality and cross-disciplinary learning.

11. Paula England, "Emerging Theories of Care Work," *Annual Review of Sociology* 31, no. 1 (2005): 381–399.

12. See Christina Maslach and Susan E. Jackson, "The Measurement of Experienced Burnout," *Journal of Organizational Behavior* 2, no. 2 (1981): 99–113.

13. Sheena Johnson et al., "The Experience of Work-Related Stress across Occupations," *Journal of Managerial Psychology* 20, no. 2 (2005): 178–187.

14. Jenny Watts and Noelle Robertson, "Burnout in University Teaching Staff: A Systematic Literature Review," *Educational Research* 53, no. 1 (2011): 33–50.

15. A. Katrin Arens and Alexandre J. S. Morin, "Relations between Teachers' Emotional Exhaustion and Students' Educational Outcomes," *Journal of Educational Psychology* 108, no. 6 (2016): 800–813; and Uta Klusmann, Dirk Richter, and Oliver Lüdtke, "Teachers' Emotional Exhaustion Is Negatively Related to Students' Achievement: Evidence from a Large-Scale Assessment Study," *Journal of Educational Psychology* 108, no. 8 (2016): 1193–1203.

16. See, for instance, Matthew Riesz, "'Email Overload' Risks 'Emotional Exhaustion' for Academics," *Times Higher Education*, January 8, 2016, https://www.timeshighereducation.com/news/email-overload-risks-emotional -exhaustion-academics.

17. Sarah Brouillette, "Academic Labor, the Aesthetics of Management, and the Promise of Autonomous Work," Nonsite.org, May 1, 2013, https://nonsite .org/article/academic-labor-the-aesthetics-of-management-and-the -promise-of-autonomous-work.

18. Gretchen M. Reevy and Grace Deason, "Predictors of Depression, Stress, and Anxiety among Non-tenure Track Faculty," *Frontiers in Psychology* 5 (2014): 1–17.

19. K. C. Ryan and L. M. Dunn-Jensen, "Stretched Thin: Stress, In-Role, and Extra-Role Behavior of Educators," in *Stress: Concepts, Cognition, Emotion, and Behavior*, ed. George Fink (London: Academic Press, 2016), 445–450.

20. "Sleep Deprivation," American Academy of Sleep Medicine, 2008, https://aasm.org/resources/factsheets/sleepdeprivation.pdf.

Acknowledgments

I wouldn't be so interested in the nature and significance of great teaching if I hadn't been the student of so many great teachers myself. Ann Meeker, Brian Doherty, William Hardy, Max Dorsinville, Mark Turner, Kasia Boddy, and Pam Thurschwell are just a few of the teachers who changed the course of my life and work. Knowing that I'll never be able to fully thank them drives me to try to make a similar difference in the lives of my own students and, I hope, my readers.

It turns out that having to write 1,000 words on pedagogy every two weeks for four years is a great way to write a book. There is no way I could have written the book without having written the columns. Gabriela Montell and Denise Magner are both exceptional editors, and I'm a better writer for having been able to work with them. They have my gratitude for their help in shaping many of the ideas that ended up in these pages.

Thank you, Andrew Kinney, for your wise counsel and stewardship of this project throughout the publishing process. Thanks to everyone at HUP for all of the work you put in to make this book a success. I received two very generous readers' reports that each helped me see better the project's flaws and strengths. Thanks to Chris Walsh, who wrote one of the reports, for the singular pleasure of having my writing responded to by an ideal reader.

I've already singled out Jim Lang for his help as I started my work on college pedagogy; he's been a source of wisdom and guidance and a role model whom I've blatantly patterned myself after. Other people from the world of teaching and learning who have made my path easier include Kevin Gannon, Josh Eyler, Sarah Rose Cavanagh, Kimberly Tanner, and John Warner. Thanks, as well, go to Mark Salisbury, for generously sharing his research and insights.

Ben Hassman once asked me, with a straight face, how long I've been bald. He has otherwise been a great friend, an inspiring colleague, and a source of much wisdom when I've had trouble thinking through some teaching challenge or another. Likewise, Charlie Williams is a much better and more dedicated teacher than he lets on, and I've gained a ton from talking to him about pedagogy. Everyone who knows Megan Knight knows that she's kind of a classroom genius; let me at least put that fact in print. I've learned so much from Megan she should really be getting a cut of this book's royalties. I'm singling out these three, but my thanks extend to all my Rhetoric colleagues for their support and camaraderie.

Thanks are also due to Jen Buckley, Adam Hooks, Naomi Greyser, Katie Hassman, Matt Gilchrist, Shea Brown, Brady Krien, and Laura Hayes. Just seeing these names in print makes me grateful all over again for having such smart and generous teachers for friends.

Jim Clements deserves special thanks for helping shape up this book's proposal, and for years of conversations about teaching that have made me a better teacher, and a better writer.

To my parents and brothers and sisters-in-law and grandmother: thank you for your love and support. To Miodrag and Natalija Perovic: thank you for treating me just like a son.

My daughters Alice and Louise have taught me more about teaching—and much else besides—than I can say. They make everything worth it. Thank you, girls, for being so *wonderful*, every day.

Katarina Perovic deserves far more thanks than I could ever express here. She supports me in everything I do, and that support has allowed me to accomplish far more than I ever could have on my own. This book is dedicated to her.

Index

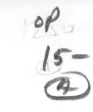

Dostoevsky and the Legend

of the Grand Inquisitor

Dostoevsky and the Legend of the Grand Inquisitor

by Vasily Rozanov

*

Translated and with an Afterword

by Spencer E. Roberts

Cornell University Press

ITHACA AND LONDON

First published 1972 by Cornell University Press. Published in the United Kingdom by Cornell University Press Ltd., 2–4 Brook Street, London W1Y 1AA.

International Standard Book Number 0-8014-0694-3
Library of Congress Catalog Card Number 79-37754

PRINTED IN THE UNITED STATES OF AMERICA
BY VAIL-BALLOU PRESS, INC.

Librarians: Library of Congress cataloging information appears on the last page of the book.

Acknowledgments

Grateful acknowledgment is made to the following publishers for permission to reprint brief excerpts from copyrighted materials: to Hillary House Publishers, Ltd., New York, and Bowes and Bowes, Ltd., London, from Renato Poggioli's *Rozanov* (1962); and to Fink Verlag, Munich, from Dmitrij Tschiževskij's "Neskol'ko slov o myslitele i pisatele Rozanove," the Introduction to Fink's reprint of *Legenda o velikom inkvizitore* (1970).

Thanks are also due to Emilia Häusler, without whose constant encouragement the translation would not have been completed.

Contents

Translator's Preface

That much quoted critic of Russian literature D. S. Mir-
sky called Vasily Rozanov "the greatest writer of his generation." Few who are well acquainted with Rozanov's
work would say that this estimate is far off the mark, although they might prefer simply to call him a writer and
thinker of genius. That Rozanov has not been published in
his native country since his death in 1919 is no reflection
on the quality of his work: He was a political conservative
and devoted much of his writing to sex and religion; thus,
from the official Soviet viewpoint, he is dangerous and sub-
versive.

In 1891, Rozanov published, in several issues of *The Russian Messenger*, *Dostoevsky and the Legend of the Grand
Inquisitor*. It was the first serious scholarly attempt to look
deep inside Dostoevsky in order to observe the workings
of his mind and discover the origins of his ideas. It was also
the first time that anyone, while considering Dostoevsky's
ideological and artistic development, had placed great stress
on *Notes from the Underground*. Indeed Rozanov shows
a remarkable understanding here of Dostoevsky's mind and
soul, certainly a far deeper understanding than anyone had
up till then. (Undoubtedly he had obtained much help in
this matter from Dostoevsky's former mistress, Apollinaria
Suslova, whom Rozanov had married.) As a critic has
noted, one senses in the book almost a spiritual kinship

between the two men. Like his contemporary Lev Shestov, who a few years later was to write his brilliantly perceptive book *Dostoevsky and Nietzsche: The Philosophy of Tragedy*, in which the influence of *The Inquisitor* is obvious, Rozanov sees Dostoevsky as a man who is without faith but who longs for it deeply, as a man on the side of his godless heroes.

The book is also noteworthy for its attempts, in the early chapters, to establish Dostoevsky's place in Russian literature and to re-examine Gogol's previously established position. According to Rozanov, Gogol was no realist: He did not portray live human beings in his works, but a long series of "dead souls." Gogol's "soulless dark genius" and strange humor repelled him, as did the writings of the positivists and radicals because of their political views. Tolstoy pleased him because of the atmosphere of domesticity in his works, but displeased him because of his tendency to teach. Chekhov left him indifferent: "He's nothing special. I can understand his success, but I don't approve." But Dostoevsky, who always moved him and whom he called a "pregnant big-loined writer," appealed to him in almost every respect. Russian literature after Gogol, he claimed, did not follow Gogol's methods of character portrayal, but represented a complete rejection of them. Because this idea met with some resistance from the critics, Rozanov included two essays [1] in the book, expanding on his argument and offering some facts to support his earlier conclusions. At any rate, *The Inquisitor*, along with Shestov's book, is one of the better studies on Dostoevsky to come

[1] They, as well as Shestov's book, appear in English in *Essays in Russian Literature: The Conservative View*, translated and introduced by Spencer Roberts (Athens: Ohio University Press, 1968).

[x]

out of prerevolutionary Russia. It set the trend, a few years later in the age of symbolism, of interpreting Dostoevsky as a kind of prophet, a source of revelation, and it gave rise to outstanding books in a similar vein, by Merezhkovsky, Berdyaev, Ivanov, and others. Thus, the book was influential, and one finds it difficult to understand why it was not translated into English long ago.

A characteristic of Rozanov's style is his constant use of italics. This is justifiable in his later works, where, along with numerous other typographical devices, it is intended to give the effect of actual speech. But here, where its purpose is merely emphasis, and where it is greatly overworked, it tends to jar. Moreover, to indicate each time in the numerous quotations the origin of the italics would be to scatter the pages with obstacles. Therefore, I have dispensed with most of them.

Here and there, while quoting Dostoevsky, Rozanov omits a word or two. As these omissions are insignificant, I have corrected them without so indicating in a footnote. In a few instances, I have also removed from the footnotes page numbers referring to early Russian editions of Dostoevsky's works, and in one case, I have shortened a long footnote. My own notes are marked [Tr.], to distinguish them from Rozanov's. Otherwise, what appears here is the complete text of the third edition of the book, minus the appendix.

SPENCER E. ROBERTS

Brooklyn College
The City University of New York

Dostoevsky and the Legend of the Grand Inquisitor

by Vasily Rozanov

And God said, "The man has become like one of us, knowing good and evil; what if he now reaches out his hand and takes fruit from the tree of life also, eats it and lives forever?"

So the Lord God drove him out of the Garden of Eden to till the ground from which he had been taken. Genesis 3

In one of his fantastic stories, Gogol tells of an old moneylender, who, as he was dying, summoned an artist and implored him to paint his portrait. Having begun the work, the artist suddenly felt an irresistible disgust for what he was doing, and mixed in with his disgust there was a kind of fear. The moneylender, however, kept a close eye on the progress of the work, his face shone with a kind of longing and anxiety—but when he saw that at least the eyes were finished, his face flashed with joy. The artist backed several steps away to take a look at his painting, but no sooner did he glance at it than his knees began to tremble: the eyes of the unfinished portrait shone with life, with real life, with the very life that was already dying out in his model, and which by some mysterious magic had been transferred to this copy. The palette and brush fell from his hands, and he ran from the room in terror. Several

[3]

hours later, the moneylender died. The artist ended his days in a monastery.[1]

For some reason or other, this story automatically came to mind when I decided to speak of Dostoevsky's famous "Legend of the Grand Inquisitor." Despite all its unreality, there seems to flash in it also a kind of truth, and, most likely, that was what had led it out into the light of my consciousness from a series of other half-forgotten stories and connected the thought of it with the subject that interests us now. Did not Gogol express in it a certain secret of the artistic soul, perhaps after having recognized it in himself? That life which had passed over to the work of art, that yearning desire not to die before such a transfer had been accomplished—all this seems to remind us of something that is of primary importance in the life of artists, poets, and composers themselves. In Gogol's story, however, the embodied and the embodier are separate, and this masks the hidden allegory. Combine the two, and you will get an idea of the fate and personality of every great creative talent.

In that place "from whose bourn no traveller returns," there is, of course, life; but we have never been told anything about it, and, in all probability, it is a life that is quite special, too abstract for our living desires, somewhat cold and spectral. That is why man so clings to the earth, so fears to be separated from it; but, since this is nevertheless inevitable sooner or later, he makes every effort to see that his separation from it is not complete. The thirst for

[1] Rozanov is referring here to the original version of "The Portrait," which Gogol had published in 1835, in *Arabesques*. A later revised version, published in 1842, presents this incident somewhat differently. [Tr.]

[4]

immortality, for an earthly immortality, is the most amazing feeling in man, and it is one that is quite obvious. Is this not why we so love our children, why we tremble for their life more than for our own, which is already fading? And when we have the joy of living to see their children as well, why we attach ourselves to them even more closely than we do to our own? Even in a moment of complete doubt as to the existence of life beyond the grave, we find here a certain consolation: "Even though we die," we say in our heart, snuggling up to our earth, which we find so dear, "our children will remain behind, and after them, their children." [2] But this kind of immortality, this life of our blood after we have become a mere handful of ashes, is much too incomplete: it is a kind of severed existence, distributed among countless generations, and it does not preserve the main thing that we love in ourselves—our individuality, the whole of our personality. The life that is attained in great works of the spirit is incomparably more complete; in them, the creator immortalizes his personality with all its special traits, with all the windings of his mind and the secrets of his conscience. At times he does not wish to reveal some side of his soul, and yet the thirst in him for immortality, for an individual life different from all others is so great that he conceals and secretes it among other things, and, all the same, he leaves in his works a reflection of this side of him. Centuries pass, the necessary feature is revealed, and there arises the complete image of one who is no longer afraid of being embarrassed before other people. "Build your pyramid to yourself higher, poor man," [3] says Gogol, as if filled with these feelings.

[2] F. M. Dostoevsky, *A Raw Youth*.
[3] N. V. Gogol, *Arabesques*, Part II, "Life."

At any rate, the feeling of joy experienced during this creative work serves at least as a sort of bright spot in the midst of the darkness that usually surrounds the soul of great poets, artists, and composers. So deeply and so often irrevocably cut off from the living world of people surrounding them, from their joys and sorrows, they feel themselves linked across the centuries with other generations of people; they mentally live in their life, they help them in their work, and they rejoice at their joys. It is a strange and somewhat fantastic life, whose features, however, we observe when we carefully read all outstanding biographies. It was not without reason that the late Professor Usov, a naturalist, but at the same time a connoisseur of art, called Gogol's world "a world of illusion."[4]

It is remarkable that with almost every creator in the field of art, we find one center, now and then several, but always few, around which all his works are grouped: these works represent, as it were, attempts to express some agonizing thought, and when it is finally expressed, there appears a creation that is warmed by the supreme love of its creator and bathed in an unfading light for others, whose hearts and minds are attracted to it by an irresistible force. Such are Goethe's *Faust*, Beethoven's "Ninth Symphony," and Raphael's "Sistine Madonna." They are the supreme products of mental activity; they are loved by mankind and known as what it is capable of in its best moments, which, of course, are as rare in world history as are moments of particular lucidity in the life of every man.

And it is on one such work that we wish to pause. It

[4] See P. Ivantsov, "Recollections of the Views of S. A. Usov on Art," in Book III of *Problems of Philosophy and Psychology* (Moscow, 1890).

[6]

is, however, permeated with a peculiar kind of agony, as is all the creative work of the writer we have chosen, as is his very personality. It is the late Dostoevsky's "Legend of the Grand Inquisitor." As is generally known, this is but one episode in his last work, *The Brothers Karamazov*, but its connection with the plot of that novel is so slight that it can be regarded as a separate work. On the other hand, instead of an outer tie between the novel and the "Legend," there is an inner one: namely, the "Legend" constitutes, as it were, the heart of the whole work, which is only grouped around it as variations are around their theme; in it is concealed the author's cherished idea, without which not only this novel would never have been written, but many of his other works as well: at least they would lack all their best and most sublime passages.

.

I

As early as 1870, in a letter to Apollon N. Maikov,[1] dated March 25, Dostoevsky wrote among other things of his plan for a large novel, which he had been turning over in his mind for the past two years and would now like to write, taking advantage of some free time. "The idea of this novel," he said in the letter, "is the same one I already wrote you about. It will be my *last novel*. In length, it will equal *War and Peace*, and I think you would praise the idea of it—at least in so far as I can judge from our earlier conversations. This novel will consist of five long stories (about fifteen signatures each; during these past two years, the plan has completely matured in my mind). The stories will be completely independent of each other, so that they could even be sold separately. The first story I have earmarked for Kashpirev: [2] in it, the action takes place in the forties. The overall title of the novel is: *The Life of a Great Sinner*,[3] but each story will have a title of its own. The main question that will be discussed in all the parts is

[1] Apollon Maikov (1821–1897), an "imaginist" poet whom Dostoevsky highly respected and whom he found a stimulating correspondent. [Tr.]

[2] The editor of the magazine *Dawn*, who had invited Dostoevsky to complete a story by autumn of that year.

[3] I have given this title (*Zhitie velikogo greshnika*) its usual English translation; I should, however, point out that it does not quite convey the Russian meaning. "*Zhitie*," an Old Church Slavic word, means rather "the life of a saint," his "*vita*," and thus provides a nuance that the English translation fails to convey. [Tr.]

[8]

the same one that has tormented me consciously and unconsciously all my life—the existence of God. During the course of his life, the hero is at times an atheist, at times a believer, at times a fanatic and a dissenter, and at times again an atheist. The second story will take place entirely in a monastery. On this second story, I have placed all my hopes. Maybe people will say, finally, that I have not always written trifles. I am confiding this only to you, Apollon Nikolaevich: I want to make Tikhon Zadonsky [4] the leading character of the second story—of course, under a different name, but there will also be a bishop living in retirement in the monastery. A thirteen-year-old boy, who had participated in the perpetration of a crime, precocious and depraved (I know the type), the future hero of the whole novel, is put into the monastery by his parents (our set, cultured) to be educated. This wolf-cub and boy-nihilist becomes a close friend of Tikhon's (you know Tikhon's character and whole person, don't you?). Here also in this monastery, I shall confine Chaadaev [5] (of course, also under a different name). Why shouldn't Chaadaev be made to spend a year in a monastery? Suppose that after writing his first article, as a result of which doctors had to examine his state of mind weekly, he could no longer re-

[4] Tikhon Zadonsky (1724–1783), a hierarch of the Russian Orthodox Church. From 1767 on, he lived as an ordinary monk, first in the Tolshevsky and later the Zadonsky Monastery, where he was admired for his piety and asceticism. He was canonized in 1860. [Tr.]

[5] Peter Chaadaev (1794–1856), a liberal aristocrat who fell under the influence of mystical Catholicism. In his first "Philosophical Letter," published in 1836, he rejected the Russian heritage and urged that the country unite with Western civilization and the Catholic Church. Tsar Nicholas I declared Chaadaev insane and had him confined to his home. [Tr.]

strain himself and published, for example, abroad, a pamphlet in French—it could very well have been that the authorities would have confined him for this for a year in a monastery. Guests and various other people could come to see Chaadaev. Belinsky,[6] for example, Granovsky,[7] or even Pushkin. (Of course, Chaadaev isn't in my novel; I'm only using his type.) In the monastery, there is also Paul Prussky, there is Golubov, and monk Parfeny (I'm an expert on this world and have known the Russian monastery since childhood). But most important is Tikhon and the boy. For heaven's sake, don't tell anyone the contents of this second part . . . I'm confiding this only to you. To others, this might not be worth a cent, but to me it is a treasure. And don't say anything about Tikhon. I wrote Strakhov [8] about the monastery, but said nothing about Tikhon. Maybe I'll portray a majestic, *positive*, and saintly figure. It will certainly not be a Kostanzhoglo [9] or the German in *Oblomov;* [10] nor will it be a Lopukhov or a Rakhmetov.[11] To tell the truth, I shan't invent anything at all,

[6] Vissarion Belinsky (1811–1848), a liberal, the founder of modern Russian literary criticism. [Tr.]

[7] Timofei Granovsky (1813–1855), a history professor, the father of the original Westerners. [Tr.]

[8] Nikolai Strakhov (1828–1896), an idealist philosopher, a literary critic, a friend of Dostoevsky and Tolstoy, and a contributor to Dostoevsky's magazine *Time.* [Tr.]

[9] The gentleman-farmer in Part II of *Dead Souls.* Gogol wanted to make him a combination of practicality and all the moral virtues. [Tr.]

[10] How do we know: perhaps it is precisely Tikhon who is the Russian *positive* type that our literature has been looking for, and not Lavretsky, not Chichikov, not Rakhmetov, etc." (A postscript of Dostoevsky's to the letter.)

[11] The latter two are the heroes of Nikolai Chernyshevsky's novel *What Is to Be Done?*

but will merely portray the real Tikhon, whom I took to my heart enthusiastically a long time ago. And if it succeeds, I'll consider even this an important achievement for myself. Now don't let anyone know. But for the second novel, for the monastery, I must be in Russia.[12]

Who does not recognize in the hasty and disconnected lines of this letter the first draft of *The Brothers Karamazov*, with its Father Zosima and its pure figure of Alyosha (evidently the divided figure of Tikhon Zadonsky), with its intelligent and depraved Ivan Karamazov (true, he is no longer a boy, but a young man now), with its trip to the monastery (the landowner Miusov is evidently the altered figure of Chaadaev), with its scenes of monastery life, etc.? But Dostoevsky's customary poverty upset his plans. Bound by urgent commitments that he had made to editorial staffs and booksellers, he was obliged to work strenuously, and although much of what he wrote at this time was excellent, nevertheless, none of it was the realization of his heart's dream and his already mature plan. Evidently, he was always waiting for the leisure time that would give him the opportunity to do his work without haste. In addition to his financial need, his sensitive nature was also a great hindrance in this matter; he could not, even for a short time, shut his eyes to current affairs, to the cares and problems of our life and literature. In 1876, he began to publish *The Diary of a Writer*, creating with it a new, original, and excellent form of literary activity, which will probably be destined to play a great role in all troubled times in the future. One might have feared that the extraordinary success of this publication would make it completely impossible

[12] See *Biography and Letters* (St. Petersburg, 1883), Part II, pp. 233–234.

for him to concentrate on some large, unified project, and, as in the case of many plans, the plan for the long novel that he had carefully thought out several years earlier would little by little be smothered and his very enthusiasm for it disappear.

But fate, so often uncharitable to great people from without, always treats with care whatever in them is inward, profound, and sincere. An idea with a future does not die with its bearers, even when death overtakes them unexpectedly or accidently. Even if only before its coming, submitting to some unconscious and irresistible urge, they tear themselves away from all that is secondary and do what is necessary—the most important thing of their life.

The disorderly and passionate Dostoevsky suddenly became silent before thousands of expectant eyes [13] and withdrew into himself, "in order to devote myself to a work of fiction." [14] He reassured the readers of the *Diary* that he needed no more than a year for the work, after which he would again return to his monthly chat with them. But the presentiment that he had expressed seven years earlier [15] was destined to come true: this piece of fiction that he was undertaking did indeed turn out to be his "last novel," and even his last unfinished literary work. In 1880 and 1881, only one issue of the *Diary* was published each year—one in a moment of particularly great animation,[16] another during a rest period between the first large

[13] For the success of *The Diary of a Writer*, see the statistics in *Biography and Letters*, Part I, p. 300.

[14] See *Diary of a Writer* (Dec., 1877): "To the Readers."

[15] See his letter above to Apollon Maikov.

[16] On the occasion of the Pushkin Celebration, the only issue for 1880. It contained Dostoevsky's Pushkin Speech and his comments on it.

section of the novel and the second, which was sup-posed "to be almost an independent whole." During this brief rest period, Dostoevsky was destined to end his days. The final volumes of this novel, which was to equal *War and Peace* in length, were not written. The fourteen books that make up the four parts (with the Epilogue) of *The Brothers Karamazov* are a full realization of the first section of this vast artistic epic. Here is what he writes in the Preface to *The Brothers Karamazov* about its overall plan: "Although there is one biography (of the hero, and which serves as the contents of the novel), there are two novels here. The main novel is the second one: it deals with the activity of my hero in our time, or at this very moment. But the first novel takes place thirteen years ago—and, properly speaking, it is no novel at all, but just a single epi-sode from my hero's early youth. It is impossible for me to do without this first novel, because much in the second one would be unintelligible without it."

Evidently, even the outer plan of this work, which he had nurtured for so long, was retained in *The Brothers Karamazov*. And everything necessary for its execution was also done now; in 1879, Dostoevsky made a trip to the famous Optina Pustyn Monastery to refresh his memory about monastery life. In the Elder of this monastery, Father Ambrosius, whose moral and religious authority guides the lives of thousands of people even to this day, he very likely found several valuable and living features for the positive character that he had conceived. But the original plan un-derwent some changes and acquired many additions. The positive figure of the Elder, whom Dostoevsky had wanted to depict in his novel, could not become its central charac-ter as he had originally intended: set in his ways and motionless, this figure could be sketched, but could not be brought into the action of the reported events. That is why Father Zosima makes only a brief appearance in *The Brothers Karamazov:* he blesses his favorite novice, Alyosha, before sending him out into the world to accomplish a spiritual feat, and then dies. Instead of Zosima, Alyosha had to become the central character of this whole complex work.[17] The moral characterization of Alyosha, as Dostoevsky depicts it, is in the highest degree remarkable. To see in this character nothing more than a repetition of the type of Prince Myshkin (the hero of *The Idiot*) would be a gross blunder. Prince Myshkin, like Alyosha, is pure and irreproachable, but he knows no inner movement, he is devoid of passions, owing to his sickly nature; he aspires to nothing, he seeks to accomplish nothing, he only observes life, but does not participate in it. Thus, passivity is his distinguishing feature. On the contrary, Alyosha's nature is first and foremost active, and at the same time it is lucid and serene. Doubts,[18] even sensual passions[19] and the susceptibility to anger[20]—there is everything in this complete human character, and at the same time he has in him a certain deep understanding of the many-sidedness of human nature: he is somehow close to and intimate with every person with whom he has to deal. His brother Ivan and Rakitin, the debauched old man his father, and the boy Kolya Krasotkin—

[17] This is definitely stated even in the Preface to *The Brothers Karamazov.*

[18] See his thoughts and words after the death of Father Zosima.

[19] One of his conversations with Rakitin, where he, "a virgin," admits that the Karamazov "storms of passion" are much too intelligible to him.

[20] The conversation with his brother Ivan about the sufferings of children.

[14]

are all equally accessible to him. But in trying to understand the inner life of another person, he always remains resolute and independent inside himself. He contains an indestructible nucleus, from which run all-penetrating fibers, capable of attaching themselves to, of struggling against, and of overcoming the inner contents of other people. And yet this person, already so strong, appears before us as a mere adolescent—an amazing figure, making an appearance for the first time in our literature. There is no doubt that with the ending (or, more precisely, the main part) of *The Brothers Karamazov* unfinished, we are robbed of many revelations about the human soul, or that it would have contained words that would indeed clarify our path of life. But that was not destined to be; in the part of the novel that we possess, Alyosha only prepares to accomplish a spiritual feat: he listens more than he speaks, from time to time he inserts remarks into the conversations of others, sometimes he asks questions, but mostly he observes in silence. However, all these features, which outline the character, but do not as yet fully express it, have been drawn so cleverly and accurately that even this unfinished figure already sparkles before us with real life. In it, we already perceive a moral reformer, teacher, and prophet, whose breathing, however, stops the instant his mouth is ready to open—a phenomenon unique in literature, and not only in ours. If we wanted to look for an analogy, we would find it not in literature, but in our painting. It is the figure of Jesus in Ivanov's well-known picture: this figure is also distant, but it is already approaching; for the time being, it is moving inconspicuously among other people standing closely together, but nevertheless it is central and dominant over them. Alyosha's image will be remembered in our literature. His name even now is mentioned whenever people encounter some rare and comforting phenomenon in life; and if we are destined some day to be regenerated to something new and better, it is quite possible that he will be the guiding star of that regeneration.

If Alyosha Karamazov is only outlined in the novel and not allowed his say, then his brother Ivan is both outlined and allowed to have his say ("The Legend of the Grand Inquisitor"). Thus, regardless of Dostoevsky's intentions, in as much as he was unable to complete his novel, Ivan became the central figure of the whole work, i.e., strictly speaking, he did so, because the only other figure (Alyosha) that overshadows him did not have a chance to step forward and engage in a moral and ideological struggle with his elder brother. Thus, *The Brothers Karamazov* is really not yet a novel, its action has not even begun: it is only the prologue, without which "what follows would be unintelligible." However, to judge from the prologue, the whole work was bound to become a powerful one, the likes of which it would be difficult to find in world literature: only Dostoevsky, who was capable of containing in himself "both abysses, the abyss above and the abyss below," could write not a funny parody, but a real and serious tragedy of that struggle which for thousands of years already has been rending the human soul—the struggle between the denial of life and its affirmation, between the corruption of the human conscience and its enlightenment. Only Dostoevsky, who had experienced this struggle both in the sheer enthusiasm with which he worked on *Poor People*,[21] in the noisy Petrashevsky Circle, in the wilds

[21] See his recollections of this in *The Diary of a Writer* for January, 1877.

[16]

of Siberia among convicts, and in his long periods of isolation in Europe, only he could tell us with equal strength both the "pro" and the "contra" [22]—the "pro" without hypocrisy and the "contra" without vain conceit.

The characters of Dostoevsky's previous novels can be regarded as preparatory: Ivan Karamazov, portrayed in *The Brothers Karamazov*, is only the last and most complete spokesman of the type that wavers now to one side, now to the other, and who had earlier flaunted themselves before us, now as Raskolnikov and Svidrigailov (*Crime and Punishment*), now as Nikolai Stavrogin (*The Possessed*), and partly as Versilov (*A Raw Youth*). Alyosha Karamazov has his prototype in Prince Myshkin (*The Idiot*) and partly in the person of the narrator of the novel *The Insulted and Injured*. Old Karamazov, "with the profile of a Roman patrician of the time of the decline," who fathers children and then abandons them, who likes to talk of the existence of God "over a bit of cognac," but who, above all, likes to ridicule everything near and dear to man, is the consummation of the type represented by Svidrigailov and old Prince Valkovsky (*The Insulted and Injured*). Dmitry Karamazov, foolish and yet basically noble, a mixture of good and evil (but not deep-seated evil), is a new character. It seems that only the eternally hurried and excited Captain Lebyadkin (*The Possessed*) can remind us of him, at least slightly—of course, only outwardly. Another new character is the fourth brother, Smerdyakov, that illegitimate offspring of Fyodor Pavlovich and "stinking" Elizabeth, a mere fragment of a human being, a spiritual Quasimodo, a synthesis of everything servile in the human mind and the human heart. But this recurrence of leading

[22] The title of the two central books in *The Brothers Karamazov*.

characters not only does not detract from the merit of the Karamazov brothers, it increases our interest in them even more: Dostoevsky is first and foremost a psychologist; he does not depict everyday life, in which we constantly seek novelty, but the human soul, with its imperceptible windings and transitions, and in them, we follow the continuity above all, we want to know how some flow of thought resolves itself, what some frame of mind leads to. And from this point of view, *The Brothers Karamazov*, as a final work, is of inexhaustible interest. But in order to understand it fully, we must say a few words about the general significance of Dostoevsky's work.

II

The view[1] that all of our most recent literature derives from Gogol is well known. It would be more accurate to say that as a whole this literature is a rejection of Gogol, a struggle against him. It does indeed have its origin in him if we look only at the surface aspect of the matter—if we compare the devices of its artistic creation, its forms, and themes. Just as with Gogol, a whole series of subsequent writers—Turgenev, Dostoevsky, Ostrovsky, Goncharov, L. Tolstoy—deal only with actual life, and not with what is created in the imagination (Pushkin's "Gypsies," Lermontov's "Mtsyri"), with situations in which we all happen to

---

[1] It is, by the way, developed by Apollon Grigoriev in his article "A View of Contemporary Fiction and Its Historical Starting Point."

[18]

be at times, with relationships into which we all enter. But if we look at the matter from its inner aspect, if we compare, from the standpoint of content, Gogol's work with the work of his alleged successors, then we cannot help seeing that the two are diametrically opposed. True, his eyes as well as theirs were equally fixed on life: but what they saw in it and what they depicted have nothing in common with what he saw in it and depicted. Could not one say that a keen understanding of the inward impulses of man is the sharpest, the most constant, and most distinguishing feature of all our more recent writers? Behind all the actions, the situations, the relationships, we see everywhere in these writers the human soul as the hidden motive force and the creator of all the visible facts. Its agitations, its passions, its fall and enlightenment—these are the object of their constant attention. That is why their works contain so much that is thoughtful; why we love them so and regard the constant reading of their works as a way of obtaining the best possible humanizing education. Now if we turn to Gogol, after having concentrated our attention on this peculiarity as the most important thing of all, we will immediately sense in his work a terrible lack of this very feature—of this feature alone and in him alone. He called his principal work *Dead Souls* and without any foresight expressed in this title the great secret of his creative work and, of course, of himself. He was a brilliant "painter" of outer forms, and to their depiction (the only thing he was capable of) he gave, through some sort of magic, such vitality, almost a sculpturesque quality, that no one noticed that virtually nothing is concealed behind these forms, that there is no soul, that there is nothing that might carry them. It may very well be that the society he depicted was base and evil; it may very well be that it deserved to be ridiculed: but surely it consisted of people. Is it possible that the great moments of birth and death, the feelings of love and hate common to all human beings, had already vanished for him? And, of course, if not, then how could these figures he depicted for us as his heroes have responded to those great moments and experienced those universal passions? What was beneath their clothing—the only thing we can see on them—that could ever rejoice, regret, or hate as human beings do? And the question arises, if they were capable neither of love, of deep hate, of fear, nor of dignity, then why, after all, did they labor and acquire things, travel about, and transfer things from one place to another? Gogol once depicted children, and those children are the same ugly figures as their fathers, figures that also are only ludicrous, and which are ridiculed just as they are. Once or twice he described the awakening of love in a person, and we see with amazement that the only thing that kindles it is mere physical beauty, the beauty of the female body when viewed by a man (Andrii Bulba and the Polish girl); it acts instantaneously, and after the first moment, there is nothing more to say about it. There are none of those feelings and words that we hear in the plaintive songs of our folk, in the Greek Anthology, in German legends, and everywhere on the whole earth where people love and suffer instead of merely taking delight in the human body. Is it really possible that this was a dream for all mankind which Gogol had exposed, after having finally stripped away the reveries and shown reality? Perhaps it would be more correct to think not that mankind had dreamed and that Gogol alone saw the truth, but, on the contrary, that mankind had felt and known the truth, which it had reflected in the poetry of all nations for thousands of years, while Gogol himself had dreamed and told us his morbid dreams as if they were reality?

"And why must I perish like a worm?" asks the hero of *Dead Souls* in a difficult moment after having been forced to leave the Customs Service:

> And what am I now? What am I good for? How can I look a respectable family-man straight in the face? How can I help being conscious-stricken when I know that I am burdening the earth for nothing? And what will my children say afterwards? "You see," they will say, "our father was a beast; he didn't leave us a fortune."
>
> We already know that Chichikov was greatly concerned about his offspring. It is such a ticklish subject! Many a person would perhaps never have thrust his hand so deeply into another man's pocket if it hadn't been for this question, which, for some unknown reason, automatically arises: "What will my children say?" And so this future father, like a cautious tom-cat, looking askance with only one eye to see if the master is watching, quickly snatches everything closest to him, whether it is soap, candles, or suet.[2]

What horror! What despair! And is this really the truth? Surely we have seen old women in city and country churchyards, sitting and crying over the graves of their husbands, even though those husbands had left them in the rags in which they themselves had lived. Have there really been children anywhere, who, as they saw their father dying, went up to their mother and asked: "Will he leave us a fortune?" Surely it is not possible that all the incom-

[2] *Dead Souls* (edition of 1873).

parable poetry of our folk lamentations,[3] by no means inferior to the poetry of *The Lay of Igor's Campaign*, is nothing but falsehood and fabrication. What images, what heartfelt grief, what hopes and recollections! And what a dull, lifeless view of reality one must have had to miss all this, to fail to hear these sounds, to fail to ponder over these sobs. Gogol had a dead view of life, and he saw nothing in it but dead souls. He did not in the least reflect reality in his works, but only drew with amazing skill a series of caricatures of it: and because of this, they stick in our memory in a way that no living images can ever stick. Look carefully at a number of the best portraits of people who are actually alive, people clothed in flesh and blood—and it is a rare one of them that you will remember; but take a look at a very good caricature—and for a long time afterward, even if you wake up in the middle of the night, you will remember it and burst out laughing. In the former, there is a mixture of various features, of both good and bad tendencies, and as they intersect they mutually soften each other; there is nothing bright or sharp in them that strikes us. But in a caricature, one character trait has been singled out, and the whole figure reflects it alone—both by a facial grimace and by unnatural convulsions of the body. It is false, and it sticks in our memory forever. Such is the method of Gogol.

And herein lies the explanation of his whole personality and fate. Acknowledging his genius, we stop before him in amazement. And when we ask ourselves: "Why is he so

---

[3] See *Lamentations of the Northern Region*, collected by Barsov. "Yaroslavna's Lament," the most poetic passage in *The Lay of Igor's Campaign*, is evidently a folk lamentation transferred to that work. Compare the language, the images, and the turns of speech.

unlike everyone else," [4] "What makes him so special," we automatically begin to think that this "specialness" is not a surplus of humanity in him, not a plenitude of strength beyond the normal limits of our nature, but, on the contrary, a deep and horrible flaw in that nature, a lack of something everyone else has, of something no one is deprived of. He was so isolated in his soul that he could not come into contact by means of it with any other soul: and that is why he so sensed all the "sculpturesqueness" of outward forms, movements, appearances, and situations. It is said that Gogol—a friend of Pushkin, a contemporary of Granovsky and Belinsky, a member of the Slavophile Circle during the best and purest time of its existence—"could

[4] In *Selected Passages from Correspondence with Friends,* one can virtually find all the information necessary to determine the inner process of his creative work. Here is one of those clear and precise passages: "I have already rid myself of many of my shortcomings by transferring them to my *leading characters,* by ridiculing them in those characters and making other people as well laugh at them . . . This will also explain to you why I have not yet depicted for the reader any comforting phenomena or chosen virtuous people as my heroes. One can't think them up in one's head. Until one begins to resemble them a bit oneself, until one acquires by persistence and by force several good qualities in one's own soul, carrion is all that will come from one's pen." ("Four Letters to Various Persons apropos *Dead Souls*"—from the third letter.)

This is a fairly clear expression of the subjective method by which he created all the characters in his works; features of his own soul are forced outward, and there is no mention at all of copying them from something outside himself. Also defined here is the very process of his creation: he takes a single defect, the essence of which is well-known to him from his subjective life, and he draws an illustration of it, or an illustration "with a moral." It is clear that every feature of this figure reflects in itself, in its own way, this defect alone, for the character being portrayed has no other purpose. And this is the essence of caricature.

[23]

not find a positive character as a model for his creations." And we ourselves sense in him the scalding, much too "visible" tears that he shed for something unrealizable, for some supposed "ideal." Is there not a mistake here in the choice of words, and once the necessary one is substituted, will we not guess his whole secret? It was not an ideal that he was unable to find and express; he, this great artist of forms, was consumed by his impotent desire to put into at least one of them some sort of a living soul. And when he nevertheless could not overcome this irrepressible need, there appeared in his works fantastic monsters such as the unnatural Ulinka and the Greek Kostanzhoglo, who resemble nothing in either the dream world or reality. And he was finally consumed by his helpless craving to come into contact with a human soul. What we are told about his last days is rather vague: a kind of madness, horrible pangs of remorse, fasting, and death from starvation.[5]

What a lesson from our history we failed to understand! A brilliant artist portrayed man all his life and yet was unable to portray the soul. He told us that the soul does not exist, and in depicting his dead characters he did it with such skill that for several decades we actually believed in a whole generation of walking corpses. We came to hate that generation, we spared no words that man can say about soulless creatures. But he, the perpetrator of this deception, suffered a punishment that still lies in store for us in the future. He died the victim of a flaw in his own nature —and the last image he left us from the whole of his strange

[5] Note what Ivan Turgenev says of him in *My Literary Memoirs:* "What a clever and what a morbid creature!" See also F. I. Buslaev's *My Leisure Time* for Gogol's historic words, addressed a few days before his death to the *comedian* Shchepkin: "Always remain as you now are."

and so extraordinary life is that of an ascetic burning his own works. "Vengeance is mine! I will repay, saith the Lord"—it is as if we hear these words from within the crackling in the fireplace into which this madman of genius has thrown his brilliant and criminal slander of human nature.

What people do not grasp with their reason, they sometimes grasp all the more strongly with their feelings. After Gogol, all our literature turned to a penetration of human nature. And was not the result of this counterforce that at no other time and with no other people have all the innermost recesses of the human soul been so thoroughly revealed as they have in the last few decades, before the eyes of us all? There is nothing more striking than the change one experiences in turning from Gogol to any of our more recent writers: it is as if one passes from a cemetery into a flowering garden, where everything is filled with sounds and colors, with sunshine, and with the life of nature. For the first time we hear human voices, we see joy and anger on people's faces, we know how funny they sometimes are: and nevertheless we love them, because we feel they are people and, consequently, our brothers. In a number of Turgenev's little stories, we find the same villages, fields, and roads over which the hero of *Dead Souls* perhaps traveled, the same small provincial towns in which he signed his deeds of purchase. But how alive all this is in Turgenev, how it breathes and moves, how it enjoys itself and loves! Before us are the same peasants, but they are no longer a couple of idiots, who, in order to separate the entangled horses climb on them for some unknown reason and hit them on the back with clubs. We see house servants and serfs, but they are not the eternally stinking Petrushka, and not Selifan, about whom we know only that he was always drunk. What a diversity of characters, sad and joyful, filled with practical cares or delicate poetry. While scrutinizing their lively and individual features, we begin to understand our history, our very selves, and all the life around us, which grew and spread so widely from the depths of this people. What a wonderful child's world unfolds before us in the daydreams of Oblomov, in the reminiscences of Netochka Nezvanova, in *Childhood and Adolescence*, in scenes of *War and Peace*, in the house of troubled Dolly in *Anna Karenina!* Is it really possible that all this is less a part of reality than are Alcides and Themistoklus, those pitiful dolls of Gogol, that vicious mockery of those whom no one has ever mocked before? And what about Bolkonsky's thoughts on the battlefield at Austerlitz, his sister's prayers, Raskolnikov's anxieties, and that whole complex, diverse world of ideas, characters, and situations that recedes into the infinite distance, and which has been revealed to us in the last few decades—what shall we say of it in connection with Gogol? What word can we use to define its historical significance? Should we not say that it is a revelation of the life that had died in Gogol, a restoration in man of the dignity which Gogol had taken from him?

III

Earlier than others, Dostoevsky began to speak about the life that pulsates behind the most stifling of forms, about the human dignity that survives under the most impossible conditions. In his tiny and charming story "An Honest Thief," we see two figures, the kind we pass by every day without noticing them. A poor little corner of a room, simple speech, an everyday event—all this is like a ray of light falling on our soul from some distant world. For a moment we forget our own thoughts and desires and carefully examine this ray. Characters whom we earlier knew only from without now become translucent before our eyes, and we see the heart that beats in them. Several minutes pass, the ray disappears, and again we return to the usual flow of our ideas. But something in our ideas has already changed, something in them is no longer possible, and something from now on and forever more has become inevitable: inevitable, a concern for human beings, however far from us they are; impossible, contempt for human beings, wherever we meet them. Despite all the wisdom we absorb, despite the high level of our intellect, we now sometimes suddenly stop and ask ourselves: is *our* inner world as pure, *our* heart as warm as the hearts in these wretched and poor folk whom we saw only for a moment and shall always remember? And the words of the Apostle become clearer to us than ever before: "Though I speak with the tongues of men and of angels, and have not charity, I am become as sounding brass, or a tinkling cymbal." We understand that in them is found the criterion of good and evil with which we shall never perish and with which we can measure all sorts of wisdom.

He who arouses understanding in us also arouses love in us. Following the author, we descend into the dreary world of human existence, hitherto concealed from us, and together with him we closely observe the living creatures swarming about down there. "You thought that they had

[27]

stopped suffering, that they no longer had any feelings," he says to us. "Listen to their talk, examine their faces: can you experience such emotion yourself, have you in a difficult moment received from the people around you such sympathy as that with which they warm each other in this darkness and in this cold? And see what faith lives in them, see how far removed they are from petty complaints, see how little they reproach each other, and see how patiently they bear their cross. Do you think they only work and eat, that they leave thinking and desiring to you? No, all your passions live also in them, and they understand a great deal that you do not. They are people, the very same people as you, people who have retained much of what you have lost, and who have managed to acquire all but a little of what you have acquired. You have seen them: now go, and if you can, forget this world."

And when you pause in doubt, he gives you a piercing look and continues: "Why don't you go? What is holding you back? Remember what has been awakened in you, and never forget conscience in your considerations—it lives in all men, and these are no exception. You see neither hands that are tired, nor feet that are cold, nor stomachs that are empty. You see before you millions of human souls, and when you get the idea that they must only be warmed, fed, and comforted, remember how you just now forgot about the food and sleep awaiting you. I have spoken. Now go and busy yourself with your philosophy or your antiquities. But I shall stay here with them, and if I am unable to share their labor, I shall at least share their sorrows, and sometime I shall perhaps rejoice at their joys."

Since then, in the midst of your philosophical and historical interests, in the midst of the whole glittering world

[28]

of beauty which rivets your attention in the arts and literature, you have sometimes experienced a feeling of alarm,
and you have recalled the strange man who once led you
into that world so different from everything you already
knew and who stayed there after having said his gloomy
words. Is he strong enough, and what will he do down in
that place over which thousands of years have rushed and
which has been covered over by our civilization? In free
moments, you pick up volumes of his stories the better to
study his face, to test the strength of his muscles and the
power of his mind.

Before you pass a number of his tales and stories. How
much in them is funny and serious, and at times impossibly
absurd:[1] he is just like a man who, in preparing to say
something, first sputters and makes inarticulate sounds. But
gradually his words begin to flow; you forget what is unnecessary and try to fathom the meaning of what he is
saying. What a wealth of feeling, what an understanding
of all that is most important for a person to understand!
Now, there unfolds before you a sad and at the same time
an amusing idyll ("A Faint Heart"); now, there is fragrant
poetry (*White Nights*); now, the burning passion of an
unfinished story, with its insane musician running down
the dark city streets accompanied by his young daughter
(*Netochka Nezvanova*); and now, a short story full of real
gaiety ("The Little Hero"); we inquire and learn that it
was written in several weeks, while Dostoevsky was confined to a fortress, awaiting trial, sentence, and perhaps
even execution. "Yes, this man is serious," we think automatically. "No matter what is contained in his inner world,
that world is stable if creative work can go on in it even

[1] For example, "A Novel in Nine Letters" and "The Landlady."

before the yawning grave." But most curious of all is the fact that he moves not only in that world where we left him; he rises easily to the one above, and here he devotes himself almost exclusively to the world of children (Princess Katya in *Netochka Nezvanova;* the tax-farmer's daughter in "A Christmas Tree and a Wedding"). In looking at that bright and innocent world, he is just as lucid and lively as he is down among the wretched poor folk. And the same concern is evident in him for that world as there is for those people who have been forgotten by everyone else: how mistrustful and gloomy his look becomes when this world of children at play is approached by adults! Here before us stands Julian Mastakovich, counting on his fingers the age of a little girl and the interest on the capital that has been deposited in her name, the amount of which he had accidentally learned at the children's party: "Three hundred, three hundred," whispers this important dignitary, ". . . eleven, twelve, sixteen . . . five years; let's say at four percent, that makes twelve, five times twelve makes sixty, and the interest on those sixty . . . No, he wouldn't invest it at four percent, the rascal, maybe at eight or ten percent . . ."

He interrupts his calculations and steals on tiptoe up to the child, who is busy with her doll, and kisses her on the head:

"And what are you doing over here, my dear child?" he says in an agitated whisper.

The children's party ends with the lively amazement of the guests, watching with tender emotion the friendly conversation of the important dignitary and the child of the rich tax-farmer. The reader's eyes close and in five years open again: a gloomy day (as always in Dostoevsky), a

[30]

parish church, a beautiful girl, barely blossomed out, and her bridegroom, who is welcoming her. A whisper passes among the people about the bride's wealth; the bridegroom's somewhat older but recognizable features explain everything to the narrator—and he recalls the children's party on that frosty New Year's Eve five years earlier.

At that same party, among the merry figures of the children, he notes a persecuted little boy, the son of the governess of the house, with his agonizing desire to go up and play with the other children, who have been avoiding him. The child's mind already understands the differences in their social positions, but his childish nature is inclined to surmount them. He is shy and ingratiating—a party as lively will not soon come again—so he presses close to the other children, pretends not to notice their insults, and obsequiously flatters them so they will not drive him away. You feel that all the tinsel and riches are of secondary importance and that the author's gaze is fixed on what lives and moves behind all this—the human soul, its first suffering, its first mutilation.

"But is he strong enough . . . ?" In a somewhat fantastic sketch, whose plot and tone will later be repeated in *The Insulted and Injured*, Dostoevsky tells of the meeting of a lonely dreamer with a jilted girl. What strange meetings, what pensive and fervent confessions, and how tightly these two lonely and pure creatures hold each other's hands! In all our literature, there is no other story that so very, very deeply penetrates the inner world of the human soul to the point where one no longer hears the sounds of human life or sees its noisy bustle. Only the bright, moonless nights of the north look down from above on these two creatures, and they themselves look each with a clear conscience into the clear conscience of the other. But then a shadow flits past them as he is talking incoherently to her and pointing to the sky. That was on the fourth night, during their fourth meeting. She presses close to him, her hand trembles. A familiar voice, which she had so loved, which she had been accustomed timidly to obey, calls to her: with a cry, she rushes to the one she thought she had lost forever—to her disrupted happiness, believing she can arouse and return ardent love. The dreamer is left alone; he returns home. How old everything seems to have grown in his lonely little corner—the walls of his room, the house next door, even himself. In a passionate and imploring letter, she explains everything, she begs him not to reproach her, not to forget, in the same way that she herself will hold him in her memory forever. The letter falls from his hands, and he covers his face:

Either a sunbeam that had suddenly peeped out from behind a cloud had again hidden itself behind a rain cloud and everything had grown dim before my eyes, or maybe the whole cheerless and melancholy perspective of my future flashed before me, and I saw myself exactly fifteen years hence, the same as I am now, only grown older, in the same room, still alone and with the same Matryona, who had not in the least grown any wiser in all those years.

But that I should nurse my grudge against you, Nastenka! That I should cast a dark shadow over your bright and tranquil happiness! That I should bitterly reproach you and thus cause your heart to anguish, wound it with secret remorse, and make it beat sadly in a moment of bliss! That I should crush even one of those tender flowers that you entwined in your dark curls when you went to the altar with him . . . Oh, never, never! May your sky always be serene, may your sweet smile be bright and tranquil, and may you always be blessed for the moment of bliss and happiness that you gave to another lonely and grateful heart.[2]

Don't you agree that these words seem to be woven of moonlight? In them is the same repose, the same self-restraint, the same readiness to reflect only the happiness of another.

And then suddenly this tone:

I'm a sick man . . . I'm a spiteful man. I'm an un-attractive man. I think my liver is diseased . . .

—and one hears a muffled grumbling from the under-ground. We turn over several pages:

I'm convinced that not only a great deal of con-sciousness, but even all consciousness, is a disease. And nothing can change my opinion about that! But let's put this subject also aside for a moment. Tell me this: Why did it always happen as if on purpose in those very—yes, in those very moments when I was most capable of being conscious of all the niceties of "the lofty and beautiful" that I not only felt, but did such ugly things—things that everyone does, but which as if on purpose occurred to me precisely when I was most conscious that they should not be done at all? The more conscious I was of "goodness" and of all that is "lofty and beautiful," the more deeply I sank

2 *White Nights.*

[33]

into my mire, and the more ready I was to get completely stuck in it.

A few pages later:

> The direct, legitimate result of consciousness is inertia . . . I emphatically repeat: all "direct" people and men of action are active only because they are mentally underdeveloped. How is that to be explained? Well, here's how: owing to their shallowness, they take immediate and secondary causes for primary ones; thus, they persuade themselves more quickly and easily than other people that they have found an infallible basis for their business at hand, and, as a result, their minds are at ease, and that is surely the main thing. After all, to start to act, you must first have your mind completely at ease and have no doubts left in it. Now how can I, for example, set my mind at ease? Where are my primary causes on which I can lean, where are my foundations? Where am I to get them? I exercise my powers of thought and, consequently, with me, every primary cause immediately draws another one after it—one still more primary—and so on to infinity. That precisely is the essence of every kind of consciousness and reflection. Consequently, these again are the laws of nature.[3]

Shameful confessions and brilliant dialectics flash by. We see the gold pins that the bored Cleopatra stuck into the breasts of her female slaves. The "poetry" of well-known verses is trampled on:

---

[3] *Notes from the Underground.*

[34]

When from the darkness of delusion,
By a passionate word of persuasion
I rescued a fallen soul. . . .

and over the helplessly collapsed body of a girl who had
been regenerated and then tormented, there appears a vile
figure without a name, without a shape, and cries: "I am a
person." [4]

Yes, you think, this man is strong enough. A soul that
could produce as many different sounds and figures, and all
those thoughts, is capable of overcoming anything that man
is able to struggle against. Perhaps he is not listened to,
perhaps he is not understood: no prophet can turn the
sands of the desert into a rapt audience. But the sands will
not lie still forever on the boundless plains of history—
and then he will reap his harvest.

Simultaneously with this writer who so attracts us, there
came to the fore a group of others. Among them, the pensive and sleepy Goncharov, with his artistic love of man,
who wanders through God's boundless world in the bright
sunlight and, without paying any attention either to the
world or the sun, closely observes just one little corner of
it as he slowly draws his genre-pictures. Also among them
is the vain and weak Turgenev, a man of such great talent,
who pondered over so much; he leads us into the enchanting world of his word, drops ideas that stick in our memory, and depicts a series of characters that are somewhat

[4] See "Apropos of Wet Snow" in *Notes from the Underground*. The only analogy to this work, one of Dostoevsky's most
profound, is *Rameau's Nephew*, by Diderot. The first draft of the
character of the "man from the underground," but only from its
comic side, is Foma Fomich in *The Village of Stepanchikovo and
Its Inhabitants*.

[35]

pallid, yet always attractive. And finally there is also Tolstoy, whose strength seems to have no bounds, who reveals to us an immense panorama of human life everywhere
that its forms are complete and stable. We hesitate: absorbed in fulfilling their mission, never turning their eyes
away from it for a moment, these great artists irresistibly
attract everyone to them. In comparison with their creations, how false is everything created by the writer whom
we would like to investigate here: his characters are often
distorted, his speech lacks harmony; it seems to be a chaos
to which measure and number have not yet been applied,
or as if all measures and numbers have already been mixed
up. Our hesitation is especially great when we look at the
world of Tolstoy: it is not only the inexpressible charm of
his creations that attracts us here; there is something else,
something more profound and arresting. It is obvious to
us that he has participated in the Eleusinian Mysteries of
nature, that he listens to muffled sounds and peers into
dark shadows while pressed close to Mother Earth, from
whom all living things grow. He tries to catch the meaning
of each birth and each death within the narrow limits of
which the poor existence of man is confined. But ancient
legends tell us that even in the real Eleusis the meaning of
life and death is revealed to the initiated in allegorical
images and only from a distance. Evidently it is man's fate
to be limited to this for all eternity.

Alluring as this world of beauty is, something else is even
more alluring: the moral degradation of the human soul,
the strange disharmony of life, which completely drowns
its few harmonious sounds. In this disharmony are played
out the millennial destinies of mankind. And if we look at
world literature, we see that the eyes of no one in it have

been turned with such insight on the causes of this disharmony as were the eyes of the writer whom we have chosen
to study. That is why, despite the chaos in his works, we find
in no one else such wholeness and fullness. There is something in him that is blasphemous and at the same time religious. He does not choose a single scene from nature in
order to recreate it with love; he is only interested in the
seams by which all these scenes are drawn together. A cool
analyst, he examines them closely and wants to learn why
the whole image of God's world is so distorted and false.
And in some incomprehensible way he combines this analysis in himself with a feeling of the most ardent love for
everything that suffers. It is as if he has experienced the
distortion to which the face of God's world has been subjected, as if his own inner world has also been deeply affected by it. Like no one else, he clearly sensed all the
suffering that man bears within himself, and he came close
to understanding its hidden nature. From this comes the
great subjectivity of his works and their passion: not from
without does he call us to come and share with him his
interests, which we can engage in just like everyone else;
his voice reaches us as if from afar, and when we draw
near, we see a strange and lonely creature, who has no one
at all around him. And this creature tells us of the unbearable suffering of human nature, of the utter impossibility of
enduring it, and of the necessity of finding ways out of it.
Hence the morbid tone of all his works and the absence in
them of an outward harmony of parts. And the world he
reveals, a world of inconsolable suffering, is entwined with
the thought of its incomprehensible causes, of its unfathom-
able purposes.

And this is precisely what gives his works an eternal

meaning, an undying significance. It would be an anachronism at the present time to analyze the characters portrayed, for example, by Turgenev, although not so many years have passed since they were created: they corresponded to the interests of the moment, they were understood in their day, and now they have an attraction that is purely artistic. We love them as if they were living people, but there is nothing in them for us to puzzle out. With Dostoevsky, however, it is just the opposite: the anxiety and doubts diffused throughout his works are our anxiety and doubts, and they will remain so for all times to come. In periods when life rolls along with particular ease, or when we are unaware of its difficulty, this writer may even be completely forgotten and unread. But every time something inconvenient makes itself felt on the paths of historical life, every time the nations traveling along them are jolted or perplexed, the name and image of this writer who pondered so much over these paths are resurrected with no loss at all in their strength.

Where he summons us, to a world of distortion and suffering, to an examination of the very seams which hold nature together, there one can indeed go, after forgetting both the world of beauty revealed in the arts and poetry and the cold spheres of science, which are much too distant from our poor earth, a thing we can by no means forget. To go there means to satisfy the deepest demands of our heart, to which suffering is somehow related, for which it has an inexplicable propensity. And to set out with such a goal means to answer the chief demand that the mind repeatedly makes, despite all that science and philosophy do to try to distract it.

[38]

IV

In 1862,[1] Dostoevsky left Paris, where he had been passing the time, to visit London and its World Exhibition for a few days.[2] In an article that seems somewhat disorderly, but that actually is extremely coherent and concentrated, he tells of the impression made on him by this city "vast as the ocean and bustling by day and by night." He describes the screech and howl of its trains, with their railways running above the houses, with their chaotic movement and boldness of enterprise:

> The polluted Thames, the air filled with coal dust, the magnificent public gardens and parks, and the terrible sections of the city such as Whitechapel with its half-naked, wild, and hungry inhabitants. . . .[3]

All of it formed a whole picture for him the parts of which could not be separated. As everywhere else, he omits particular and transitory interests and ponders over the general meaning of the scene, over its eternal significance:

> You feel the terrible force that has brought together into a single flock all these countless people, who have

[1] Rozanov writes "1863," but this date is wrong. [Tr.]

[2] This was his first trip abroad. His first impressions of Europe are described *directly* in *Winter Notes on Summer Impressions* (1863) and also *indirectly* in many of his novels, where he even more completely and vividly expresses his general feelings toward Europe, as, for example, in parts of *A Raw Youth*, which are of great autobiographical significance.

[3] *Winter Notes on Summer Impressions.*

come from all over the world. You are conscious of a gigantic idea; you feel that something has already been achieved here, that there is victory and triumph here . . . For some reason or other you become terrified. You think: Can this, in fact, be the final realization of the ideal? Is this the end by any chance? Perhaps this is actually the realization of the "one fold" of the prophecy? . . . It takes your breath away: it is all so grand, so triumphal, and proud. You look at these hundreds of thousands, at these millions of people submissively streaming here from all over the world—people who have come with one thought in mind, calmly, stubbornly, and silently thronging in this colossal Crystal Palace,[4] and you feel that something final has been accomplished here—accomplished and completed. It is rather like a scene from the Bible, something having to do with Babylon, a sort of prophecy from the Apocalypse being fulfilled before your very eyes. You feel that a good deal of constant spiritual resistance and rejection is needed not to give in, not to succumb to impression, not to bow down before fact, and not to idolize Baal, i.e., not to take the actual for the ideal.

In everything that meets his eye, he looks for what has sprung up independently and which is, consequently, strong; everything borrowed, and, consequently, weak he disregards. In Rome he wanted to see the Pope, but in London he did not even take a look at St. Paul's Cathedral. On the other hand, he visited the "Sabbath of White Negroes," as he called Saturday night in the workers' quarters of the city:

[4] The Crystal Palace at the Exhibition.

Half a million male and female workers, with their children, spread like the ocean all over the city and celebrate the whole night long until five in the morning, eating and drinking enough to make up for the whole past week. All these people bring their weekly pay with them, everything they have earned by hard labor and cursing . . . Great jets of gas burn brightly, illuminating the streets. It is as if a ball is being given for these white negroes. The people throng in the taverns and in the streets. Here, too, they are eating and drinking. The pubs are decked out like palaces. Everyone is drunk, but without merriment; everyone is grim and gloomy, and everyone is strangely silent. Only now and then do curses and bloody brawls destroy this suspicious silence, which has such a sad effect on one. All these people hasten as quickly as possible to drink themselves unconscious . . . The wives do not lag behind their husbands in getting drunk; the children run and crawl about among them.

Dostoevsky notices that there is something in this loss of consciousness that is "systematic, resigned, and encouraged." With his generalizing mind, he tries to catch the hidden meaning of this observation as well and connect it with what he saw in the city during the day and with what cut such a proud figure with its completeness and perfection: this sweat, this sullen dissipation, this eagerness to forget oneself, if only for several hours a week—it all seems to him as if millions of human souls have been put in a corner of a tower that is being raised. True, this tower almost reaches the sky, but on the other hand, it presses heavily against the earth! For these social pariahs, it will be a long time before the prophecy comes true; it will be a long time before they will be given palm branches and white garments; and for a long time yet they will have to cry out to the throne of the Almighty: "How long, O Lord?"

This biblical imagery is, after all, only the greatest possible generalization of facts that history and philosophy could think up; and the "palm branches and white garments" are nothing but the thirst of millions of crushed beings for joy and light, of beings who now are the necessary appendages of monstrous machines, with completely useless remnants in themselves of a certain kind of consciousness. Dostoevsky sees only the whole of this matter: he does not see feet that are cold, nor hands that are tired, but a man who is crushed, and he asks: "Doesn't he also thirst for spiritual joy, isn't he worthy of it, in the same way that all of us are who cannot live without it?"

But these creatures are only crushed; they are not yet perverted: God's image has grown dim in them, but at least it is not disfigured. Dostoevsky visited the Haymarket, an area to which thousands of prostitutes flock at night. Brightly lit streets, cafes adorned with mirrors and gilt decorations . . .

> There are festival halls and night lodgings. It is terrifying to enter this crowd. And how strange is its composition! There are old women, and there are beautiful girls before whom you stop in amazement. In all the world, there are no women so beautiful as those in England. As there is not room enough for all these people on the sidewalks, they move into the streets and become a dense crowd. They are all on the lookout for prey and throw themselves with shameless

cynicism at the first person they come across. You see magnificent, expensive clothing and what almost amounts to rags, and a sharp difference in age—everything is all mixed together. In this terrible crowd, the drunken tramp strolls along beside the man of wealth and title. You hear cursing, quarreling, touting, and the enticing whisper of a still timid beauty. And what beauty you sometimes see here!

He describes a young woman of striking appearance, with a thoughtful and intelligent face, drinking gin; beside her sits a young man, evidently an unaccustomed visitor to this quarter.

> There was something repressed in her beautiful and somewhat proud look, something pensive and sad. She was—she could not but be—above this whole crowd of unfortunate women in her mental development; otherwise what is the significance of the human face?

It was obvious that the young man had sought her out here, that this was a prearranged meeting. Both of them were thoughtful and sad, they spoke in fits and starts, frequently lapsing into silence. Evidently something important remained unsaid between them. Finally, he got up, paid for the drinks, shook her hand, and left; she, her pale face covered with red blotches, mixed in with the crowd of prostitutes and disappeared.

> In the Haymarket, I noticed mothers who bring their very young daughters to walk the streets. Little girls of about twelve grasp you by the arm and ask you to go with them. I remember, one time I saw a girl of

about six, no older, all in rags, dirty, barefoot, drunk, and beaten up: her body, visible through her rags, was covered with bruises. She walked along as if unaware of what she was doing, hurrying nowhere. God only knows why she was staggering about in the crowd; maybe she was hungry. No one paid any attention to her. But what struck me most was the fact that she walked along with a look of such sorrow, of such hopeless despair on her face, that to see this little creature, also bearing in herself so much execration and despair, was somehow unnatural and terribly painful. She kept shaking her tousled head from side to side, as if she were discussing something; she would spread her little hands apart, gesticulate with them, and then suddenly clasp them together and press them to her bare little breast. I went back and gave her a sixpence. She took the silver coin, then shyly, with timid amazement, looked me in the eyes and suddenly took to her heels, as if afraid I would take the money from her.

And we can repeat: "How long, O Lord?" The World Exhibition, the Crystal Palace, somewhere in it a lecture by a famous physicist, accompanied by brilliant demonstrations —is all this worth the grief of that tiny creature, beating its thin little hands against its breast, and those women who bring their very young daughters to give to anyone who will toss them a coin? People will say: "That's the way it always was, and even worse." They are saying it already as justification and offer as proof the cannibalism of savages, saying that if we do not wish to return to that, we must put up with the evil in our society, the specific poison of civilization. But that is not true—it was not always like that.

With the nation that lived according to God's commandments, there was neither cannibalism, nor were there mothers who traded in their children's bodies: there, there were mothers who gathered the wheat that the rich had intentionally left behind on the fields for them.[5] And that would not happen with us, it would not dare happen if we carefully followed the words: "Seek ye first the kingdom of God . . . and all these things shall be added unto you."

But when the night passes and day begins, the same proud and gloomy spirit again sweeps regally over the gigantic city. It is not alarmed over what happened in the night, nor is it alarmed over what it sees around it during the day. Baal reigns, and does not even demand obedience, because he is convinced that he already has it. His faith in himself is boundless; he calmly and scornfully gives organized alms only to be left in peace. He does not close his eyes to the savage, suspicious, and alarming phenomena of life. The poverty, the suffering, the discontent, and the torpor of the masses do not in the least alarm him.

All these facts, as well as concern about their causes, can be formulated as follows: the aim of every normal process of development is the prosperity of the developing beings themselves. Thus, a tree grows in order to realize the completeness of its forms—and the same can be said about everything else. Of all the processes that we observe in nature, there is but one in which this law is violated, and that is in the historical process. Man is the developing element in it, and, consequently, he is its aim; but this is only in theory: in reality, he is a means, while the aim is the in-

[5] See the Book of Ruth.

stitutions, the complexity of social relations, the flowering
of the arts and sciences, the power of industry and trade.[6]
All this grows irresistibly, and it never occurs to the poor
man to oppose this trend, to refuse to lie down in front of
this triumphant chariot of Baal and to bespatter its wheels
with his blood.[7]

[6] There is a fact in history particularly suitable for an explanation of this idea: in Germany, by the time of the rebellions of the
knights and the peasants, Roman law had already spread over a
considerable part of the country, having supplanted the local
feudal customary law. The burden it placed on the entire population was so great that the insurgents, poor jurists and only simple
people, demanded, among other things, the abolition of Roman
law in juridical practice. But who would doubt that Roman law
was immeasurably superior not only to medieval legal customs, but,
in general, to everything that world history had ever known in this
field? It did not, therefore, cease to spread. It was natural and, so
to say, inwardly necessary. This example shows that the perfection
of individual branches of life is by no means necessarily linked
with a diminution of human suffering, that it has an inner regularity
and is outwardly autonomous; therefore, it is achieved in history
independently of all else.

[7] A specific example can here, too, conveniently explain the
general historical process: (1) for a country to maintain its international position, it must have several hundred thousand men
engaged specifically in the art of war, and for their greatest possible perfection in it, they must be freed from the cares of family
life; (2) it is necessary that the people who keep the country up
to the mark in its spiritual and material prosperity prepare themselves as well as possible to carry out their mission and that they
enter as deeply as possible into the complex and difficult world of
the pure and applied sciences. Thus, a huge contingent of people
is formed for whom a family is possible and convenient only at a
somewhat late age. For reasons unnecessary to explain, a corresponding contingent of single women arises—the difference being,
however, that for the former, a family is something belated, and
its temporary absence is a convenience, whereas for the latter, a
family becomes impossible forever, and they are an impersonal

[46]

And the nations go on stretching themselves out in front of it. After crushing millions in its own country, the chariot is already crossing over into other countries, to those cannibals who thus far have been naïvely devouring each other one by one, and whom Europe is evidently now preparing to devour at a single stroke.

In an amazing way, Dostoevsky's enormous talent for generalization was combined with a keen receptivity to the particular and the individual. Therefore, he not only understood the general and the primary significance of what takes place in history, but also was conscious of its unbearable horror, as if he himself had experienced all the personal suffering caused by violation of the principal law of development. Immediately after *Winter Notes on Summer Impressions*,[8] he published the gloomy *Notes from the Underground*,[9] which we mentioned above.

In reading it, one is unexpectedly struck by our need for annotated editions—annotated not from the standpoint of the form and origin of literary works, as is already done, but from the standpoint of their contents and meaning—in order finally to decide the question of whether the idea contained in them is true, or whether it is false, and why, and to decide this by joint efforts, to decide it thoroughly

----

means of a comfortable life for others. In the same way that a large river attracts small rivers and streams and by the evaporation at its basin creates moisture and rain that finally collect in it again, so into this large stream of unmarried life flow many of its smaller streams, which to a considerable extent are produced simply by its massiveness, its easiness, its convenience for everyone, and its habitualness.

[8] Published in 1863 in the magazine *Time*.

[9] Published in numbers 1, 2, and 4 of the magazine *Epoch*, which, in 1864, had replaced the suspended *Time*.

and rigorously, in a way accessible only to science. For example, every line of *Notes from the Underground* is important; it is impossible to reduce the book to general formulas. Moreover, no thinking person can pass over the assertions made in it without considering them carefully.

There never was a writer in our literature whose ideals were so completely divorced from present-day reality. The thought never for a moment occurred to Dostoevsky to try to preserve this way of life and merely improve a thing or two in it. Because of the generalizing cast of his mind, he directed all his attention toward the evil concealed in the general system of a historically developed life; hence his hatred of and disdain for all hope of improving anything by means of individual changes; hence his animosity towards our parties of progressives and Westerners. Perceiving only the "general," he passed directly from reality to the extreme in the ideal, and the first thing he encountered there was the hope of raising, with the help of reason, an edifice of human life so perfect that it would give peace to man, crown history, and put an end to suffering. His criticism of this idea runs through all his works; it was expressed for the first time, and moreover in the greatest detail, in *Notes from the Underground.*

The man from the underground is a person who has withdrawn deep within himself. He hates life and spitefully criticizes the ideal of the rational utopians on the basis of a precise knowledge of human nature, which he acquired through a long and lonely observation of himself and of history.

The outline of his criticism is as follows: man carries within himself, in an undeveloped state, a complex world of inclinations that have not yet been discovered—and their discovery will determine his future history just as inevitably as the existence of these inclinations in him now is certain. Therefore, the predetermination of history and its crown by our reason alone will always be empty talk without any real importance.

Among those inclinations, in so far as they have already revealed themselves during the course of history, there is so much that is incomprehensibly strange and irrational that it is impossible to find any intelligent formula that would satisfy human nature. Is not happiness the principle on which this formula can be constructed? But does not man sometimes crave suffering? Are there really any pleasures for which Hamlet would give up the torments of his consciousness? Are not order and regularity the common features of every final system of human relations? And yet, do we not sometimes love chaos, destruction, and disorder even more passionately than we do regularity and creation? Is it possible to find a person who would do only what is necessary and good his whole life long? And would he not, by limiting himself to this for so long, experience a strange weariness; would he not shift, at least briefly, to the poetry of instinctive actions? Finally, will not all happiness disappear for man if there disappears for him the feeling of novelty, of everything unexpected, everything capriciously changeable—things to which he now adapts his way of life, and in so doing experiences much distress, but an equal joy? Does not uniformity for everyone contradict the fundamental principle of human nature—individuality—and does not the constancy of the future and of the "ideal" contradict his free will, his thirst for choosing something or other in his own way, sometimes contrary to an external, even a rational, decision? And can man really be happy

[49]

without freedom, without individuality? Without all this, with the eternal absence of novelty, will not instincts be irresistibly aroused in him such as will shatter the adamantine nature of every formula: and man will wish for suffering, destruction, blood, for everything except that to which his formula has doomed him for all eternity; in the same way that a person confined too long to a light, warm room will cut his hands on the glass of the windowpanes and run naked out into the cold, merely so as not to have to remain any longer in his former surroundings? Was it not this feeling of spiritual weariness that led Seneca into intrigue and crime? And was it not this that made Cleopatra stick gold pins into the breasts of her black slave girls, while eagerly looking them in the face, watching their trembling, smiling lips, and their frightened eyes? And finally, will the never-changing possession of the achieved ideal really satisfy a person for whom wishing, striving, and achieving is an irresistible need? And does rationality, on the whole, exhaust human nature? But obviously that is the only thing that its very creator—reason—can give to a final formula.

By nature, man is a completely irrational creature; therefore, reason can neither completely explain him nor completely satisfy him. No matter how persistent is the work of thought, it will never cover all of reality; it will answer the demands of the imaginary man, but not those of the real one. Hidden in man is the instinct for creation, and this was precisely what gave him life, what rewarded him with suffering and joy—things that reason can neither understand nor change.

The rational is one thing; the mystical is another thing again. And while it is inaccessible to the touch and power of science, it can be arrived at through religion. Hence the development of the mystical in Dostoevsky and the concentration of his interest on all that is religious, something we observe in the second and chief period of his work, which began with *Crime and Punishment*.

V

Dostoevsky is acknowledged the most profound analyst of the human soul. He became so because he saw in the soul a concentration of all the enigmas over which man ponders, as well as a solution to all the difficulties that man thus far in history has not been able to surmount.

Earlier, we called Count Leo Tolstoy the artist of life in its fully developed forms which have acquired stability. The spiritual world of man within the bounds of these forms is exhausted by him with unrivaled perfection: the slightest movements of the heart, all the most imperceptible buddings of thought in these forms of fully developed life and fully developed spiritual types are portrayed in Tolstoy's works with a clarity that leaves nothing to be desired. But two great moments in a historically developing life, its genesis and decomposition, are not touched on by him. These moments undoubtedly carry in themselves something morbid; they often contain something anomalous and sometimes something criminal. Tolstoy turns away from all this with irresistible disgust. Dostoevsky, on the contrary, is irresistibly attracted to it; he complements Tolstoy, and, unlike him, is an analyst of what is unsettled in human life and the human spirit.

Dostoevsky's complete aloofness from present-day reality, the absence in him of any organic ties whatsoever with reality or any sympathy for it is, of course, the main reason for his dwelling exclusively on moments of genesis and decomposition. Filled with expectation or regret, he always directs his attention to the future or the past, but never to the present. Therefore, to observe how the present dies while decomposing or how, in the midst of this process of dying, a new life comes into being is always the greatest satisfaction for him. In the long series of his novels, from *Crime and Punishment* to *The Brothers Karamazov*, we see fully developed types only in glimpses, and almost from a distance; in the foreground move people belonging to no definite category whatsoever—they are alarmed, they seek, they destroy, they create.

Because of this, his psychological analysis has certain pecularities about it: it is the analysis of the human soul in general, in its various states, stages, and transitions, and not that of an individual, discrete, and fully developed inner life (as with Count L. N. Tolstoy). They are not finished characters, each with his own inner center, that move before us in Dostoevsky's works, but a series of shadows of one particular thing; it is as if they are various transformations or inflections of a single spiritual being in the process of being born or dying. Therefore, the characters portrayed by him move us mainly to meditation rather than observation. He reveals to us the innermost recesses of the human conscience, and, I dare say, in so far as he is able he undoes and reveals that mystical knot which is the center of man's irrational nature.

But, in any case, in the order of the emergence of his interests, psychological analysis was only secondary and conditioned; and it began to develop only with *Crime and Punishment*. The main and all-determining thing for him was: human suffering and its connection with the general meaning of life. It already appears, even if only personified, in his first work, *Poor People*, and it is discussed dialectically in his last, *The Brothers Karamazov*.

As has already been noted above, the fundamental evil of history lies in the incorrect relationship in it between the ends and the means: the human personality, regarded as only a means, is sacrificed in order to raise the edifice of civilization, and, of course, no one can determine to what extent and how much longer this can go on. The lower classes have already been crushed by civilization everywhere, it is now preparing to crush the primitive peoples, and there is an idea in the air according to which the present generation can be sacrificed for the good of the future, for an indefinite number of generations to come. Something monstrous is taking place in history; a sort of phantom has seized and perverted it: for the sake of something that no one has ever seen and which everyone is only awaiting, an intolerable wrong is being wrought: human beings—today, as in the past an eternal means—are being sacrificed, no longer individually, but in whole masses, in whole nations, in the name of some general and distant goal that has not yet revealed itself to a single living person and about which we can only guess. And where will it all end? When will man as an end-in-himself appear—he for whom so many sacrifices have been made? No one knows.

It was against this powerful idea, which is never voiced, but which is everywhere governing facts as it is being put into practice, that Dostoevsky began his struggle, perhaps feeling and sensing it more than being fully conscious of it.

[53]

The criticism of the possibility of a final idea was only the first half of the task that faced him. Having revealed the irrationality of human nature and consequently the imaginary nature of the final goal,[1] he came to the defense not of the relative but the absolute value of the human personality—of every last individual, who never, under any circumstances, must be only a means.

Closely connected with this were a number of his religious ideas. The coincidence that proved to exist between the results of his impartial analysis of human nature and what was required by the tasks of his struggle was remarkable and fortunate. The analysis showed the irrationality of the human being and revealed the existence in him of something mystical, of something that had doubtless been transmitted to him during the very act of creation. And this was in the highest degree in keeping with the view that man is immeasurably superior to what we thought him to be, that he is something religious, sacred and inviolable. As an aggregate of physiological functions, one of which is consciousness, man is, of course, only a means—at least every time a different and greater number of similar physiological aggregates demands it. We see something completely different in him when we acknowledge his mystical origin and his mystical nature: he carries in him a reflection of his Creator, he has in him God's image, which never tarnishes, which never submits, but which is always precious and invulnerable.

It should be noted that the importance of the human

[1] Thus, *Notes from the Underground* is the first cornerstone, as it were, of Dostoevsky's literary work, and the ideas expounded in it form the first basic line in his world outlook.

personality is revealed only in religion. In law, the personality is but a fiction, a necessary center to which contractual obligations, possessory rights, and so on, refer; its importance is neither explained nor proved there, and if it is defined in one way or another, the definition is primary and arbitrary: it is a condition to which we need not agree. The personality in law can serve as the subject of a contract—and slavery, in general, is the natural result of a pure judicial system. In political economy, the personality completely disappears: there, one finds only manpower, to which the individual is an unnecessary appendage. Thus, it is impossible, by means of science and learning, to reconstruct the personality in history: we can respect it, but there is no necessity to do so; we can also ignore it—particularly when it is depraved and evil. But the very introduction of these conditions undermines the idea of an absolute personality: to the Greeks, all barbarians were bad; to the Romans, all non-citizens; to the Catholics, all heretics; to the humanists, all obscurantists; to the people of 1893, all conservatives. But none of this conditionality or these vacillations and doubts are known to religion: in it, every living personality is God's image and thus is absolute and inviolable.

That is why slavery, for example, always increased under religion the weaker or more perverted religion became; on the contrary, under law, it increased the more consistent, pure, and unalloyed law was. In history, it was most terrible with the Romans, the nation with the most thorough understanding of law: they chopped up slaves and fed them to the fish in their ponds. And it was most human with the ancient Jews, who lived according to strict religious laws:

in their jubilee years, all slaves had to be set free, i.e., they were an object of temporary use, but not possessions in the strict sense of the word, not property.

In *Crime and Punishment*, Dostoevsky reveals in detail for the first time the idea of the absolute significance of the individual personality.[2] Surrounded by hopeless suffering, faced with people who are perishing or about to perish, the chaste soul of the hero of this novel rebels and decides to transgress the law of the inviolability of human life. He underpins his idea with a brilliant dialectic and then carries it out. And as soon as this happens, there begins a mystical interaction between the murderer, the woman he murdered, and all the people around them. Everything that goes on in Raskolnikov's soul is irrational; up to the very end he does not know why he should *not* have killed the old pawn-broker. And we, too, do not understand intellectually or dialectically the various states of his conscience or the nature of his deed. But with our whole being, we quite clearly sense the necessity of all the consequences of the deed. Scarcely had he smashed the reflected image of God (true, it had already been disfigured by its bearer) than he began to feel that this image, and along with it all nature, had died out in himself as well. "I didn't murder the old woman," he says in one place, "I murdered myself." It is as if something had changed in his soul, and with that change, everything took on a different aspect, and what he had formerly known became hidden from him forever. He felt that he no longer had anything in common with or

[2] Thus, this novel, as far as literature is concerned, Dostoevsky's most severe and, consequently, best work, constitutes the *second* cornerstone in the development of his world outlook. He expresses his idea in this novel positively and defends it, but he expresses it negatively as early as in *The Possessed*.

anything that linked him to any living people who remained on this side of crime; nor would he ever have in the future. He had crossed to another shore; he had left all people, apparently to go to a place where he would have no one with him but the murdered woman. It was as if the mystical knot of his being, which we conventionally call the "soul," had been joined by an imperceptible bond to the mystical knot of the other being whose outer form he had smashed. It seems as if all relations between the murderer and the murdered woman are ended—yet they continue; it seems as if all relations between him and the people around him are maintained, that they are only slightly changed—and yet they are broken off completely. Here in this analysis of criminality, in this display of, as it were, the husks or spiritual shells surrounding every "I," which at times interact and at times cease to interact, it seems that the deepest secret of human nature has been divined, that the great and sacred law of the inviolability of the human being and of its absolute nature has been revealed. In so far as this mystical phenomenon lends itself not so much to explanation as to a simple designation by words, it can be expressed thus: that which we observe in man, his acts, words, desires, everything that others know about him and he knows about himself, do not exhaust his complete being. There is something more in him beyond all this, and, moreover, it is the main thing, something others know nothing about.[3] We must attach ourselves to, we must love this most important thing in man: this is why we sometimes love him despite everything that we see in him; on the contrary, we can

[3] The fact that atavism occurs or the fact that parents of average intelligence give birth to a genius proves the existence in man of something he is aware of neither in himself nor in others.

only hate in man that which is external and unimportant, a kind of disfigurement to which he has subjected himself. But when we confuse the one with the other, or more precisely, when we know nothing of the existence in man of something beyond what meets our eye, and we smash his image, we smash a whole, the existence of which we never suspected in him. Suddenly we touch the main thing, which we had never thought about before, and we become aware of a change that has unexpectedly taken place inside us and which had never before entered into our considerations. Thus, only after having violated the personality of another do we understand its complete significance: but, too late. By having made such an experiment unnecessary, by having revealed with all the persuasiveness of his brilliant powers of depiction the state of a criminal conscience, Dostoevsky rendered us a great historical service.

As a matter of fact, with the solution of these two problems, he was fulfilling his task, in so far as it related to man as a suffering and scorned being. But immediately thereafter, a theoretical interest developed in him, and in pursuing it, he entered that boundless field that examines what might be called the seams of the universe. We find the first glimmer of this mental tendency as early as in *Crime and Punishment.*

In the unspeakably painful scene between Raskolnikov and Sonya, in the latter's stuffy room, he tells her of the possibility of her becoming infected and diseased and of how her family, for which she had sacrificed herself, would then of necessity perish:

> "Isn't it possible to save up something, to put something aside for a rainy day?" he suddenly asked, stopping in front of her.

[58]

"No," whispered Sonya.

"Of course not. But have you *tried?*" he added almost with a sneer.

"I've tried."

"And it didn't work out! Well, of course not! What's the use of asking!"

And again he started to pace the room. There was another moment of silence.

"You don't get money every day, do you?"

Sonya was more embarrassed than before, and the blood rushed to her face.

"No," she whispered with an agonizing effort.

"It will probably be the same thing with Polechka [her little sister], he said suddenly.

"No! No! That's impossible. No!" Sonya shrieked loudly, like a woman in despair, as if she had suddenly been stabbed with a knife. "God—God won't let such a terrible thing happen!"

"But He *lets it happen* to others!"

"No! No! God will protect her," she repeated, completely beside herself.

"But perhaps there isn't any God," answered Raskolnikov with a sort of malicious joy. He began to laugh and then looked at her. Sonya's face suddenly underwent a terrible change.[4]

In the same novel, there is a conversation between Raskolnikov and his *alter ego*—his second and worse half, Svidrigailov—about ghosts and life beyond the grave:

[4] *Crime and Punishment.* The horrible significance of the words about trying to save money lies in the rush and the eagerness for depravity to which this girl, who is only outwardly corrupt, is driven. Here, Dostoevsky, with a sort of diabolical torment, observes how physical need, in striking against the soul, as it were, pierces it and opens the way for the entry of inner vice.

"I agree with you," says Svidrigailov, "that ghosts only appear to sick people; but, after all, that only proves that ghosts can appear to no one but sick people, and not that they *don't exist* in their own right. Ghosts are, so to say, wisps and fragments of other worlds, their beginning. Of course, there is no need for a healthy person to see them, for a healthy person is, above all, a terrestrial being and, consequently, for fullness and for order must live only the life on this side of the grave. But no sooner does he fall ill, no sooner is the normal terrestrial order in the organism upset than the possibility of another world immediately makes itself felt; and the sicker the person becomes the more contact he has with the other world, so that when he dies completely, he passes directly into that other world. I've been thinking about this for a long time now. If you believe in a life to come, you can also believe in this argument of mine."

"*I don't believe in a life to come,*" said Raskolnikov. Svidrigailov sat lost in thought.

"But what if there is nothing but *spiders or something like that* up there?" he said suddenly.

"He's insane," thought Raskolnikov.

"Eternity always seems to us an idea that can't be understood, something vast, incredibly vast! But why must it definitely be vast? What if, instead of all that, there is nothing up there but a little room, such as a village bathhouse—sooty, and with spiders in all the corners—and that is all there is to eternity? You know, it sometimes seems to me as if it is like that.

"Is it possible, is it really possible that you imagine nothing more consoling and just than that?" shouted

Raskolnikov with a feeling of pain [earlier, he had not wanted to say anything at all to Svidrigailov].

"More just? Who can tell, *perhaps that is just;* and, you know, I would definitely make it like that on purpose," answered Svidrigailov with a vague smile.

A cold shudder seized Raskolnikov at this outrageous answer.

We sense the stifling atmosphere of strange ideas and feelings. If in this same novel there is a dialectic that justifies crime, and, nevertheless, the soul in its entirety is chastised for it, then here we see a dialectic that ascends to an acknowledgment of "new worlds," while feelings about eternal retribution descend to the level of spiders. The "trembling creature," as man is several times called in this book, deserves, both on account of the meanness of his crimes and the uselessness of his virtues, neither more nor less than this.

From here on, the religious question never disappears from Dostoevsky's works: he touches on it in every novel, but in such a way that we keenly feel that he is merely setting it aside until he is able to work on it freely and leisurely, without any outside interference. Finally, that moment came, and there appeared *The Brothers Karamazov.*

VI

The very time when this novel appeared was most remarkable: it was near the end of the reign of Alexander II; conspiracies of the anarchists; vacillation on the part of the Government; a loud and influential press—everything was spreading anxiety and expectation throughout society. The struggle of the various parties was at its most intense, and of those parties the one that coincided with the trend of Russian history over the past two centuries, i.e., the party of Westerners and advocates of reform enjoyed immeasurable dominance in literature and society. That all the hopes and almost all the demands of this party were destined to be realized was scarcely doubted, even by its opponents, and all the latter tried to do was to delay, at least for a short while, its final victory.

At this time, the three most influential writers—Turgenev, Tolstoy, and last of all Dostoevsky—came out in rapid succession with their final word. Whoever reads these works, even superficially, without even trying to analyze them, immediately senses the uncertainty of the period in which they appeared and the insecurity of the society whose mood called them forth.

As always, Turgenev, in *Virgin Soil*, responded to the trends of the time, having toned them down somewhat and limited them. The many-sidedness and breadth of his education, his lack of primitive strength, and his never-expressed but quite obvious indifference to everything but art—all this made him try now as earlier to enter into a realm of ideas and aspirations with which he obviously had nothing in common. This man, who had once said that there is something more indisputable and lasting about the Venus de Milo than about the principles of the First French Revolution, wanted, in his declining years and despite everything to which he had devoted his life, to share the tastes of people for whom the whole world of art and beauty had no meaning or importance whatsoever. But this unnatural attempt, as was to be expected, turned out to be so forced and pitiful that everyone to whom he had been dear for his earlier works could not regard it with anything but a feeling of the deepest sadness. This sadness could not help being sensed by the author himself, and it was this sadness that gave his last works a liveliness and a special coloring. Everyone, ordinary men and writers alike, carries within himself the gifts that nature has bestowed on him, both the bitterness and the sweetness of his life. Turgenev happened to be the first of our writers to win fame in Western Europe; and after he had won it, and there was no longer any time for him to aspire to anything more, he suddenly saw that he had won extremely little: everything important and valuable had slipped away from him.

On the contrary, the other two writers, who had hitherto been somewhat pushed into the background by Turgenev, began to speak more strongly than ever before, and their voices seemed to contradict everything that society wanted and everything it was thinking. If we should have to look for an example in history where the significance and influence of the individual personality was as incontestable and clear, we would find no better one than that represented by the last phase of the work of these two writers. At the very height of the general passion for external reforms, at a moment when everything in life and in man that is inward, religious, and mystical was being unconditionally rejected, these writers rejected as completely insignificant everything outward and turned their attention to the spiritual and the religious. And society, at first surprised and indignant, but at the same time enchanted by what they had to say, in the beginning singly and then in masses, let itself be dragged along by them in a direction opposite from the one it had been going in; a fundamental change took place in the life of our society, and we now stand on paths completely different from those we stood on only a short time ago.

In *Anna Karenina*, a deep and austere subject matter was combined with an unrivaled perfection of form. In it, more so than in *War and Peace*, the author's idea dominates all the groups of characters portrayed; it moves them more closely together and gives the entire work more unity and integrity. The groups and the scenes are less widely dispersed, they do not live so freely, and everything seems to be directed toward a single invisible center that lies up ahead. Instead of the epic calm that reigns in *War and Peace*, giving all the events and characters of that novel such a leisurely pace, we sense in *Anna Karenina* the presence of something that is anxiously seeking. This gives the whole work a lyric quality. On laying down *War and Peace*, the reader has a distinct feeling of satisfaction; on the contrary, on laying down *Anna Karenina*, he feels alarmed and confused. A feeling of sorrow, spiritual horror, hatred of life, and pity for man's fate—all this is mixed up in him to the point where it becomes unbearable; lacking the strength to struggle with himself, he looks for help from this great artist who has so disturbed his peace of mind. And the latter does not make him wait long for his answer. *Anna Karenina* proved to be but a great prologue to the doctrine that its author had been developing for ten years, sometimes directly, sometimes in allegories. Shifting from doubt to faith, falling from faith again into doubt, firm only in rejection, and wavering in affirmation, he seems in the whole series of his later works to personify the quest for the answer to skepticism. What he seems to be saying in his last works is: "I feel that I believe in some sort of God; but I am unclear as to what sort of God I believe in."

Dostoevsky's sprawling and episodic novel, while it differs sharply from *Anna Karenina* in form, resembles it very much in spirit and meaning. It, too, is a synthesis of psychological analysis, philosophical ideas, and the struggle of religious aspirations against doubt. But now the problem is attacked on a broader scale: whereas *Anna Karenina* shows how inexorably and horribly a person perishes once he has departed from paths predetermined for him, *The Brothers Karamazov* discloses the mysterious inception of a new life in the midst of a life that is dying. The old Karamazov is, as it were, the symbol of death and decay. All the elements of his spiritual nature seem to have lost their binding center, and he gives off the smell of putrefaction. There is no longer a regulating norm in him, and everything fetid in the human soul has irresistibly begun to ooze out, soiling everything he touches. There has never been a character in our literature for whom both the inner and outer laws have existed less than they do for him: iniquitous man, reviler of all law, defiler of all that is sacred—such is his name, such is his kind. Our society, advancing without traditions, failing to develop in itself a religion or any sense of duty, and nevertheless thinking that it has outgrown every religion and every duty, broad only because of an inner slackness, is in its basic features accurately, although too severely, symbolized by this character. We are shown his chief characteristic, the lack of an inner restraining norm, and the result of it, his naked lust for everything, his insolent sneer in answer to anyone who would stand reproachfully in his way.

It is in the stench of this decomposing corpse that his

offspring grow up. Between all four of Karamazov's sons, one can find an internal relationship subject to the law of the attraction of opposites. Smerdyakov, that nest of miasmas, that decaying hull from a grain of wheat that "has fallen into the ground and died," is, as it were, the opposite pole of the pure Alyosha, who carries in himself a new life, in the same way that a fresh sprout brings forth from its dark little grave into the sunlight the life and law of the dead mother organism. The mystery of the rebirth of all that dies is beautifully conveyed in this contrast. The third son, Ivan Fyodorovich, is reserved and sullen; he is the opposite of the expansive and garrulous Dmitry, who has good intentions, but who lacks any kind of norm—whereas that norm is to the highest possible degree concentrated in Ivan. Just as Dmitry is strongly attracted to Alyosha, so something in Ivan binds him to Smerdyakov. Ivan "highly values" Alyosha, but only, of course, as his opposite, and, moreover, as his equal. But he has nothing in common with Dmitry. The relations between Ivan and Dmitry are purely superficial, and this is more important than the fact that they finally grow hostile to each other. On the contrary, there is a kinship between Smerdyakov and Ivan: they understand each other at once, on the basis of no more than a hint; they begin to talk with each other as if, even after a silence between them, their contact was never broken. Thus, the bond between them is as obvious as is the bond between Alyosha and Dmitry. And in the same way that the power of affirmation and life stands out in its purest form in Alyosha, so is the power of negation and death, the power of evil, concentrated in its purest form in Ivan. Smerdyakov is merely his outer shell, his decaying offal. Of course, the evil in human nature is not so slight that it can assume only monstrous forms. It is also strong, it is also charming, and strength and charm are concentrated in Ivan. Dmitry is destined to be regenerated. Through suffering, he will purify himself. Even as he readies himself to face this suffering, he senses a "new man" in himself, and he prepares to strike up "a hymn to God" out in cold Siberia, from the mines to which he has been exiled to hard labor. Along with his purification, there will be an awakening of the life force in him: "In thousands of torments—I *am*; writhing in agony—I *am*," he says on the eve of his trial at which he feels he will be found guilty. In this thirst for life and this insatiable desire to become worthy of it, even through suffering, Dostoevsky has again divined the most profound, vital, and perhaps the central feature of history. Perhaps in this thirst alone has there been preserved in man the preponderance of the good over the evil in which he is so dreadfully immersed and which reveals itself in his every deed, his every thought. But despite them all, despite all the slime through which man has been crawling for thousands of years, there is nevertheless an insatiable desire to crawl farther on in order some day to see the light—and this raises man high above all else in nature and is a pledge that he will not completely perish in the midst of all suffering, of any misfortune whatsoever. Herein also lies the explanation of why we shudder and turn away at the sight of a suicide, why it seems to us even more gloomy than murder. It violates an even higher law—and religion condemns it as a crime for which there is no atonement. From a rational point of view, we should regard it indifferently, leaving everyone to decide whether it is best for him to live or to die. But the universal and supreme law, which is, of course, of mystical origin, forces

[67]

us all to live, it demands this as an obligation, whose burden we can never throw off. If the depraved and unfortunate Dmitry Karamazov is restored to life because deep down inside him there is, nevertheless, something good, then Ivan, to whom a broad path of life is open from without, stands, despite his great mental development, despite his strong character, on the edge of the abyss into which Smerdyakov fell and died. A powerful champion of negation and evil, he will struggle long and violently against death, that natural result of negation; and, nevertheless, the eternal laws of nature will overcome his strength; he will grow weary, and he will die in the same way that Smerdyakov died.

The last days of Smerdyakov, known to us from his first, second, and third meeting with Ivan, are striking. Here, too, as in *Crime and Punishment*, we are plunged in a peculiar way, the secret of which was known only to Dostoevsky, into a special psychological atmosphere, stifling and gloomy, and before we can make anything out, even before we come to the deed itself, we experience a mystical horror at the approach of a violation of the laws of nature, the approach of something criminal; and we shudder in expectation. The hatred with which Smerdyakov now regards Ivan, who had suggested to him that "everything is permitted"; the book *The Sayings of the Holy Father Isaac the Syrian*, which has replaced the French vocabulary lists under his pillow; the fits of delirium, of which his alarmed landlady tells although we ourselves notice nothing peculiar about him; the wad of banknotes that he pulls out of his stocking, at the sight of which Ivan trembles and backs up against the wall without knowing why, and the story itself of how the murder occurred, with the victim's unconscious fear of his murderer—his illegitimate son and trusted servant, a weak coward and idiot—all this is in the highest degree startling and painful, and once again it leads us into the world of criminality. It is remarkable that just as the law of nature violated here is higher than the one violated in *Crime and Punishment,* so the atmosphere surrounding the criminal is somehow more stifling and unbearable than that which we sense around Raskolnikov. This is why the latter did not commit suicide; his life still had some meaning, and after several years of expiation, he could go from this atmosphere into the light and sunshine. But Smerdyakov's life had no meaning; and although there may have been light and sunshine somewhere or other for him, it is quite clear that he did not have the strength to reach the place where they were, and he fell and died at his first steps in that direction. His final parting with Ivan, when he gives him the money for which the murder had been committed, and his words about Providence—all this lets us look into the soul of this man shortly before his suicide: a mystery never before depicted by anyone, never before reproduced by any of the living.

I should say a few words here about the nature of the fits suffered by these two brothers, the one of whom is a parricide, the other an accomplice in parricide. The latter, as we know, complains of having been visited by the devil, "a rotten, insignificant devil"; the former speaks of Providence, of having been visited by God. Earlier, both of them were atheists, and, moreover, quite confirmed ones. In reading Dostoevsky's story carefully, we have no difficulty in seeing that it is precisely hallucinations that are Ivan Fyodorovich's main trouble. Recall what he says to Alyosha: "It was *he* who told you that." And how he becomes animated every time his interlocutor's vague words give him

[69]

reason to think that the latter also knows that it is possible for the devil to show himself. ("Who is he? Who's here? Who's the third person here?" he asks Smerdyakov in alarm.) And, finally, recall the icy chill that suddenly grips his heart as he draws near his house after the third meeting with Smerdyakov, when he thinks that the "visitor" is already waiting for him there; and the almost whining tone of his complaints after his hallucination: "Yes, he knows how to torment me . . . he's beastly cunning." "Alyosha, who dares put such questions to me?" "He was the one who frightened you . . . you pure cherub," etc. If we recall the cold and severe tone of this atheist, and his genuinely powerful nature, then this transformation of a strong man into a grumbling child, into a whining woman, can give us the clearest possible idea of how greatly he is tormented by his hallucinations. "Tomorrow the cross, but not the gallows," he decides after this same hallucination, while preparing to tell all at the trial. By analogy, we must assume that Smerdyakov was tormented by something similar. As a matter of fact, Smerdyakov's recollection of the murder and his remorse should have been most intense the first few days after the deed had been committed, and yet at that time, he was still quite calm; his sickness and delirium do not begin until several weeks later. And they, too, as with Ivan Fyodorovich, are not continuous, but intermittent. The only difference is that "the third person," of whose presence he is certain even when his visitor is with him, is God, "Providence" Itself, although he answers Ivan's question of whether he believes in God by saying: "No sir, I've never believed." Evidently, what they had conversed about earlier and what they had agreed on was something completely different from what they experienced after they violated the law of nature. Therefore, once the one had sensed the presence of what he calls "the devil," and the other of what he calls "Providence," they both experienced something quite unexpected. All their earlier words about life beyond the grave and about God proved to be irrelevant. Continuing the analogy with Ivan, we must imagine that it was precisely the horror of expecting a "visit" that threw Smerdyakov into his frenzied confusion and also drove him to suicide. As always with man, Smerdyakov took the path of least resistance and suffering. To bear the physical pain of strangulation was evidently easier for him than to feel once again the icy touch of the apparition that had been tormenting him.

Smerdyakov's fits, obviously more severe, are not described for us; we are given only a detailed description of Ivan Fyodorovich's. We are told that when *The Brothers Karamazov* was first published, a certain psychiatrist wrote Dostoevsky, expressing his amazement at how closely Dostoevsky's artistic description corresponded to what is revealed during the objective observation of such fits. The psychiatrist did not, of course, know the substance of hallucinations, and this is precisely what is provided by Dostoevsky. The author gives his description a somewhat scoffing tone, but if we read all his works carefully, we will see that he always gave his favorite ideas, at the beginning and the end, a slight touch of irony [1]—at least he did so every time he expected them to be subjected to ridicule. Evidently, he did not want to set the great mass of readers

[1] Such, for example, in *The Brothers Karamazov*, is the public prosecutor's speech in court, which is presented with a tone that slightly ridicules the prosecutor. Nevertheless, many of the ideas in this speech are a repetition of ideas expressed by Dostoevsky in *The Diary of a Writer* in his own name.

against him—but he also found it difficult to leave anything unsaid. Ivan Fyodorovich, all during his hallucination, refuses to believe that it really exists, i.e., he does not believe in it when he is sick; on the contrary, he believes in its reality all the time he is well, when he is no longer experiencing it; and it is the only thing he fears, the only thing he thinks of. The sick man's words are overserious precisely when he is in a healthy state, and the author becomes too insistently focussed as soon as he approaches them. All this makes us see the duality and the hidden nature of Dostoevsky when he tells of Ivan Fyodorovich's nightmare. Did he really want to give us only a description of the hallucination? Is it not possible that behind his mocking tone is concealed his true conviction? And Svidrigailov's very clever idea (see above) about the possibility of other worlds, wisps of which are revealed to sick people—is this not Dostoevsky's own idea? At any rate, here is what he has Father Zosima say, and this time without any irony:

> Much on earth is concealed from us, but in return for that, we have been given a mysterious inner sense of our living tie with another world, with a higher and heavenly world, and the roots of our thoughts and feelings are not here, but in other worlds. That is why philosophers say that we cannot understand the true nature of things here on earth. God took seeds from other worlds and sowed them on this earth, and He made His garden grow, and everything came up that could come up, but things that grow live only through the feeling of their contact with another mysterious world; if that feeling becomes weak or is destroyed in you, then what has grown up in you will also die.

[72]

Then you will become indifferent to life and will even come to hate it.[2]

These words are striking both for the profundity of the idea contained in them, the beauty of their images (which seem very closely to correspond to the hidden reality of things), and their power of conviction. This is the second time that our fiction, which has so immeasurably out-stripped our sluggish science, has risen to a height of contemplation that only Plato and a few others were able to attain. In what a criminal senses, Dostoevsky unquestionably saw this contact with "other worlds" suddenly becoming clear and perceptible, whereas for everyone else, who has not transgressed the laws of nature, this contact, of course, exists, but it is not sensed; it is completely imperceptible and unclear.

That Dostoevsky is far from guilty of making a gross error, and that we, too, are not falling into it by revealing his unexpressed idea, becomes evident from the answer we must give to two questions that automatically arise in a reading of both *Crime and Punishment* and the description of the meetings of the parricides in *The Brothers Karamazov:* why is it that we so clearly sense the accuracy of the depiction of the emotional state of these criminals even though we have never experienced it ourselves? And why is it that a criminal, once he has committed a crime and consequently has suddenly fallen so low in the eyes of the people around him, on the contrary, rises in one respect so high above them all? Smerdyakov is a trembling insect in front of Ivan before the crime; but, once he has committed the crime, he speaks with him as if he has a certain power over

[2] *The Brothers Karamazov.*

[73]

him, as if he is his master. Ivan himself is amazed at this and says: "You're really in earnest, you're more clever than I thought." Raskolnikov, who is only *primus inter pares* among other people before the crime, definitely rises above them all after it. Only Svidrigailov, also a murderer, speaks with him as an equal, derisively pointing out that they have a certain point of contact between them. This all demands an explanation, and I shall now give the one that seems most likely to me. If we who have never committed murder clearly understand the mental state of the criminal, and if in reading Dostoevsky we wonder not at the whimsy of his imagination but at the skill and depth of his analysis, then is it not perfectly clear that we have a means of evaluation with which we pronounce our judgment on the plausibility of depicting something that should be completely unknown to us? Is it not obvious that such a means can only be *a priori* knowledge of this state, although we are not aware of it in ourselves? Someone depicts feelings for us that we have never experienced—and in response to what he says, there is awakened in us a knowledge that was previously hidden. And only because this newly awakened knowledge merges and coincides with what has been provided us from without are we able to draw a conclusion about the plausibility, about the truthfulness of these new feelings. In case it does not coincide, we say it is false— we say this of something about which we apparently can have no idea whatsoever. This strange fact reveals to us a most profound mystery of our soul—its complexity: it consists not only of what can be clearly observed in it (for example, our mind consists not only of knowledge, thoughts, and ideas of which it is conscious); in it is much that we do not even suspect in ourselves, but all this begins to function perceptibly only at certain very exceptional moments.

And, for the most part, we do not until our very death know the true contents of our soul; we do not even know the true image of the world in which we live, in as much as it changes in accordance with the thought or the feeling that we apply to it. With crime, there is revealed one of these dark sources of our ideas and feelings, and we immediately become aware of the spiritual threads that bind the universe to everything living in it. It is precisely the knowledge of this, something that is still hidden from all other people, that in a certain sense raises the criminal above everyone else. The laws of life and death become perceptible to him as soon as he transgresses them, and suddenly he feels that in one place he has severed one such thread, and, having severed it, he himself has strangely perished. What destroys him, what can be felt only by violating a law of nature, is in its way another world with which he has come into contact. We, however, have only a presentiment of it, we guess at it with our rather vague knowledge.

We said that in *The Brothers Karamazov* a great analyst of the human soul depicted for us a new life emerging from an old one that is dying. According to certain inexplicable and mysterious laws, all nature is subject to such regeneration; and the main thing that we find in this is the inseparability of life from death, the impossibility that one can come about before the other has occurred. And here is the explanation of the epigraph that Dostoevsky took for his last work: "Verily, verily, I say unto you, Except a corn of wheat fall into the ground and die, it abideth alone: but if it die, it bringeth forth much fruit." (John 12:24.) The fall, death, decay—this is merely a pledge of a new and better life. This is how we must look at history. We must accustom ourselves to this point of view in watching the elements of decay in the life around us: it alone can

[75]

save us from despair and fill us with the firmest of faith in moments when it seems that the end of all faith has come. It alone is in keeping with the real and powerful forces directing the flow of time, and not the weakly glimmering light of our mind, not our cares and fears with which we fill history and by which we do not in the least guide it.

But Dostoevsky's broadly conceived canvas remained unfinished. With this understanding of darkness, chaos, and destruction, there was undoubtedly connected in the soul of the artist himself a certain lack of harmony, order, and consistency. As a matter of fact, *The Brothers Karamazov* shows only how the old dies; the regeneration is, of course, outlined, but only briefly, and from without. But just *how* this regeneration comes about—that is a secret Dostoevsky took with him to the grave. To judge from the last page of *Crime and Punishment*, it was his life-long intention to depict this, and it was finally to appear in the subsequent volumes of *The Brothers Karamazov;* but, because of the author's death, that was not to be. Dostoevsky had outlined the most important task of his life but had failed to complete it.

But what stood on its threshold he executed with a breadth of plan and a depth of understanding unequaled both in our literature and in those of other countries. We mean "The Legend of the Grand Inquisitor." It was already noted above that each life is a combination of good and evil, and as it dies, it precipitates in itself, in pure form, both the good and the evil. It is precisely the latter that will, of course, perish, but not before it wages a stubborn struggle against the good, and this is what is depicted in the "Legend" with unparalleled strength.

VII

Behind a partition in a small inn, the two brothers get together for the first time: the dreamy and religious Alyosha, Father Zosima's favorite novice, who had so calmly turned from the beaten track of life to the path of monastic reclusion, and Ivan, older than he in both years and experience. Of all four brothers, only these two were born of the same mother; Dmitry and Smerdyakov are their brothers only through their father. Four months have passed since Alyosha and Ivan met for the first time after a long separation—and only now, on the eve of a new separation, perhaps forever, do they get together and speak privately. During those months, Alyosha had observed his brother with curiosity; he already knew of his convictions and superior education. And, for his part, he had sometimes noticed Ivan's searching look on him. Up to now, both of them had remained silent, although it was only to one another that they had anything of moment to impart. With the others, they had spoken either indifferently or submissively (Alyosha with Zosima) or domineeringly (Ivan with Miusov). They were bound together by a certain point of departure, and although they had separated at its very beginning to go in opposite directions and later had no contact with each other at all, still their friendship through this common point of departure was more significant and more vital than their friendship through lateral branches of the family or through the heights of their spiritual development, the only thing they had in common with everyone around them. This is well expressed in the following introductory episode of their conversation:

"Why are you worried about my going away?" said Ivan to Alyosha. "We have God only knows how much time before I leave. A whole eternity of time, immortality!"

"But if you're going away tomorrow, what kind of eternity is it?"

"Of what concern is that to you and me?" said Ivan, laughing. "We'll have time to talk over what we have to say to each other, the things we've come here to talk over, won't we? Why are you looking at me with such surprise? Tell me: for what purpose did we meet here? To talk about love for Katerina Ivanovna, about the old man and Dmitry? About travel abroad? About the disastrous situation of Russia? About the Emperor Napoleon? Was it for that?"

"No, not for that."

"So then you do know for what purpose it was. The others have one subject of conversation, and we greenhorns have another; we have first of all to decide the eternal questions. All young Russia is talking about nothing but the eternal questions now. Especially now, when the old men have all suddenly begun to occupy themselves with practical questions. Why have you been looking so expectantly at me all these three months? To ask me: 'What do you believe in, or don't you believe in anything at all?' That's what your glances have meant these last three months, isn't it?"

"That's probably what it was," Alyosha smiled. "You're not laughing at me now, are you, brother?"

"I, laughing at you? As if I would want to distress my little brother, who has been looking at me expectantly for three months now. Alyosha, look me in the eye: after all, I'm exactly the same sort of little boy as you, only I'm not a novice. What have Russian boys been doing up to now—that is, some of them? For example, take this stinking tavern—they get together here and sit in a corner for hours on end. They haven't known each other all their lives, and when they leave the tavern, they won't know one another again for forty years. Well, what will they talk about, now that they have seized the opportunity in a tavern? Naturally about nothing but questions of world importance: is there a God, is there immortality? And those who don't believe in God—well, they will talk about socialism and anarchism, about the transformation of all mankind in accordance with some new order. So you see, it will be the same damned thing, the same questions, only they start from the other end. And an enormous number of the most original Russian boys do nothing today but talk about eternal questions. Isn't that so?"

"Yes for real Russians, questions as to whether there is eternity, or, as you say, questions from the other end, of course, take precedence over all else, and so they should," said Alyosha, looking intently at his brother with the same peaceful and searching smile.

And on this "so they should" the brothers agreed. The passage just quoted will always remain an historic one.

It seems there really was a time when people became close friends or parted company because of "eternal questions." And these mutual interests brought them closer together than did their ties of kinship, not to mention a similar status or wealth. Happy times, happy people: how far they were from moral corruption! But it seems that all this has passed, and possibly for good. How it could happen with us that the most interesting thing could so quickly turn into the least interesting of all will be learned when future history pronounces its judgment. Only one thing is certain: that intellectual indifference, indifference to all questions, has never been so brazen as it is with the generation that will soon replace ours.

The two brothers, sensing that they see eye to eye about the most important thing, lose all shyness before each other in regard to everything else, and Ivan reveals his true nature to the novice Alyosha: the main thing he finds in himself is a thirst for life.

"Let's suppose that I didn't believe in life," he says, "that I lost faith in the woman I loved, that I lost faith in the order of things, even that I was convinced that everything was, instead, disorderly, damned, and perhaps, devilish chaos,[1] even that I was stricken by all the horrors of man's disillusionment—I would still want to live! [2] And having

[1] In *The Possessed*, Kirillov says just before his suicide: "Our whole planet is a lie and rests on a lie and stupid mockery. The very laws of the planet are a lie and a vaudeville of devils. What's the point in living? Answer me, if you're a man!" It is obvious from the repetition and the passionate tone that Dostoevsky has injected into his passage his own doubt, against which he had struggled long and hard.

[2] In *Biography and Letters*, one can find a great many indications of Dostoevsky's own unusual tenacity of life. It was the only thing that gave him the strength to bear all that fell to his

once tasted of the cup, I would not tear myself away from it until I had drained it to the dregs. However, when I reach thirty, I'll probably cast the cup aside even though I haven't emptied it, and I'll turn away . . . where, I don't know." This thirst for life is spontaneous and instinctive: "There is still a lot of centripetal force in our planet," he remarks, finding it difficult to explain. "I have a longing for life, and I go on living, even if it is contrary to all logic."

There is something in man that is related to the life of nature and to that other life which unfolds in its bosom and which we call history. And man sticks to all this: threads much stronger and more vital than the cold ties of reasoning bind him to the earth, and he loves it with a love inexplicable and deep:

> "The sticky little leaves that come out in spring are dear to me; so is the blue sky; so are some people— you know, you sometimes love people without knowing why; so are some great deeds of man in which you have perhaps lost faith long ago, but which your heart still reveres by force of habit . . ."
>
> "I think that everyone must love life more than anything else in the world," says Alyosha thoughtfully.
>
> "Love life more than the meaning of it?"

Aloysha says "yes," that a spontaneous love of life is always followed by an understanding of its meaning— sooner or later.

Ivan's love for the life of slumbering nature, for "the sticky little leaves that open in spring," is inseparably connected with his love for that other nature which is fully

lot during his life. "I have in me a cat's tenacity of life, don't I?" he says at the end of one of his letters.

conscious: i.e., man and the wonderful world created by him.

"I want to make a trip to Western Europe," he says.

He has two thousand rubles that have been bequeathed to him by the woman who had raised him and Alyosha out of pity and love for their mother after their father had abandoned them. Now, having graduated from the university, Ivan is planning to use this money for a trip abroad.

> "I'll be going abroad from here," he continues. "And yet I know I'll be going to a graveyard, but it's the dearest graveyard there is, of this I'm certain. Dear are the corpses that lie there; each stone over them speaks of such an ardent life in the past, of such a passionate faith in one's own great deeds, in one's own truth, in one's own struggle, and in one's own knowledge that I know in advance I'll fall on the ground and kiss those stones and cry over them [3]—at the same time convinced with all my heart that all this has long been a graveyard and nothing more. And I shall cry not from despair, but simply because I'll be happy about my tears."

These moving words reveal to us a man with a great heart and a great mind, as well as all the sadness that such a soul must inevitably carry within itself. The sadness here results from a powerful love and, at the same time, from a deep intellectuality, which is inseparable from it and which, nevertheless, contradicts it. Dialectical rejection without attachment or unconscious attachment without under-

[3] Here, too, Dostoevsky has inserted his own feelings toward Europe. Compare this with Versilov's words in *A Raw Youth* (pp. 453–454, edition of 1882) and Dostoevsky's remark on p. 295 of *Biography and Letters*.

standing—these are the two equally simple attitudes toward Europe that almost exclusively predominate with us in Russia. Very few people are able to combine the one with the other, and, of course, such a combination cannot help causing the deepest possible suffering. But in it alone is the truth, and however difficult it may be, everyone who wants to be right must try to develop in himself a capacity for both this feeling of love and for an awareness of the fact that what one loves is already dying.

Anyone who has a great interest in something outside himself, in something not directly connected with himself personally, cannot help being sincere and truthful. Such a person's thoughts are too strongly focussed on this interest for him to concern himself with all the petty things with which a person usually tries to surround himself in order to hide his own insignificance. For that reason, true greatness is always so very simple; and also for that reason, of course, it never in its lifetime wins the recognition that always falls to the lot of false and, therefore, feigned greatness. Spiritual loneliness, the impossibility of sharing one's thoughts, is merely the necessary result of this state of affairs, and ultimately it turns even into reticence, into a reluctance to share them. And yet the need to speak one's mind nevertheless exists—and herein lies the explanation for those meetings and deep confessions that even a moment before could not have been foreseen, and which leave in one's interlocutors an impression for the rest of their lives.

"I'd like to be friends with you, Alyosha," says Ivan, "because I have no friends."

Everything that had caused such an unbridgeable gap between him and everyone else now suddenly disappears. Alyosha jokes with him, with this person with whom no one has ever joked before, and Ivan himself tells him, laughing "like a meek little boy:"

"My dear little brother, I don't want to corrupt you or push you from your firm foundation; perhaps it is I who would like to be cured by you."

Alyosha looks at him in amazement. He has never seen him like this before.

VIII

"Well, what are we to begin with? With God?" asks Ivan—and he develops his idea of the incompatibility of a compassionate God with suffering humanity and of a just God with unavenged crime.

"An old sinner said in the eighteenth century," begins Ivan, "that if God did not exist, He would have to be invented." "*S'il n'existait pas Dieu, il faudrait l'inventer.*" [1] And man indeed invented God. The fact that God really exists is not strange—that would not be so amazing. What is amazing is the fact that such an idea, the idea of the necessity of God, could have entered the head of such a savage and vicious animal as man: it's so holy, so touching, and so wise, and it does man such great credit."

Thus, what Ivan is trying first of all to establish is the corruption of man and the sanctity of religion. Religion is something lofty: and to make it accessible to man, for him to be able to penetrate its world outlook—this is the highest

[1] This idea was first attributed to Voltaire.

goal, the greatest satisfaction he can ever achieve. But he can truly and sincerely achieve this, not despite his learning capacities, but only by acting in accordance with them as they have been arranged for him by the Creator, about Whom religion itself teaches.

Thus, there is not even a trace here of hostility, arrogance, or scorn for what will soon be so vigorously contested; and therein lies the very profound originality of the method itself. In world literature, we find frequent attempts to deny the existence of God, but here we feel that we are approaching something special, something that has never before appeared in any literature, a point of view that has never been taken by any man. And we also feel that this point of view is the only serious one for the attacking side and very likely the only menacing one to the side being attacked.

And this originality of thought is maintained farther on as well: God's existence, the indemonstrability of which is usually considered (in both science and philosophy) as the first stumbling-block to the human mind on the path to a religious outlook, is here passed over as if it were no hindrance at all. That which religion tries most of all to defend, that which it finds difficult to defend, is not in the least subjected to attack, but is conceded without dispute. And it is impossible not to acknowledge the strictly scientific nature of this method: the relativity and conditionality of human thought is a most subtle and profound truth that for thousands of years remained hidden from man, but now it has finally been revealed. A striking and graphic illustration of this relativity in recent times was the doubt as to whether real space is confined solely to what man

[85]

knows, solely to what is thinkable and imaginable for him. The rise of so-called non-Euclidean geometry,[2] which is now being worked out by the best mathematicians of Europe and in which two parallel lines intersect and the sum of the angles of a triangle is somewhat less than two right angles, is an indisputable fact clear to everyone and a sure proof that the reality of being is not covered by what is conceivable to the mind. And God's existence, the indemonstrability of which is no refutation of its reality, can also belong to those things that are inconceivable, but which, nevertheless, exist. Proceeding from this relativity of human thinking, Ivan refuses to judge whether the claims of religion are correct or not about Him who is the source of all being and the determiner and legislator of all thought. "I humbly admit," he says, "that I have no faculty for settling such questions. I have only a Euclidean, an earthly mind, so how am I to judge about something that is not of this world? And I advise you, too, my friend, never to think about that, and particularly about God: whether He exists or not. All those are questions that are quite inappropriate to a mind created with an understanding of just

[2] It was first discovered by Lobachevsky, and Kazan University, where he was a professor, honored his memory by publishing in its own name and at its own expense his complete works (in one volume, Kazan, 1883). Contained in it are his "Hypothetical Geometry," "New Principles of Geometry with a Complete Theory of Parallels," and "Pangeometry." For a detailed discussion of non-Euclidean geometry and information on its literature, see Professor Vyashchenko-Zakharchenko's *Euclid's Principles, With an Explanatory Introduction and a Commentary* (Kiev, 1880). [*Translator's note:* Contemporary mathematicians would be quick to point out that J. Bolyai (1802–1860) and K. Gauss (1777–1855), each working independently in Hungary and Germany respectively, developed the theory of non-Euclidean geometry almost simultaneously with N. Lobachevsky (1793–1856).]

three dimensions. And so I accept God, and not only with willingness—no, it's more than that—I accept both His infinite wisdom and His purpose—which are utterly beyond our comprehension; I believe in the underlying order and the meaning of life; I believe in the eternal harmony into which it is said we shall all merge someday; I believe in the Word, to which the universe is striving, and which itself was 'with God' and which is God. . . ." [3]

IX

"But I do not accept God's world," says Ivan, as he ends his confession.

Again we encounter a completely unfamiliar turn of thought: the creature does not reject its Creator—it knows and acknowledges Him; but it revolts against Him, it rejects what He has created, and along with it, its own self, having sensed in the underlying order of this creation something incompatible with the way in which it is created. The supreme and wise will that has been poured over the universe from an inscrutable source, rebels in one of its tiny particles called man— it rebels against its own self and grumbles about the laws according to which it functions.

"I must make a confession to you," says Ivan. "I never

[3] The reference is to the opening words of the Gospel according to St. John: "In the beginning was the Word [*logos*—reason, sense, word as an expressed thought], and the Word was with God, and the Word was God. He was in the beginning with God; all things were made through Him, and without Him was not anything made that was made" (John 1:1).

could understand how people can love their neighbors. In my opinion, it is precisely their neighbors they can't love; at most, they can love those who live far away. I once read somewhere about John the Merciful (a saint), who, when a hungry and frozen passerby asked him to warm him, lay down with him in his bed, put his arms around him, and began to breathe into his mouth, which was festering and which stank from some terrible disease. I am convinced he did so from anguish that originated in a lie, for the sake of love arising from a sense of duty, for the sake of a self-imposed penance. In order to love a person, it is necessary that he be hidden. . . . In theory, of course, it is possible to love one's neighbor, and sometimes even at a distance, but in proximity, almost never."

In these words, one detects a terrible hatred, at the base of which lies a great bitterness. No one will hate one's own flesh; everyone will feed and warm it—this is said to be a general rule of man's nature. But here we see that very hatred of one's flesh, the desire not to feed and warm it, but, on the contrary, to lacerate and destroy it. The example is an unhappy one, chosen in confused haste: of course, John the Merciful did his deed happily and joyfully; this needs practically no explanation. But this error in a character who appears only for a moment changes nothing; we skip it, and listen further:

"I had to make you see my point of view," continues Ivan. "I wanted to speak about the suffering of man in general, but maybe it's better if we limit ourselves to the sufferings of children. . . . First of all, it is possible to love children even in proximity, even those who are dirty, even those with ugly faces (however, it seems to me that children never have ugly faces); secondly, I won't speak

[88]

about adults, because, in addition to their being disgusting and unworthy of love, they have a compensation: they have eaten the apple, and know good and evil, and have become 'like gods.' And they continue to eat it, even now. But the children have eaten nothing, and for the time being are guilty of nothing. Do you like little children, Alyosha? I know you like them, and you will understand why I want to speak only of them. If they, too, suffer horribly on earth, it is, of course, because of their fathers; they are punished for their fathers, who have eaten the apple—but that is an argument from another world, and, of course, it is incomprehensible to the human heart here on earth. An innocent person must not suffer for another, and, more-over, not such innocent ones! Go on, Alyosha, be surprised at me—I, too, am terribly fond of little children. And take note, cruel people, passionate ones, carnal ones, in short Karamazovs, are sometimes very fond of children. Children, as long as they are children, up to the age of seven, for example, are extremely different from other people: it is as if they are a different type of creature, with a different nature. I knew a robber in prison; during his career, he happened to murder whole families in houses he had broken into at night to rob, and among his victims were, of course, several children. But when he was in prison, he had a strange affection for them. He would spend his time at the window of his cell watching the children playing in the prison yard. He got one little boy accustomed to come up to the window, and the boy even became friends with him . . . You don't know why I'm telling you all this, do you, Alyosha? I have a headache, and I feel sad."

"You look so strange as you speak," observed Alyosha uneasily, "as if you were almost mad."

The desire to cause suffering in order to be able to show compassion is a mysterious and inexplicable feature of the polarity of the human soul, and Dostoevsky reveals it to us here. He himself, as is well known, frequently and with extreme agony dwells in his works [1] on the sufferings of children, portraying them in such a way that it is always obvious that he too is suffering what they suffer and that he has a keen insight into their suffering: the scene depicted, with all its windings, is like a knife piercing a trembling body; it sinks deeper and deeper into the struggling, innocent creature, whose tears burn the artist's heart in the same way that blood burns the hand of a murderer. One can feel the criminality of all this, one can long to lacerate one's body, which has been disposed like this, but so long as this flesh is not completely lacerated, so long as the perversion of the human soul is not corrected, it would be a useless endeavor to close one's eyes to the fact that all this exists, or at least that one encounters it through some inexplicable law of nature. But, of course, once one acknowledges this, one can go mad realizing that the history

[1] In *The Insulted and Injured*, the character and fate of Nelly; in *The Possessed*, Stavrogin's conversation with Shatov, as well as his conversation with Kirillov, when the latter is playing ball with the little child; in *Crime and Punishment*, Marmeladov's children; in *The Brothers Karamazov*, in two chapters: "Heartache in the Hut" and "In the Open Air," where the child's suffering is almost unbearable, even in reading about it. ("Papa, papa, dear papa, how he humiliated you!" Ilyusha says hysterically to his father.) There is something burning and passionate in this pain. In this same chapter, people are constantly called "invalids" and "children." Immediately following these scenes begins "Pro and Contra," the great dialectic of every religion, Christianity included, which, although it had been conceived by the author many years earlier, suddenly seems to pour out of him here with no connection whatever to the course of the action in this novel.

of mankind is not yet complete and that this "unsettled" flesh will have to live on, to torture, and to suffer for thousands of years to come.

"People sometimes speak of man's bestial cruelty," continues Ivan, recovering himself, "but that's terribly unjust and insulting to the beasts: a beast can never be so cruel as a man, so artistically, so cleverly cruel. A tiger only gnaws and tears its victim to pieces—that's all it knows how to do."

On the contrary, man puts a refinement, a secret, voluptuous, and malicious joy into his cruelty. Neither nationality nor education rid him of this trait, nor, on the contrary, does primitiveness or even religion; it is eternal and ineradicable in man. When Cleopatra, a refined Greek woman,[2] grew weary of the monotony of an eternally happy life, she varied it, sometimes with a page from Sophocles or Plato, sometimes with the changing smile on a slave girl's face, into which she would look and which would look her in the eyes as her hand stuck a pin into the girl's black breast. The Turks, Mohammedans and barbarians, even when busy with a troublesome rebellion, would still snatch the time to enjoy man's greatest pleasure—the pleasure of seeing another suffer greatly. In the example quoted here, they enter a hut and find a frightened mother with her suckling child.

"They fondle the child," says Ivan, "and laugh to amuse it. They are successful: the child begins to laugh. At that moment, a Turk points his pistol a few inches from the child's face. The baby laughs with joy and holds out its little hands to grasp the pistol, when suddenly the artist pulls the trigger, right in the baby's face and blows its little

[2] She is said to have been able to converse in seven languages. [Tr.]

head to bits. Artistic, isn't it? By the way, they say the Turks are very fond of candy." [3]

"Brother, what is the point of all this?" asks Alyosha.

"I think that if the devil doesn't exist, and, consequently, that man created him, he created him in his own image and likeness."

"In the same way as he did God?" observed Alyosha.

"It is amazing how good you are at 'cracking the wind of the poor phrase,' as Polonius says in *Hamlet*," laughed Ivan. "You've caught me there. All right, I'm glad. Yours must be *some* God if man created Him in his own image and likeness."

And Ivan goes on to develop the picture of human suffering. In peaceful, industrious, and Protestant Switzerland, just five years earlier, an execution had taken place, remarkable for its details. A certain illegitimate child, Richard, had been given away by his parents to some shepherds when he was still a baby. The shepherds took him so as to have additional manpower in the future. He was given to them as a thing, and he was treated by them as a thing. In wet and cold weather, almost naked and always hungry, he would tend their cattle in the mountains.

"Richard himself testified how in those years, like the prodigal son in the Gospel, he longed to eat the mash given the pigs that were being fattened for sale. But he was not even given that; and when he stole some of it from the pigs, he was beaten. Thus, he spent his whole childhood and youth, until he grew up, became strong, and went out to

[3] The reference to the Turks' fondness for "candy" has a more general meaning: everywhere that Dostoevsky depicts man's propensity to cruelty he connects it with that which is sensual and depraved.

steal. This savage began to earn his living as a day laborer in Geneva. He drank up what he earned, lived like an animal, and ended up by killing and robbing an old man. He was caught, tried, and condemned to death."

Once he is condemned and lost, society, the Church, and the State surround him with attention and care. Clergymen come to visit him in prison, and for the first time the light of Christ's teaching is revealed to him. He learns how to read and write, he confesses his crime and writes to the court, saying he is a monster and that finally it has been vouchsafed to him by the Lord to see the light and to obtain grace. Society is touched and disturbed; people go to him, they kiss and embrace him: "And you have been visited with grace, you, too, are our brother in the Lord!" Richard weeps. New impressions that he had never before experienced enter his soul, they soften and move it. This savage, this young beast, who had stolen food from pigs, suddenly learns that he, too, is a person, that he is not a stranger to everyone and completely alone, that he, too, has friends who love, warm, and console him. "I, too, have been visited with grace," he says, moved with emotion. . . . "I am dying in the Lord." "Yes, yes, Richard, die in the Lord. You have shed blood and must die in the Lord. Even though it was not your fault, because you did not know the Lord when you coveted the pigs' food, and when you were beaten for having stolen it (what you did was very bad, because it is forbidden to steal), but you shed blood and must die." And then comes the last day: "This is my best day," he says. "I am going to the Lord." "Yes," they tell him, "this is your happiest day, for you are going to the Lord!" The cart on which he is brought to the square is surrounded by countless people, all of whom look

[93]

at him with tender emotion and love. Now they stop before the scaffold: "Die, brother, die in the Lord, you who have been visited with grace," say the people surrounding him. They take leave of him and cover him with kisses; he mounts the scaffold and lays his head on the guillotine; the knife slides down, and his head, which had for so long been in darkness, but which had finally been enlightened, falls severed at the feet of his weeping brothers, who had enlightened him.[4] This combination of a feeling of love with warm blood, which warms and excites the people even more, is a delight to man's unsettled soul, and, in its way, just as refined as the combination of playful innocence with the jeering scheme in a moment to smash this innocence to bits.

[4] A pamphlet was prepared in Geneva with a detailed description of this event. It was translated into foreign languages and distributed in various countries, Russia, by the way, among them, as a free supplement to newspapers and magazines. Dostoevsky remarks that such an incident was to the highest degree a local one (so far as nationality and religion are concerned) and would be completely impossible in Russia: "Although," he shrewdly mentions later on, "it seems that it has begun to take root here, too, ever since Lutheranism has begun to be propagated in our high society." This remark is profound: there is a certain correlation between the various faculties of the human soul, and once any one of them is affected by progress, education, or religion, all the others are, without fail, changed in conformity with it, according to the new form that it has assumed under this outside influence. Tearful pietism, that typical offspring of Protestantism, also needs to be aroused by crime and suffering, but only in its own way, as do other types of mentality produced in other historical conditions. In Catholic countries, for example, it would be impossible to have a case such as the one with Richard; on the other hand, in Protestant countries, it would be impossible to have the refined, varied, and sinuous system of torture devised in Catholic countries by the Inquisition. Everywhere, in one's own special way, but, nevertheless, everywhere, man is tortured by man.

Man not only suffers and is corrupt himself, he introduces corruption and torture everywhere he can into all of nature. In adapting animals to himself, he has perverted their very instincts; [5] he has forced unheard-of forms out of both them and plants by subjecting them to unnatural interbreeding,[6] all of which would have known no bounds, had he not met with stubborn resistance on the part of the mysterious laws of nature. A villainous transgressor, he stands before these laws, still trying to devise ways of violating them, ways of extending all limits, so that his depravity and evil can overstep them. He quickly grasps at every deformity and every sickness in nature; he guards and cherishes all this and increases it even more.[7] He has intermixed climates, changed all our living conditions, mixed that which is incompatible and has separated that which is related, removed God's image from nature and replaced it with his own distorted face. And in the midst of all this destruction, he composes poetry about the works of his hands.

Shifting from distant lands and different types of suffering to our native soil and our own suffering, Ivan also dwells in passing on this poetry. True, if one does not understand the deformity that man introduces into nature, one can also fail to understand the great evil that he carries within himself. "Although we Russians may find it absurd to cut off the head of a brother merely because he has become our brother and has been visited with grace, we

[5] Byron in one place, quite rightly and with great insight, calls tamed and domestic animals perverted.

[6] See the startling details about this, for example, in Bogdanov's *Medical Zoology,* I (Moscow, 1883).

[7] See Danilevsky, *Darwinism: A Critical Study* (St. Petersburg, 1885), (on pigeon breeds).

have something of our own that isn't much better. Our historic, direct, and dearest pleasure is torture by beating. Nekrasov, in one of his poems, tells of a muzhik who whips his horse across the eyes, 'its gentle eyes.' Now who has not seen this happen? It is typically Russian. He describes how a weak nag, whose overloaded cart becomes stuck in the mud, tugs and tugs, but is unable to move it. The muzhik beats it, beats it in a frenzy, beats it finally without realizing what he is doing, and, intoxicated by the very act of beating, he whips it mercilessly, a countless number of times. 'Even if you are too weak, go on and pull, even if you die doing it!' The nag strains—and then he starts to lash the poor defenseless thing across its weeping 'gentle eyes.' Beside itself with pain, it finally tugs with all its might, pulls the cart out of the mud, and starts off down the road 'trembling all over, hardly breathing, moving sideways, with a sort of skipping motion, unnaturally and shamefully.' "

The horror here is precisely in the unnaturalness and shame that man has introduced into a child's nature. But if the beating of a horse across its "gentle eyes" can make one's blood boil, then it will boil all the more at the cries of a child, of one's own child seeking protection in one from the punishment that one is meting out to it. An intelligent, educated gentleman and his wife flog their own daughter, a child of about seven. The father chooses birch rods with twigs on them: "It will sting more," he says. "They flog the child for a minute, they flog it for five minutes, they flog it for ten minutes; the longer they flog it, the more stinging the blows become. The child screams; finally, when it can scream no longer, it gasps: 'Papa, papa, dear papa.' " [8] Another time, most respectable and well-educated parents of high social standing had for some reason or other grown to hate their child, a five-year-old girl; they would beat her, kick her, and finally they even went so far as to "lock her up all night in the cold and frost in the outhouse; and all because she had not asked for the chamber pot during the night (as if a five-year-old child, sleeping its sound, angelic sleep could be trained at such an age to ask for the pot)—and for that they smeared her face with excrement and even made her eat it: and it was her mother who made her do it! And this mother could sleep, hearing in the night the groans of her poor child locked up in that foul place!"

"Do you understand," says Ivan, "what it means when a little creature, not yet able even to comprehend what is being done to her, beats her aching breast with her tiny fist, in that foul place, in the dark and cold, and cries her agonizing, forgiving, and gentle tears to 'dear, kind God,' asking Him to protect her—do you understand this nonsense, my friend and brother, you humble servant of God— do you understand why such nonsense is so necessary and why it has come about? They say that without it man could not even have existed on earth, for he would not have known good and evil. But why must we know that devilish good and evil when it costs so much? Surely, the whole world of knowledge isn't worth this child's tears to her 'dear, kind God.' I'm not saying anything about the suffer-

[8] This is obviously a reference to the trial of M. Kroneberg and Mme. Jesing, an analysis of which, as well as of M. Spasovich's speech for the defense, was made by Dostoevsky in the February, 1876, issue of *The Diary of a Writer*.

ing of adults—they have eaten the apple, and to hell with them, let them all go to the devil, but the children, the little children! Am I tormenting you, Alyosha? You don't seem yourself. I'll stop if you want me to."

"That's all right; I, too, want to be tormented," murmured Alyosha.

"One small scene more, just one," continues Ivan irrepressibly, and he tells how, in the darkest days of serfdom, a boy of about eight, the son of one of the house servants of a retired General, threw a stone and accidentally hurt the foot of the General's favorite hound; and for that, the General ordered the boy torn to pieces by the hounds, before the very eyes of the boy's mother.[9] The General went out the next morning to go hunting with his countless hounds and their keepers. The entire staff of servants had been assembled in the cold "for their edification." The boy's mother was made to stand in front: the child himself had been taken from her the night before. He was led out and stripped naked. "He shivers, panic-stricken, not daring to utter a word." "Make him run," shouts the General. "Run, run," cry the huntsmen. And when the boy, beside himself with fear, begins to run, the General sicks the whole pack of wolfhounds on him. In a moment, they tear him to pieces.

"Well, what should be done with this man? Should he be shot? For the satisfaction of our moral feelings—should he be shot? Tell me!"

"Yes, shot," Alyosha said quietly, raising his eyes to his brother with a pale, distorted sort of smile.

[9] This incident actually happened, as, by the way, did all the others mentioned here. It was reported in one of our historical journals.

"Bravo," shouted Ivan, delighted. "If even you say so, then . . ."

"What I said was absurd, but . . ."

"That's just it, that 'but' . . ." shouted Ivan. "Let me tell you, novice, that absurdities are only too necessary on this earth. The world is founded on absurdities, and without them, perhaps, nothing would come to pass in it.[10] I know what I know!"

"What do you know?"

"I don't understand anything," Ivan continues, as if delirious. "I don't even want to understand anything now. I want to stick to facts. Long ago, I decided not to understand. For if I'd want to understand something, I'd immediately be false to the facts, and I've decided to stick to the facts."

"Why are you testing me?" exclaimed Alyosha sadly, as if his heart were breaking. "Will you finally tell me?"

"Of course, I'll tell you. That's what I've been leading up to," says Ivan. And he draws his conclusion: "Listen, if I chose children only, I did it to make everything absolutely clear. I'm not saying a word about all the other human tears that soak the earth from crust to core. I limited my subject on purpose. I'm a bedbug, and I confess in all humility that I can't understand why everything has been arranged as it is. . . . Oh, all that my pitiful, earthly, Euclidean mind can grasp is that suffering exists, that no one is to blame, that effect follows cause, simply and directly, that every-

[10] For a similar passage in *The Brothers Karamazov*, see the chapter "Ivan Fyodorovich's Nightmare," where the devil jokingly explains that he exists "solely so that events will happen," and as much as he would like, he simply cannot join in the chorus and shout "Hosannah" with the rest of nature—for after that, things would stop happening.

thing flows and finds its level—but surely this is nothing but Euclidean nonsense—I know it is; moreover, I just can't agree to live by it! [11] What do I care that no one is

[11] This is an extraordinarily elevated passage, one of the sad and great confessions of the human spirit, the truth of which cannot be denied. Its meaning is that there is a disharmony between the laws of outward reality, according to which everything in nature and human life happens, and the laws of moral judgment that are hidden in man. As a result of this disharmony, man is faced with either renouncing the laws, and along with them his own personality, the spark of God in him, and then merging with external nature, blindly submitting to its laws, or with retaining the freedom of his moral judgment—of being in conflict with nature, of being in eternal and impotent discord with it. We find the first glimmer of this idea in Dostoevsky in 1864, in *Notes from the Underground*, Part I, Chapter IV, where it is expressed nervously and confusedly, but most characteristically: "Good Lord, what do I care about the laws of nature and arithmetic, when for some reason or other I don't like these laws and this business of two times two equaling four? To be sure, I won't be able to break through such a wall by butting my head against it if I really don't have the strength to knock it down, but I won't reconcile myself to it, merely because it is a stone wall, and I don't have the strength.

"As though such a stone wall really were a comfort, and really did contain some word of conciliation, merely because it is as true as two times two equals four? Oh, absurdity of absurdities! How much better it is to understand everything, to acknowledge it all, all impossibilities and stone walls; not to reconcile yourself to a single one of those impossibilities—those stone walls if it disgusts you to reconcile yourself to them; to come by means of the most inevitable, logical combinations to conclusions about the everlasting subject that you yourself are, as it were, to blame even for the stone wall, although again it is clearly evident that you are not in the least to blame for it, and consequently, silently grating your teeth, to sink voluptuously into inertia, brooding over the fact that you do not even have anyone to be angry with; that there is not, and perhaps never will be, an object for your spite; that it is a sleight of hand, but despite all these unto blame, and that I know it—I need retribution, or I'll destroy myself.[12] And retribution not somewhere and sometime in eternity, but right here on earth, so that I myself can see it. I have believed, and I want to see for myself; and if I'm dead by then, let them resurrect me, for if it all takes place without me, it will be too great an outrage. I certainly didn't suffer so that with myself, my crimes, and my sufferings I would provide manure for the soil of someone else's future harmony. I want to see with my own eyes the deer lie down with the lion and the murdered man rise up and embrace his murderer. I want to be there when everyone suddenly finds out what the point of all this has been. All religions on earth are based on this desire.[13] And I believe. But then there are the little children, and what am I to do about them? That is a question I cannot answer. . . . If all must suffer, so that by their suffering they can purchase eternal harmony, then tell me, please, what have

---

certainties and jugglings, it still hurts you, and the more you don't know, the more it hurts."

In the mockery and suffering of these last words is already the germ of the idea of "The Legend of the Grand Inquisitor."

[12] I.e., if, in the case of suffering and criminality, there is no retribution, and along with it satisfaction, then I, in seeking satisfaction, will destroy my own flesh, as it is criminal and suffering. Here we have an explanation of suicide. There are parallel passages in *The Diary of a Writer* (October and December, 1876).

[13] In these words, it is acknowledged that all religions, without exception, had their origin in the depths of the human soul, in the contradictions inherent in it and in the desire in some way or other to resolve them, and that they were not provided man from without. I.e., their origin is acknowledged as mystical only to the extent that man's soul itself is mystical, and no more. This view contradicts all the usual theories of the origin of religion—both those that say it was absolutely mystical, as well as those that say it was natural.

the children to do with it? It is completely incomprehensible why they, too, must suffer, and why they must purchase harmony with their suffering. Why should they, too, be material to fertilize the soil for someone else's future harmony? I can understand the solidarity in sin among men; I can also understand their solidarity in retribution, but there can't be solidarity in sin with children! And if there is indeed righteousness in their being jointly responsible with their fathers for all their fathers' crimes, then, of course, that righteousness is not of this world, and it is beyond my comprehension. Some joker would probably say that it is all the same—that this child would grow up and would certainly sin; [14] but you see he did not grow up, he was torn to pieces by hounds at the age of eight. Oh, Alyosha, I'm not blaspheming! I certainly understand what a cataclysm of the universe there is bound to be when everything in heaven and on earth blends in one hymn of praise and everything that lives and has lived exclaims: 'Thou art just, O Lord, for Thy ways are revealed!' And when that mother embraces that tormentor who had her son torn to pieces by the hounds and all three cry out in tears: 'Thou art just, O Lord,' then, of course, the crown of knowledge will be reached, and everything will be explained. But there's the rub—that is just what I can't accept. And while I am on earth, I hasten to take my own measures. You see, Alyosha, if it actually happens that I live to that moment, [15]

[14] In philosophy and so-called moral theology, there is such an explanation, but, to tell the truth, it is totally unsatisfactory.

[15] For a parallel passage, see the chapter "Ivan Fyodorovich's Nightmare," where the devil says: "I, of course, know that there is a secret here, but they won't tell the secret for anything . . . After all, I know that I shall finally be reconciled, and that I, too, shall walk my quadrillion miles and shall learn the secret. But until

or rise from the dead to see it, I myself will perhaps cry aloud with all the rest, looking at that mother embracing her child's torturer: 'Thou art just, O Lord!' But I do not want to cry aloud then. While there is still time, I hasten to protect myself against it, and, therefore, I absolutely renounce the supreme harmony. It is not worth a single tear of that one tortured child who beat herself on her breast with her tiny fist and prayed in that stinking toilet, with her unexpiated tears to 'dear, kind God!' It is not worth it, because her tears remained unatoned for. They must be atoned for, or there can be no harmony. But how, how are you to atone for them? Is it really possible? Surely not by the fact that they will be avenged? But why do I need them to be avenged? Why do I need a hell for torturers? What can a hell put right when they have already been tortured? And what harmony is there if there is a hell? I want to forgive, and I want to embrace. I do not want there to be more suffering. And if the suffering of children goes to make up the sum of the suffering necessary to pay for the truth, then I insist in advance that the whole truth isn't worth such a price. Finally, I do not want that mother to embrace the torturer who had her son torn to pieces by his hounds! How dare she forgive him? If she wants, she can forgive him for herself, she can forgive the torturer for her boundless suffering as a mother; but she does not have the right to forgive the suffering of her tortured child; she dares not forgive the torturer, even if the child itself were

---

that happens, I'll sulk, and I'll reluctantly fulfil my destiny: namely, to destroy thousands for the sake of saving one . . . No, until the secret is revealed, there are two sorts of truths for me: one that is theirs, and which for the time being is completely unknown to me, and the other my own."

to forgive him! And if that is so, if they dare not forgive, then where is the harmony? Is there in the whole world a being who could or who would have the right to forgive? I don't want harmony; I don't want it out of my love for humanity! I prefer to remain with suffering that is un-avenged. I prefer to remain with my suffering unavenged and my indignation unappeased, *even if I am wrong.* They've put too high a price on harmony. It is beyond our means to pay so much for admission. And therefore I hasten to return my entrance ticket. And if I am an honest man, I'm bound to return it as soon as possible. And this I am doing. It isn't God I don't accept, Alyosha; only I most respectfully give Him back my ticket."

X

"This is rebellion," says Alyosha quietly, with down-cast eyes.

The words of Ivan just quoted are the most bitter to have been forced from man in his entire history. Without rejecting God, he turns his face from Him; without doubt-ing ultimate retribution for his suffering, he no longer wants that retribution. Something so precious in him has been perverted, something so sacred in him has been out-raged that he raises his eyes to heaven and, filled with sor-row, prays that in the end this outrage not be atoned for, that this perversion not be removed. "You, who have im-planted in my nature the lust for torturing my neighbor, and because of that lust have had my children snatched from me and had them tortured—why have You given me a love for them that has even begun to murmur against You? Why have You confounded my soul, torn asunder all its beginnings and endings, so that I can neither love nor hate, neither know nor remain in ignorance, neither be only righteous, nor only sinful? And if You have confounded the issue of my soul which entered into me from the tree of the knowledge of good and evil, why did You create that tree to tempt me? Or why did You not surround it with an insurmountable barrier? And finally, why, when You created me, did You give me less firmness of obedience than lust for temptation? Most likely so that You could later forgive me; but look here, my children have perished —so let your forgiveness pass me by. Extinguish the consciousness in me, and with it give me oblivion; return me to the dust from which You took me. But if my consciousness is not extinguished, then I prefer to weep over my tortured children rather than to see the triumph of Your righteousness. I want no comfort; I prefer in the torments of my heart to share for all eternity the torment of my children who have perished."

We see here the inadequacy of human strength, man's inability to continue along the path down which he is led by Providence from an unknown beginning to a dark end. He has been travelling this path for thousands of years, submissively enduring all in the hope that ultimate knowledge and the ultimate triumph of God's righteousness will some day bring comfort to his heart. But finally this suffering has grown so great that he stops involuntarily, and can go no farther. He looks back over all this path that he has already covered, he recalls everything, he weighs his burden and the remainder of his strength, and asks: "Where am I going, and am I able to get there? My hope was folly, and the will that instilled it in me, evil."

Without a doubt, the loftiest contemplation of the destinies of man on earth is contained in religion. Neither history, philosophy, nor the exact sciences have in them even a shadow of the unity and the completeness of presentation contained in religion. That is one of the reasons why it is so dear to man, why it so ennobles his mind and so illuminates it. If we know the "whole" and the "universal," it is easier to orient ourselves, to define ourselves in the details; and, on the contrary, no matter how many details we may know—and this is all that is provided by history, science, and philosophy—it is always possible to meet new ones that perplex us. Hence the steadfastness of life, its stability, when it is religious.

Three great mystical acts [1] serve in religious contemplation as points of support to which the destinies of man are, as it were, fastened, on which they are mounted. These are the fall: it explains what is; redemption: it helps man to bear what is; and eternal retribution for good and evil, the ultimate triumph of righteousness: it attracts man to the future.

Only by shaking one of these supports can one shake the destiny of man. Without that, no matter what misfortunes may befall man—war, famine, pestilence, the annihilation of whole nations—he endures it all, because in it all, his very essence is preserved; *people* may perish, but *man* remains, and people will be revived; the change touches mani-

[1] Rozanov uses the word "act" in a rather strange way, both here and throughout the remainder of the book. I have retained the word only because there seems to be no adequate substitute. [Tr.]

festations, but it does not touch the manifested essence. The leaves may be torn off, but the ovary and pistil will remain. But there is one thing that man will not stand, and that is the severance of his being and his consciousness from these three mystical acts, by faith in which he lives. Without any misfortunes, completely content, he would somehow become confused and would perish; manifestations that had existed for some time would disappear, because the essence concealed behind them would disappear; people would not revive, because man would die.

Hence, one can understand the hatred with which man views every hostile approach to these bases of his existence. "Don't touch that—it's my life," he seems to say to everyone who tries to approach them, to anyone who wants to weigh, measure, improve, supplement, or purify them. In this feeling of instinctive hatred lies the explanation of all the religious persecutions that have taken place in history— persecutions that have aroused the greatest sympathy among the broad masses of the people, no matter how cruel they were.

And it is precisely these three acts, these three bases of man's earthly destinies—the source of his knowledge about himself, the source of his strength—that are shaken by the dialectic, a part of which we already cited above. The act of redemption, the second act linking the first and third, has not yet been touched on here. But the first act—the fall of man—is subjected to doubt, and the last one—the act of eternal retribution for good and evil, the act of the ultimate triumph of divine truth—is completely rejected. It is rejected not because it is no longer needed, but because it will not be accepted by man.

It should be noted that a dialectic has never before been

directed against religion in so powerful a way as here. Usually it has come from a feeling of malice toward religion and has been peculiar to a few people who have fallen away from it. But here it comes from a man obviously more devoted to religion than to anything else in nature, life, or history, and it rests on the positive and good sides of human nature. One can say that what rises up against God here is the divine element in man: namely, his feelings of justice and his consciousness of his own dignity.

And that is what gives this dialectic a dangerous, a somewhat satanic nature. It has been said that the first fallen angel was "higher than all the rest," that he stood "closer than they to God," that is, he bore a particularly close resemblance to Him—of course, in his purity and holiness. This dialectic has a certain religious nature about it, and the feeling of devotion that every religion inspires for itself, and the hatred that everyone arouses for oneself who touches it with intent to harm become, as it were, an integument over this dialectic too, even though it is directed specifically against religion. It seems that the only one who could try to destroy this dialectic, which comes entirely from a trembling love for man, would be someone who does not love him. It undermines the foundations of human existence, and it is done in such a way that one finds it impossible to defend those foundations without arousing in man a bitter feeling of outrage. Man himself is involuntarily drawn into the defense of his own destruction, and it is not one that is individual or temporary, but universal and final.

To construct a refutation of this dialectic as profound and severe as it is will undoubtedly be one of the most difficult tasks of our philosophical and theological literature in the future—of course, if this literature ever recognizes its duty to resolve the troubling doubts that are wandering through our society instead of serving only as a certificate of literacy in German for a few people who for some reason or other are indeed obliged to be acquainted with it. Without attempting such a refutation, I should like to make a few remarks in this connection.

Ivan Karamazov's refusal to accept retribution or even only to see the triumph of God's truth is actually based, in the words cited above, on a true and shrewdly noted peculiarity of the human soul: whenever its suffering is too great and its outrage unbearable, there is aroused in the soul a desire not to part with that suffering, not to be relieved of that outrage. There is some consolation in the awareness that the suffering is undeserved (the sufferings of children, it is assumed) and that it is not compensated for; and as soon as the compensation appears, the consolation disappears, and the pain of suffering becomes unbearable. Thus, the compensation is accompanied by a new and different kind of joy; but it by no means takes the place of the earlier bitterness, it does not in the least force it out. And this is a law of the human soul, this is its nature. One cannot deny that this characteristic has a good deal that is noble about it and that it results from man's awareness of his own dignity, from a certain pride, and at the same time from humility, but it is without the slightest admixture of anything evil.

Thus, as long as man remains in those forms of his spiritual and physical being in which he is now confined, he will indeed "prefer to remain with his suffering unavenged" than to accept retribution for it and reconcile himself to it. But to think that these forms of his being are something

[109]

absolute and eternal, that they are not conditioned by anything, would be a gross error. The human spirit, with its ideas, notions, and feelings, is closely, much too closely linked up with the mysterious organization of its body; it is fixed to it, fettered and conditioned by it as a foetus is by its mother's womb. But this constrained state is only temporary, and if the flow of our ideas changes with every change in our organization, then we find it difficult even to imagine what our spirit will feel and what it will think when it is freed from that organization and is pure. In the same way as reconciliation is impossible, truly impossible, for it now, so perhaps will it be necessary and automatic for it then. There will be "a new heaven and a new earth," it is said of the last day, on which "God shall wipe away all tears from their eyes," [2] and these words indicate a solution to this difficulty which, for the time being, we find insurmountable.

Furthermore, the suffering of children, apparently incompatible with the functioning of a higher justice, can be somewhat more understandable if we take a stricter view of original sin, the nature of the human soul, and the act of procreation. We said earlier that in addition to what is clearly and distinctly expressed in the human soul, there is also contained in it a whole world of what is unexpressed and unrevealed. When man commits a crime, his action is only a secondary act of lesser importance, whereas what is primary and of greatest importance is the spiritual impulse that preceded it and from which the criminal act was born. It makes an indelible mark on the human soul and subjects it to a certain mutilation. The question now arises: is this mark and are the effects of this mutilation made only

[2] Revelation 21: 1, 4.

[110]

on what is clearly expressed in the soul: on the memory and all the information contained therein, on the routine desires and transient feelings? Obviously not: the evil enters the whole of it, and its entire contents are mutilated —both the part that is perceptible, as well as that which is not yet revealed. We know that everything criminal originates in man in ways that are unclear, that it comes from the darkest depths of his soul. Furthermore, during the act of procreation, there is doubtless transmitted by the procreator to the future child not only its organization, but also that which serves, as it were, as its law and its binding center, i.e., the soul itself. The inheritance of character, of special talents, or of depraved tendencies is too well-known a fact now for us to doubt it even slightly. The multiplicity of the acts of procreation and the individual characteristics of the children born give us reason to think that in every separate act of procreation, there is transmitted a certain part of the complex contents which enter the soul of the child being created. Moreover, when perceptible parts are transmitted, the heredity is noticeable; when nonperceptible ones are transmitted, the heredity, apparently, is lacking. Every part, precisely by virtue of its nature, has in itself the ability to restore itself to the whole, to cause the appearance of the missing parts, which, just like their order of succession, are all pre-established in the part precisely by its earlier relation to the whole from which it came; thus, for example, in the smallest arc remaining from a circle all its missing parts are predetermined, and from it, they can be restored. These restored parts of the psychical make-up of each new organism can be regarded as something new; but among them is undoubtedly also an earlier part that is not newly-developed, but merely transmitted. This part bears within itself the general distortion that was inherent in the soul of one of the parents, and at times also some special deep evil, some crime that had been a part of that soul and which had been lost among all the rest, but which now stands alone and has reconstructed about itself the "whole." Bearing the crime within itself, it also bears its guilt, and the inevitability of retribution. Thus, the purity of children, and consequently their innocence, is only seeming: in them the depravity of, say, their father is already concealed, and along with it, the father's guilt. However, this does not manifest itself in any destructive acts, i.e., it does not bring new guilt with it: but the old guilt remains in the child so long as there has been no retribution. And the children receive this retribution through their suffering. Their father's offense may be so serious that it cannot even be atoned for by him, not even through his death: he has, let us say, seduced a child, a pure creature who had approached him trustingly. Can he answer for this crime with his life? No, and his crime remains hidden and unpunished. Generations come and go, and finally the retribution appears—in suffering that apparently is incomprehensible and which violates the laws of righteousness. But in reality it complements righteousness.

One very profound phenomenon in man's spiritual life finds its explanation here: the purifying significance of all suffering. We carry within ourselves a great amount of criminality, and along with it a terrible guilt that has not yet been atoned for; and although we do not know it exists in us, although we do not clearly sense it, we are deeply oppressed and our soul is filled with inexplicable gloom. And every time we experience suffering, a part of our guilt is atoned for; something criminal leaves us, and we have a feeling of joy and light, we become nobler and purer. Man should praise each sorrow, for he is visited in it by God. On the contrary, he whose life passes without difficulty should worry about the retribution that is postponed for him.

The possibility of such an explanation did not occur to Dostoevsky, and he thought that the sufferings of children are something absolute, something that has sprung up in the world without any previous guilt; hence his question is understandable: "Who can forgive the perpetrator of this suffering?" This difficulty is connected with the question of redemption, the second and central of these mystical acts, and with it are connected the destinies of man. Our very religion is named "Christianity" after the Redeemer; and it, too, is drawn into the discussion here, in the dialectic that follows. Redemption is called into question in the same way that the fall and eternal retribution were earlier. This second part of Dostoevsky's dialectic, which, in contrast to the first or biblical part, can be called, after its subject, evangelical. And it has been put in the somewhat odd form of "The Legend of the Grand Inquisitor."

With the criticism of the act of redemption in Dostoevsky, there has been combined an account of the hidden idea of Catholicism.[3] Namely, this idea, in revealing its contents, pronounces in it its judgment on the life and teachings of Christ and at the same time proves the necessity of its own appearance on earth. In analyzing man's nature and contrasting it with Christ's teachings, the aged Inquisitor re-

[3] Perhaps the first draft of this idea is found in *The Idiot* (1868), and Dostoevsky returns to it very often in *The Diary of a Writer*, for example, in the May–June issue, Chapter III, 1877.

veals the idea of his Church; and between the former and the latter, he finds a discrepancy. The gifts that Christ bestowed upon the world are too elevated and cannot be grasped by man; therefore, man is unable to accept them, i.e., he can neither comprehend Christ's word nor carry out His precepts. Because of this discrepancy between demands and capabilities, between the ideal and reality, man must eternally remain unhappy: only a few who are strong in spirit have been and are able to seek salvation by following Christ and understanding the mystery of redemption. Thus, Christ, who treated man with such great respect, acted "as if He did not love him at all." He overestimated man's nature; He did something great and holy, but at the same time impossible and impracticable. Catholicism is a correction of His work, it is a reduction of the heavenly doctrine to an earthly understanding, an adaptation of the divine to the human. But, this done, Catholicism kept the secret of the change to itself: and the various peoples who follow it think that they are following Christ. It costs great suffering to bear the secret of this deceit, one side of which is directed toward God, the other toward man; and a few leaders of the Western Church have taken it on themselves in order to save all the rest of mankind from suffering, to settle mankind's earthly destinies. Here, too, love for man is the motive principle of the whole dialectic, and its instrument is an analysis of his nature.

But the general meaning of all this lies in the fact that there was no act of redemption: there was only an error. And there is no religion as the custodian of religious mysteries; there is only an illusion, by which it is necessary that man be deceived in order that he can in some way or another establish himself on earth.

[114]

And the final implication of all this dialectic is that religion lacks reality and is absolutely impossible because it lacks an outer basis: the mystical acts of the fall, redemption, and the Last Judgment.

Now let us turn to a detailed consideration of this idea, only the theme of which we have stated. To Alyosha's exclamation: "This is rebellion," Ivan answers earnestly:

"Rebellion? I'm sorry to hear you call it that. One can't live by rebellion, and I want to live. Tell me frankly, I beg of you—answer me: Imagine that you yourself are raising the edifice of human destiny [4] with the purpose of making people happy, of giving them peace and quiet at last, but that in order to do it, it was necessary and unavoidable to torture to death just one tiny creature, for example, that same little child who beat her breast with her little fist, and to found this edifice on her unavenged tears, would you agree to be the architect on these conditions? Tell me, and don't lie!"

"No, I wouldn't agree," Alyosha said quietly.

"And can you admit the idea that the people for whom

[4] In the Pushkin Speech (*Diary of a Writer*, 1880), Dostoevsky examines Tatyana's character and her refusal, for the sake of gratifying her own feeling of love, to hurt her elderly husband, and he asks, this time in his own name: "Is it really possible for a person to base his happiness on the unhappiness of another? Happiness . . . lies in the greatest possible spiritual harmony. How can one calm one's spirit, if behind this happiness stands a contemptible, ruthless, and inhuman deed? . . . Now just imagine that you yourself were raising the edifice of human destiny for the purpose of finally making people happy, of giving them peace and quiet at last. And then also imagine that in order to do this it was necessary and unavoidable to torture only one human being. . . . Would you agree to be the architect of such an edifice on this condition?" From this comparison, it is obvious that everything that Ivan Karamazov says represents Dostoevsky's own views.

you are building it would themselves agree to accept happiness based on the unjustly shed blood of a little tortured child, and, having accepted it, would remain happy ever after?"

Thus, it is to such a great and noble feature of the human conscience, the one thing that raises its possessor above merciless nature to merciful God, that the question of rebellion against God Himself is reduced. There must be no hesitation in one's answer: if humanity says: "Yes, I can accept it," then it immediately ceases to be humanity, "the image and likeness of God," and turns into a pack of wild animals; but a negative answer approves and justifies the rejection of eternal harmony—and thus turns everything into chaos . . .

Alyosha is confused; he rejects the possibility of accepting universal harmony on this condition, and suddenly says with flashing eyes: "Brother, you just said: Is there in the whole world a being who could or who had the right to forgive? But there is such a being, and He can forgive everything, everyone and everything, and for everything, because He gave his innocent blood for everyone and everything. You forgot about Him, but it is on Him that the edifice is built, and it is to Him that people will call out: "Thou art just, O Lord, for Thy ways are now revealed."

"Ah, so it is the only one without sin and His blood," says Ivan, and instead of an answer, he offers to tell his brother a legend that came to mind as he was pondering over these questions. Alyosha is ready to hear it, and Ivan begins.

XI

The scene shifts to a distant land in the far West of Europe, the centuries draw apart and reveal the sixteenth century, a period when various elements of European civilization were mingling with and struggling against each other. It was the time of the first journeys to recently-discovered America, the religious wars, Luther and Loyola, the noisy humanists, and the first Generals of the Jesuit Order. The tumult and disorder of this struggle take place, however, in the center of the continent, while down beyond the Pyrenees in Spain, the people see the struggle only in the distance; they shrink further into themselves and remain motionless. Still farther back in the dark depths of time, one sees the poor sun-parched land where the great mystery of redemption took place, where blood was shed on the earth for the sins of that earth, for the salvation of suffering mankind. Fifteen centuries have already passed since that mystery took place; an enormous empire has fallen, and on its ruins, there has sprung up a world of new and different nations and states, who were enlightened by a new faith and strengthened by the redeeming blood of their God and Savior. With unquenchable thirst and hope, they await His coming; they await the fulfilment of the promise made them by His disciple: "And, behold, I come quickly," [1] and they recall that His disciple, while on earth,

[1] Revelation 21:12. "And, behold, I come quickly; and my reward is with me, to give every man according as his work shall be."

had said that only His Father in heaven knew the day and hour. They await Him with ever greater faith, because "fifteen centuries have passed since the pledges given to man from heaven had ceased:

> Believe what your heart may tell you,
> There are no pledges from above . . ."

And the only thing that sustains them is their infinite trust in the sanctity of the Word. "But the devil does not slumber, and men were already beginning to doubt the truth of those miracles. And at that very time, a terrible new heresy appeared in the North, in Germany. A huge star, resembling a lamp, fell upon the fountains of waters, and they were made bitter.[2] But those who remained faithful were all the more ardent in their faith. The tears of mankind rose up to Him as before; the people awaited His coming, they loved Him, they relied on Him, they longed to suffer and die for Him as before. And for so many centuries they called on Him that He, in His infinite mercy, longed to come down to His worshipers."

The scene shifts, and the story becomes more focussed. We see Seville, on whose hot streets a quiet evening is descending. Crowds of people move here and there; and suddenly He comes quietly, unnoticeably, and in the same human form in which He had walked for thirty-three years

[2] "I.e., the Church," remarks Dostoevsky. The image of a star falling from heaven is taken from Revelation 8:10–11, as are some of the later comparisons by which the fate of the Christian Church on earth is represented. The passage above expresses the view that the Reformation was a likeness of the Church and attracts people by its apparent similarity to it, thus drawing them away from the true Church. The "fountains of waters" here represent the purity of faith contaminated by this "likeness" of the Church.

among the people fifteen centuries ago. In appearance, He in no way differs from the rest, but, strangely enough, everyone recognizes Him. The people are drawn to Him by an irresistible force, they surround Him, their number around Him grows larger and larger, they follow Him. "He silently walks among them with a gentle smile of infinite compassion. The sun of love burns in His heart, rays of Light, Enlightenment, and Power stream from His eyes, and as they pour over the people, they move their hearts with responsive love. He stretches out His hands to them, blesses them, and from contact with Him, even with His garments, there comes a healing force. An old man in the crowd, blind since childhood, calls out: 'O, Lord, heal me that I, too, may see You'—and it is as if scales fall from his eyes, and the blind man sees Him. The people cry and kiss the ground on which He walks. Children throw flowers before Him, sing, and cry out to Him: 'Hosannah! It is He.' 'It is Himself,' repeats everyone. 'It must be He! It can be no one but He!' He stops on the steps of Seville Cathedral at the very moment when weeping mourners are carrying into the Cathedral a child's little white open coffin: in it is a seven-year-old girl, the only daughter of a prominent citizen. The dead child lies covered in flowers. 'He will raise your child from the dead,' people call out from the crowd to the crying mother. A priest, who has come out to meet the coffin, gives them a puzzled look and knits his brows. But suddenly there is a cry from the dead child's mother; she throws herself down at His feet, stretches out her arms to Him, and cries, 'If it is You, then raise my child from the dead!' The procession halts. The little coffin is set on the steps at His feet. He looks at the child with compassion, and His lips once again say quietly:

'*Talitha cumi*'—'and the damsel arose.' The little girl raises herself in the coffin to a sitting position; smiling, she looks about her [3] with astonished, wide-open eyes. In her hands is a bouquet of white roses that had been placed in the coffin with her. There are cries, sobs, and commotion among the people."

[3] It is amazing how much vitality Dostoevsky has instilled in this wonderful scene: it is as if we are not reading lines of print, but seeing a vision of the second coming of Christ to the people, and almost in our own time. In Dostoevsky's *Biography*, there are certain passages that to a certain extent can explain the strange, incomprehensible vitality of this imaginary supernatural scene. "Once," it is said there, "Dostoevsky was with a group of people who were alien and even hostile to every religion. Unexpectedly, one of the conversants referred to Jesus Christ, and he did it without sufficient respect. Dostoevsky suddenly grew terribly pale, tears came to his eyes. This was still in the days of his youth, and evidently even then he was deeply pondering the image of Christ." Subsequently, during his exile, the only book he was allowed to have was the Gospel. In constantly rereading the Gospel stories, he evidently acquainted himself with them to the point where he had a clear perception of everything told in them. Finally, the resurrection of the little girl, which is described in such a way that we seem to see the performance of the act itself, also has a biographical explanation. Here is what we read in his biography: "The birth of a daughter (February 22, 1862) brought great happiness to both husband and wife and very much cheered up Fyodor Mikhailovich. He would spend every free moment at her baby-carriage, he rejoiced at her every movement. But this went on for less than three months. The child's death was a terrible and unexpected blow to him. For the rest of his life, Fyodor Mikhailovich could not forget his first little daughter; his heart ached whenever he thought of her. Once, when he was staying in Ems, he made a special trip to Geneva in order to visit her grave." Undoubtedly, when he was writing the scene quoted above, he vividly imagined what his own feelings would be if his beloved little daughter were, through some miracle, to rise suddenly from the dead.

[120]

At this very moment, an old man of ninety, with an emaciated face, and dressed in a coarse hair cassock, walks past the Cathedral. Although he is a cardinal of the Roman Catholic Church and also the country's Grand Inquisitor, he stops and from a distance watches everything that takes place; his face darkens. The cries of the people reach his ears, he hears the sobbing of the old men and the shout of "Hosannah" from the lips of the children, he sees the child raised from the dead; and then, turning around, he summons with a gesture the sacred guard and points to the one responsible for the commotion and exultation. And the people, "cowed into submission and trembling obedience to him" make way for the guards, who go up to Christ, seize Him, and lead Him away. The crowd bows down to the ground before the gloomy old Inquisitor. He blesses it and passes by. The prisoner is taken to the dark dungeon of the Sacred Court and locked up.

The evening draws to a close, and night follows, "a quiet and breathless" southern night. The air is still hot and suffused even more with the fragrance of the blossoming laurel and lemon trees. In the silence of the night, the rusty hinges of the prison door suddenly begin to creak; the door opens, and into the dungeon comes the old Inquisitor. The door is immediately locked after him, and he is left alone with his prisoner. For a long time he looks into His face; then he sets the dim lamp on the table, approaches the prisoner and whispers:

" 'Is it You? Really You?' But, receiving no answer, he quickly adds: 'Don't answer, keep quiet. And what could You say anyhow? I know well enough what You would say. And what is more, You have no right to add anything to what You said when You were on earth before.

Why, then, did You come to hinder us? For You did come to hinder us, and You know You did. But do You know what is going to happen tomorrow? I don't know who You are—I don't want to know whether it is You or only a likeness of You, but tomorrow I am going to condemn You and burn You at the stake as the worst of heretics, and those very people who today kissed Your feet, will, at the mere beck of my hand tomorrow, rush to rake up the hot coals about Your bonfire—do You know that? Yes, maybe You do know it,' he added, deep in thought, without tearing his eyes from his prisoner for a moment."

In these tense, vehement words are anticipated all the variations of the ensuing dialectic: there is an acknowledgment of the divine that amounts to a clear perception of it, to contemplation, and, on the other hand, a hatred for it that amounts to a threat—to destroy it on the following day, to burn and trample it under foot. Never before has there been a greater union, and a simultaneous disunion, of the human soul with its Eternal Source. In the distance, as if in the background, one notices a rather strange attitude toward the people, toward those millions of shepherded souls; in this attitude, there is undoubtedly an anxious feeling of concern: there is, of course, love, but at the same time, there is scorn, and also a kind of deceit, something concealed. In the Prisoner's silence and in the words: "Yes, maybe You do know it," there is a hint of the blasphemous idea that in this opening scene something new and unexpected is being revealed to the Savior, some great secret that He did not know before and which He is beginning only now to understand. And it is man who wants to tell Him this secret: the "trembling creature" feels in himself such a strength of conviction, gotten from all of his past fate, that he is not afraid to rise up with it and for it before his Maker and God.

In all of the remainder of the Inquisitor's confession of faith, there is revealed the motive idea of the Roman Catholic Church. One finds it very difficult to dismiss the thought that this idea is at the same time the confession of all mankind, the wisest and most penetrating acknowledgment of its destinies, and moreover of both those past and, mainly, those future. The Western Church is, of course, only the Latin conception of Christianity, in the same way that the Orthodox Church is its Greek and Slavic conception, and Protestantism its Germanic one. But the fact is that of these three branches into which the Universal Church has split, only the first has developed to its full strength; the other two are still in the process of development. Catholicism is complete, it is well-rounded in its inner make-up, it is clearly aware of its significance, and up to now has been irresistibly striving to put it into practice, to subject history to it. On the contrary, the other two Churches lack such a clear awareness of themselves.[4] That is why, I repeat, it is

[4] Protestantism, the first to allow an individual interpretation of Christianity, not only is not final and complete at present, but it evidently never will become so in the future. As for Orthodoxy, it has found itself up to now in such difficult historical circumstances, being at one time hampered from without by barbarism (the Tatar Yoke), at another by Mohammedanism (the Turkish Yoke), and finally by Catholicism itself, that it has had to direct all its efforts throughout history toward defending its existence and somehow doing everything necessary to save the souls of its insulted and injured peoples; it has not yet had the means to concern itself with bringing its hidden inner contents into the light of clear consciousness. The attempts of the Slavophiles (Khomya-

impossible to refrain from generalizing to an extreme degree and having the strange confession made by the Grand Inquisitor in private to Christ cover all of mankind and all of history.

He begins with the assertion that all of the teaching bequeathed to us by Christ, as it has been preserved by Providence, is something eternal and fixed, and in the same way that nothing can be removed from it, so can nothing be added to it. It has become a cornerstone of that edifice of world history that has already been raised; and it would be too late now to correct, explain, or limit it in some way or other: that would shake fifteen centuries of constructive work. And that is not only in relation to mankind, which cannot constantly reorganize itself, but also in relation to God. What would a new revelation or an addition to what was already said be but an acknowledgment of the inadequacy of what was said before—and by whom? By God Himself! Finally, and this is the most important thing of all, such a supplementation would be an infringement of human freedom: Christ left mankind His image, which it could follow with a free heart as an ideal in keeping with its (secretly divine) nature and answering to its confused inclinations. This decision of whether or not to follow Him must be a free one, and it is precisely in this freedom of choice that its moral virtue lies. But every new revelation from heaven would appear as a miracle, it would introduce compulsion into history, and would take this freedom of

kov and Yu. Samarin, for example) and of Dostoevsky himself to explain the peculiarity and the idea of the Orthodox Church in history can be explained by this condition and would have been impossible in any other state of affairs.

choice away from man, and along with it its moral virtue. Therefore, as he looks at Christ and thinks of His promised second coming, the Inquisitor says: "Now go, and come no more . . ." "at least do not meddle for the time being," he corrects himself, thinking of his own work on earth which he has not yet completed.

He is strangely thoughtful all the time. Before the face of the Savior, the contrast between reality and His great precepts seem to him particularly striking, and this arouses in him a sad feeling of irony. He reminds Christ of how often the latter had said to men fifteen centuries ago: "I want to make you free," and he adds: "So now You have seen these free people." The irony of this remark relates not only to those whom Christ wanted to ennoble with his teachings, but also to Himself: "This business has cost us dear," he continues, "but we have finally completed it—in Your name. For fifteen centuries, we have been tormenting ourselves with this freedom, but now it is finished, and finished for good."

He is speaking here of the principle of authority which has always permeated the Roman Catholic Church and which has been the reason for its being much more intolerant of all deviations from its dogma than that which was inherent in the other Churches. In the sixteenth century, the time the scene being depicted takes place, the necessity for authority and unquestioning submission was especially strongly understood by Rome in view of the threatening movement of the Reformation, which had destroyed a thousand years of spiritual unity in Western Europe. Phenomena in which it displayed itself were the introduction of the Inquisition and the censorship of books. Champions of these ideas were the Council of Trent and the Jesuit Order, with its doctrine of unconditional submission [5] to one's superiors and of the complete suppression of the individual will.[6] But, as everywhere in the legend under consideration, reference is made to the main feature of Catholicism only because it answered one of mankind's eternal needs and, consequently, expressed in itself an everlasting and necessary feature of man's history. This becomes clear from the Inquisitor's subsequent explanations. He says:

"Only now that we have conquered freedom has it become possible to think for the first time of man's happiness. Man was created a rebel; and how can rebels be happy?" he asks.

Christ brought truth into the world; but the Inquisitor says that man's earthly life is governed by the law of suffering, of perpetually running away from it, or when that is not possible, of eternally following the path of least suffering. Between the truth, which is absolute and characteristic only of an absolute God, and this law of suffering to which man is subjected as a result of his relative nature lies an unbridgeable gap. Whoever can, let him attract man to the first path; man himself will always take the second. And this is precisely what the Inquisitor says: without denying the sublimity of the truth given man by the Savior, he denies only that this truth corresponds to man's nature and, at the same time, he denies the possibility of man's following it. In other words, he rejects the possibility of basing man's earthly destiny on the Savior's precepts and there-

[5] "Be as submissive in the hand of a superior as is the staff in the hand of a pilgrim," etc.

[6] "*Cadaver esto*," i.e., be as impersonal and inert as a corpse.

[126]

fore asserts the necessity of basing them on some other principles.

And it is to them that he immediately shifts his words. But before turning to a consideration of them, let us note that a fundamental change had taken place in Dostoevsky's attitude toward human freedom after publication of his *Notes from the Underground*. There, as here, man's free will is advanced as the chief obstacle to the final arrangement of man's destinies on earth; but, because of that, only the necessity and possibility of such an arrangement are denied, while freedom of will itself is defended as man's most precious feature. In his view of this freedom in *Notes from the Underground*, there is something approbatory, and in this approbation, Dostoevsky with obvious pleasure draws a picture for himself of how, at the moment when universal prosperity is finally achieved, a man "with a retrograde and sarcastic physiognomy will suddenly appear and say to his happy, but somewhat bored, brothers: 'Well, what about it, shall we give all this rationality a good kick and smash it to pieces—with the sole purpose of sending these logarithms to the devil and letting us again live according to our own stupid will?' " [7] After that, a good deal in Dostoevsky's views changed; there was no longer the cheerfulness in his tone, nor was there the mockery or the jokes. How much suffering for man he endured and at the same time how much hatred for him! This is attested to

[7] *Notes from the Underground*, Part I, Chapter IX. See also Chapter X, regarding the preference for a temporary "chicken coop" in the socio-historical system, precisely because it is not final and does not do away with freedom forever, to the "Crystal Palace," which is detestable precisely because of its indestructibility.

by the whole series of his later works, among them *Crime and Punishment*, with its meek martyrs and its senseless tormentors. Fatigue and sorrow replace his earlier confidence, and there is a desire for peace, which is evident most of all in the "Legend." The sublime gifts of freedom, truth, and moral heroism—all this is now pushed aside as burdensome and unnecessary, and one thing only is called for: some kind of happiness, some kind of rest for the "pitiful rebel," for this creature who is nevertheless weary and sick, and for whom compassion stifles all else in his heart, every aspiration to the superhuman and the divine. The "Legend of the Grand Inquisitor" can to a certain extent be regarded as his idea for a final arrangement of man's destinies, something that had been unconditionally rejected in *Notes from the Underground*—the difference being that in the latter he spoke of a rational settlement based on a subtle and detailed study of the laws of physical nature and social relations, but in the "Legend," he speaks of a religious settlement coming from the deepest possible penetration of man's psychical make-up.

"You were warned," says the Inquisitor to Christ. "You had no lack of signs and warnings, but You did not heed them, and You rejected the only way by which men might be made happy." And then he tells his idea, which, if seriously pursued, could not help arousing a feeling of horror in man; and this horror would become greater and greater the more clearly man sensed the idea's irrefutability. The threads of world history, as it has already been played out; the future destinies of man, as they might be foreseen; the mystical demimonde, and the incomprehensible combination of an unquenchable thirst for faith with a despair of there being any object for it—all this has been interwoven here in an amazing way and as a whole forms a statement that we cannot help taking as the wisest, the most profound, the most penetrating that, from the only point of view possible for man, man has ever thought up about himself.

XII

"That terrible and wise spirit, the spirit of self-destruction and non-being," so begins the Inquisitor, "the great spirit spoke with You in the wilderness, and we are told in the books that he supposedly tempted You . . . Is that so? And could anything truer have been said than what he revealed to You in three questions and what You rejected and in the books are called temptations? And yet if ever there was on earth a genuine prodigious miracle, it took place that day, the day of the three temptations. And the miracle was precisely the statement of those three questions. If it were possible to imagine, just for the sake of argument, that those three questions of the terrible spirit had been lost without leaving a trace in the books and that they would have to be restored and invented anew so that they could again be set down in writing, and if in order to do that, we had to assemble all the sages of the earth—rulers, pontiffs, scholars, philosophers, poets—and set them the task of thinking up and formulating three questions, and moreover ones that would not only be in keeping with the magnitude of the occasion,[1] but, in addition, would express in three

[1] How vividly one senses its reality! We note this quality because, in varying, it changes in different places of the "Legend" to

words, in just three human sentences, the whole future history of the world and of humanity—do You think that all the great wisdom of the earth, combined, could have thought up anything equal in depth and force to those three questions which were really asked of You at that time by the wise and mighty spirit in the wilderness? From those questions alone, from the miracle of their statement alone, one can see that we have to do here not with a human, commonplace mind, but with one that is absolute and eternal. For it is as if all the further history of mankind is combined into one whole and foretold in those three questions, and in them are revealed three images in which all the irresoluble historical contradictions of human nature in the whole world will meet. At the time, it could not be so clear, for the future was unknown; but now that fifteen centuries have passed, we see that everything in those three questions was so accurately divined and foretold and has proved to such an extent to be true that nothing can be added to them or taken from them."

Only because the conversation of the Inquisitor with Christ is presented as taking place in the sixteenth century are fifteen centuries of past history mentioned here; but it was written in the nineteenth, and if it could have been done without grossly violating plausibility, the Inquisitor should have agreed to all nineteen centuries: everything he speaks of later and which he referred to in the words "at the time, it could not be so clear" has been completely revealed only in our present century. There were not even any harbingers of it in the period when this scene takes place. Strange as that may be, the transference of historical

the point where one has a completely clear feeling that the "event" never happened.

contradictions that were revealed only in the nineteenth century to a conversation taking place in the sixteenth does not make a bad impression at all; it is not even noticed: everything transitory in the "Legend" recedes into the background and to the foreground come features only of what is deep and eternal in man, so that the mixture in it of past, present, and future—as it were, a combination of all historical time in one moment—not only seems not monstrous, but, on the contrary, completely appropriate and, apparently, necessary. In the Inquisitor's words quoted above, we feel that he himself seems to forget that he is addressing his words to another: they sound like a monologue, like the confession of faith of a ninety-year-old man, and the more they develop the more clearly there emerges from behind his "tall and erect figure" the small and emaciated figure of a man of the nineteenth century, who had borne in his soul much more than this old man ever could have, even though the latter had "fed on honey and locusts in the wilderness" and afterward burned heretics by the hundreds *"ad majorem Dei gloriam."*

From the standpoint of the three temptations, which figuratively represent the future destinies of man, the Inquisitor begins to speak of those destinies and to analyze the meaning of the temptations themselves. Thus, the revelation of the meaning of history and, as it were, the measurement of man's moral strength is presented here in the form of an extensive commentary on a brief text from the Gospel. Here is what is written by the Evangelist Matthew about the temptation itself and the spirit's first question:

> Then was Jesus led up of the spirit into the wilderness to be tempted by the devil.

And when He had fasted forty days and forty nights, He was afterward an hungered.

And when the tempter came to Him, he said: If Thou be the Son of God, command that these stones be made bread.

But he answered and said: It is written, a man shall not live by bread alone, but by every word that proceedeth out of the mouth of God. (Matthew 4:1–3)

"Now decide for Yourself who was right," says the Inquisitor. "You or the one who questioned You then? Recall the first question; its meaning, although not in these words,[2] was as follows:

"You want to go into the world, and You are going with empty hands, with some sort of promise of freedom which men in their simplicity and innate unruliness cannot even understand, which they fear and dread—for never was there anything more unbearable for man and human society than freedom![3] Do you see these stones in this naked and

[2] It is indeed remarkable that the spirit tempted the God-man not during His ministry of saving mankind, but before He had entered upon that ministry, and consequently this ancient fighter against God and enemy of mankind tried, as it were, to lure Him to other possible methods of salvation, he pointed out ways of achieving this other than through His divine teaching and His death on the cross. The temptations related precisely to Jesus' ministry as a whole, and therefore the bread, miracle, and authority offered by the tempter are actually three modes of a different kind of salvation—one that is neither heavenly, divine, blessed, nor mysterious.

[3] This profound idea was first expressed by Dostoevsky in 1847, in one of his most disorderly works, "The Landlady." Here is what he says: "A weak person cannot hold out alone. Give him everything, and he will come and give it all back; give him half the kingdoms of the earth to possess, just try it—and what do you

[132]

parched desert? Turn them into bread, and mankind will run after You like a flock of sheep, grateful and obedient, though eternally trembling with the fear that You might take away Your hand and cut off Your supply of bread. But you did not want to deprive man of freedom, and You rejected the offer; for, You reasoned, what kind of freedom is it if obedience is bought with bread? And Your answer was: 'Man shall not live by bread alone.' But do You know that for the sake of that earthly bread, the spirit of the earth will rise up against You, and will fight You, and overcome You, and everyone will follow him, crying: 'Who is like this beast? He has given us fire from heaven!' "

Here in this apocalyptic image is presented the rebellion of everything earthly, of everything in man that gravitates downward, against everything in him that is heavenly and which is directed upward. And we are shown the victorious outcome of this rebellion, of which we all are the sad witnesses. Poverty, anguish, the pain of unwarmed limbs and of an empty stomach will smother the divine spark in man's soul, and he will turn away from all that is holy and bow down before some new "sacred" thing, before something crude and even base, so long as it feeds and warms him. He will ridicule his former righteous men as unnecessary people and will bow down before new ones, and from them he will begin to compile new calendars of

think? He will then and there hide himself in your boot—so small will he make himself. Give a weak man freedom—and he himself will tie it up and bring it right back to you, etc." This shows how early all of Dostoevsky's basic ideas were conceived, and it was only in accepting or rejecting them that he later hesitated for several decades, but he did not discover anything in them that was essentially new.

saints and celebrate the birthdays of these "benefactors of mankind." Auguste Comte, for example, tried to devise in place of Christianity, which he considered moribund, something like a new religious cult, with feast days and the honoring of the memory of great men. And the cult of service of mankind is spreading more and more today as the service of God declines. Mankind idolizes itself, it now considers only its own suffering, and with weary eyes it looks around for someone who might bring it comfort, help, or at least relief. Timid and trembling, it is ready to rush after anyone who will do something for it, ready to bow down reverently before the one who will lighten its work with successful machines, fertilize its field with a new compound, or ease its temporary pain, even with something that will poison it for life. Confused and suffering, it seems to have lost its sense of the whole, it is as if it does not see behind the petty details of its life the main and monstrous evil approaching it from all sides: that the more man tries to overcome his suffering the more the suffering grows and the more all-embracing it becomes—and people are already perishing not just individually, not by the thousand, but by the million and by whole nations, faster and faster, more and more inexorably, having forgotten God, and cursing themselves.

I should like to quote here the majestic scene from the Revelation of Saint John—a revelation of the destinies of God's Church on earth and also of mankind in agitation around it, trying to devour it. The imagery here expresses allegorically the stages in the development of those destinies and by its nature determines the general meaning of those stages, free of all details:

[134]

And I stood upon the sand of the sea, and saw a beast rise up out of the sea, having seven heads and ten horns, and upon his horns ten crowns, and upon his heads the name of blasphemy. . . . and the dragon [4] gave him his power, and his seat, and great authority.

And I saw one of his heads as it were wounded to death; and his deadly wound was healed: and all the world wondered after the beast.

And they worshiped the dragon [5] which gave power unto the beast: and they worshiped the beast saying, who is like unto the beast? Who is able to make war with him?

And there was given unto him a mouth speaking great things and blasphemies; and power was given unto him to continue forty and two months.

And he opened his mouth in blasphemy against God, to blaspheme His name, and His tabernacle, and them that dwell in heaven.

And it was given unto him to make war with the saints, and to overcome them: and power was given him over all kindreds, and tongues, and nations.

And all that dwell upon the earth shall worship him, whose names are not written in the book of life of the Lamb slain from the foundation of the world.

If any man have an ear, let him hear.

He that leadest into captivity shall go into captivity: he that killeth with the sword must be killed with the

---

[4] According to Revelation, the first spirit to renounce God.

[5] We should expect here "the beast"—but how wonderfully sustained is the accuracy of the apocalyptic images, their conformity with their true sense!

sword. Here is the patience and the faith of the saints. (Revelation, 13)

A knowledge that feeds but no longer enlightens man, a great exchange of spiritual gifts for material ones and of a clear conscience for a full stomach—this is what is represented in those amazing words. With this concern for "bread alone," churches will close, the great regulating force will disappear, and people will again set about raising buildings on sand, constructing with their own strength and their own wisdom the Tower of Babel of their life. It is to all this that the Inquisitor refers in his moving words, and at the same time he predicts how it will all end: "Do You know," he says, "that ages will pass and mankind will proclaim through the mouths of its representatives of science and wisdom that there is no crime and, consequently, no sin, that there are only hungry people. 'Feed them, and then ask virtue of them'—this is what will be written on the banner that they will raise against You and with which Your temple will be destroyed.[6] In the place where Your temple stood, a new building will rise;[7] the terrible Tower

[6] The reference is to the theory of the relativity of crime, according to which it in no way differs from any of the rest of man's deeds, for like them all it is caused by the influence of environment, upbringing, and external circumstances in general. The will, completely determined by these circumstances, is incapable of not performing some act, in the given instance a criminal one; therefore, it is not free, and, consequently, "there is no sin." *Crime and Punishment* (in certain of its episodes) and finally *The Brothers Karamazov* can be regarded as an artistic-psychological critique of this idea of the nineteenth century, to which the greatest minds in it are somehow attracted, and also as its rejection, for being contrary to the nature of things and untrue.

[7] Because of the theory of the innocence of the individual will, all crimes, as well as all evil, are attributed to an incorrect social

of Babel will be raised again, and although, like the first one, it will not be finished, yet You could have prevented this new tower and have reduced men's suffering by a thousand years; for, as You know, they will come back to us after having tormented themselves for a thousand years with their tower! [8] Then they will seek us out again, underground, hiding in the catacombs—for we shall again be persecuted [9] and tortured; they will find us and cry out to us: 'Feed us, for those who promised us fire from heaven [10] did not give it to us.' And then we shall complete the construction of their tower, for the one who feeds them will complete it. And we alone shall feed them, in Your

---

order. Therefore, the question of the struggle against evil boils down to the question of the best possible organization of human society—and this introduces into history a theoretical idea as the creative principle, in place of the unconscious forces operating in it.

[8] Dostoevsky frequently and persistently pointed out (for example, in *The Possessed*) how science, by rejecting free will in man and absoluteness in crime, will drive people to cannibalism—and then, in despair, "the earth will begin to cry for its old gods," and the people will again turn to religion. Thus, their turning to God, he thought, would crown history, and the greater the misfortunes awaiting man in the future the more certain this would come about.

[9] The reference here is to a period of unbearable persecutions to which self-determining and unhappy mankind will subject religion for a certain time, precisely just before it turns to God. The persecutions—not against the Church, but against the religious principle itself in man—which occurred at the end of the eighteenth century in France, and which even now flare up here and there, can be regarded as the first mild harbinger of an attempt to eradicate religion completely, to eradicate it everywhere on earth.

[10] I.e., the rationalist theoreticians who propose to arrange man's life on earth without religion, and particularly the theoreticians of new organizational forms of labor and property.

name, declaring falsely that it is in Your name. Oh, they will never, never feed themselves without us! No science will give them bread so long as they remain free. But it will all end by their laying their freedom at our feet and saying to us: 'It doesn't matter if you enslave us, just give us enough to eat.' [11] They themselves will finally understand that freedom and earthly bread sufficient for everyone are inconceivable together: for they will never, never be able to share with each other! [12] They will also be convinced

[11] Despair from economic catastrophes will lead (it is already leading) to the neglect of all other ideals that were originally inseparable from the ideal of an even distribution of wealth: thus, even now, the radical democrats are growing indifferent to the precepts of political and social freedom (constitutionalism), as well as to the progress in the sciences and education, and are ready to join up indifferently with both military despots and the Church triumphant over the State, as long as some force, be it military or ecclesiastical—it is all the same to them—solves the economic problem and "feeds everyone."

[12] With this concern "about bread alone," the conscience dies out in man, and along with it, compassion: for it is impossible either to trace these feelings to "bread" or to derive them from "concern about it." Everyone will take for himself as much as he has a right to according to the quantity and quality of his work, and the genius will demand that the untalented be removed from the banquet, because they take too much from him. As for the question of the organization of society according to economic principles, the distribution of the products of production according to right—"*suum cuique*"—and according to the justice of the human heart—"God is for all"—presents the main and, in a strict sense, an unsolvable difficulty. It precisely is already the subject of endless disagreements among theoreticians of society, and if they are so irreconcilable in their thinking, so incompatible in their books, then it is difficult even to imagine the chaos of conflict to which the unsolvability of this question will lead in reality, where passions prevail, where indignation and anger fail to subside when necessary and pity has its cogency, and, finally, where every dialectic is shattered against the honest failure to understand

that they can never be free, because they are weak, vicious, worthless, and rebellious. You promised them the bread of heaven, but, I repeat again, can it compare with earthly bread in the eyes of the weak, the eternally vicious, and the eternally ungrateful [13] race of man? And if for the sake of the bread of heaven, thousands and tens of thousands will follow You, then what will become of the millions and tens of thousands of millions of creatures who will not have the strength to give up the earthly bread for that of heaven?"

XIII

"Or is it only the tens of thousands of the great and the strong that are dear to You," continues the Inquisitor, "and the millions of others, numerous as the sands of the sea, who are weak but who love You, are to serve only as material for the great and the strong?"

These words mark a turning point in his thought: its shift to the eternal meaning of history, which is incompatible with absolute truth and mercy. For the time being, this

---

men of good heart. Even now it is possible to foresee that if the social crisis is solved in accordance with the inner wishes of these theoreticians, then a new one will arise with two diametrically opposed slogans: "Do away with the untalented; hide them, reduce them to zero, enslave them" and "We don't need geniuses, geniuses are superfluous, they insult our poverty with their spiritual beauty, and they are dangerous." Nietzsche's philosophy, now being propagated in Europe before our eyes, is an early, but a very bold expression of the first slogan.

[13] The word in Dostoevsky is *neblagorodnogo*—ignoble. [Tr.]

meaning is only pointed out in passing, but later the Inquisitor will base his rejection precisely on it.

It is a well-known view that the greatest flowering of culture is brought about by only a few select people of great ability; and in order that they be able to carry out their mission freely and leisurely, they are provided with security and spare time by the labor and suffering of the vast masses of the people. We shall pass over this view, as it is too crude to dwell on, and in order to make clear what the Inquisitor says next, quote the words from the Revelation of St. John 14:1–5, about the small number of the chosen and justified on Judgment Day. Evidently, it is this sublime and heart-piercing image that the Inquisitor has in mind as he further develops his idea:

> And I looked, and, lo, a Lamb stood on the mount Sion, and with him an hundred forty and four thousand, having his Father's name written on their foreheads.
>
> And I heard a voice from heaven, as the voice of many waters, and as the voice of a great thunder: and I heard the voice of harpers harping with their harps:
>
> And they sang as it were a new song before the throne, and before the four beasts, and the elders: and no man could learn that song but the hundred and forty and four thousand, which were redeemed from the earth.
>
> These are they which were not defiled with women; for they are virgins. These are they which follow the Lamb whithersoever he goeth. These were redeemed from among men, being the first fruits unto God and to the Lamb.

And in their mouth was found no guile: for they are without fault before the throne of God.

What a wonderful, alluring ideal is in this image; how it arouses yearning desire in us; how little we are surprised, after merely a glance at it, at the profound and quick upheaval the Gospel brought about during the transition from the ancient world to the modern one.

And yet, precisely because the beauty of this ideal is so great that the mere desire to achieve it provides happiness, there is immediately aroused in us an irresistible feeling of pity for those human beings "as numerous as the sands of the sea," who, after separating off from themselves those "hundred and forty and four thousand," remain somewhere behind, forgotten and trampled under foot in history.[1]

This feeling of pity also fills the soul of the Inquisitor, and he says firmly: "No, we cherish the weak, too," and the thought quickly flashes across his mind of how he and

[1] In the chapter "Ivan Fyodorovich's Nightmare," which on the whole can be regarded as variations on "The Legend of the Grand Inquisitor," the devil says: "How many souls it was necessary to ruin . . . in order to obtain just one righteous Job!" Leaving aside the superficial idea that for the free leisure time of the few who would "cultivate the arts and sciences" (they are really cultivated by poor people whose lives are filled with hard work), it is necessary to have the back-breaking and excessive work of everyone else, we should like to point out another correlation that does indeed exist between the salvation of one at the expense of the destruction of many. . . . Higher education, for example, is a fine thing, it is respected by everyone, and it attracts everyone to it, but, as it is impossible in childhood to tell whether someone has a talent for it, thousands and tens of thousands of children are crippled by difficult and complex schooling, in order that from their number can be separated a score or so of truly educated people. The others crowd around them not only as an uneducated mass but as a corrupted one.

those who will understand him must regulate the lives of those weak ones: and they will do it completely alone, without *Him*, although, for the lack of another organizational idea, it will be done in His name:

"They are depraved and rebellious," he says, "but in the end, they, too, will become obedient. They will marvel at us and look on us as gods because, having become their leaders, we agreed to endure freedom and to rule over them—so terrible will it finally become for them to be free! But we shall say that we are obeying You and are ruling in Your name. We shall deceive them again, for we shall never again let You come to us. In this deceit will be our suffering, for we shall find it necessary to lie."

And then he shifts to the unquenchable desires of the human soul, by means of which, if one knows and answers them, one can and should raise the final and everlasting edifice of man's earthly life: "In the first question in the wilderness," he says, "lay the great secret of this world. Had You chosen the bread, You would have satisfied man's universal and everlasting yearning—both that of the individual and that of mankind as a whole: to know whom he should worship. Once man is free, he has no more incessant and agonizing anxiety than to find as soon as possible someone to worship. But man seeks to worship what is indisputable, so indisputable that all people at once agree to worship it together. For these pitiful creatures are concerned not only with finding something that I or another person can worship, but with finding something that *everyone* will believe in and worship; and it must without fail *be done by all together*. This longing for *community* of worship has been the chief torment of every person individually as well as of mankind as a whole since the beginning of time. In the name of common worship they have destroyed each other with the sword.[2] They have created gods and have called out to each other, 'Abandon your gods and come worship ours, or else it will be the death of you and of your gods.' And so it will be to the end of the world, even when the gods have disappeared from the world, the people will just the same fall down before idols. You knew, You could not help knowing this fundamental secret of human nature; but You rejected the only absolute banner that was offered You in order to make everyone worship You incontestably —the banner of earthly bread; and You rejected it in the name of freedom and bread from heaven. And look what You did further—again all in the name of freedom! I tell You man has no more excruciating anxiety than to find someone to whom he can as quickly as possible turn over the gift of freedom with which the unfortunate creature is born. But the only one who can take possession of man's freedom is he who can soothe his conscience. With bread, You were given an incontestable banner: if You give him bread, man will worship You, for there is nothing more in-

---

[2] In *A Raw Youth*, Makar Ivanovich, an old man and a type similar to that of Father Zosima in *The Brothers Karamazov*, says: "Man cannot exist without worshiping something, such a person couldn't put up with himself, no person could at all. And if he rejects God, he will worship an idol, a wooden one, a golden one, or one that exists only in his imagination." By "idols" that people fall down before after rejecting the true God are understood here imaginary ones: intellect deified and its products— philosophy and the exact sciences; or, finally, idols that are completely crude, such as certain individual ideas of that same intellect, that science, or that philosophy: for example, the idea of utilitarianism. In this passage of the "Legend," however, is meant the mystical or religious worship of, for example, Christ, Mohammed, and so on.

contestable than bread; but if at the same time, someone other than You gains possession of his conscience—oh, then he will even give up Your bread and set out after him who has seduced his conscience. You were right about that. For the secret of human existence is not only to live, but to have something to live for. Without a clear idea of the object of life, man will not consent to go on living, and will rather destroy himself than remain on earth—even if there is bread all around him.[3] This is so. But what came of it? Instead of taking possession of man's freedom, You increased it more than ever! Or did You forget that peace of mind and even death is dearer[4] to man than freedom of choice in the knowledge of good and evil? Nothing is more enticing to man than the freedom of his conscience, but nothing is more agonizing either. And so instead of firm foundations for soothing man's conscience once and for all You chose everything that is unusual, conjectural, and vague; You chose everything that was beyond man's strength; there-fore, You acted as if You did not love him at all—and who was it who did that? You, who came to give Your life for him! Instead of gaining possession of man's freedom, You increased it and burdened man's spiritual kingdom with its torments forever. You wanted man's freely-offered love; You wanted him to follow You freely, charmed and capti-vated by You. Instead of relying on the firm ancient law,[5]

[3] A characteristic correctly noted, and the only one, with its idealism, that balances all the baseness attributed to man in this "Legend."

[4] This is undoubtedly a slip of the tongue, which should read: "more convenient, more advantageous, more necessary, and better."

[5] I.e., the law of the Old Testament, which does indeed differ from that of the New in the detail, clarity, and firmness of its in-structions and the precision of its punitive measures for violation

man in the future was supposed to decide for himself with a free heart what is good and what is evil, having only Your image before him as his guide.[6] But did You not think that he would finally question even Your image and Your truth, and reject them, too, if he were oppressed by such a terrible burden as freedom of choice? They will at last cry out that the truth is not in You—for they could not have been left in greater confusion and torment than that caused by You in giving them so many cares and unsolvable problems. Thus You Yourself laid the foundation for the destruction of Your own kingdom, so don't blame anyone else for it."

In other words, the doctrine that came to save the world has through its very loftiness destroyed it; it has brought into history not reconciliation and unity, but chaos and

---

of what is fixed by it (see Deuteronomy). One can say, transposing everything to legal terms, that in the Old Testament are given rules, and in the New, principles.

[6] In these three lines is expressed Dostoevsky's conception of the nature of Christianity and is indicated the guiding principle for a Christian's actions: always mentally connect each of your intended acts with Christ and ask yourself if He would have done it, or, if He had seen it, would He have approved of it—and do this without violating in your mind the totality of His image as passed on to us by the Evangelists, or the aggregate of all His features. I think this principle is the true one, and if it had been observed, His Gospel could never have been subjected to those forced applications to which it has been subjected in history by those who have singled out individual statements from it. Thus, on the expression *compelle intrare*—"compel them (the invited) to enter" to the marriage feast, in the "Parable of the Invited and Uninvited" —the Catholic Inquisition based its right of existence. On the expression "My Kingdom is not of this world," many, even now, base their demand that the Church take an indifferent attitude toward sin, toward the crime of the "world" (the entire sociohistorical system).

hostility. History has not yet come to an end; and yet it must come to an end. This is precisely what the nations are seeking in their thirst to find an object of common and harmonious worship. They are even destroying one another so that, even if by means of the destruction of the many who are irreconcilable, the remainder can finally be united. Christianity did not satisfy this need of the human heart by leaving everything to be decided by the individual and by falsely relying on man's ability to distinguish between good and evil. Even the ancient law, which was not so lofty, but which was precise and strict, satisfied this need more than Christianity does: all who deviated from it were stoned and cast out, and the people remained united, even if by force. An even better way to satisfy this need—true, it is quite a crude one—would be by "earthly bread," the concealment from man's eyes of everything heavenly. By satisfying his hunger, it would lull the anxieties of his conscience.

We will probably not depart very far from the truth if we say that with the attempt to resort to "earthly bread" in gaining control over the destinies of mankind, there is understood here a terrible, but a really powerful way out of the contradictions of history: namely, the lowering of the psychical level in man. By extinguishing in him all that is vague, disquieting, and tormenting, and by simplifying his nature ⁷ to the point where it will know only the serenity of short-lived desires, by making him know in

⁷ In *The Possessed*, one of the characters who appears only in passing (Shigalyov) expounds the idea of this simplification of human nature and the lowering of its psychical level. This can be regarded as an early and more thoroughly motivated account of the given passage in the "Legend."

moderation, feel in moderation, and desire in moderation—
this is the way to satisfy him finally and to set his mind at
rest.

XIV

In shifting his words more and more from the chaos
into which Christianity and its doctrine of freedom have
plunged man to a description of man's future and final
pacification on earth, the Inquisitor turns to an analysis of
the two remaining temptations of the devil. Here are the
words in which they are recorded by the Evangelist Matthew:

> Then the devil taketh Him up into the holy city,
> and setteth Him on a pinnacle of the temple,
> And saith unto Him, If Thou be the Son of God,
> cast Thyself down: for it is written, He shall give His
> angels charge concerning Thee: and in their hands,
> they shall bear Thee up, lest at any time Thou dash
> Thy foot against a stone.
> Jesus said unto him, It is written again, Thou shalt
> not tempt the Lord thy God.
> Again the devil taketh Him up into an exceeding
> high mountain, and sheweth Him all the kingdoms of
> the world, and the glory of them;
> And saith unto Him, All these things will I give
> Thee, if Thou wilt fall down and worship me.
> Then saith Jesus unto him, Get thee hence, Satan,

for it is written, Thou shalt worship the Lord thy God, and Him only shalt thou serve.

Then the devil leaveth Him, and, behold, angels came and ministered unto Him. (Matthew 4:5–11; see also Luke 4:5–13.)

Having spoken of the elements of self-destruction with which Christianity is filled, the Inquisitor continues, addressing himself again to Christ: "And yet, is that what was offered You? There are three forces, the only three forces on earth that can conquer and hold captive forever the conscience of these weak rebels for their happiness. Those forces are: *miracle*, *mystery*, and *authority*. You rejected all three, and You Yourself set the example for it. When the wise and terrible spirit set You on a pinnacle of the temple and said that if You want to know whether You are the Son of God, You should cast Yourself down, for it was said concerning Him that angels would take and bear Him up, and He would not stumble or fall;[1] then You would know whether You are the Son of God, and would prove how great is Your faith in Your Father. But You listened and then rejected his offer. You did not succumb and did not cast Yourself down from the pinnacle. Oh, of course, You acted in this instance proudly and splendidly, like God. But what of men, that weak, rebellious race of men—are they gods? Oh, You understood very well then that if You had taken just one step, had made just one move to cast Yourself down, You would immediately have tempted God and would have lost all Your faith in Him, and would have been dashed to pieces against that earth

[1] In Dostoevsky, this word is *rasshibyotsya* ("injure Himself"). [Tr.]

which You came to save. And the wise spirit, who was tempting You, would have rejoiced."

Surprising here is the disbelief in the mystical act of redemption, expressed in the *first* words we noted, and its combination with a complete belief in the temptation of Jesus and even in the mystical importance of that temptation, in the devil's attempt to prevent His coming into the world as the Savior, which is expressed in the *last* words we noted.

"But, I repeat," continues the Inquisitor, "are there many like You? And could You really assume, even for a moment, that man, too, could withstand such a temptation? Is human nature so constituted that it can reject a miracle, and at such terrible moments of life, the moments of its most terrible, fundamental, and agonizing spiritual difficulties [2] remain with only the free decision of his heart? Oh, You knew that Your spiritual feat would be preserved in the books, that it would be remembered to the end of time [3] and reach the farthest ends of the earth, and You hoped that man, following You, would stay with God without the need of a miracle. But You did not know that as soon as man rejects miracle, he immediately rejects God as well,[4] for man seeks not so much God as miracles. And

[2] This refers to man's attitude toward the mystical act of redemption, by faith in which man lives, and the fact that this faith and this life would have to be supported by something more than what is provided by merely the sublime image of Christ.

[3] Again, what astonishing faith resounds in these words!

[4] Dostoevsky is speaking here, and with justifiable contempt, of how in history—even to this day—the struggle against religion has almost been identified with the struggle against the miraculous, and vice-versa; and of how man had no sooner puzzled out something in nature that had previously seemed supernatural than he cowardly deserted faith for unfaith.

as man is unable to remain without a miracle, he will create for himself new miracles, miracles of his own,[5] and will worship the miracle of the sorcerer and the witchcraft of old women,[6] even though he is a rebel, a heretic, and an infidel a hundred times over. You did not come down from the cross when they shouted to You, jeering You: 'If Thou be the Son of God, come down from the cross, and we will believe that Thou art He.' You did not come down, for, again, You did not want to enslave man by a miracle, and You thirsted for a faith that was given freely, and not based on miracle. You thirsted for freely-given love and not for the servile raptures of the slave before the might that has once and for all terrified him.[7] But here, also, You rated men too highly, for they are, of course, slaves, although they are born rebels. Look around and judge for Yourself: fifteen centuries have gone by—go and take a look at them. Who is it You raised up to Yourself? I swear, man is weaker

[5] This refers to the latest discoveries of science and, even more, to the technological inventions that man so marvels at in our day and likes to repeat over and over to himself, scarcely believing that they actually exist and that he discovered them himself.

[6] The reference here is to the particular interest with which people in godless times listen to everything strange and exceptional, in which the law of nature seems to have been violated. One might say that in such times nothing is so avidly sought after by man as precisely the miraculous—but only with the indispensable condition that it not also be divine. The craze for spiritualism, referred to derisively in *A Writer's Diary*, was undoubtedly called to Dostoevsky's mind by the universality and constancy of this psychic trait in man. Compare the superstitious state of Roman society when it lapsed into total atheism in the second and third centuries.

[7] The reference here is to the ineffable superiority of Christianity, with its simplicity and humanity, to all the other religions of this earth, in which the element of the miraculous so predominates over everything else and which arose historically out of a fear of that "miraculous."

[150]

and baser by nature than You believed him to be! [8] Can he, can he really do what You did? By respecting him so much, You acted as if You had ceased to feel any compassion for him, for You demanded too much of him—and who did that? You, who loved him more than Yourself! If You had respected him less, You would have demanded less of him, and that would have been more like love, for then his burden would have been lighter."

Because the Savior's precepts were too lofty, they were misunderstood by man, whose heart is perverted and whose mind is darkened. He scoffs and jeers at their great purity, at their wonderful simplicity and holiness—and he does this at the same time that he worships what is vulgar and coarse, but which impresses his timid imagination. With powerful words, the Inquisitor draws a picture of the rebellion against religion, only a small segment of which has as yet been seen by world history, and with a penetrating eye he notes what will follow it:

"Man is weak and base. What does it matter that he is now [9] rebelling everywhere against our authority and is proud that he is rebelling! It is the pride of a child and a

[8] The basic idea of the "Legend." Later we shall also mention several sentences in which its meaning seems to be concentrated, or more precisely, in which its points of departure are indicated.

[9] He is not speaking here of the Reformation movement, which was contemporary with the dialogue of the "Legend," for the spirit of deep faith that permeated that movement was too great to be referred to contemptuously (see the few words about that spirit in Dostoevsky's Pushkin Speech, apropos the lines: "Once while wandering in the savage wilderness," etc.). Undoubtedly, the words of the "Legend" were called forth by the antireligious movement, partly of the eighteenth, but mainly of the nineteenth century, in which as few efforts and as little seriousness were expended on the struggle against religion as were on the struggle against some superstitions or other.

schoolboy. They are little children who have rebelled in class and driven out the teacher. But an end will also come to the enthusiasm of the children,[10] and it will cost them dear. They will tear down the temples, and drown the earth in blood.[11] But they will see, at last, the stupid children, that although they are rebels, they are impotent rebels, unable to bear their own rebellion.[12] In a flood of

[10] And it is happening, for example, in our time in respect to the recent antireligious movement, just as it happened in every other more serious time in respect to every previous rebellion against religion. Thus, the Reformation itself, as a personal quest for the Church, came into being after the age of humanism and its blasphemous attitude toward religion. And after the period of the French Revolution came the times of Chateaubriand, Joseph de Maistre, and others, with their bizarre ideas and confused feelings. The true attitude toward those and analagous movements is correctly pointed out by Dostoevsky: in their followers, there is no genuine faith, simple and strong, but the fear and confusion of yesterday's blasphemous schoolboys; this is not a case of God acting in man, but of man imitating outwardly the words and impulses of those in whom He truly acted, those whom He at one time called to Himself (the righteous).

[11] This refers not to the time of the First French Revolution, as one might think, but to what will definitely happen in the future —an attempt forcibly to suppress the religious consciousness in all of mankind. These words correspond to certain of the passages of the "Legend" already quoted above.

[12] Dostoevsky, who always stands above his heroes (whom he never portrays out of admiration, but rather to express one of his ideas), likes to observe how, despite their great strength, they weaken under the pressure of spiritual torment, how they cannot bear their own "breadth" and criminality, although they had earlier made a theory of it (for example, Stavrogin's last conversation with Liza in *The Possessed* and Ivan Karamazov's last meeting with Smerdyakov). Almost everywhere in Dostoevsky the depiction of a very strong man, if he does not finally end by repenting (as with Raskolnikov), ends with a description of a sort of weakening of his strength and the humiliation and mockery of the "former strong man."

silly tears, they will finally admit that He who created them rebels must, without doubt, have wanted to ridicule them. They will say this in despair, and their words will be blasphemy which will make them even more unhappy, for human nature cannot bear blasphemy, and in the end always avenges it on itself."

Then, summing up world history, the Inquisitor turns to the disclosure of his secret, which consists in correcting the act of redemption through acceptance of all three counsels of the "wise and powerful spirit of the wilderness," which, in turn, he does out of love for mankind, in order to settle its earthly destinies. His justification of this criminal correction derives from the image of the few who are redeemed, which we cited above from Revelation 14. Recalling it, he says: "And so unrest, perplexity, and unhappiness—this is the present-day lot of man after You suffered so much for his freedom! Your great prophet tells in a vision and an allegory that he saw all the participants in the first resurrection and that there were of each tribe twelve thousand.[13] But if there were so many of them, they, too, must have been not like men, but gods. They had borne Your cross, they had endured scores of years in the hungry and naked wilderness living on locusts and roots—and, of course, You can point with pride to those children of freedom, of freely-given love, of free and splendid sacrifice in Your name.[14] But remember that there were only a few

[13] In Revelation 7, there is a preliminary enumeration of those who are saved—twelve thousand from each of the tribes of Israel, who, in chapter 14, are named in the overall figure of 144,000.

[14] What an amazing, profound, and correct understanding of the true meaning of spiritual freedom—freedom from ourselves, from the baseness in our nature, in the name of what is higher and sacred, and which we felt and acknowledged to be our better side. This is the freedom referred to here, in contrast to the crude un-

thousand of them, and what is more, they were gods—but what about the rest? And how are the others, the weak ones, to blame for not being able to receive such terrible gifts? [15] Did You really come only to the chosen and for the chosen? If so, there is a mystery here, and we cannot comprehend it."

XV

With this inability to comprehend why the mystery of redemption took place in such elevated forms and why it failed to include the innocently weak, the Inquisitor's dialectic enters a new and higher sphere: the rejection of redemption itself. As above, in the confession of Ivan Karamazov, the rejection of a future life and the Last Judgment is based on the incomprehensibility of the mystery of innocent suffering. The Inquisitor does not deny the existence of these acts; [1] on the contrary, he has a dazzlingly keen perception of them. There is rather a *rebellion* against them, a *fall* from God—the second, near the final arrangement of man's destiny, at the close of history, but in every way similar to the first fall, which took place at the very beginning of man's destiny—however, with a deeper consciousness of all its burden.

---

derstanding of it, according to which the baseness in ourselves is independent of guidance by or subservience to some higher principle lying outside us.

[15] The second central idea of the "Legend."

[1] That is, redemption and retribution. [Tr.]

"And if it is a mystery," says the Inquisitor, "then we, too, had a right to preach a mystery and teach them that it is not the free decision of their hearts that is important,[2] nor is it love, but a mystery to which they must submit blindly, even against their conscience. And that is what we have done. We have corrected Your great work and founded it on *miracle, mystery,* and *authority.* And the people rejoiced that they were again led like a flock of sheep and that their hearts had finally been relieved of the terrible gift that had brought them so much suffering.[3] Were we right in teaching and doing that? Tell me! Didn't we love mankind when we so meekly acknowledged its weakness, when we lovingly lightened its burden, and permitted its weak nature even to sin, so long as it was with our permission? Why have You now come to interfere with us? And why are You looking so silently and searchingly at me with Your meek eyes? Get angry! I don't want Your love, because I don't love You myself. And what do I have

[2] This thesis, as is generally known, is indeed a feature of Catholic doctrine, and it is what has led to all the formalism in the Western Church and to the moral corruption of the nations shepherded by it. From it came the so-called doctrine of "good works," which, no matter how they are done, even if quite mechanically, are equally salutary for the soul. Thence the Indulgence, i.e., the forgiveness of sins, at first to those who participated in the Crusades in order to lay down their lives for their faith and Church, later to those who in some way or other supported the Crusades, and finally to those who, in general, contributed money for the needs of the Church: whence it was but one step to the sale at various prices of Letters of Indulgence. And it was precisely over this means of absolution that Protestantism parted company with the Old Church: to the latter's formal method of saving men's souls through dead works it opposed absolution through faith, i.e., through an act of live inner movement.

[3] I.e., freedom and the free distinction between good and evil.

to hide from You? Or don't I know to whom I am speaking? Everything I have to say to You is known to You already—I can read it in Your eyes. And would I hide our secret from You? Maybe You really want to hear it from my lips. Then listen: we are not with You, but with *him*—that is our secret! For a long time now we have not been with You, but with *him*—eight centuries already. Just eight centuries ago, we took from him what You rejected with scorn: that last gift he offered You after showing You all the kingdoms of the earth: we took from him Rome and Caesar's sword . . ."

With just these words begins the disclosure of the special Catholic idea in history. Everything said earlier is of general significance, i.e., it represents the dialectic of Christianity in its basic idea, which is the same for all believers in connection with the revelation of human nature, condemnation of it, and compassion for it. But as it develops further and further and finally ends with the idea of a religious arrangement of human destinies on earth, one that is final and universal, this dialectic, hitherto completely abstract, coincides with a historical fact that answers to it; and it automatically draws it into itself, clinging with its turns of thought on to outstanding features of reality. That historical fact is the Roman-Catholic Church with its universal aspirations, with its external power of unification—a Christian seed that germinated on the soil of ancient paganism.

Pointing out that their work "has not yet been brought to completion," that it "has only begun," the Inquisitor, nevertheless, expresses his firm belief that it will be completed: "We shall have to wait a long time for that," he says, "and the earth will suffer a great deal in the meantime, but we shall achieve our goal and be Caesars, and then we

shall think about the universal happiness of man.[4] And yet
You could even then have taken up Caesar's sword. Why
did You reject that last gift? If You had accepted that
third counsel of the mighty spirit, You would have accomplished everything that man seeks on earth, that is, whom
to worship, whom to hand his conscience to, and how to
unite everyone finally in one unanimous and harmonious
anthill.[5] Because the need for a world-wide union is the

[4] An idea exclusively Dostoevsky's and by no means one of
Rome's. Even if Rome, both in ancient and modern times, did
aspire to world supremacy, it was certainly not for "the happiness
of man." From this example, one can best of all see how Dostoevsky intertwines his own particular and personal idea into historical
fact, making it, as it were, its soul.

[5] The language and the ideas here were specially worked out
by Dostoevsky, and they sound somewhat strange in the mouth
of the sixteenth-century Inquisitor. The "anthill," the "Crystal
Palace," and the "chicken coop" are three metaphorical expressions
of the idea of a world-wide union of men and of their pacification,
first discussed by Dostoevsky in *Notes from the Underground*.
The "chicken coop" is poor and unpleasant reality; it is, however,
preferable to all else, because it is fragile, it can always be changed
or destroyed, and, consequently, although it fails to answer the
secondary requirements of human nature, it does answer its chief
and most essential feature—free will and capricious desire, which
do not die out in the individual. The "Crystal Palace" is the artificial edifice of human life, raised on the principles of reason and
art, and it is worse than any reality, for, while it satisfies all human
needs and demands, it does not answer the most important one—
the need for individual, particular desire; it crushes the personality.
In *Notes from the Underground*, the second formula is rejected
and the first retained, in the absence for man of the third—the
"anthill." By it is understood the universal and harmonious union
of all living creatures of one species, based on the presence in them
of a general and infallible instinct for constructing a common
dwelling. All animals living in societies (ants, for example) are
endowed with such an instinct, but man lacks it; therefore,
whereas they always build alike, everywhere the same and always

[157]

third and final torment of man.[6] Mankind as a whole has always aspired to organize itself into a universal state. There have been many great nations with great histories, but the higher those nations stood, the more unhappy they were, for they were more acutely aware than other people of the craving for a world-wide union of men. The great conquerors, the Tamerlanes and Genghis-Khans, swept like a whirlwind over the earth, trying to conquer the universe; and they, too, although unconsciously, expressed the same great craving of mankind for universal and world-wide unity. If You had accepted the world and Caesar's purple, You would have founded the universal kingdom and given universal peace. For who is to rule over men if not those who possess their conscience and in whose hands is their bread? And so we have taken up Caesar's sword, and having taken it up, we have, of course, rejected You and followed *him*."

Thus, the counsels of the "wise and powerful spirit," who tempted Jesus in the wilderness, contain the secret of universal history and the answer to the deepest aspirations

---

peacefully, man everywhere builds different things, eternally changing his desires and notions. And no sooner does he set about building a common dwelling than he disagrees over his representatives, individual persons, and, moreover, he does it with deadly animosity and hatred. One must constantly keep these three formulas in mind when reading Dostoevsky's works.

[6] One must distinguish this "union" from the "common worship" of something or other by the human conscience, about which we spoke earlier. That was an internal, spiritual union of men, but this refers to their external union, to a harmonious socio-historical life. There is a relationship between these two ideas, but they are not identical; corresponding to each other like body and soul, they are two parts of a third—the universal harmony of human life.

of human nature. Those counsels were criminal, but that is because man's very nature is already perverted. And there is no means except through crime to answer its aspirations; there is no other possibility of satisfying, protecting, and pitying this race of perverted creatures than by accepting this very perversion as its basis—by gathering together their scattered flock by means of a perverted idea, the falsity of which would answer the falsity of their nature.

XVI

Never has there been a greater despair than that with which this strange and almost irrefutable idea is infused. One might say it is the saddest thought ever to pass through human consciousness and that the page just quoted is the most painful in all of world literature. And it ends with complete despair—with the fall of the lie, behind which stands no truth, with the annihilation of the deceit, the only thing that people can live by. This is said in explanation of the mysterious words of the twelfth, seventeenth, and eighteenth chapters of The Revelation of St. John, in which, according to the interpretations of theologians, the earthly destinies of the Old and New Testament Churches are allegorically represented by the figure of the "woman." Here are those words:

> And there appeared a great wonder in heaven; a woman clothed with the sun, and the moon under her feet, and upon her head a crown of twelve stars:

And she being with child cried, travailing in birth, and pained to be delivered.

And there appeared another wonder in heaven; and behold a great red dragon, having seven heads and ten horns, and seven crowns upon his heads.

And his tail drew the third part of the stars of heaven, and did cast them to the earth: and the dragon stood before the woman which was ready to be delivered, for to devour her child as soon at it was born.

And she brought forth a man child, who was to rule all nations with a rod of iron: and her child was caught up unto God, and to His throne.

And the woman fled into the wilderness, where she hath a place prepared of God, that they should feed her there a thousand two hundred and threescore days. . . .

A few lines later the fate of the dragon is described:

And the great dragon was cast out, that old serpent, called the devil, and satan, which deceiveth the whole world. . . .

And I heard a loud voice saying in heaven, Now is come salvation, and strength, and the kingdom of our God, and the power of His Christ: for the accuser of our brethren is cast down, which accused them before our God day and night.

And they overcame him by the blood of the Lamb, and by the word of their testimony; and they loved not their lives unto the death. . . .

And when the dragon saw that he was cast unto the earth, he persecuted the woman which brought forth the man child.

[160]

And to the woman were given two wings, a great eagle, that she might fly into the wilderness, into her place, where she is nourished for a time, and times, and half a time, from the face of the serpent.

And the serpent cast out of his mouth water as a flood after the woman, that he might cause her to be carried away of the flood.

And the earth helped the woman, and the earth opened her mouth, and swallowed up the flood which the dragon cast out of his mouth.

And the dragon was wroth with the woman, and went to make war with the remnant of her seed, which keep the Commandments of God, and have the testimony of Jesus Christ.

Then the images change; a new vision appears: from the waters of the sea comes a beast to which the dragon gives its strength and power. Evidently it is through this strength and power that the beast rises up against those who "keep the commandments of God." The whole earth watches it with wonder; the nations bow down before its marvelous strength, for it does all sorts of wonders and even makes fire come down from heaven. It puts its mark on people, and it is accepted by all "whose names are not written in the book of the Lamb." The vision changes again: the Lamb appears, "slain from the foundation of the world," and with it are one hundred and forty-four thousand "having his Father's name written in their foreheads." They were redeemed by its blood, for they were not defiled by the filth of the earth. An angel, in whose hands is the everlasting gospel, flies by in order to preach unto them that dwell on earth, and to every nation, and kindred, and tongue, and people. After it comes another angel, saying: "Babylon is fallen, is fallen, that great city, because she made all nations drink of the wine of the wrath of her fornication." This is the first harbinger of the great fall, the depiction of which still lies ahead, but it is already imminent. There appears a bright cloud, and on it is one "like unto the Son of Man," holding a sharp sickle. The angel says to Him: "Thrust in Thy sickle, and reap: for the time is come for Thee to reap; for the harvest of the earth is ripe." And a great harvest was reaped. Thereupon begins a new vision: "And them that had gotten the victory over the beast, and over his image, and over his mark, and over the number of his name, stand on the sea of glass, having the harps of God. And they sing the song of Moses the servant of God, and the song of the Lamb, saying, 'Great and marvellous are Thy works, Lord God Almighty; just and true are Thy ways, Thou King of saints. Who shall not fear Thee, O Lord, and glorify Thy name? For Thou only art holy: for all nations shall come and worship before Thee; for Thy judgments are made manifest.' "

After this come seven angels holding seven vials of the wrath of God, which they pour upon the earth. All sorts of torments are inflicted on those people who had worshiped the beast's image and accepted its mark; all nature is altered, and the suffering continues to grow. "And they blasphemed the name of God, which hath power over these plagues: and they repented not to give Him glory." After the fifth angel had poured out his vial, the kingdom of the beast "was full of darkness; and they gnawed their tongues for pain, and blasphemed the God of heaven because of their pains and their sores, and repented not of their deeds." When the last vial of God's wrath is poured upon the earth, there comes a great voice out of the temple of heaven, from the throne, saying, "It is done." And after that begins the vision of the judgment of the whore:

> And there came one of the seven angels which had the seven vials, and talked with me, saying unto me, Come hither; I will shew unto thee the judgment of the great whore that sitteth upon many waters:
>
> With whom the kings of the earth have committed fornication, and the inhabitants of the earth have been made drunk with the wine of her fornication.
>
> So he carried me away in the spirit into the wilderness: and I saw a woman sit upon a scarlet colored beast, full of names of blasphemy, having seven heads and ten horns.
>
> And the woman was arrayed in purple and scarlet color, and decked with gold and precious stones and pearls, having a golden cup in her hand full of abominations and filthiness of her fornication:
>
> And upon her forehead was a name written, MYSTERY, BABYLON THE GREAT, THE MOTHER OF HARLOTS AND ABOMINATIONS OF THE EARTH.
>
> And I saw the woman drunken with the blood of the saints, and with the blood of the martyrs of Jesus: and when I saw her, I wondered with great admiration.
>
> And the angel said unto me, Wherefore didst thou marvel? I will tell thee the mystery of the woman, and of the beast that carrieth her, which hath the seven heads and ten horns.
>
> The beast that thou sawest was, and is not; and shall

ascend out of the bottomless pit, and go into perdition: and they that dwell on the earth shall wonder, whose names were not written in the book of life from the foundation of the world, when they behold the beast that was, and is not, and yet is.

And here is the mind which hath wisdom. The seven heads are seven mountains, on which the woman sitteth.

And there are seven kings: five are fallen, and one is, and the other is not yet come; and when he cometh, he must continue a short space.

And the beast that was, and is not, even he is the eighth, and is of the seven, and goeth into perdition.

And the ten horns which thou sawest are ten kings, which have received no kingdom as yet; but receive power as kings one hour with the beast.

These have one mind, and shall give their power and strength unto the beast.

These shall make war with the Lamb, and the Lamb shall overcome them: for he is Lord of lords, and King of kings: and they that are with him are called, and chosen, and faithful.

And he saith unto me, The waters which thou sawest, where the whore sitteth, are peoples, and multitudes, and nations, and tongues.

And the ten horns which thou sawest upon the beast, these shall hate the whore, and shall make her desolate and naked, and shall eat her flesh, and burn her with fire.

For God hath put in their hearts to fulfill his will, and to agree, and give their kingdom unto the beast, until the words of God shall be fulfilled.

And the woman which thou sawest is that great city, which reigneth over the kings of the earth.

After this comes a vision of the judgment of the triumphant whore, by whose "sorceries were all nations deceived," (18:23), and who "corrupted the earth with her fornication" (19:2). The kings of the earth who have committed fornication with her and the merchants who grew rich from her "shall stand afar off for the fear of her torment, weeping and wailing" and beating their breasts, saying in sorrow and amazement: "What city is like unto this great city!"

In order that all these words may be clearer, let us note that after the judgment of the whore, the "Lord of lords and King of kings" descends for the final struggle with the beast and the nations who worshiped it. (Although they were covered with sores, they were still not vanquished.) And the same words are repeated about Him (19:15) that were said about the child whom the dragon wanted to devour, but who was taken to God.

Now we shall continue with the Inquisitor's words, this time almost without interruption. Having said that he and those of the same opinion as he, who had rejected Christ and accepted the counsels of the devil, will gain possession of the consciences of men by both the word and the kingdom of Caesar, he describes as follows the attitude toward him of mankind, for whom all this was done.

"There will yet be ages of the excesses of their free thought, of their science and cannibalism, for, having begun to put up their Tower of Babel without us, they will end with cannibalism."

Science, as the exact knowledge of reality, does not contain any insuperably restrictive moral principles, and in raising with its help the final edifice of human life, one can by no means deny that when necessary it will take some measure that is cruel and criminal. Malthus's idea (shared even by a thinker such as John Stuart Mill), according to which the only way for the working classes to maintain their wages at a certain level is for them to abstain from marriage and having a family, so as not to increase their number—or in other words, for them to degrade the huge mass of women to the extent that they become merely an adjunct of a certain male function—can serve as an example of the cruelty and immorality that theoretical thought can lead to when unrestrained by firm religious laws. And in fact, since science has already found painless ways of dying (increased doses of anesthetics), why shouldn't a second Malthus appear, one just as inspired by the "love of one's neighbor" as the first, one who will say "let there be marriages, but let the children from them be eaten." This can be done "not necessarily by the parents," it will cause no suffering, and it will be "of benefit to all mankind."

"But then the beast will crawl up to us," continues the Inquisitor, "and will lick our feet and spatter them with tears of blood. And we shall sit upon the beast and raise the cup, and on it will be written: 'Mystery.' But then, and only then, will the reign of peace and happiness come to men. You are proud of those You have chosen, but You have only Your chosen ones, whereas we will give solace to everyone. And that is not all: how many of those chosen ones, of those mighty ones, who could have become the chosen ones, have finally grown weary of waiting for You and have carried and will continue to carry the powers of their spirit and the fervor of their heart to another camp, and will end up by raising their *free* banner against You? But You Yourself raised that banner."

What striking words, what a profound understanding of the whole antireligious movement of great European minds of recent centuries, with an acknowledgment of their power and magnanimity, with a feeling of sadness for them, but at the same time with an indication of their fallacy.

"But with us, all will be happy and will no longer rebel, nor will they destroy each other as they do everywhere under Your freedom. Oh, we will convince them that they will become free only when they have renounced their freedom in our favor and have submitted to us. Now tell me: will we be right or will we be lying? They themselves will be convinced that we are right, for they will recall the horrors of slavery and confusion to which Your freedom had led them. Freedom, a free mind, and science will lead them into such a labyrinth and bring them face to face with such wonders and unsolvable mysteries that some of them, the refractory and fierce ones, will destroy themselves,[1] others, refractory but weak, will destroy one another,[2] while the rest, weak and unhappy, will crawl to our feet

[1] The theoretical idea justifying "self-destruction," which Dostoevsky expounded in *The Diary of a Writer* apropos a certain suicide.

[2] For a corresponding idea, see Kirillov's words to Peter Verkhovensky just before the former's suicide in *The Possessed:* "To kill *another* would be the very lowest point of my self-will. And this [suggestion] is something that could only come from a person like you. But I am not you: I want its highest point, and therefore I shall kill *myself.*"

and will cry out to us: 'Yes, you were right, you alone possessed His mystery, and we are returning to you: save us
from ourselves!' " [3]

In the absolute submission and the weak will of the
masses, this salvation will reveal itself. Nothing new will
be given them by the wise men who have taken away their
freedom; but what was previously unattainable to them,
they will attain, by having their will guided and their labor
distributed:

"In receiving bread from us, they will, of course, clearly
see that we take from them the bread made by their own
hands, in order to distribute it among them, without any
miracle; they will see that we do not turn stones into bread,
but, in truth, they will be more glad to get it from our
hands than they are about the bread itself! For they will
remember only too well that previously, without us, the
bread they made turned into stones in their hands, but when
they returned to us, the very stones turned into bread in
their hands."

This is a reference to our times, when, under free competition, despite the vast amount of goods produced, the vast
number of the popular masses are scarcely able to eke out
a meager existence, and everything slips away, is squan-
dered, disappears on account of a lack of coordination between man's desires and actions. On the contrary, when
the desires of those now living on the fat of the land are
curtailed and the labor of all mankind coordinated into one

[3] The basic problem of history, and one which, with its merging of the subject and object into one (both the "saved" and the
"savior" are man), is unsolvable. It can be solved only when they
are separated (in religion, where the "saved" is a person and his
"savior," God).

whole, even if it is not as burdensome as it now is everywhere, there will be sufficient goods produced for a comfortable existence for all.

"Too, too well will they appreciate what it means to submit once and for all! [4] And until people understand this, they will be unhappy. Now, tell me, who contributed most to this lack of understanding? Who scattered the flock and sent it astray on unknown paths? But the flock will come together again and will submit, and this time it will be for good. Then we shall give them quiet, meek happiness, the happiness of weak creatures, such as they are by nature.[5] Oh, we shall finally convince them not to be proud, for You exalted them, and this taught them pride; we shall prove to them that they are weak, that they are only pitiful children, but that a child's happiness is sweetest of all. They will become timid and will snuggle up to us in fear as chicks to a brood hen. They will marvel at us and be terrified of us, and will be proud of our being so powerful and intelligent that we could subdue such an impetuous flock of thousands of millions. They will tremble impotently before our anger, their minds will grow timid, their eyes will be as tearful as those of women and children, but at a sigh from us they will just as easily shift to merriment and laughter, to radiant joy and happy childish song.[6] Yes,

---

[4] "There's one thing lacking in this world of ours, there's one thing that has to be established, and that is obedience," says Dostoevsky in *The Possessed* (through the mouth of Peter Verkhovensky).

[5] These words and the ones immediately following constitute the third central idea of the "Legend."

[6] This "weakening" of human nature is virtually identical with the artificial "reduction" of its psychic level; it will, however, be brought about not forcibly, but peacefully.

we shall make them work, but in their leisure time, we shall make their life like a child's game, with children's songs, choirs, and innocent dances. Oh, we shall also allow them to sin; [7] they are weak and helpless, and they will love us like children because we allow them to sin. We shall tell them that every sin will be expiated if it is committed with our permission; that we allow them to sin because we love them, and as far as the punishment of these sins is concerned —well, so be it, we shall take that upon ourselves.[8] And we shall take it upon ourselves, and they will adore us as benefactors who have taken on ourselves their sins before God. And they will have no secrets from us. We shall permit or forbid them to live with their wives and mistresses, to have or not have children—always according to whether they have been obedient or not—and they will submit to us gladly and cheerfully. The most agonizing secrets of their conscience—everything, absolutely everything—they will bring to us, and we will decide everything, and they will gladly believe in our decision, for it will relieve them of great anxiety and the terrible torments they now experience in making a free decision for themselves."

The last words contain a hint of the possibility even of regulating the population, its increase or diminution, all depending on the needs of the current historical moment. But the general idea of this passage is that the whole range of passion will be removed from mankind, that men will be left with only the details and trivia of sin, and that only

[7] The criminal element in history, once it is provided for and permitted within the bounds of the "necessary," will immediately lose its dangerous and menacing character.

[8] This whole picture of a future semi-sinless life had earlier appeared in Dostoevsky's *A Raw Youth*—in Versilov's conversation with his son.

those able to endure every range and every burden will take sin on themselves. Thus, both the unsolvable contradictions of history and the incomprehensible secret impulses of the human soul—everything that hinders man's life on earth—will be concentrated on the shoulders of a few, who will be able to bear the knowledge of good and evil. One might say that history will lapse into silence, and there will remain only the secret history of a few great souls, which, of course, is never destined to be told.

XVII

"And everyone will be happy," concludes the Inquisitor, "all the millions of creatures, except the hundred thousand who rule over them. For only we, we who guard the mystery, only we shall be unhappy. There will be thousands of millions of happy infants and one hundred thousand sufferers, who took on themselves the curse of the knowledge of good and evil. They will die peacefully, they will pass away peacefully in Your name, and beyond the grave they will find nothing but death.[1] But we shall keep the secret, and for their happiness we shall entice them with the reward of heaven and eternity. For even if there were anything in the next world, it would not, of course, be for the likes of them."

The pride of these words, spoken so simply, is ineffable: behind them one senses a power that indeed freely surveys

[1] Compare this with the tone and ideas of the passage from *A Raw Youth* already pointed out above.

the endless paths of history and resolutely weighs in its hand the measure of the human heart and the human mind. And we are not surprised when we subsequently hear the following words referring to the passage from the Revelation of St. John quoted above:

"It is said and prophesied that You will come and again triumph, that You will come with Your elect, with Your proud and strong ones, but we shall say that they have saved only themselves, whereas we have saved everyone. It is said that the whore, who sits upon the beast and holds in her hands the *mystery*, will be disgraced, that the weak will again revolt, that they will tear to pieces her purple mantle and strip naked her 'vile' body. But I will then stand up and point out to You the thousands of millions of happy infants who have known no sin. And we, who have taken their sins upon ourselves for their happiness, will stand before You and say 'Judge us if You can and dare.' Know that I do not fear You. Know that I, too, was in the wilderness, that I, too, lived on locusts and roots, that I, too, blessed the freedom with which You blessed men, and I, too, was preparing myself to join the number of Your elect, the number of the strong and powerful, eager to 'complete the number.' But I recovered my senses and did not desire to serve madness. I went back and joined the multitude of those *who had corrected Your work*. I left the proud and returned to the humble for the happiness of the humble. What I am telling You will happen, and our kingdom will be built. I repeat, tomorrow You will see that obedient flock, which at the first sign from me will rush to rake up the hot coals about the stake on which I shall burn You because You came to hinder us. For if ever there was someone who deserved our fire, it is You. Tomorrow I shall burn You. *Dixi*."

The Inquisitor pauses. In the deep silence of the arched dungeon, he looks at his prisoner and awaits His answer. He is distressed by the silence and distressed by the sincere and gentle way in which the prisoner continues to look at him, the same way He looked at him during his speech. He might at least say something, even something bitter, something terrible—so long as He does not leave him without any answer at all. Suddenly the prisoner draws near to him and silently kisses him on his pale, aged lips. "This is His only answer." The Inquisitor shudders, his lips move as if trying to say something. He goes to the door, opens it, and says to Him: "Go, and come no more . . . come never again . . . never, never!" The prisoner goes out into the "dark streets of the city." The Seville night still holds its breath. From the dark skies, the bright stars pour down their gentle light on the tranquil earth. The city sleeps; only the old man stands at the open door with the heavy key in his hand, looking at slumbering nature. The kiss burns in his heart, but . . . "he persists in his idea," and . . . his kingdom will be built.

With this, the "poem" ends. The centuries again move together, the dead return into the earth, and before us once more is the little tavern where the two brothers an hour earlier had begun to speak about various disturbing questions. But no matter what they say now, we shall listen to them no longer. Our hearts are filled with other thoughts, and our ears all the time seem to ring with a kind of Mephistophelian song, sung from a celestial height above our poor earth.

[173]

We have broken the work up into parts and pondered its every word; but now that they have all resounded we are left with only a memory of the whole, of which we have not yet rendered an account.

Above all, we are struck by its unusual complexity and variety, combined with a very great unity. A most ardent love of man merges in it with a complete disdain for him, boundless skepticism with fervent faith, doubt about man's unsteady strength with a firm belief in the adequacy of his strength for any heroic deed, and finally, a scheme for the greatest crime ever committed in history with an inexpressibly great understanding of what is righteous and holy. Everything in it is unusual, everything is strange. It is as if those unsteady streams of good and evil that flow and overflow in history, weaving its complex pattern, had suddenly come together and merged; as if at that first moment when man for the first time learned to distinguish them and began his history, we again see them undivided—and just as he had been then, so are we now struck with terror and doubt. "Where is God, the truth, the way?" we ask ourselves, because suddenly, as never before, we sense our irresistible destruction. We sense the approach of a terrible and disgusting creature about which so much had been told us in prose and poetry that we had seriously begun to regard it as a mere play of fancy; but now we suddenly feel its icy touch and hear the sound of its voice. One man, who lived among us, but who, of course, resembled no one of us, sensed in an incomprehensible and mysterious way the actual nonexistence of God and the existence of another, and before he died, he reported to us the horrors of his soul and of his lonely heart, feebly beating with love for the One who is not, and feebly fleeing from the one who is. All his life he preached God, and of those who heard him, some laughed at his constancy and were indignant at his importunity, while others were moved by it and pointed him out in admiration. But it was as if he noticed neither the indignation nor the sympathy. He always said one and the same thing, and the only thing that surprised everyone was why he, who had such a joyous and comforting idea in his heart, was so desperately gloomy, so melancholy and troubled himself. He spoke of the joy in God, he pointed to religion as the only salvation for man, and his words rang out fervently and passionately, and although he usually never mentioned nature, it was as if he was beginning to love it then, to understand its trepidation, its beauty, and life.[2] It was as if it withered from the breath of some icy feeling in his soul and would revive when he forgot about it, at least in the sound of his words. There were also confessions in his words, but they were all misunderstood. He let slip that a man who does not really have God in his heart is terrifying, because "he comes to you with God's name on his lips." [3] People read these words, but no one understood their meaning. And he went to the grave unknown, but he did not take the secret of his soul with him. As if urged on by some instinct, not at all sensing the approach of death, he left us an amazing image, one look at which and we finally understand all. "*You, too,* are with him." These words, which Alyosha sorrowfully addresses to his brother after hearing the story

---

[2] Compare the description of nature (or more precisely the scanty words about it) in *Poor People, Notes from the Underground,* etc., with the words about it of Father Zosima in *The Brothers Karamazov* and of Makar Ivanovich in *A Raw Youth.*

[3] *A Raw Youth.*

of the Grand Inquisitor, we irrepressibly address to the author himself, who so obviously stands behind him: "You, too, are with *him,* with the wise and powerful spirit, who offered the tempting counsels in the wilderness to Him who came to save the world—counsels that you understood and explained so well that one might think you had thought them up yourself!" The confession that Dostoevsky made in a private letter long before writing this novel and which we pointed out above, the words he wrote in his notebook shortly before his death: "*My* hosannah has passed through the crucible of ordeal," the reference on that occasion specifically to the "Legend," and finally the complete independence of the "Legend" from the novel itself, and at the same time its central position not only in it, but also in the long series of his other works—all this leaves no further doubt in our mind as to its true meaning. The author's soul evidently became interwoven in all those amazing lines that we quoted above, before our eyes the characters become mixed up with each other, the one becoming visible behind the other, we forget the person speaking behind the Inquisitor, we do not even see the Inquisitor—before us stands the evil spirit with his fluctuating and nebulous image, and just as two thousand years ago, he unfolds his tempting idea, which had been expressed so concisely then. But, as a matter of fact, he must speak in greater detail: he is being listened to now by men, and before them, one must not cover all of world history in just two or three words.

XVIII

His subtle, tempting, and powerful dialectic begins exactly as it should. He is called a "slanderer"—and it is with slander of man that his words begin.

Is human nature fundamentally good and merely perverted by evil added to it from without, or has it been evil from the very start and only feebly tried to rise to something better? This is a difficult question that he has decided in one specific direction, and on it he now bases his whole idea. Is man a dying spark, or is he cold ashes that can be ignited only from without? What is he in his heart of hearts? This is what we must answer before deciding to struggle with his nature further.

Only once does the Inquisitor falter, only once does he make a slip of the tongue: when he remarks that man will even give up his bread and run after the one who entices him with truth. "You were right about that," he says. Is it not possible that in this momentary confusion, the truth revealed itself, only to conceal itself immediately again? And if so, are there ways of bringing it out into the light of our clear consciousness?

His dialectic develops temptingly: he takes what is most important—man's attitude toward God—and by that attitude measures man's baseness and the permanence of his fall. Standing before the face of God, between Him and mankind in its millennial destinies, he points to His holy image, and after showing that man was able to jeer even at Him, he asks what could the measure of his true worth be? It seems that to defend oneself means here not to sense the sanctity of the image, that the mere attempt to justify oneself means to forfeit every right to justification; just as in a similar way, earlier in the book, the mere failure to repudiate God's justice seemed a horrible insult to those who suffer innocently. The words before us are indeed strange: the Deity and man, who is bound up with Him, are irrevocably separated, and every effort to prevent this seems a rebellion precisely against the Deity or against man himself.

But, by facts showing man's temporary apostasy from God, one cannot decide the question of whether his nature is fundamentally good or evil. Are there not just as many facts showing man's irresistible attraction to God? Did not those martyrs whom the Inquisitor burned at the stake on the eve of his monologue die for the very reason that they refused to submit to his diabolical idea and to the end remained loyal to the truth? Do not the sobs that rang out in the crowd, when it seemed to them that "He Himself had come down to see their sorrows and suffering," tell us anything about the human heart? Do not fifteen centuries of unwavering expectation mean anything? Who dares, after considering the moments of man's fall, even if they had lasted for centuries—or let us put it more clearly, directly answering the author's veiled question: who dares, in seeing the degradation and baseness of one's century and, raising this indignation to law, slander all of human history and deny that as a whole it is a wonderful and sublime manifestation, if not of human wisdom (which one might doubt), at least of an unselfish striving for truth and a powerless desire to realize some sort of justice?

[178]

But even by facts showing the sublimity of the human spirit, no matter how many of them we assemble, we can only shake the conclusiveness of the facts pointing to the contrary, but by no means can we decide the question of what exactly man's nature is, the thing to which all these series of contrary and mutually negating phenomena rise as if to their common node.

There is another sound way to shed the clearest possible light on this difficulty, on the solution of which in one direction or another depend so many of our hopes and beliefs. By eliminating the mixed and contradictory facts of history, by removing, as it were, their incrustation from man, we can capture his nature in its primordial purity and determine its necessary relation to eternal ideals, the aspiration to which can never be questioned: to truth, to good, and to freedom.

What was the order of precedence in man's consciousness: first falsehood and then truth, or truth and then falsehood? This is a simple question, the answer to which marks the beginning of an irresistible solution of the general question of human nature as well. We can have no doubt here: falsehood in itself is something secondary, it is a violation of the truth; and it is clear that before truth could be violated, it certainly had to exist. Thus it is protoplastic, something that has existed from the very beginning; but falsehood was introduced from without, something that appeared later. It has its origin entirely in history; but truth has its origin *in man himself*. It proceeds from him, and it alone would eternally proceed from him if he did not encounter on his path obstacles diverting him from it. But this shows only that the origin of every falsehood lies outside him. Man's first impulse is always an impulse toward

[179]

truth, and we cannot imagine it otherwise if he is free, i.e., if he is free from all outside influences, and he acts only in accordance with his abilities. Can we possibly imagine that when the first man looked at the world around him and for the first time experienced delight he told a falsehood about that world: that he pretended not to see it, or that he suppressed in himself his feeling of awe and said that he felt disgust? And also, every time man is not afraid, when he is not trying to achieve some end, when no outside influence distracts him from simple contemplation, does he not tell only the truth about that contemplation? And when, influenced by fear or yielding to some impulse, he tells a falsehood, does he not each time experience a certain distress, a certain inward pain, which comes from the fact that his thought, on its way to its outward expression, was subjected to a certain distorting influence? And in order to produce this in himself, in order to suppress something about the truth or to add something to it, does it not each time require a certain effort? And from where would that come if human nature from the very beginning was indifferently inclined to both falsehood and truth?

Thus, between man's reason on the one hand and truth, as an eternally aspired-to object on the other, there exists not a simple relation, but a *correlation*. Truth is just as imperceptibly pre-established in reason as there is imperceptibly pre-established in a line toward which another line has been deflected a point of distant junction with it. Falsehood and error, i.e., evil, are merely a hindrance to this junction or a deflection from it; but they are not something independent, self-contained, or whole, which would be torn asunder by truth. Truth is absolute; it is the simple and normal interaction between man's reason and the world in which he lives. On the contrary, falsehood is always relative and partial: namely, it has to do with some particular thought, the truthfulness of which it violates. Therefore, in the same way as the world is a whole, so can a world outlook, i.e., a system of harmoniously combined truths, be a whole. On the contrary, falsehood cannot be arranged into any system whatever, and particularly not into one in which the principles on which the system is constructed would also be false. With every attempt to create thoughts that are definitely false and definitely to combine them falsely, the mind experiences unbearable suffering—and even if the mind manages to overcome its suffering, it will still not be able to achieve its goal: somewhere into the system, it will automatically introduce truth. On the contrary, the creation of true thoughts and their combination into a true system has always given reason the greatest of pleasure, and the closer that which is being constructed by it comes to the irreproachable truth, the greater it becomes. This suffering and this joy is an indication of the true nature of man; they define it as lofty and good, but only in its primordial state; on the contrary, in its present state, after it has been changed by history, they show it to be tarnished.

That is why, when we sometimes find something in science or philosophy that appears to be evil, something that our nature irresistibly opposes, we can without preliminary investigation assume that the part of it that arouses such indignation in us contains something false. And a more careful study of that part, a study of the way in which it originated, will always certainly reveal that behind it lay not a pure thought, but one distorted by some feeling introduced from without, by some fear or inclination. Thus, in Malthus's Law, mentioned above, the only thing that is true is its basis, according to which in *certain* periods the population increases in geometric progression, whereas the goods produced increase only in arithmetical progression; but what is completely false is the antinatural demand that the working classes refrain from marriage. Behind this demand lies the anxiety that those living on the fat of the land might lose the right to luxury and also the fear that the poor might finally begin to die from starvation. One can say that the first fear is vain and the second, rash, because other and deeper laws, those governing the birthrate itself, apparently guard people against such a misfortune; and although a sufficient amount of historical time has already elapsed for Malthus's Law to begin to function, nevertheless, parents have never eaten their children, nor have they remained unmarried, but have always and everywhere found food for themselves and their children as well.

But pure thought, in its abstract activity, can create only "good"; and every science and philosophy, in so far as it does not betray its own nature, is perfect and good before God and man. The mixing of the fields of thought and feeling, the distortion of the former by the latter or vice-versa, is what produces all the evil that has ever been able to cause dissatisfaction even with one's own nature, to complain about the excessive depth of consciousness or the intractability of one's own passions.

On the contrary, when these fields are not distorted by interference from one another, they seem to us to be free of evil. Having examined the first of them, the field of thought, we shall now proceed to the second.

Does feeling in its primordial nature aspire to good, is

[182]

it inclined to do good, or does it aspire to evil and seek out evil? This is a question the answer to which will continue the disclosure of man's primordial nature begun by us above. And here again the solution of the difficulty cannot give rise to doubt. The thirst to do evil to another is always responsive, it is provoked by suffering caused us by another. Thus, the nature of a bad feeling is as necessarily secondary and derivative as is the nature of falsehood. Just as it is impossible to imagine that the first man took a look at nature and then lied about it, so is it impossible to assume that that same first man, having become aware of a second human being near him and having in some way or other learned what pain and suffering are, would want to subject him to them; that he would not push him away from a tree that was threatening to crush him, warn him of the depth of the water in which he himself almost drowned, or invite him to share the shade of the only bush in the neighborhood during the parching noonday heat. And everywhere, as in these examples, where we find someone who has not yet absorbed evil from his environment or from some previous evil, we find that his nature is *inclined only to "good."* It is the *first thing* to which human feeling is attracted, whereas evil is always the second, something always brought in from without. Feelings of inner suffering or inner joy can here, too, serve as the same infallible signs of truth as they do in the field of consciousness. Suffering vaguely and irresistibly takes possession of man and grows as his soul is possessed by evil; on the contrary, radiant joy accompanies a benevolent life, no matter how many physical misfortunes have oppressed it. Suffering, here, comes from the incompatibility of evil with human nature, while serenity of spirit comes from their harmony.

[183]

On this retaliatory origin of all evil is also based the profound doctrine of nonresistance to it: and indeed the more this doctrine is carried out the more evil disappears from life. By not returning evil for evil, we eradicate it. Little by little this calms at individual points the agitation of passions that latch on to each other and with which all life is filled and by which the will of each individual is ensnared. Difficult at first and completely unnoticeable so far as its results are concerned, this doctrine becomes easier with every step and its results more perceptible. The passions, ceasing to arouse one another, gradually subside, and every evil caused by some other person, since it fails to provoke a response, inevitably dies. For those accustomed to think that history and all the charm of life consist precisely in the play of passions, and that it is better to suffer evil than to be deprived of its free and fascinating beauty, one might point out that the joy of sensing one's inner purity and sensing one's spirit in harmony with all life around it will more than compensate the human heart for the loss of what it now so painfully and blindly enjoys.

As for the third side of human nature, the *will*, we can settle the question of its original purity or depravity by the following investigation: by deciding whether it is in keeping with the last great ideal to which man can aspire —freedom. Here, too, mental experience provides a clear solution. Freedom is outward action that corresponds to inward action, and it is fully realized when the former is completely the result of the latter. It is clear that if man could be separated from the past and from his environment, then his outer activity, which must, of course, have its cause, could have it only in inner psychic activity: that is, without outside influences, his will is absolutely free. But in reality, since he is connected with the past and his environment, his outer activity ceases to be in harmony with his inner activity, and moreover always in proportion to the force acting on him from without. This means that a decrease in human freedom, its curtailment or suppression, comes not from within his nature, but from without. The suffering that always accompanies this feeling of suppression, here, too, shows the true nature of this side of the human spirit.

Truth, goodness, and freedom are the main and the constant ideals toward the realization of which human nature in its chief elements—reason, feeling, and will—directs itself. Between these ideals and man's primordial constitution, there is a correspondence, by virtue of which human nature irresistibly aspires to them. And as these ideals can by no means be regarded as bad, human nature, as originally constructed, must be regarded as benevolent and good.

XIX

And this undermines the foundation of the Inquisitor's dialectic. "For my yoke is *easy*, and my burden is *light*" (Matthew 11:30), said the Savior about His teaching. Indeed, since it is filled with the loftiest truth, since it summons all men to unity through love, and since it leaves it to man freely to follow good, it corresponds in its entire purport to man's primordial nature and awakens it again from the thousand years of sin that had burdened it with an odious and oppressive yoke. To repent and follow the

Savior means to remove this odious "yoke" from oneself; it means to feel as joyful and free as man felt on the first day of his creation.

And herein lies the secret of the moral regeneration that Christ brings about in each of us when we turn to Him with all our heart. There are no other words but "light," "joy," and "rapture" by which one can express this special state experienced by true Christians. And because of this, despondency is regarded by the Church as so grievous a sin: it is the outward seal of estrangement from God, and no matter what the lips of a man who has fallen under its influence may say, that man's heart is remote from God. That is why all losses and all outer misfortunes are the same for a true Christian and a society of people leading Christian lives as the howling of the wind for people sitting in a sturdy, well-heated, and well-lit house. Society is immortal and indestructible so long as and to the extent that it remains Christian. On the contrary, every life that once became Christian and then turned to other sources of being and life is permeated with elements of destruction. Despite its outward success, despite all its outward power, it is filled with the spirit of death, and this influence inexorably puts its seal on each individual mind and each individual conscience.

"The Legend of the Grand Inquisitor," so far as history is concerned, can be regarded as a great and powerful reflection of that peculiar spirit. Whence, all its sorrow; whence, the utter darkness that it casts over the whole of life. If it were true, man could not go on living; after he had pronounced this harsh judgment on himself nothing would remain for him except to die. And it is with despair that the "Legend" ends. One can imagine the horror that seizes man when, after finally arranging his life in the name of a higher truth, he suddenly learns that this arrangement was based on a deception, and that this had been done because there is no truth at all except the truth that one must nevertheless save oneself, but there is nothing to save oneself by. In effect, this is precisely the gist of the Inquisitor's last words, which he is preparing to address to Christ on the day of the resurrection of nations: "Judge me if You can and dare." The darkness and despair here is the darkness of ignorance. "Who am *I* on this earth? What is this *earth? Why* do *I* and *everyone else* do what we do?" These are the words that are heard coming through the "Legend." And this is what is expressed at its end. When Alyosha tells his brother: "Your Inquisitor simply doesn't believe in God," the latter answers: "You've finally guessed it."

And this determines the "Legend's" historical position. For more than two centuries the people of Europe have been acting directly counter to the Savior's great precept: "But seek ye first the kingdom of God and His righteousness; and all these things shall be added unto you." Yet these people continue to call themselves Christians. One cannot and should not conceal from oneself the fact that underlying this phenomenon is a secret unvoiced doubt about the divinity of the precept itself: one believes in God and submits to Him blindly. But that is just what we do not find: the interests of the State, even the progress of the arts and sciences, and finally the mere increase in productivity—one gives all this precedence, without any thought of opposition to it; and everything in life that stands above it—religion, morality, the human conscience—is pushed aside or throttled by those interests that are re-

[187]

garded as most important for mankind. All of Europe's great progress in the field of outward culture is explained by this change. The attention paid to what is outside man, once it became undivided, naturally grew more intense and more refined; discoveries followed which were not even dreamed of earlier; inventions came along that rightly dumbfounded the inventors themselves. All this is much too explainable, too clear, all this was to be expected as far back as two centuries ago. But something else indissolubly combined with it is also much too clear: the gradual obscuring and finally the loss of a higher meaning of life.

A vast number of details and the lack of something primary to bind them together—this has been the characteristic peculiarity of European life as it has taken shape in the last two centuries. No common idea binds the nations together any longer, no common feeling guides them —everyone in every nation works only at his own particular job. The lack of a coordinating center in our incessant work, in our eternal creation of parts that are meant for nothing in particular, is merely the outer result of this loss of the meaning of life. An inner result is the universal and inexorable disappearance of an interest in life. The grand image of the Apocalypse, where it tells of something "burning as it were a lamp" and falling on the earth at the end of time, as a result of which the earth's waters become wormwood, is not so much applicable to the Reformation as to the civilization of the most recent centuries. The result of so many efforts on the part of the loftiest minds of mankind, this civilization no longer satisfies, and least of all does it satisfy those who toil at it. Just as the flame that has burnt brightest leaves the greatest number of cold ashes, so does this civilization increase the amount of inexplicable

[188]

sorrow the more eagerly one applies oneself to it at the beginning. Hence the deep sadness of all new poetry, which alternates with blasphemy or spite; hence the peculiar nature of the prevailing philosophical ideas. Everything sad and gloomy inexorably attracts contemporary man, for there is no longer any joy in his heart. The tranquility of the old short story, the gaiety of early poetry, whatever the beauty that may have accompanied it, no longer interests or attracts: people strangely shun everything like that; they cannot bear the disharmony between the bright impressions that they receive from the outside and the absence of any light in their soul. And one after the other, with spiteful or jeering remarks, they "abandon" life. Science records the number of those "abandoning" life, it shows in which countries and in which periods the figures rise or fall, and the contemporary reader in his lonely corner automatically thinks to himself: "What does it matter if they rise or fall, when I haven't the wherewithal to live—and no one wants or is able to give it to me!"

Hence the turn to religion, troubled and sad, combined with an ardent hatred of all that impedes it, and at the same time a sense of being unable to join in a religious mood with millions of people who have not been touched by the enlightenment of the last few centuries. Ardor and skepticism, muffled despair and high-flown words by which, for want of something better, the longing of the heart is stifled —everything is amazingly intermixed in these outbursts of enthusiasm for religion. Life dries up at its sources and falls apart, irreconcilable contradictions appear in history and unbearable chaos in the individual conscience—and religion seems to be the last untried way out of it all. But the gift of religious feeling is acquired with perhaps greater difficulty than all other gifts. There are already hopes—the countless windings of the dialectic sustain them; there is also love, with a readiness to give everything to one's neighbor, to sacrifice for his slightest joy all the happiness of one's own life; and yet there is no faith. And the whole edifice of arguments and feelings, which are piled one on top of the other and fastened the one to the other, proves to be something like a beautiful dwelling in which there is no one to live. Centuries of excessive clarity in concepts and relationships, the habit (already a need) of occupying one's mind solely with what is demonstrable and clear, have so destroyed every capacity for mystical perceptions and feelings that even when salvation depends on these perceptions and feelings, they are not aroused.

All the aforementioned features are deeply imprinted on the "Legend"; it is the only synthesis in history of a most ardent thirst for religion with a total incapacity for it. Along with this, we find in the "Legend" a deep awareness of human weakness verging on contempt for man, and simultaneously a love for him that is ready to abandon God and to share man's degradation, his brutality and stupidity, but at the same time his suffering as well.

XX

It remains for us to note the last feature of this "Legend": its attitude toward the great forms that have been assumed by the religious consciousness of the European nations. In character and in origin, this attitude is highly independent: it is very much like a man who, after having broken away from the religious forms of every nation and every period, develops a religion of his own based solely on his own troubled feelings. Strictly speaking, this religion contains only a passing reference to Christianity and Catholicism; but from the former there has been taken for criticism the lofty concept of man, and from the latter, disdain of him and the horrible attempt to fetter his destinies and will through individual wisdom and force. The idea, developing tempestuously and inexorably, as if having sensed in these two facts of history something similar to itself, drew them to itself, twisting and grinding them up in the convolutions of the dialectic, governed by nothing but the laws of the soul in whose depths it originated.

The abstract, generalizing nature of this soul reveals itself in the fact that the "Legend" only rests on the inward needs of human nature, but instead of answering them, it answers the historical contradictions. Its plan is to fashion the destinies of mankind on earth by taking advantage of man's weaknesses. And this side of it coincided with what could be assumed to be a feature of one of the established forms of religious consciousness—that of the Roman-Catholic Church. Hence the story of the "Legend" is merely the fabric in which its ideas are woven. But, here, having begun to speak of the attitude of the "Legend" toward an assumed Catholic idea, we must give our opinion in general of the interrelation of the three main Christian Churches. In it will also be revealed the final viewpoint from which one should regard the "Legend" as a whole.

The tendency to strive for the "universal" is the most common and most constant feature of the Catholic Church, in the same way that the tendency to strive for the "in-

[191]

dividual" and the "particular" is the basic feature of Protestantism. But if we were to assume that these fundamentally different features are characteristic of these Churches themselves, or that they in any way derive from the spirit of Christianity, we would be deeply mistaken. Universality is a characteristic feature of the Latin *races,* in the same way that individualism is a characteristic feature of the Germanic ones; and only because of this did Christianity, as it spread through Western Europe and came into contact with these two contrary types of people, acquire these particular features. No matter what we take, whether we examine individual facts or the general trend of history, whether we turn to law, science, or religion, we shall everywhere note that the leading idea is in one case the tendency toward the "general" and in the other the tendency toward the "particular." The legal formulas of ancient Rome, as abstract as its gods, are also valid for every nation and every period, as are the principles of 1789, with their appeal to man, with their desire to establish on human law the law of the French as well. The striving of the "general" boldly to underpin itself with the "particular" is clearly evident here. The philosophy of Descartes, the only great one developed by the Latin races, also tries to reduce all the variety of living nature to two great modes of being, "extension" and "thought"; in the same way that Horace and Boileau tried to reduce fits of poetic rapture to simple and clear rules; in the same way that Cuvier reduced the animal world to a few eternal types; in the same way that a number of the great mathematicians of France who considered even geometrical drawings too concrete reduced the knowledge of nature

[192]

to the knowledge of algebra. It is the interest in and the attraction to the universal, plus a certain blindness toward the particular, that have produced all these great facts in the intellectual world of the Latin races; and no less in keeping with them are the great facts of their political history. The thirst to unite, first by embracing and finally by wiping out what is individual, is the undying wish of Rome and of all that grows from its soil. It was this deep, unconscious, and inexorable instinct that made the Roman legions, contrary to clear calculations, cross from country to country, farther and farther, and finally to a point that neither the eye nor the mind could grasp; and this was what led the Roman missionaries first to Germany and England, and several centuries later to the distant and unknown countries of Central Africa, to the interior of China, and to remote Japan. The Roman Catholic Church itself, because of its irresistible aversion to all that is particular, dispersed, and solitary, rolled itself up, as it were, into great monastic orders—a phenomenon completely exceptional in world history, not connected with any feature of Christianity, and one that sprang up in all its various forms and at various times on Latin soil alone. It was as if the spirit of monasticism, the spirit of asceticism and retirement from the world, once it was transplanted to this soil, decided to go out into the world to subject it to its demands, its ideas, the forms of its outlook and of its way of life. While the ascetics of all countries, of all times, and of all nations turned their backs in disgust on sinful mankind and fled from it into the wilderness to seek salvation there, the ascetics of the Catholic Church united amicably into a single unit and went out among this same mankind to lead it to what it could never hope to arrive at by itself. Inseparably combined with this striving of the Latin races for the universal was a failure to understand all that is individual, a sort of blindness to it, an inability closely to examine its nature or to sympathize with its suffering. The words of the Roman Legate who told his soldiers: "Kill them all; God at the Last Judgment will separate the Catholics from the heretics" were perhaps said with too great thoughtfulness; at least, we know for certain from the chronicles that the army of crusaders that set out for Languedoc [1] was inspired by such religious fervor and fanaticism and that it was so serious that every desire on our part to take these words as cynical blasphemy must be abandoned. The teachings of Calvin, which spread with difficulty through France, threatened it much less than the flame that was kindled by Luther threatened Germany; and, nevertheless, "Bartholomew's Night" occurred precisely in France. Members of one and the same family destroyed each other so that the French would all be the same; in the same way that three centuries later, for different principles, but with the same brutality, members of the National Convention destroyed those French people who differed from themselves and later even those in their own ranks as well, feeling that the slightest difference of opinion was a crime. Contempt for the human personality, only a feeble interest in the conscience of another, force used against man, against the race, against the world—all this is a fundamental and indestructible characteristic of the Latin races, and it has revealed itself in the great facts of the Roman Empire, French centralism, the wars of ag-

[1] A reference to the Crusade proclaimed in 1208 by Pope Innocent III against the Albigenses. [Tr.]

gression of the Catholic Reaction and the First Revolution, the Jesuit Order, the Inquisition, and socialism.[2]

At all times and in all places, with the cross or with cannons, under the banners of the Republic or under the eagles of Caesar, in the name of various truths in various periods, these nations have sensed the Roman blood in their veins and have attacked other peaceful nations in order, without looking deeply into their soul, to make them accept the forms of their thinking, their faith, and their social order. A ruthlessness toward man and an inability to understand him, together with a great talent for organizing mankind, have made these nations a sort of cement that binds together into a great whole other parts which are sometimes immeasurably more valuable, but always smaller. Nothing in itself great, true, or holy has ever been produced by the Latin genius; except for one thing: the bond between everything great, true, and holy that was created by other nations, but which in its entirety makes up history. Hence the magnetic force of the forms of all Latin civilizations; hence the lyricism, the endless yearning for something or other which strikes us, for example, in Catholic music. Other nations, even those that are by nature

[2] We mean here the ideas of Fourier, Saint-Simon, Cabet, Louis Blanc, etc., in which socialism arose as a dream, as an ardent and yearning desire before it was subsequently founded scientifically, thus justifying that dream. One can, in general, say that in the same way that the Republic of the Fabians and the Empire of the Augustans was a Latin attempt to unite mankind by law, so Catholicism was a Latin attempt to unite it through religion; and socialism is the desire, also originating in the Latin races, to unite it on an economic basis. From this it is clear that even though the means have changed, the goal of the Latin spirit has remained the same over a period of two thousand years, or throughout the whole period of these races' historical existence.

more profound and richer in content, are irresistibly attracted to these civilizations, to this Church, science, and literature. In all of them is aroused a secret instinct for unity; and with a feeling of sadness, they stifle their superior genius and go to merge with this strange edifice, eternal, ever-growing, cold, but also beautiful.

The spirit of the Germanic race, on the contrary, everywhere and always, no matter what it is engaged in, is directed toward the particular, the specific, the individual. In contrast to the all-embracing view of the Latin man, the view of the Teuton is penetrating—hence all the peculiarities of his law, science, Church, and poetry. The human conscience instead of the destinies of mankind, family life instead of political conflicts, contemplation of the depths of one's own "I" instead of cognition of the world—all these are different results of a single fact. One can regard the fact that the Germanic peoples belonged to the Catholic Church as the result of a great misunderstanding. And they did so for so many centuries only because they did not see the true aspirations of Rome, nor did Rome examine in too great detail or at close hand what went on on the other side of the Alps. The Reformation movement, which covered two centuries and divided Europe into two camps blazing with hostility, was only the discovery of this misunderstanding; and the misunderstanding was equally surprising to both sides, who since then have parted company forever. When Luther, a poor Augustinian monk, forgetting his Order, the Empire, the Universal Church, and heeding only the anxieties of his own conscience, said firmly that he would not admit he was wrong until this was proved to him "by the word of God," the German essence manifested itself in him for the first time, in this stubborn opposition of his "I" to the whole world, and it became an indomitable factor in history, no longer submitting to others, but making them submit to it. The world of religious sects that sprang up from this, that strange profession of faith in God in one's own way in almost every locality, without any desire to adapt one's faith to the faith of others, is, in the sphere of religious consciousness, the same thing that feudalism [3] was earlier in the socio-political sphere—another strange desire everywhere to make one's personal "I" the center of one's ideas and interests, to make it something absolute, which adapts itself to nothing at all, but which makes everything else adapt itself to it. Finally, the third great factor that the Germanic race introduced into history—its special way of looking at nature, its philosophy—is also a result of this mentality. As in the religious and political spheres, so in this purely intellectual one the individual's own "I" was acknowledged by the greatest spokesmen of that race as the source of the norms, bounds, and ties that we observe in nature. And that deeper study

[3] The essence of feudalism is perhaps best of all expressed in this medieval saying: *Chaque seigneur est souverain dans sa seignorie,* in which not political or economic relations, but the provincialism—if one can put it that way—of the will is shown to be the main feature of this whole system of life. It is remarkable that this formula was expressed in French, i.e., it originated in a mind especially capable of generalization, capable of discerning the unifying traits in a complex of heterogeneous phenomena, although its subject is an institution of indisputably Germanic origin. (The territory over which feudalism had spread was at the same time the territory on which the Germanic people had settled. In the early centuries A.D., they had wandered into countries that had hitherto been exclusively Latin ones.) Feudalism, which has disappeared in all countries of predominantly Latin blood, has, however, survived to this day in purely Germanic ones as political particularism.

of the world, which for all peoples from the beginning of history was a curious examination of the world and reflection on what had been seen, became for a number of great German scholars, beginning with Kant, only the cognition of the innermost movements of one's own inner being. "Reason dictates its laws to nature," "the world is *my* idea," it is "the development of my idea, of my cognition" —all these words which Europe listened to with amazement and then repeated, were deeply predetermined by the special mentality of the Germanic race. Examining them and the long series of arguments on which they apparently impartially rest, we finally lose complete sight of the boundary between objective knowledge and subjective illusion and ask: "What means then does man have to break through the limitations of time, place, and race? And how, when he is so bound even by these limitations, can he ever hope to surmount the limitations of his own human organism and to acquire a knowledge of absolute and complete truth?"

And no matter what else we single out, even if it is less significant, we shall everywhere note in it this same gravitation of the Germanic spirit toward the particular. Its poetry, in contrast to the heroic poetry of the Latin peoples, has chosen as its subject the world of private relations—the family instead of the forum, the heart of the simple bürgher instead of the lofty duty and the complex cares of a king, a conqueror, or their advisers. Bourgeois drama, the novel of manners, the work of Lessing and Addison, bordering on them, and finally even Goethe and the world of vague inner anxieties of his Faust—all this, on which we would like to see the stamp of personal genius, bears on itself only the stamp of the genius of its people.

The understanding of the "individual" in law created in the remote darkness of the Middle Ages the court of twelve jurors, who decide their verdict in the depths of their conscience, instead of finding it in a pre-established norm of a law the same for all cases. For the same reason, the English people refused to codify their laws, which went as far back as a thousand years, and the German scholars made deep studies of medieval law and its historical development and finally of the law of all nations, where side by side with the most sublime things the most primitive are carefully considered. When the great Herder said: "Each time and each place lives for itself alone," he inaugurated the era of the true understanding of history, by having pointed out the world of the "individual" and "particular" that must be discerned in it. And how wonderfully in keeping with those words are the words of another German thinker addressed to the conscience of all that lives: "So act as to treat humanity, whether in your own person or that of another, in every case as an end in itself, never as a means." This realm of "ends in themselves," this ethical monadology of Kant (what a striking connection it has with the ideas of Leibniz!), and the whole of it, this Germanic world, which seems to have been dispersed into myriad centers, each of which is aware only of itself and which through itself perceives everything, believes everything, and acts on everything—how wonderfully this world corresponds to that other world [4] about which we said earlier that it envelops everything, dominates everything, and determines forms, but is incapable of creating any sort of contents. It is as if these two opposite and congruent races represent the edges of a huge foot, the move-

[4] I.e., the Latins. [Tr.]

ments of which make history, drag the centuries behind it, and separate nations, who, in their free genius only reflect the will of something higher, whose thinking they are never destined to get to know.

The boundless mysticism of Protestantism, the thirst to still the great sorrow of one's heart by means of a spiritual feat somewhere among savages—this is the same yearning in the Germanic race that we find in the sounds of Latin music, its poetry, and in the indefatigable activities of its great politicians. Unbridgeably separated, each eternally conscious of the shortcomings of the other, they are full of inner discord, and this discord they carry from the depths of their spirit into life and into the history that they make. Their eternal struggle and indefatigable creation is only the struggle of opposites, who will never be able to understand each other, and the preparation of form and content, which never merge to produce a living whole. Hence the feeling of dissatisfaction which is diffused throughout all of history; hence the eternal striving and the discontent with all that is finally achieved.

XXI

The introduction of harmony into life and history, a combination of the paints and the canvas into a living picture—this is what man has not accomplished on earth, and something that he terribly needs. He needs the "palm branches" and "white garments," the inner peace and joy to praise God and his own destiny, to praise his fellow man, and every work of his own hands.

Through what inner impulse this will be achieved, how one will feel the rapture of the soul that will suffice to soothe every sorrow and to reconcile every hate—this we cannot tell. We can only long for it and look forward to it; and it is already being longed for and looked forward to by all nations as something right and necessary.

The race last to enter the historical arena and to which we Russians belong has in the peculiarities of its mentality the greatest capacity for carrying out this important task. Alien equally to the desire for the external unification of heterogeneous elements and to the unlimited withdrawal of each element into itself, it is filled with serenity, harmony, and a desire for inner harmonization of itself with all things surrounding it, and also of all things surrounding it with each other and through itself. Instead of the forcible tendency of the Latin races to unite everything through unity of form, without considering the individual spirit and without showing mercy for it, and instead of the stubborn tendency of the Germanic races to separate themselves from the whole and withdraw into the endless world of details, the Slavic race enters as an inner unity into the most diverse and apparently irreconcilable contradictions. A spirit of compassion and endless patience and simultaneously an aversion to all that is chaotic and gloomy makes it, without any force, slowly but also perpetually, create harmony that will sometime be felt by other nations as well; and instead of those nations destroying that harmony, and with it themselves, they will submit to its spirit and set out, weary as they are, to meet it halfway.

An awareness of the inadequacy of those ideals pursued by the other races can most of all concentrate our energies on our own ideal. Finally, we must understand that the in-calculable amount of suffering man has borne in history and which was a blessing to him because it supposedly gave him "the knowledge of good and evil," has actually been borne in vain, and he is just as far from that knowledge as he was on the day when he first stretched out his hand for it. Unexceedable limits, by which he is defined and fet-tered, let him have only a tiny glimpse of that knowledge that worries and teases him; but it is no more than a glimpse, and therefore he is never destined to look directly at the "sun" of truth. And we must also understand that the tireless striving to "unite the scattered flock" of man-kind has only divided it even more with irreconcilable hostility, and the more passionate and forcible have been the attempts at unification the more violent this hostility has always become. Once we understand this, we shall real-ize how deceptive is that greatness to which man has aspired in his history. Once we tame our spirit, we shall see that its tasks on this earth are more limited. Once we stop eternally directing our thoughts and desires toward something distant, we shall again sense a fullness of strength, which has returned to us after its fruitless wan-dering. And as soon as this happens, we shall understand the sublimity of those tasks we had earlier thought so in-significant and uninteresting. We shall realize that to calm a single troubled heart, to soothe someone's anguish is greater and loftier than to make the most brilliant dis-covery or astonish the world with some useless spiritual feat. Our spiritual feats will become dear to us, they will lead to an alleviation of that sorrow in which the world has drowned itself in its fruitless quests. And at the same time as our pride is conquered, our true dignity will increase.

Having realized how weak is our strength when confronted with great goals, we shall stop sacrificing the human personality to them. We shall no longer pile suffering on suffering in order to rise to a height from which we may be seen by the most distant peoples and the most distant times of the future. We shall understand the absolute significance of man, we shall understand that the joy and light in his heart and on every individual face is the most sublime, the most precious, and the best thing in history.

To bring about this harmony and to spread it throughout life is by no means now acknowledged as man's loftiest task on earth. It will be a long time before "swords will be beaten into ploughshares," and, of course, when that is done, it will be done through the power of inner joy and not by means of outer logical reasoning. The latter, even though it prefers the "ploughshares," will first make swords in order to drive the people to the ploughshares. But let us not turn again to disquieting thoughts—they were exhausted by the "Legend." Instead, in searching for something by which we can overcome them, let us turn to an examination of the third great branch into which the Christian world is divided.

In the same way that Catholicism is the Latin conception of Christianity and Protestantism the Germanic conception, so is Orthodoxy its Slavic one. Although its roots lie in Greek soil,[1] and it was on that soil that its dogmas were formed, nevertheless, the whole of the special spirit it radiates in history reflects vividly the features of the Slavic race. And precisely this spirit is what is significant in the

[1] We must, however, keep in mind the extent to which this soil in the early centuries A.D., in the period of the migration of peoples, was saturated with Slavic elements.

historical destinies of nations, and not the dogmatic differences, which, to all appearances, is the only thing that separates the Churches and seems so easily eliminable. Undoubtedly it was not *filioque* [2] that gave rise to the Inquisition, even though the Inquisition existed only where there was also *filioque*. The dogmatic difference coincided with a character, tendency, and a spirit that had no connection with it and which came solely from the racial peculiarities of the Latin peoples. Even if that difference had not existed, one could be certain that the Germanic and Slavic peoples would still have differed irreconcilably from the Latin peoples over their interpretation and practice of Christianity and would then have disagreed among themselves as well. Even now, each Church stubbornly resists union with the other, not essentially because of dogma, but because of the fact that each one inwardly, in every feature of its character, is something highly original and completely different from the other Churches. And that is why the life that pulses in them pulses in each one in a special way.

Still, there is but one Gospel and but one spirit that shines in it. If we look deeply into the matter of which of these three types of life most closely corresponds to Christianity, we shall automatically say that it is the spirit of Orthodoxy. If we are shown the ineffable grandeur of Catholicism, the unlimited amount of thought with which it is filled, with which it is entwined, and on which it has been based since the earliest days of Scholasticism down to the present, we shall agree with all that and also admit that our Church and its history has nothing like it. If we

[2] A controversy about whether the Holy Spirit came from the Father and the Son, or from the Father only. The Western Church took the former position, the Eastern, the latter. [Tr.]

are shown all the fruits of Protestantism, its God-fearing life, its freedom of criticism, and the great enlightenment that has resulted therefrom, we shall say we see all that, that we have never closed our eyes to it. We shall only ask: "But what about Christianity, what about the evangelical spirit, what about that which the Savior taught us in word and deed?" We have nothing, neither lofty spiritual feats, nor the glitter of intellectual achievements, nor schemes to determine the paths of history. But here before us stands a poor church; on all sides, close to it, are small scattered houses. Enter it, and listen to the discordant singing of the Deacon and some boy who has come from God knows where to help him. A tall, grey-haired priest is celebrating evening mass. In the middle of the church, on a lectern, lies an icon toward which several old men and women are slowly moving. Look closely at the faces of all these people, listen closely to their voices. And you will see that what has already been lost everywhere else, what no longer comes to the aid of love and no longer sustains hope elsewhere—*faith*—continues to live in these people. That treasure, without which life inexorably dries up, which wise men never find, which flees from those impotently thirsting and perishing, still shines in these simple hearts; and those terrible thoughts that trouble us and press heavily on the world apparently never trouble their minds and consciences. They have faith, and with it they hope, with its help they love. What does it matter that the Deacon reads the prayers from the choir indistinctly: he believes in their meaning, and those who listen to him do not in the least doubt that he would if necessary die for his faith, and that he would enter the Kingdom of Heaven. Like everyone else, they will die, and according to their deeds, they will receive the reward for which they are now preparing themselves.

Can the exaltation of Protestantism and the universal designs of the great but declining Catholic Church be compared with this peace of heart, with this stability of life? Are not the despondency of the former and the yearning desire of the latter symptoms of the loss of something, without which a church is only a building and a crowd of worshipers only a gathering of people? And is not all the glitter of the arts with which they surround themselves —those incomparable paintings, that enchanting music, those majestic cathedrals—is not all this the result of a desire to arouse in oneself something that never went to sleep in those poor worshipers? To find something that has been lost, but which in that wretched little church was never lost at all? Are not all those unbounded transports of longing with which Europe is filled and with which it throbs merely the desire to drown a great sorrow, which it wants to overcome but cannot? And all the beauty, majesty, and diversity of its life and civilization—does this not remind you of a magnificent chasuble in which our priest would never array himself?

Thus, that profound and inexplicable phenomenon occurred in history, according to which "it was taken from the poor and given to the rich." In the wonderful evangelical image of Mary and Martha, who welcomed the Savior into their home, it seems as if those inscrutable destinies of the Church have been expressed. When Jesus entered, Mary "sat at Jesus' feet, and heard His word. But Martha was cumbered about much serving, and came to Him, and said, Lord, dost Thou not care that my sister hath left me to serve alone? Bid her therefore that she help me." And then Jesus uttered those words in which the meaning of all life and history resounds: "Martha, Martha, thou art careful and troubled about many things: But one thing is needful: and Mary hath chosen that good part, which shall not be taken away from her."

Through the inscrutable ways of Providence, our Holy Church was destined to choose this "one thing that is needful." It has only believed in the Savior and heeded His word. Let us pray that this faith will never be taken from us, and let us not, in accordance with the precept of the Savior, regret that our busy sisters have managed to accomplish so much.

XXII

The more the treasure of our faith dries up in us the more we are alarmed about the ideals by which the other Churches live [1]—the boundless development of inner feeling and subjective thinking or anxieties about the destinies of mankind and its outer organization. With these anxieties we try to fill the emptiness that forms in our heart from the loss of faith, and this happens every time we for some reason or other lose close ties with our people. "The Legend of the Grand Inquisitor" is an expression of such an anxiety—the loftiest ever to make an appearance—because the emptiness that it fills is a yawning abyss whose bottom

[1] Here we see an explanation for that irrespressible urge to unite with the other Churches which some of our people express from time to time.

is not only very deep, but apparently does not even exist at all. (Recall Ivan's words: "You've finally guessed it," when Alyosha tells him: "Your Inquisitor simply doesn't believe in God—that is his whole secret.")

In this sense, i.e., in respect to our historical life, the "Legend" is the most poisonous drop ever to fall to earth after having finally separated itself from that phase of spiritual development through which we have been passing for two centuries already. We not only have never before experienced greater bitterness, despair, and, let us also add, greatness in the denial of our own foundations of life, but, and there can be no doubt about this, we shall never experience it again. The "Legend," on the whole, is something unique in its kind. The facetious and equivocal words that Faust uses in evading Margarete's questions about God, the darkness of the religious consciousness in Hamlet—all this is but poor prattle in comparison with what was said and what was asked behind the partition in that little tavern into which our great artist had whimsically led the spokesmen of his thoughts. And then, having pushed aside the centuries, he showed us that wonderful scene of Christ's appearing "to stinking and suffering mankind"; then, having led Him into the dark dungeon of the Inquisitor, he showed from there that distant wilderness of fifteen hundred years earlier, and in it, Christ, ready to set about saving mankind; facing Him is the Tempter, saying that that is not necessary, that Christ will not be able to save men without knowing their true nature, and that sooner or later he himself will have to undertake that salvation, as he knows their nature better, and . . . he loves them no less than Christ does.

Truly satanic features—not something man might think

up about the evil spirit lying in wait for him, but something the evil spirit might say about himself—manifest themselves in this "Legend" in an amazing and incomprehensible way. Alyosha—poor, trembling Alyosha, still in the process of growing, helplessly raising his hands to heaven, the true personification of a small shoot springing from that huge decaying seed of life—is as if defeated and crushed by this powerful profession of evil, by these confessions of "the clever spirit of the wilderness, the spirit of death and destruction." Let us repeat, the images of the Inquisitor, the student, the artist himself, and the tempting spirit, who stands behind them all, flash, the one from behind the other; they lose the sharpness of individual contours, and finally merge into one being, whose voice we hear and understand, but whose face and name we are unable to make out. As if confused, finding support in nothing at all, Alyosha clutches at his heart, at the life that pulses in him, whose laws he does not know—he only knows that it is good. In the incomprehensible strength and beauty of life that has been given us and which is praised by us, but which also remains incomprehensible and mysterious to us, he finds that support against the evil spirit:

"But, brother, how will you live?" he asks.

In this cry lies the whole meaning, the whole strength of the refutation: the recognition of the limited nature of our mind, which not only cannot understand, but also come anywhere near understanding even such a near and dear phenomenon as life. How could it comprehend the organization of the universe and sources of good and evil? Fettered to life, unable even to grasp its meaning, we irresistibly begin to think that there is something in it immeasurably deeper than the pitiful meaning that we would like to see in it, and that if only we could find it, we would be ready to reconcile ourselves to it, to "accept it." The sense of the mystical, in which our life is rooted, even though we cannot see it, fills our heart, calms our mind, but also gives us back again the strength to live. "Thou art righteous, O Lord, and inscrutable are Thy ways," we involuntarily say in our heart when, after all the inexplicable anxieties and torments of our consciousness, we again return to the peace of a simple faith, the stable result of our acceptance of the incomprehensible.

With the stability of this faith, our hopes are also connected. In the "Legend," which we have been analyzing, there is one omission: while it speaks of the "justified," it says nothing of the "forgiven." Yet, immediately after the words in Revelation, where it is said that there will be one hundred forty-four thousand of the former, a joyous promise is made also about the rest. We should like to quote that promise, and may its holy words overcome the darkness and despair that have surrounded us for such a long time while we have been speaking of the "Legend." St. John says of his vision:

> After this I beheld, and lo, a great multitude, which no man could number, of all nations, and kindreds, and people, and tongues, stood before the throne, and before the Lamb, clothed with white robes, and palms in their hands;
>
> And cried with a loud voice, saying, Salvation to our God which sitteth upon the throne, and unto the Lamb.
>
> And all the angels stood round about the throne,

and about the elders and the four beasts, and fell before the throne on their faces, and worshiped God.

Saying, Amen: Blessing, and glory, and wisdom, and thanksgiving, and honor, and power, and might, be unto our God for ever and ever. Amen.

And one of the elders answered, saying unto me, What are these which are arrayed in white robes? And whence came they?

And I said unto him, Sir, thou knowest. And he said to me, These are they which came out of great tribulation, and have washed their robes and made them white in the blood of the Lamb.

Therefore are they before the throne of God, and serve Him day and night in His temple: and He that sitteth on the throne shall dwell among them.

They shall hunger no more, neither thirst any more; neither shall the sun light on them, nor any heat.

For the Lamb, which is in the midst of the throne shall feed them, and shall lead them unto living fountains of waters: and God shall wipe away all tears from their eyes.

In this great image is displayed the end of all the earthly destinies of man. In the words of the book of Genesis quoted by us in the epigraph of our book is shown the starting point of man's wandering. The "Legend" itself is his bitter cry when, after losing his innocence and having been abandoned by God, he suddenly realizes that now he is completely alone, with his weakness, with his sin, with the struggle of light and darkness in his soul.

To overcome this darkness, to help this light—this is all that man in his earthly wandering can do, something he must do in order to soothe his troubled conscience, which is so burdened, so sick, incapable any longer of bearing its sufferings. A clear knowledge of whence this light and whence this darkness come can best of all strengthen him in the hope that he is not destined to remain the arena of their struggle forever.

About Rozanov: An Afterword

by Spencer E. Roberts

Rozanov was born in 1856, in the small Russian town of Vetluga. A few years later the family moved to Kostroma, where the father soon died, leaving only a small pension of three hundred rubles a year. According to Rozanov, the atmosphere in the house was one of unrelieved gloom. Disgruntled and weary, the mother paid little attention to the upbringing of her children, and they in turn regarded her with hostility, especially after she invited her lover, an impoverished artist, to move in with them. Rozanov was thirteen when she died, and one of his first thoughts afterward seems to have been that now he could smoke openly. Later he realized that the children's negative feelings toward her had not been justified, for she had worked hard and selflessly to feed and clothe them on her scanty income.

As a child, Rozanov read a great deal and daydreamed. He completed the gymnasium and attended the University of Moscow, where he ridiculed the professors, slept through the lectures, and cheated in the examinations. At this time he also made an error he was to regret for the rest of his life by marrying Apollinaria Suslova, a former mistress of Dostoevsky. She was forty, Rozanov twenty-four.

What mainly intrigued Rozanov about Suslova was her intimacy with Dostoevsky, a writer whom Rozanov had long idolized; and marrying Suslova, he thought, would be a way of getting to know him, if only vicariously. But whatever knowledge was acquired through this union was paid for dearly. Suslova, who had bedeviled Dostoevsky and then abandoned him when he refused to leave his dying wife, made Rozanov's life a constant hell: besides tormenting him, she even beat him at times, and when she finally left him for good, six years after they were married, she refused to give him a divorce. Even her father seems to have been at her mercy, for when Rozanov asked for help, he wrote back: "The enemy of the human race [Suslova] is settled here in my house, and I can stay in it no longer myself." Rozanov characterized her as a regular Catherine de' Medici, who would have calmly shot at the Huguenots on St. Bartholomew's Eve, and he used the following passage from Dostoevsky's *Insulted and Injured* to describe her more fully: "My lady is so perverse that the Marquis de Sade could have taken lessons from her . . . yes, she was the devil incarnate."

What attracted Suslova to this awkward and undistinguished student is difficult to understand. She still had vestiges of her once dazzling beauty; she was intelligent, sophisticated, and financially independent; and she was always active, engaged in either writing, study, or social work. What she probably lacked at the time was a person she could dominate, someone she could make submit to her strong, proud will. In this respect, Rozanov was an ideal partner, for his own will was exceedingly weak, and, as he tells us later in regard to his life in general, he often longed for nothing so much as humiliation.

Meanwhile, Rozanov was teaching history and geography in a gymnasium in the provinces. There he fell in love with

Varvara Rudneva, a simple, uneducated petty bourgeoise, who, he felt, could give him peace after his bout with the tempestuous Suslova. At Varvara's insistence, he agreed to a secret marriage ceremony. Fortunately the Government never learned about this bigamy, for if it had, the consequences would have been grave indeed. Nevertheless, Rozanov was right in his judgment of Varvara: she provided him with a comfortable home, bore him five children (he had to adopt them, since they were illegitimate in the eyes of the State), and gave him the peace of mind so necessary for his writing.

Rozanov began to write soon after leaving the university. By 1886, he had published his first book, *On Understanding*, a long, anti-rational philosophical study and a bitter polemic against the University of Moscow. It was a failure, but at least it attracted the attention of the conservative critic Nikolai Strakhov, who recognized Rozanov's talent and took it upon himself to act as a sort of mentor to him. The book's lack of success did not discourage Rozanov. His words flowed on and on, article followed article, and thanks to Strakhov's efforts, they were published, for the most part in *The Russian Messenger*. Some of them, particularly those attacking the Russian system of education—under which, he argued, everything was done by rote, no attempt was made to pay attention to individuality, the students were turned into automatons, and so forth—did not go down at all well with the Minister of Education, and Rozanov was reprimanded. But even if he had lost his job over this, it would not have mattered very much, for teaching had always been little more than torment for him: he was never at ease before audiences, he felt stifled by having to follow rigidly set methods, and most of all he was bored with living in the provinces. The only advantage of the job was that it gave him time to write.

His talent continued to mature, and when, in 1891, he published *Dostoevsky and the Legend of the Grand Inquisitor*, it attracted considerable attention. Two years later, he brought it out at his own expense in book form, and it soon went through the edition. What struck the public about the book was its fresh critical approach to Dostoevsky.

The earlier criticism of Dostoevsky, particularly that which appeared during his lifetime, had either praised or damned his works according to the social or political views they supposedly advocated. This method of evaluation had, of course, been started by Belinsky in 1846, when he hailed *Poor People* as a humanitarian work that inspired sympathy for the "insulted and injured"; and it was continued by Dobrolyubov, Pisarev, and later by other radical critics, the difference being that as Dostoevsky's views shifted to the right, the radicals gradually came to regard him as more of an enemy of the people than the people's friend. Moreover, they considered Dostoevsky's characters too aberrant to be understandable to the average Russian reader. The characters could be of interest only as clinical cases to psychiatrists.

To this social and political approach, the noted populist Nikolai Mikhailovsky added a new dimension when, in 1882, he published his article "A Cruel Talent." While acknowledging Dostoevsky's genius, Mikhailovsky bitterly attacked his personality, which, he insisted, determined the themes of his work and his treatment of them. He called

Dostoevsky a sadist who enjoyed the humiliation and suffering to which he subjected his characters, and he argued that the social protest of the early works had given way to meekness and passivity, and the former humanitarian sympathy to gratuitous violence and the praise of suffering.

A year later, the philosopher Vladimir Solovyov gave three lectures in which he presented Dostoevsky as a mystical seer, thus temporarily removing him from the social-political arena and placing him on a religious pedestal. In very general terms, such was the background of Dostoevsky criticism when Rozanov's book appeared.

Strakhov was pleased with *The Inquisitor*. It, along with various articles that appeared soon afterward, showed that he was right in his earlier judgment of Rozanov. Therefore, in 1893, he made it possible for Rozanov to give up his teaching job, to move to St. Petersburg, and to work there as a very minor official of the Civil Service. The salary was small, but Rozanov had free time to write and the opportunity to meet stimulating people. He seems to have gravitated toward the conservatives and arch reactionaries, and in many of his articles he reflected their views and supported the die-hard policies of the Government. Unfortunately, much of what he wrote at this time was so obviously hypocritical and fawning that it incensed not only the liberals but some of the conservatives as well. For instance, after an article in which Rozanov had opposed religious toleration, Solovyov labeled him a new Porfiry Golovlyov (the sentimental, unctuous hypocrite in Saltykov-Shchedrin's *The Golovlyovs*) and added that there was not a word of truth in what he had written. To a considerable extent Solovyov was right at the time, but when Rozanov laid polemics aside, as he did for the most part in his more serious works, even his detractors such as Ivanov-Razumnik had to admit his greatness.

Rozanov's big opportunity came in 1899, when he was appointed to a well-paid job on the staff of the popular, and reactionary newspaper *New Times*. Here one of the many paradoxes about the man becomes clear: for a time, while he was publishing article after article supporting the conservatives, he was also contributing articles expressing totally opposite views, under a pseudonym, to the liberal *Russian Word*. Moreover, after the Revolution of 1905, he published in his own name *When the Authorities Went Away*, a book in which he derides the impotence of the Government and hails the power of the revolutionaries. It was not surprising that the liberal Peter Struve accused Rozanov of "moral insanity."

What was the reason for Rozanov's ambivalence? One critic says it was probably because Rozanov's mind was so broad that he had to consider all sides of a question; another attributes it to his disintegrated personality; another to his skepticism and cynicism; and still another wonders whether Rozanov may not have simply wanted to remain a completely free individual.

Rozanov was indeed enigmatic. Nevertheless, he does provide us here and there in his works with clues to his behavior. For one thing, he says that he had no convictions, that he "spat on convictions." For another, he says that his duty was to write, and it made no difference for whom he did it. And late in life, he explains that he never worried about having accommodated himself to falsehood, for it was none of anyone's business exactly what he thought; but, he added, there was one area in his life where truth always prevailed: "My deep subjectivity . . . had the effect that I went through my whole life as if behind a curtain, immovable, untearable. No one dared touch that curtain. There I lived, there with myself I was truthful." Thus, it is futile to try to determine from any of Rozanov's individual works just what his true views were. Unlike most writers, who ponder their subject for years on end and then come to firm conclusions which they publish, Rozanov seems to have jotted down his ideas and to have published them hurriedly. That they frequently contradicted one another did not bother him at all. For example, while preparing the third edition of *The Inquisitor*, he wrote an introduction, drawing partly on the introduction to the second edition. But he decided not to include it, for some of his ideas had changed, and to publish the introduction in the new edition, he said, would cause literary cacophony. Nevertheless, he had no compunction about publishing this same introduction, now called an afterword, almost simultaneously in one of the leading magazines. But we need not, as a matter of fact, be too concerned about the fluctuation of Rosanov's ideas. Each of his books may be taken on its own terms, without consideration of what he says elsewhere. Regarded in this way, as individual entities, the books stand up well indeed.

By the time Rozanov began to work for the *New Times*, he was a highly controversial and widely known figure in Russian cultural life. But he was eager to reach an even wider audience than that provided by the newspaper and also to increase his earnings; therefore, he collected some of his earlier articles and had them published in book form under the title *Literary Sketches* (1899). The success of this project led him to republish other of his articles in *The Twilight of Enlightenment* (1899), *Religion and Culture* (1899), and *Nature and History* (1900).

By the end of the nineties, Rozanov had struck upon the themes to which he would devote most of his later work. Motivated by his own personal conflict with the stringent divorce and illegitimacy laws, he began to reflect upon marriage and the family in Russia; this in turn led him to question the reaction of the Church to these matters, and ultimately to examine Christianity in general. The first of his books devoted to these themes, *In the World of the Obscure and Uncertain* (1901), was an assemblage of earlier articles, plus letters from his readers and his detailed comments on them. It was promptly banned because of the last few pages, in which one of the correspondents describes how he rescued his marriage and found new happiness through circumcision. A book of earlier articles dealing mainly with divorce came out under the title *The Family Problem in Russia* (two volumes, 1903), and articles on Jesus and Christianity followed a few years later in the books *Around the Church Walls* (1906) and *The Dark Face* (1911). *Moonlight People* (1913), dealing with Christianity, monasticism, and sexual anomalies, was held up for several years by the censor.

The central point around which these matters revolved for Rozanov was sex, which he discussed with an openness unknown in the Russia of the time (and, for that matter, in the Russia of today). Although the censor periodically made excisions, much of what Rozanov wrote, both on sex and the equally sensitive matter of the Church, managed to be published. Since these themes dominated Rozanov's work more or less to the end of his life, since they embrace ideas for which he is usually remembered today, and since *The Inquisitor,* coming as it does at the beginning of Rozanov's literary career, contains not even a hint of them, they need some explanation.

Sex, he said, existed before the word and is holy, the soul and sex being one. "The tie of sex with God is stronger than the tie of intellect, or even conscience, with God." During intercourse, according to Rozanov's theory, man actually comes into direct contact with God, and from this act he causes souls to be brought from the higher world into this one. The child that results completes the family, the most aristocratic, the most sacred unit of society. Given the holiness of the relations between the husband and wife, it was wrong, he insisted, for the State to force them to remain together once their love had died and no further relations between them were possible. Therefore, he called for—and, according to some scholars, helped to achieve—less rigidity in the matter of Russian divorce.

"How," Rozanov asked, "can marriage, a physical phenomenon, be religious, i.e., of the other world, when our 'bones' and all our 'physical decay' are so obviously of this world? Precisely because sex is by no means the body, because the body, such a temporal phantom, comes from sex and wraps itself around it, with sex remaining hidden as the immortal noumenon of that body, as the face of the order of the 'I am' in us."

Since sex is closely linked with God, Rozanov found atheists to be completely sexless creatures who are unable to understand it and who pay no attention whatever to it in their thinking and writing. He regarded the genitals, both male and female, also as holy and eventually developed what amounted to a fixation about them. "If I can't smell and kiss the sex of a woman," he says in one of his letters, "then let me suck the udder of a cow." And elsewhere he frankly admits that during his researches for his book on Egyptian religion, the sight of the phallus drove him to ecstasy.

Poor Varvara, his simple bourgeois wife—his "friend," as he always referred to her—and his modest daughters were shocked by all this talk of sex, and quarrels over it sometimes disturbed the peace of the household. The Decadents and Symbolists, however, whose work dominated the Russian cultural scene at the time, were highly enthusiastic about it and his ideas in general; but, although Rozanov met with them often and published in their journals, he did not really agree with or like them, a fact he pointed out in the *New Times* and in the preface which one Vilinskaya-Minskaya had asked him to write for her book: "This poetess," he wrote, "belongs to the Symbolists. I am not in sympathy with that school. . . . I cannot tolerate disorder and cannot recommend this book." [1]

Basically, Rozanov's asystematic philosophy is a worship of life, and this is precisely what led him to reject Christianity. Christ, he said, never laughed, never sang, never danced, never married; He preached the renunciation of the world and its joys for those of heaven; His teachings cultivate pessimism, despair, death, and destruction. "A merry Christian," Rozanov said, "is the same *contradictio in adjecto* as a circular square." And elsewhere: "The pain of the world conquered the joy of the world—

[1] This remark is rather amusing when one thinks of the disorder in some of Rozanov's own books.

this is Christianity." But, he wondered, if the world is of God's making, then wasn't Christ really in opposition to Him?

The true religion, in Rozanov's eyes, is the one that glorifies life, a religion he found in the teachings of the ancient Hebrews and the primitive religion of early Egypt. What attracted him to them most was the fact that they were primarily religions of the flesh, that they supposedly placed great stress on the moral and sexual behavior of man, that they urged man to be fruitful and multiply, and that they were mainly concerned with the here and now. But then, he said, Christ appeared, "Our Sweetest Lord Jesus," and the fruits of the world turned bitter. A severe monasticism sprang up in imitation of Jesus's life, and this became the Christian ideal. The flesh became the Christian's cross. Sex and the family were accepted, but only grudgingly.

Also unacceptable to Rozanov was the Christian concept of resurrection and life everlasting: "There is absolutely no need for the dead to leave their graves, because the earth is not a wasteland; on the graves, new flowers have sprung up, with a memory of the original ones, with a reverence for the original ones, even virtually repeating in themselves those original ones. Death is not a death that is final, but merely a means of renewal: after all, in my children, I live completely, in them lives my body and blood, and therefore, literally I do not die at all, only my present name dies. My body and blood continue to live, and in their children again, and then again in their children—eternally! . . . I work in mankind with a thousand hands, I smell all the fragrances of the world, I practice all professions, I am slave and tsar, genius and madman.

[223]

What riches in comparison with any kind of personal existence! And, in general, is it really possible that the vine is poorer than a single grape?"

And yet Rozanov was not sure about all this. His struggle against Christ was difficult, and it caused him frequently to waver. When faced with inconsolable sorrow, he was particularly drawn to Christ; when filled with joy, he rejected Him. "Christ," he wrote, "manifests Himself only in tears. He who never cries will never discover Christ; but he who cries will definitely discover Him. . . . And how understandable is its [Christianity's] silence about marriage, the flesh, and useless circumcision. When there is a sick person in the room in danger of dying, would we say to him: 'Disrobe, and cut off your foreskin'? It wouldn't even occur to us."

It must be noted that Rozanov's critics, and they were many, had no trouble finding flaws in his religious thinking; some, for instance, pointed out that monasticism and asceticism are not typical of Christianity as a whole; others, that one cannot overlook the unity of the Father and the Son; and Nikolai Berdyaev added that if Rozanov had taken the Christian idea of resurrection seriously, he could not have characterized Christianity as a religion of death. Authorities of the Russian Orthodox Church also raised objections, but they never went so far as to excommunicate Rozanov, as they did, for example, Tolstoy. Perhaps they sensed that Rozanov was not really being his true self in all this, that despite all his words of rejection, despite all his ridicule, despite all his praise of the Old Testament and disparagement of the New, he was actually more attracted to than repelled by Jesus and His teachings, and that he probably took his position at times simply to shock, to have something different to write about, to see a subject through the eyes of another. In this connection, it is interesting to note that in one place he plainly tells us that when he dies, it will, of course, be in the Church. And in another, he asks:

"What monument would you like raised to yourself?"

"One simply showing me sticking my tongue out at the reader."

Still another of the strange paradoxes of Rozanov reveals itself in his attitude toward the Jews. Although time and again he held up the life and philosophy of the ancient Hebrews as the model to be followed, he felt no sympathy for the Jews of the present; indeed, he vilified them mercilessly and even urged pogroms against them. For this and for his anti-Semitic articles in general he was finally expelled from the highly respected Religious and Philosophical Society, an organization of clergy and intelligentsia. His expulsion did not, however, seem to bother him very much for he continued his attacks, and in 1914, in connection with the Beilis case (1911–1913), he published his most viciously anti-Semitic work, *The Attitude of the Jews toward the Smell and Touch of Blood.* The book was destroyed by the Soviets soon after they came to power, but for some strange reason was republished in Stockholm in 1934.

But, after *The Inquisitor*, the works for which Rozanov is mainly remembered today, and rightly so, are his *Solitaria* (1912; English translation, 1927), *Fallen Leaves* (1913; English translation, 1929), and *Fallen Leaves, Another Basketful* (1915). Written in a disconnected aphoristic style, they contain recollections, meditations, dreams, random thoughts, intimate revelations of his past, and the like,

[225]

all supposedly jotted down on the spur of the moment in such prosaic places as "the railway station," "the bath," "the toilet," wherever he might have been when they struck him. They seem to be dictated entirely by mood, with no workings of the will involved, and despite their chaotic and disjointed nature they have a decided charm about them and have led one critic aptly to describe them as little poems in prose.

After the Revolution, the Government closed the *New Times*, and Rozanov found himself without means of livelihood. He moved his family to Sergiev-Posad, the village outside the Trinity Monastery, near Moscow, where his main efforts were directed at collecting cigarette butts from the street to satisfy his smoking habit and at finding enough food to keep his family alive—circumstances not very conducive to writing; nevertheless, he managed to produce some articles and to complete a rather large part of a book, *The Apocalypse of Our Time*, which he brought out in short installments. Here he continued to brood over Christianity and also to seek the causes of the Revolution, which he had at first half-heartedly welcomed, but now rejected. At fault, he said, were both the State and the Church, for they had not served the people, and therefore the people had abandoned them. But the Russian people, he felt, were also to blame, for they had been guilty of vice and folly and were now being punished.

Rozanov's style here differs completely from that of *The Inquisitor*. Fragmented, jerky, and colloquial, it is intended to give the effect of actual living conversation, to establish a close rapport with the reader. The following excerpt well illustrates not only this later style but also Rozanov's reaction to the Revolution:

[226]

Well, what of it: death came, and consequently the time for death had come as well. . . . It means that God didn't want Rus' to exist any longer. He is driving it away from under the sun. "Away with you, you useless people."

Why are we "useless?"

For a long time now we've been writing in "our golden literature": "The Diary of a *Superfluous* Man," "Notes of an *Unnecessary* Man." Also "—of an *Idle* Man." We thought up all sorts of *"undergrounds"* . . . We had somehow hidden ourselves from the light of the sun, as if we were ashamed of ourselves.

A person ashamed of himself? Won't the sun also become ashamed of him? The sun and man are tied up with each other.

Consequently, we are "of no use" in the world, and we are withdrawing into a kind of night. Night. Nonexistence. The grave.

We are dying like braggarts, like actors. "Without the cross, without prayer." And if there was ever a death without the cross and without prayer, it was the death of the Russians. Strange. All our lives we crossed ourselves, we prayed: then suddenly, death—and we had cast aside the cross. "It is simply that the Russian had never lived as an Orthodox believer." The transition to socialism and consequently to complete atheism was accomplished in the soldiers and peasants as easily "as if they had gone into the bathhouse and drenched themselves with fresh water." That's exactly the way it was, it is reality, and not some wild nightmare.

As a matter of fact, why are we dying? . . . We are dying for a single and fundamental reason: *lack of respect for ourselves*. We are, as a matter of fact, committing suicide. It isn't so much that the "sun is persecuting us," as it is that we are persecuting ourselves. "Go away, you devil."

Nihilism . . . Yes, this is nihilism—the name the Russian long ago baptized himself by—or more accurately the name he took when he renounced Christianity.

"Who are you wandering there through the world?"

"I'm a nihilist."

"I only *pretended* that I prayed."

"I only pretended that I *lived in the Empire*."

"As a matter of fact—I'm a completely independent person."

"I'm a worker in a pipe factory, and nothing else concerns me."

"I'd like to work a little less."

"I'd like to have a good time a little more often."

"And I don't want to fight."

And the soldier throws down his gun. The workman leaves his bench.

"The land—it must bear fruit on its own."

And he leaves the land.

"Everybody knows that the land is God's. It belongs to everyone alike."

"Yes, but you're not a man of God. And the land in which you trust, will give you nothing. And because it will give you nothing, you will stain it with blood.

The land is Cain's, and the land is Abel's. And your land, Russian, is Cain's. You cursed your land, and your land has cursed you. There you have nihilism and its formula. . . .

It is remarkable that we are going to the grave enraptured. We also began the War enraptured with ourselves. . . .

But if there was one thing that we were enthusiastic about, it was revolution. "The complete fulfillment of our heart's desire." No, as a matter of fact: what aren't we satiated with? "If ever there was a time when the thirsty had their thirst quenched and the hungry their hunger satisfied, it was during the Revolution." And the revolutionary has hardly worn out his first pair of boots than he falls into the grave. Isn't he an actor? Isn't he a braggart? And where are our prayers? And where are our crosses? "Not a single priest would conduct a funeral service for such a corpse."

It is a sorcerer, a werewolf, and not a live human being. There is no living soul in it, there never was.

"Nihilist."

They don't conduct funeral services for nihilists. They limit themselves to saying: "To hell with him."

Cursed was his life, and cursed is his death.

One-sixth of the earth's surface. The Revolution was enraptured, enraptured was the War. "We'll win." Oh, definitely. Now isn't it a terrible fact that one-sixth of the earth's surface somehow always produced "thistles and thorns" until the sun said: "I don't need you any longer." "I'm bored shining down on the barren earth."

Nihilism. "What grows from you?"

"Nothing."

And about this "nothing," there is nothing more to say.

"We didn't respect ourselves. The main thing about Rus' is that it does not respect itself."

That is quite clear. One can respect work and sweat, but we didn't sweat, we didn't work. And the fact that we didn't work and didn't sweat is the reason that the land has cast us from it, that the planet has cast us from it.

Did we deserve it?

Far too much. . . .

Russia is like a fake general over whom some fake priest is conducting a funeral service. "As a matter of fact, it was a runaway actor from a provincial theater."

The most striking thing about the whole affair, the main point of it, lies in the fact that "virtually nothing happened." "But everything went to pieces." What did they do to cause the downfall of the Empire? Literally, it fell on an ordinary day of the week. It was a Wednesday, no different from any of the rest. Not on a Sunday, nor a Saturday, nor even a Mussulman Friday. Literally, God spat and put out the candle. There had been a shortage of food, and lines had formed at the shops. And there had been opposition. And the Tsar had been capricious. But then when in Rus' had there ever been enough of anything without the work of the Jew and without the work of the German? And when wasn't there opposition with us? And when wasn't the Tsar capricious? Oh, dreary Friday or Monday, Tuesday . . .

Can one really die so dully, so stinkingly, so horridly? "Actor, you might at least make some sort of gesture. After all, you were always ready to play Hamlet." "Remember your lines." . . .

Yes, if ever there was a "dull affair," it was "the fall of Rus'."

The candle was put out. And it wasn't even done by God . . . A drunken peasant woman was walking along, she stumbled, and fell flat on her face. Stupid. Vile. "Don't play us a tragedy, give us a vaudeville instead." . . .

The Apocalypse of Our Time was never completed, for Rozanov's health failed rapidly. Near the end, when he realized he was dying, he underwent a profound spiritual change and renounced all that he had written against both the Christians and the Jews. At his request, priests from the monastery gave him communion four times, extreme unction once, and three times read the prayers for the dying over him. Shortly before death, he said: "Everyone embrace—everyone. Let us kiss each other in the name of the resurrected Christ. Christ has risen! How joyful, how wonderful . . . Miracles are indeed happening inside me; what those miracles are I'll tell you later, sometime . . ."

He died on January 23, 1919 (Old Style), and, as he had requested, was buried in the monastery cemetery beside Konstantin Leontiev, a fellow conservative, an aesthete and writer. Shortly afterward, his wife also died, one of his daughters hanged herself, and his son froze to death while searching for food.

Shifty, insincere, servile, inconsistent, contradictory, prejudiced, blasphemous—all these pejoratives and more describe Rozanov. Certainly few Russian writers can so antagonize. Yet, even while disagreeing with him, scholars read him with delight, marveling at his inventiveness, at his brilliant verbal gift, at his clever dialectic, at his candor in revealing the sordid details of his narcissistic soul. If the Soviet Union ever decides to publish him, along with a considerable number of other writers it now regards as skeletons in its closet, the Russian people will realize that their literary past is even richer than they ever thought it was. And Rozanov will introduce them to a strange world they have never known before: a world dominated by the idolatry of the soul; a world where man comes into direct contact with God through sex; a world where the individual counts for more than anything else in history and where the most satisfying thing a person can do is just to sit at home in his round, warm little nest and watch the sun go down. But this is dangerous stuff for a collective society, and the chances of it being published in the present circumstances are slim indeed.

Therefore, one can only hope that the present volume will encourage publishers in the English-speaking world to bring out other works of Rozanov's, thus rescuing him from the obscurity of the few research libraries to which he has been relegated for the past fifty years.

*Dostoevsky and the Legend
of the Grand Inquisitor*

Designed by John H. Warner.
Composed by Vail-Ballou Press, Inc.,
in 11 point linotype Janson, 3 points leaded,
with display lines in monotype Janson.
Printed letterpress from type by Vail-Ballou Press
on Warren's No. 66 text, 60 pound basis,
with the Cornell University Press watermark.
Bound by Vail-Ballou Press
in Columbia BSL book cloth
and stamped in All Purpose foil.
Endpapers are Weyerhaeuser Torino Blue Spruce.

Library of Congress Cataloging in Publication Data
(For library cataloging purposes only)

Rozanov, Vasiliĭ Vasil'evich, 1856–1919.
  Dostoevsky and the legend of the Grand Inquisitor.

  Translation of Legenda o Velikom inkvizitorẽ.
  "What appears here is the complete text of the
third edition [1906] of the book, minus the appendix."
  Includes bibliographical references.
  1. Dostoevskiĭ, Fedor Mikhaĭlovich, 1821–1881.
Brat'ĩa Karamazovy. Book 5, chapter 5. 2. Gogol',
Nikolaĭ Vasil'evich, 1809–1852. I. Title. II. Title:
Legend of the Grand Inquisitor.
PG3325.B73R613   1972   891.7'3'3   79-37754
ISBN 0-8014-0694-3